NATURE IN OUR CULTURE

A Study in the Anthropology and the Sociology of Knowing

Friedrich W. Sixel

in cooperation with Baldev R. Luther

University Press of America,® Inc.
Lanham · New York · Oxford

Library of Congress Cataloging-in-Publication Data

Sixel, Friedrich W.
Nature in our culture : a study in the anthropology and the
sociology of knowing / Friedrich W. Sixel in cooperation
with Baldev R. Luther.
p. cm
Includes bibliographical references and index.
1. Human ecology—Philosophy. 2. Knowledge, Sociology of.
3. Goethe, Johann Wolfgang von, 1749-1832—Views on human
ecology. I. Luther, Baldev R., d. 1998. II. Title.
GF21 .S556   2001   304.2—dc21   2001023355 CIP

ISBN 0-7618-2002-7 (pbk. : alk. paper)

Contents

Chapter 7: Goethe's Praxis and Concept of Science

Preface

The book "Nature in Our Culture" is not the result of a singular research project. To the extent, however, that it culminates in the practical-critical examination of a mode of thinking, namely that of modernity, it can be categorized as a study in the anthropology and the sociology of knowing.

The investigations, thoughts, ideas and, indeed, experiments brought together in this book have many roots, some of them less clear to us than others. Yet, two are rather obvious to us. First, there is the "Political Economy Group" that existed around 1980 for quite a few years at Queen's University (Kingston, Ontario). Its most active members were Drs. Muhammed Fayyaz, Robert Gaucher, Jayant K. Lele and Friedrich W. Sixel. The focus of this group's attention was the predisposition of European states and societies for the creation of the capitalist state and its expansion. Second, there was a growing interest among a few of this group in what became increasingly known as the "environmental" issue. Dealings with this issue grew since the mid-80s into the central concern of another study group, this one consisting of Drs. Hans J. Kummer, Baldev R. Luther and Friedrich W. Sixel (with a few occasional hangers-on). Without the work done in these groups, the present book would not have been possible. We acknowledge this with a great deal of gratitude and with fond memories.

In 1996, Baldev Luther and Friedrich Sixel began to write the first draft of this text. Its progress was temporarily slowed down when Baldev was struck by a sudden and serious illness in the fall of 1997. On the day we wanted to start writing up that portion of the text to which both of us had been looking forward so very much, namely the affirmative ideas that make up chapter 7, Baldev passed away. This was on April 10, 1998.

Slowly recovering from the loss of such a friend, Friedrich Sixel finished the first version of "Nature in Our Culture". Prior and after Baldev's death, this draft or whatever was completed of it, had been given for comments to a few of our friends and colleagues. Some aspects of it have also been presented at conferences. These discussions induced many re-considerations and led to the writing of several new drafts until the final version was completed.

At this point, we also would like to admit that we have not incorporated all the literature we have studied in connection with the different aspects of our concerns. The simple reason for this omission rests on our belief that much of what has been said or has been published on the relationship of modern man to Nature is quite far from the point we think needs to be made.

Among those who have commented on our specific position directly as we have presented it in various drafts and at conferences, the following deserve particular mentioning: Richard N. Adams, Heinz Eidam, Zain Ghadially, Hans J. Kummer, Joyce Melbourne, Carlos Neves, Frank Pearce and Wolfdietrich Schmied-Kowarzik. While their sharp-minded and helpful comments made quite a number of revisions necessary, we have accepted these suggestions always with a great deal of gratitude, temporary resistance notwithstanding. Whatever conceptual flaws the text may still contain, it is now mainly I who has to take responsibility for them. [*]

My friend Zain Ghadially, while completing his graduate studies at Queen's, took it upon himself to edit the text. His main task was to put thoughts perceived as complex by the modern mind into an at least somewhat straightforward English. His thorough understanding of the ideas expressed did not make his task any easier. My appreciation for the job he did increases, when I take into consideration how, at times vociferously, I clung to the initial wording of the text.

Shirley Fraser formatted the whole book. And again, she did her job with her usual competency and promptness. I would like to thank her very much indeed.

---

[*] The reader may very well notice a stylistic inconsistency in the last chapter. "We", "our" and "us" often interchange with "I", "my" and "me". This reflects my inability to distinguish between Baldev's and my thoughts and also relates to my desire not to burden Baldev with problems he might have helped to avoid.

Financial support for the editorial and clerical work came from Queen's University. This is gratefully acknowledged.

My thanks also go to members of my family.

Graziano Hueller drew my attention to both literary and philosophical writings on Goethe. As artists, he and Caroline Sixel-Hueller, have such a sense for the Nature of things that they cannot help but be living reminders of what life could be for all of us. Friederike and Katharina, the medical and scientific minds in the family, have told me so often how the brain "really" works and what physicists "really" do. In different ways, passages of this book continue conversations I had with them over the years.

Margrit Sixel proofread the whole text. Of course, I state this with a great deal of gratitude. It is, however, an entirely different matter how much her whole being influenced me and the thinking that went into this book. Whatever she has been and is for me cannot be expressed in a few lines. Let me just say this: she has always brought me back to a life grounded in the here and the now. This cultivates more than just gratitude.

Friedrich W. Sixel, May 2000.

Introduction:

The Argument

Contemporary variations of Darwinism assume that all parts of Nature stand in competitive relation to one another. The form of this competition may vary depending on the level of evolution, yet each part of Nature is confronted by the alternative of either dominating others or being dominated by them. This constellation does not exclude the occurrence of symbiosis, parasitism, co-operation, compromises, even friendliness depending on the benefits that accrue. Mutual checks may lead to balances, but not necessarily so. Controlling too much may be detrimental to the controllers, be these individual bodies, groupings of them or whole species. Some species have become extinct, not because of their lack of success but, often in combination with other factors, because of the excess of their success.

Human beings are no exception in this scheme, so we are told. The only difference is that man is capable of culture, other parts of Nature are not. This is to say that culture is "man's secret adaptive weapon" in survival (Richard N. Adams). This weapon yields a degree and kinds of power and control which are unparalleled in the evolution of the universe, as far as we know. And yet, gains to be made from the use of this weapon do not exclude the possibility of our self-inflicted extinction; suicide is perfectly thinkable also at the level of our whole species. Such suicide, as a result of our increasingly pyrrhic victories over one another or over Nature out there, does not imply the destruction of Nature, as some say. Nature itself will definitely survive us, and might very well be indifferent to the event of our disappearance.

It may be comforting to some, if not to most of us, that this distinctive weapon, namely culture, can also be intentionally used for increasing our chances of survival. We could use our knowledge, our values and norms against blind growth in our exploitation of Nature, i.e. relate to Nature out of a "well understood self interest". Would this kind of smartness, so we wonder, not go against the Nature built into us? If we are little more than part of a ruthlessly competitive Nature, then controlling our weapon of culture would require the development of ever stronger weaponry against her. This kind of social control will easily turn into a growth industry and become self-defeating. Nonetheless, this proposition is considered to be realistic, and everything else utopian.

But is it?

There is no doubt in our mind that everything else appears to be utopian for the dominant thinking of today of which Darwinism is, after all, a major part in whatever variation. It is our contention, though, that the major quality of this dominant mode of thinking is just its sheer dominance. Even the tradition within which this mode of thinking emerged and became increasingly dominant has always contained in it other modes of thinking. Examples would be mysticism, the traditions often associated with Johannes Duns Scotus (the victim of Thomas Aquinas), the young Martin Luther, Jean-Jacques Rousseau and Friedrich Nietzsche. Yet other examples would be represented, perhaps singularly so, by Johann Wolfgang von Goethe, or by a contemporary thinker like Ernst Bloch. Common to some of these undercurrents is a sense for at least the possibility of a culture founded on a trust in Nature within and around us.

Since all we can know must be of this world in order to be known, it would follow that the commonality of Nature in all there is would clearly imply the primacy of Nature in culture. This proposition indicates that the double meaning of the title that we give to the considerations presented here is intended. We do not just want to speak about the concept that our culture has of Nature, but also about how Nature itself is contained in our culture. Appreciating the containment of Nature this way could entail a different way of understanding of what would be a kindred Nature and of what would be the fellow human being. In this sense, Nature would not be just a resource; our knowledge of her would constitute a new science of Nature. Society would not be a system of power and its constraints; it would be the locus of mutual cultivation. Understanding society would not be an expert analysis, but a socializing and, thus, a mutually refining event itself.

Cultivation in this sense would lend strength, time and again, to a sensuously grounded understanding of the circumstance that we are more than raw Nature. Such kind of understanding would also keep us aware that even our most cultivated ideas are still manifestations of Nature.

Repression of Nature would be alien to us. Culture would not be a weapon against Nature, nor would it make her a slave to be dominated. Every moment, be it the one of understanding or the one of creating, would be a celebration of Nature and thus of ourselves.

This sense of Nature and of us being part of it, we discovered not only in Goethe the poet, but more surprisingly, in Goethe the thinker and the student of Nature. To an astounding degree, his observing and writing, and indeed his living, anticipate what Ernst Bloch calls in our times, "Allianztechnik", i.e., a technology in alliance with Nature. However awkward this term may be, it is intended to capture an understanding of and a working with Nature in which both Nature and we are elevated to mutual cultivation. Our agency in evolution would then not be suicidal; instead it would be an enhancement of evolution thinkable nowhere else but on this earth. We agree with Ernst Bloch "that we and a God are thwarted is the one and only Last Judgement on us and Him, and this is gruesome enough".[1]

With an eye to man's potential future, we wish, after critical examination of our culture, to present and comment on an essay by Goethe. This essay written more than 200 years ago and published under the title of "The Experiment as Mediator of Object and Subject", is of interest to us today, because it practices the primacy of Nature in the act of coming to know and of being in and with Nature.

Most certainly we do not present this essay in order to propagate yet another new methodology, i.e., another set of instruments to manipulate Nature and thus, man and society. We discuss this essay publicly in the hope that it would strike a cord in our readers. And yet, it is not our intention at all to deliver a sermon for making converts.

Note

[1] Bloch, 1973, p 338; our translation

Part I: The "Environmental" Issue

Chapter 1

Our Problems with Nature Reveal Our Problematic Nature

Environmental problems are being discussed in the media, among concerned citizens, and are raised as issues by politicians. Even industry is joining in. Anyone can feel the problem by him/herself. One of us did when he smelled the odor of the drinking water from his faucet; what he smelled was not chlorine alone; it smelled foul. This happened in the summer of 1998 right on the shores of Lake Ontario from which the water was pumped and purified. He remembered that his friend, - was it in 1973 or 4 ? -, drank water from the same lake directly while canoeing on it about a mile off shore. Would he be willing to do that again today?

Recently, people in the Midwest of the US were advised not to use tap water for human consumption, definitely not for babies. Instead of this contaminated water, the use of bottled water was strongly recommended. A few days later, the news in our hometown Kingston, Ontario, warned the public against health hazards in bottled drinking water. With a certain amount of shelf life, bacteria could develop easily in it.

The reason given for the contamination of water in the American Midwest was the heavy use of fertilizers and pesticides in agriculture. This is by no means a singular or localized phenomenon. While we do not know what makes the water of Lake Ontario smell, we cannot exclude the possibility that it originates in man's interference, be it an industrial or agricultural one. In a place far away from North America and much more densely populated, namely, in Germany's Bavaria, the groundwater has reached such a dangerous level of contamination that an economically viable possibility of deriving drinking water from it no longer exists.[1] Fertilizers and pesticides flowing down our rivers have polluted the Baltic Sea and the Gulf of Mexico, to name just a few examples. 18 000 km² in the Gulf of Mexico are dead and that area appears to be growing. The Baltic Sea is for major parts "eutrophied"; this is what experts call the overgrowth of weeds. The Black Sea is not better off.[2] Needless to say that many of the rivers that carry the water to the sea are equally threatened, as are the lakes. In fact, there is a growing scarcity of drinking water all over the world. 40% of the world's population, at the present time, have no access to clean water and 80 countries have serious shortages of it. If the current trend in our dealings with water continues, then water is likely to become, not in the long run, but quite soon, the effective constraint on agricultural yield, while being at the same time unusable for direct human consumption.[3] Presently, deliberations are under way to ship drinking water from the Great Lakes, the world's largest resource of such water, to other parts of the world. The impact of this on the Lakes has not been studied.

Chemical fertilizers and pesticides applied to the soil in quantities that plants cannot even absorb or make use of have a direct damaging influence on the soil. Nutrients forced out of the soil and into the plants by chemical fertilizers, besides excessive mechanical "cultivation", turn humus into unproductive dust. It is being estimated that, as a consequence of this, 1000 to. of soil are washed away per second at the global level.[4] Anyone who has ever seen a field on which corn has been grown for only a limited number of years will know that the soil, oftentimes having turned gray, has hardly any other purpose or ability beyond holding the stalks upright so that the plant can still grow towards the light of the sun. Fields that have reached that stage will need more as well as additional kinds of chemical fertilizers.[5] To a large extent, this is why agriculture gets increasingly "hooked" onto the chemical industry.[6]

Leaving aside what is happening to the plants and their fruits, we would like to point out that chemicals unused in this process do not only seep via the soil into the water, but that they also evaporate into the air. In general, approximately 60 000 different chemicals, some of which of unbelievable and yet known toxicity, are presently released into the biosphere, a good many of them in large quantities.[7] The effects of them on plants, air, soil and water are unknown, particularly their cumulative effect, e.g., how they might get compounded and the subsequent result thereof. Oftentimes, not knowing the precise chain of events in this regard - a widespread feature of our knowledge of Nature[8] - we must assume that the damage they do to plant life, and directly or indirectly, to animals and human beings is substantial. Acid rain is only one of the many examples of this. Other effects of air pollution include respiratory problems among humans which are most pronounced in urban agglomerations like Mexico-City, Delhi and Tokyo.[9] The release of CFC into the air has created some depletion of the ozone layer leading to growing danger of skin cancer. CO_2 and other industrial and agricultural gases have contributed through the greenhouse effect to global warming.[10]

If this can be known so widely and easily, why is it that so little is being done about this problem? In order to answer this question, we need to remind ourselves that maximizing profits is the intent in modern agriculture as it is in the economy in general. As a result, the farm has been turned into a capital intensive business, depending on excessive use of fertilizers, herbicides and pesticides besides heavy mechanization.[11] The latter, of course, adds to further deterioration of the soil (compaction, inability to retain water, etc.). We leave aside that this form of food production uses up far more energy than it makes available for human consumption.[12] Surprisingly, though, we consider this a cost efficient way of producing food. The impression of cost efficiency would vanish, not only in agribusiness, but also in other businesses, if monetary costs were calculated in terms of energy units.[13] Not doing that, "cost efficiency" manifests itself, among other forms, at the individual level in the relatively small portion of the household income that is spent on food and transportation, most strikingly in the "developed" countries.

It is common knowledge that - particularly in the "developed" countries - a quite small and yet still shrinking proportion of the population is involved in food production. This is one of the major reasons that urbanization occurs at an increasingly rapid pace. Conservative estimates expect that there will be about 100 cities on our planet with over 20 million inhabitants each not too far in the future,[14] while today there are only a few. This look into the future allows us to anticipate how the treatment of the land and its resources is, in all likelihood, going to develop. Less and less of an individual's budget will go into foodstuffs[15] meaning agriculture has to become ever more "efficient" through the application of means mentioned above. This, of course, implies that the agriculturally used land will be even more ruinously exploited at a yet accelerating rate. This pattern will also apply to other natural resources; as an example, one could think of the ludicrously low prices for gasoline in most "developed" countries.

On the other side of this coin, the last several decades have demonstrated how a rapidly increasing portion of the consumer income is spent on such man made "amenities" as luxurious housing,[16] vastly inefficient modes of transportation,[17] tourism,[18] entertainment, leisure time activities in general, household gadgets and the like. This form of consumerism spreads like a wildfire all over this planet, although in the "developing" countries it is only a small minority that can participate in this behavior, however at times quite excessively so.[19] Evidence for all this is abundantly available through the common media. Could it not be that the obviously insatiable demand and desire for this "life-style" indicates a pseudo-satisfaction incapable of yielding contentment?

The serious impact of this "life-style" on agricultural production and thus on the agricultural land and beyond is, as can easily be seen, marked. To this must be added the onslaught on Nature by industrial production. The depletion of natural resources is certainly a serious problem, but one which to some extent can be compensated for. In more than one respect, the replacement of today's more commonly used fuels by nuclear energy may be a good example. But this also exemplifies that technical solutions of such a kind generate their own problems. We do not really know what to do, for instance, with nuclear waste.[20] For reasons like this, the pollution and degradation of Nature around us is in all likelihood a far greater threat to our survival than the depletion of raw materials.

The buildup of cities, industries and arteries connecting them implies a serious degree of soil sealing, let alone deforestation and its consequences.[21] The spatial distances between centers of production and consumption, a global phenomenon, make the development of vast transportation systems, their energy consumption and, in some cases, further sealing of the soil, a necessity[22] (not to mention the further pollution of our air and water). As far as the water run-off is concerned, soil sealing together with the compaction of agricultural land are the major culprits in some of the recent extraordinary floods. Deforestation can not be ascribed only to industrialization, urbanization and transportation, but also to agricultural extension, for instance, to cattle ranching caused by an increasing demand for beef particularly in the "developed" countries. Speaking of the cattle industry brings to mind various forms of globalizing costly production, consumption and transportation. Car makers, for instance, do not only produce cars worldwide, they also ship them worldwide. Examples of this kind could easily be multiplied. They would describe in ever new variations, how we get deprived of the means to regenerate not only the air, but also water and soil. For instance, if Shell and Monsanto, as the world's largest producers of grain seeds offer fertilizers without which their seeds would not sprout,[23] then this only further illustrates the global accumulation and complexity of the problems that our dealings with Nature have created.

Some forms of pollution may very well be avoidable and/or be kept in limits by means available today. But we must not lose sight of the circumstance that some kinds of waste, though potentially deadly, are unavoidable only given our lifestyle. In a number of respects, our present way of living has already done irreversible damage to the life sustaining abilities of this planet.[24]

The use of energy could, undoubtedly, be reduced in numerous ways in many of our activities. However, to the extent that any energy turnover will release heat, there will be an unavoidable degree of heat waste. While the problem of harnessing energy from Nature may be a solvable problem (particularly if we succeed in nuclear fusion), the unavoidable waste of heat[25] and of the spent nuclear fuel present increasingly unsolvable problems. In the foreseeable future, the amount of heat released into the biosphere by human activities will go beyond the amount intercepted by our planet from solar radiation.[26] This is, in all likelihood, the main culprit, particularly in conjunction with the aforementioned CO_2 release, for what has come to be known as the greenhouse effect.

There is much talk about the probability of some damages done to Nature having become irreversible. True, whole species of plants and animals have disappeared through our onslaught on Nature and no gene technology will be able to recreate them.[27] While we do not deny that there are damages that can be reversed - polluted rivers have been cleaned up - we wonder whether reversibility is that much of an issue, let alone the reversibility of the sum total of our intervention into Nature. Species have always died out; energy has always been turned over, irreversibly. It is not even exactly the point to lament that there is and has always been a growth in energy turnover. Closer to the issue is that the balance in the turnover of energy and in the dying out and evolution of new species has become negative for the first time in history. This is exclusively the consequence of our doing. More species vanish than do emerge;[28] more of the energy intercepted and stocked over the millennia on earth is turned over than the earth is able to replenish from the sun, the ultimate source of all life. Besides the killing of species done by us unintentionally, the shrinking of bio-diversity is also intentional, at least since the emergence of modern biotechnology. The productivity of whole species of plants and animals edible by humans has seen massive cost efficient increases, not to a small extent by limiting their variety. And yet, cost efficiency is not an indisputable criterion, as we have indicated a few moments ago. In addition, the short term effects of these interactions with Nature are relatively well known. Once again we have to ask: do we know the long term effects of this for our survival as a species?

There is yet another aspect that does not enjoy frequent attention in the literature on the man - Nature - relation, namely, the aspect of our relation to our own inner Nature.

We have often wondered - in order to start with a quite mundane example - about the raison d'être of fast food. While a permanent shortage of time is inevitable under the present social conditions,[29] the willingness of all too many people to ignore the longing of our taste buds seems to suggest a lack of sensuousness unbelievable to a few of us. Has the sensuousness of these people not been cultivated, or has it been aborted from day one in their lives? Or, how is it possible that a music melodically, rhythmically and harmonically impoverished to a yet again unbelievable degree has become so popular? Is it because of this poverty that electronic amplification has to come to its help? What does the need for amplification tell us about people's sense of hearing? Or: We all know that death and violence are an integral part of today's entertainment. People can "handle" several such acts per show without any problems, yet a death witnessed on the highway affects them strongly, albeit only for the next few kilometers on the road.

As we become less and less sensuous about our own bodies, we are bound to relate to other human beings - essential parts of our environment - in a form of sensuousness strongly affected by this. While so many of us seem not to have experienced a cultivation of their senses, a process about which Rousseau knew so much, it is not surprising that they would treat their fellow human beings violently if they are not forced to repress their uncultivated senses. We need not elaborate on this pattern, since Hobbes has done this already. Sexuality in combination with extreme deprivation of other kinds of sensuousness, as we find it in the slums of this world, be it the "developing" or the "developed" countries, may very well be an adequate explanation for the population growth that we are experiencing.[30] We would feel quite strongly about this suggestion, since the population growth can hardly be explained, as is often tried, by hygiene, medical progress or improved nutrition. These are out of reach for the impoverished and deprived masses.[31] To be sure, it is not our intent to ascribe the modest reproduction rate of the rich to the higher cultivation of their senses; they handle their desires simply more smartly.

In this context, we would like to stress that it is certainly not our view that the population growth in "developing countries" is the main culprit for our ecological problems. To conceive of population growth this way is all too often grounded in the tacit assumption that the Western "standard of living" should be globalized - a ludicrous idea in the first place. Let us remember that the "developed countries", though barely representing 20% of the world's population consume well over 60% of the world's energy and produce a pollution quite in keeping with this.[32]

Certainly, a technological solution to the problem of population growth could, as in the case of other problems that we have with Nature, be attempted. And yet, proposing to treat population growth and other ecological problems in such terms is culture bound and, for reasons soon to be inspected, inadequate to the issue at hand.[33]

In order to make an attempt at getting closer to what it takes to resolve our problems with Nature, we would like to submit the following consideration.

There is obviously ample reason to believe that a continuation on our present course will imply a threat to our survival.[34] Despite knowing that we are constituted to exist within very limited survival conditions, we seem to be intent on destroying these conditions. To say it again, Nature will live on without us and will be indifferent to our extinction.[35] Nature out there will adjust to unlimited changes, e.g., in temperature, while we have to make sure that our body temperature has to stay within the incredibly narrow range from 28 to 42 degrees Celsius. While it would seem undoubtedly consistent with the logic of modern technology to apply itself even to the engineering of our own species,[36] it still remains to be seen, whether this would imply better chances for the survival of us, or whether it would merely create new problems. Instead of advocating potentially dubious technological fixes we wonder whether all our ecological problems are not trying to teach us the following: if we want to survive as a species, then the Nature around us and our understanding and treatment of her must be in keeping with the Nature that we ourselves are.

This question announces the possibility that our present problems could stem from our now problematic Nature. Inspecting this possibility more closely will inform us about three internally connected aspects of the man-Nature-relationship. At the obvious level, the production and consumption of objects implies that the man-Nature-relation is a synthetic one, meaning that our interaction with Nature, i.e. our understanding of and interference in Nature is grounded in the material commonality between the Nature in us and the Nature around us. This, in turn, suggests that this synthesis is an aspect of a materially concrete dialectic in which the human being as a symbolizing part of Nature is the "Transcending Other" (Marx) to her. This dialectic, while going beyond a merely material relation to Nature remains grounded in her and thus defies a merely philosophical explication. And thirdly, this formulation entails our hope that a lived appreciation of this dialectic would facilitate greater clarity on the question of what it takes to establish peace between our species and the Nature around us and in us. Of course, our understanding of the man-Nature-relationship, as it is the central issue of our considerations, will require a good deal of further unpacking. This much, however, should be clear: the threat to our survival through our own actions is a glaring indication of the material foundation of man's synthetic relationship to Nature. If our relationship to Nature were not a materially synthetic one, how could it then be a negative one in the sense of being suicidal for us?

Assuming that our considerations are not completely mistaken, we think it is obvious that turning our negative synthesis with Nature into a positive one is a matter entirely different from merely applying technological, legal or political remedies. These measures would only result in a vastly intensified social control which in turn would devour enormous costs, i.e., would require an ultimately energetic input that would in all likelihood exceed all potential savings. As some of the more thoughtful writers on today's environmental problems know,[37] real solutions to these problems will take qualitatively different approaches than what is involved in the application of remedies created by the mode of thinking presently dominant. A positive synthesis with Nature would in all likelihood require a fundamental change in our mode of thinking, indeed, in our culture. This, in turn, demands clarification of what precisely today's mode of thinking is. In other words, the human subject involved in today's synthesis with Nature needs to be understood, before his problematic Nature can be determinately negated and changed by an alternative proposal for living. Without such clarification (and more, as we shall see), an attempt to solve contemporary issues remains superficial.

The weight of the problem before us can be grasped by going through the following considerations.

Today's natural sciences do not normally acknowledge the synthetic Nature of their wisdom. That is to say that they, for the most part, do not even consider what used to be a strong line of thought in Western philosophy namely, that all knowledge is grounded in the structural commonality between the human mind and the objects around him. The above mentioned significance of the *material* commonality between man and Nature for the creation of knowledge about her is, of course, not even remotely contemplated by the practitioners of these disciplines. At the same time, one cannot deny that the sciences "as are" have generated a vast body of knowledge of which one cannot simply say that it is incorrect. This means that those like us, who see today's environmental problems as an indication of a problematic relation between man and Nature, have the burden of sorting out how a knowledge that is as correct as classical scientific findings are, could turn out to be so untrue to Nature around us and in us. At any rate, our suicidal treatment makes it clear *that* there is today a fundamental falsity in our relation to Nature. *What* precisely this falsity consists of and what it takes to remedy it is a somewhat different matter. We strongly suspect that this falsity begins at the level of our ways of understanding Nature.

Over the years, there have been numerous voices in the natural and social sciences, and also in philosophy, who have tried to link the increasingly more serious environmental problems to the modern social structure and the kind of human being living in it.[38] Among these voices, the American Anthropologist Richard N. Adams has been, in our view, the most articulate one in placing culture and society squarely into the realm of Nature. For him, all socio-cultural constructs are merely the highest stage in natural evolution so far attained. Culture is elevated matter for Adams of which he admits, however, that the precise details of this elevation can probably never be identified. Culture is nonetheless understood by him as that weapon in survival that is fully part of Nature and yet is by far the most advanced aspect in her evolution.[39]

Since the Paleolithic, human individuals have, according to Adams, competed with one another for control over natural resources, energy being the quintessential one among them.[40] Growth in socio-cultural complexity has finally allowed our species to solve the problems of energetic supply. At the same time, disposing of waste, nowadays conspicuously of heat waste and nuclear materials no longer usable, keeps posing problems of suicidal dimensions. As Adams puts it, the problem is not "...where the energy will come from, but where it is leading us".[41] While it is beyond doubt, for Adams, that human interaction has embarked on a fatal trajectory, he also thinks that "(I)t is, perhaps, a little much to ask of man that, in order to survive, he cease to be human".[42] In other words, a positive synthesis between Nature and the Nature that we are is unthinkable for him.

Even only noting this problem allows us to indicate that Adams' theory of evolution may also in other respects turn out to be a product of the modern mode of thinking. By assuming that man has not changed since the Paleolithic, i.e., has always been what he is now, Adams is in the danger of projecting his culture bound ideas back into previous stages in evolution. This brings up a quite complex dilemma which we share with Adams in a way. Though its inspection has to be delayed for the moment, its emergence adds to the urgency to at least sketch it here.

On the one hand, Adams does not contemplate the possibility that cultural constructs, e.g., religions or other world views, could fascinate individuals, even their "inventors", to such a degree that these constructs limit, even incapacitate the further evolution of that social system in which they exist. They may very well do so by limiting the level of individuation and thus of competition. According to Max Weber, it is due to this reason that otherwise highly developed societies like ancient China and India never developed a capitalist social structure. On the other hand, Adams' lack of genuine understanding of societies which do not think along his lines and yet are interpreted by him in his way, does not limit his ability to explain advantages, and lack thereof, in the course of evolution. Great yet stagnating cultures have been destroyed by others that were more interested in the growth of power. Adams may not do justice to these great cultures, but he explains them.

It is our contention that Adams' hopeless pessimism stems from his one-sided concept of the human individual and, consequently from his one-sided concept of culture. To the extent that Adams' views reflect today's praxis very well - as we shall try to establish - he is also limited by them. And yet, a thorough understanding and critique of the ideas presented by him would be quite helpful for our considerations.

The instrumentality of culture, already indicated in Adams' view as the human weapon in survival, comes clearly to light even more when one analyzes his concept of power. For him, all social relations are power relations.[43] Power as a social relation is elevated beyond and distinguished from control by Adams. Even at lower levels of evolution than the one of homo sapiens, parts of Nature control one another, as cows, a somewhat mundane example, control the growth of grass. At the human level, this control is a matter of correct understanding measured in terms of the ability to manipulate things advantageously. This understanding already implies that one among other requirements for culture has to be in place, namely that of cognitive symbolization. Power, as a quintessentially social relation goes beyond control. It requires that control can be used to control objects of which the power seeker knows that they are valued by others who lack control over these objects. This indicates that power cannot be without a minimal set of symbolizations, i.e., an at least incipient cultural system of concepts and values.

It is additionally important, according to Adams, to retain awareness of the often taken for granted circumstance that our species comes in segregated individual bodies[44] which, like all bodies in Nature, have to compete for survival. This competition implies that the weapon of culture, though shared in an however antagonistic fashion, turns the materially concrete human body with abilities found nowhere else in Nature, into the basic unit in the struggle for life. This does not exclude co-operation among individuals in a variety of forms, i.e., the build-up of social arrangements like families, communities, corporations, etc. as "survival vehicles",[45] particularly as long as they serve the egofocal interests of each involved. While this, in turn, makes an understanding of historically ever more complex social, or better, power structures, a necessity for the social analyst, it is the human individual which remains for Adams, the anthropologist, the basic unit of that analysis.

Since power is the issue in the world of man, gaining as much of it as possible is the task of any individual. This accelerates, for Adams, the irreversible growth direction in socio-cultural evolution beyond what happens on less advanced levels of Nature that lack the capacity for culture. Power allows one to take away power from those who have less - not nothing (!) - of it. This inevitably leads to power structures in a multitude of forms of exploitation. At any rate, given the competition among all individuals, power (like profit in the merely economic realm) flows inevitably to the top.[46] Those who have more of it are in the position to get more of it and have to behave accordingly. Adams quotes the bible at St. Matthew, chapter 13, verse 12: "For whosoever hath not, from him shall be taken that he hath". Adhering to this principle too literally would, however, be quite detrimental to the exploiter's interests in the long run. Profits in power imply the same danger that Marx saw with regards to economic profits: the destruction of "buying power" at the bottom end. Power can only be gained from those who have at least some of it. Since power, however, depends ultimately on control over material/energetic objects, their extraction from Nature provides, up to a point, a way out of the emerging problem of society ending up with too many individuals from whom power can hardly be gained. As a remedy, society simply needs to increase the rate of extracting material/energetic objects from Nature and pump them into society. Control over these and thus power will, of course, be unevenly distributed. The growth in power in such an expanding society will occur at an increasing rate and is a process that cannot be reversed. Trying to do so would mean, as we read before, to force man to be non-human. One important form of this power struggle in modern capitalist societies is the attempt to keep levels of employment high. The promise of ever more growth must, therefore, not be absent from public statements of political and economic leaders. High, even growing rates of production and consumption and, thus, of profits and buying "power" are an obvious consequence. As long as the "little guy" has that kind of power (sometimes also expressed in strike action), the social, or better the power system will flourish. As a consequence, this kind of growth will, sooner than later, turn Nature around us into an environment uninhabitable for our species.

The culture driven growth of power structures is unique in the universe and has, according to Adams,[47] once upon a time, rung in the "Eighth Day" of creation. This notion emphasizes that with the inevitable growth of power, comes an inevitable growth in an ever more creative interpretation of the environment, including human beings, as resources. This is merely a consequence of the interest inherent in power, namely to gain more of it.

As Adams puts it, high culture cannot be had at low energy costs.[48] It follows from here that levels of cultural complexity are proportionate to the level of energy turn-over. This, in turn implies that the more power there is in a system. i.e., the more complex the competition for power is, the more powerful that system will be in comparison to other social systems with less complexity. Therefore, a system of greater complexity can exercise power over other less developed social systems, should it decide to channel its power flows into external competition. To do just that became inevitable at some point in time. This took on an entirely new quality with the emergent supremacy of Western society a few hundred years ago.

The rules ("norms") in the competition for power are, needless to say for Adams, set by those in power, although this activity will seldomly go unchallenged by competitors in the field.[49] With the increasing complexity of social or power structures, the enforcement of normative regulations of the power games would become too costly, if internalization of norms could not be instilled via an increasingly elaborate set of mental constructs, or ideologies as some might say. It is in this sense that, for Adams, power holders have, in evolution, to rely increasingly on what he calls the belief in the cultural potential of the exercises of direct power by those who have it. Of course, this potential needs to be backed up with real power, should the need arise. Ultimately, so Adams notes, the question remains: "who holds the knife".[50]

With the growth of ever more complex power structures accompanied by numerical growth of human bodies available to compete in these structures, cultural complexity has to grow itself. The media of integration at the cultural level have to change as well along the lines of social evolution. One could think in this connection of a sequence leading more or less from kinship, religion, to philosophy, theories of the state and, nowadays, to science and technology, all usually accompanied by artistic and legal forms compatible with them. All of these media in which cultural integration has been expressed at one stage of evolution or another had their times of emergence and dominance. Their eventual supersession over time has not necessarily meant their abolition. Even modern man recognizes some sort of kinship and religion. Although they no longer provide societal integration, they have survived only in rudimentary, yet at times useful forms.

According to Adams, it is one of the important functions of refined forms of culture that they help to distract people to some extent, if not totally, from striving for power. While this greatly contributes to social control, at times even at relatively low costs in energetic terms (remember: internalization of norms and values !), they may also serve as means for gaining power by those who choose to see these areas this way. Preachers, teachers, entertainers and scientists fall into this category. For them, the arts, religion, science or education serve as "survival vehicles".[51] Obviously, the amount of energy flowing within developed systems has to be such that it enables them to differentiate out such cultural systems and to have people specialize in them. We could speak here, following Adams, of a societal thermodynamics that permits the scientist, for instance, to pursue his specific interests. These, like other specialized interests, are, of course, part of the social competition for power. Sticking to the example of the scientist we could say that his interests are focused accordingly: he works on what is in demand, i.e. is valued by others. This, after all, is the foundation of whatever limited power he can find within the "survival vehicle" of science.

Science as an example of a specialized cultural system allows us to point out that the conceptualization of such systems have their impact on how the man-Nature-relation is seen. In this sense, we could say that certain thermodynamic conditions have to be met by society before it could develop a field such as physics and, later yet, of – thermodynamics in it. We cannot let the reference to this circumstance pass without hinting that it provides one with a possibility for a critique of Adams' views. To the extent that Adams places culture squarely into Nature and thus into her thermodynamics, serious conceptual problems for his understanding of culture may be anticipated; his own theory is relative to its own position in the evolution of societal thermodynamics. This, to say the least, relativizes Adams' theory clearly.

In view of Adams' concept of "survival vehicles", we have to remember that they play their role in social institutions other than the sciences as well, such as economics, politics, religion, etc. (e.g. modern corporations, trade unions, political parties, churches, etc). Competition, though not eliminated, is highly regulated in these structures and is surrounded by normative expectations like honesty, loyalty, openness, or simply "team-spirit". The costs of breaking the rules by which one is expected to play in these "survival vehicles" are usually set so high that breaking them may not be gainful, in power terms. Similar constraints permeate other types of "survival vehicles" as well, such as marriages, friendships or neighborhoods. These "vehicles" survive for no other reason than to generate what is valued. In other words, power requires constraints but is not absent from whatever pacified subsystems a society may retain. Therefore, the somewhat contradictory situation emerges that, in terms of Adams' theory, power cannot be without that which negates or at least limits it: constraints. In this case, we would agree with Adams that as long as there is power, there have to be norms – and the other way around.

As we saw, for Adams, culture is a conglomerate of meaning, values and norms. It is a constitutive aspect in the exercise of power. This tells him that culture has to be materially concrete itself, otherwise it would not work within this material world. At the same time, Adams is aware that there is a difference between what is merely the matter-energy-complex and that special form of it we call culture. That is why he speaks of culture as being *elevated* matter or energy. His problem is, and he admits to it, that the precise form and process of that elevation has so far escaped our observation, and might do so forever.[52] For this reason, he has to operate with what he calls an "as-if-methodology".[53] By this he means to say that he treats, for methodological reasons, the mental sphere "as if" it were different from the material one, although he would not subscribe to that distinction at the theoretical level.[54] Adams believes that he can live with this inconsistency, since cultural phenomena can only be dealt with to the extent that they "materialize" themselves, i.e., appear in a material-energetic form. He does not feel compelled to raise the old philosophical question for the conditions on the basis of which concepts - or culture as a whole - could work in this material world. Raising this kind of question is, for Adams, a slipping away into the rather non-rewarding field of philosophy.[55] *That* culture works in this world, is for him as a student of social relations a sufficient reason to inspect it.

In anticipation of considerations to be presented later in this essay, we should note an observation at this point which may very well baffle a good many of our readers: there are striking similarities between the American anthropologist Richard N. Adams and the German poet and thinker Johann Wolfgang von Goethe. Both speak of the realm of symbols as being an elevation of Nature and both have kept their distance from philosophy. Having said that we hasten to add that these similarities, while undoubtedly present, do not diminish telling differences. In particular, the two differ fundamentally in their views on the elevation of Nature to culture. The differences in this regard rest with the circumstance that Goethe takes the commonality of Nature in all there is to be primarily the foundation for the possibility of elevating this commonality to an ever more refined level of a Nature grounded social togetherness. At the same time, he knows of forces, conditions and consequences of an individuated elevation of Nature to a supplier of tools in power relations and fears them. Thus, cultivation and, for that matter, culture have a quite different meaning for Goethe than they have for Adams. For Goethe, they allow for a positive synthesis between man and Nature; for Adams, they do not.

All this notwithstanding, it is important for our considerations to understand Adams' concept of culture better yet. After all, it is our intent to understand those who argue that our species can only live in what we have to call a negative synthesis with Nature. A very convenient way of accomplishing such better understanding of Adams' concept of culture would be to examine his concept of human communication. We shall see then how culture as communicative interaction among humans accelerates, in Adams' view, evolutionary growth and does so to a degree nowhere else to be found than in our species.

Adams[56] is aware that getting an informational message requires getting it materially. Messages are, for Adams, flows of structured matter/energy, like sound-waves or light-waves. Their reception by the compatible organ of the human body does not, however, guarantee that they would be understood. In the non-human world (of animals, plants, rocks etc.) and also among machines including computers, the sheer reception of the informational energy will trigger a definite response. This is why one speaks of communication taking place at that level in a 100% feedback fashion. Humans do not only stand in the flow of information at the material level, they also elevate that flow to symbolic understanding, if not all the time, then very often. This double relationship to "material" objects (so reminiscent and yet so different from Marx's concept of it) requires human physiology in two aspects. It requires, on the one hand, the urge (neuronal firing) of the human brain to elevate information to meaning and this has to be carried out, on the other hand, by the brain working in terms of a cognitive frame of reference. Adams perceives of this frame of reference as having been built up in the sedimentation of previous experiences. How and why neurons fire and how that symbolic framework has emerged in the course of evolution (or in an individual's life) is as unclear to Adams as it is to neuro-physiologists, the scientific experts on this matter.[57] Since meaning in itself is of zero-dimension,[58] i.e. is outside space and time, Adams does not even attempt to deal with it. Thus, we have reason again to understand that and why Adams is only dealing with culture when it manifests itself within this three dimensional world. In other words, culture, for Adams, can only be dealt with in the moments of it being "done".

To the extent that humans come in different bodies, their experiences and the sedimentation of these experiences are, by necessity, individually different. Since meaning will never be identical between any two humans, human speech and other forms of communication among members of our species cannot be a matter of 100%-feedback and cannot exist without interpretation. Otherwise, the receiving of a message would be its understanding. This, however, is obviously not the case. By the same token, cultural communication is always a matter of mutual surprises. These surprises remain bearable, as long as they can be responded to by those involved. In other words, the degree of novelty in communication as in all other human interaction requires flexibility in one's reactions. In this sense, culture requires constant learning and this has added so enormously to the dynamics of cultural evolution.

In the course of socio-cultural evolution, power structures got ever more complex and came to depend more and more, as we indicated above, on the control of abstract means rather than on obviously material ones. Accordingly, the manipulation of meaning systems, e.g. bureaucratic procedures, religious beliefs, the interpretation of the law etc., grew in significance in the exercise of power. This implies that retaining or gaining power is increasingly contingent on the purposive re-definition of meaning, values and norms. This ability becomes the most significant means in the competition for power. Power thus takes on a new kind of alertness and, as a mental stance, teaches us to see ever more objects, concrete or abstract ones, as means to the end of power. To be sure, not even power itself is the goal; it too is only a means for getting more of it.

The art of instrumentally re-defining social reality has been explored by the German Sociologist Niklas Luhmann in his Theory of Sense Systems[59] in greater detail than Adams has done in his theory of power structures. This makes him important for our considerations.

Similar to Adams, Luhmann speaks of communication as a flow of information that is elevated to sense through the process of interpretation. Interpretation requires the presence of a sense system, i.e. a framework of concepts, in terms of which incoming signals are understood. Exposure to an environment is for Luhmann experience in so far as that environment gives off information.[60] Regardless of whether the environment consists of people, Nature, the media, the interior of a car, or whatever, the information coming from it may turn out to be momentarily "indigestable", i.e. too complex. Succeeding in the interpretation of such kind of information, i.e. learning, can only be accomplished through restructuring the sense system so far at work in the attempts of interpretation. Higher levels of interpretive ability require higher levels of abstraction in sense systems. If so, experience can again be "cut down to manageable size". In order to attain a higher level of comprehensiveness, the process of re-structuring requires self-examination, i.e., reflexion on the part of the sense system. This enables the improved sense system to regain its ability to participate in communicative interaction with other sense systems. The function of sense systems, thus, lies with their ability to "handle", if need be via internal re-structuring, the surprises experienced by them and, in doing so, to produce new experiences for other sense systems outside of it.

It is at this point, where Luhmann's and Adams' theories could speak to one another gainfully, especially since communicative interaction is growth oriented for Luhmann as well. Luhmann understands his theory of sense systems as a science which has the potential of providing other sense systems in society – e.g. politics, the legal system, the mass media, etc., including other sciences – with strategies for communicative interaction.[61] Such a science has become, at least in praxis, though perhaps unacknowledged, the leading subsystem of society today. It overarches other systems like economy, politics, religion, etc. It promises to improve the abilities of these other systems to react to surprises coming from their environment and thus helps them to retain cognitive control. As we saw, Adams too is aware that with higher levels of social evolution, power depends increasingly on improved abilities to create re-definitions.

Regardless of whether one speaks of the ability of re-definition (Adams) or of strategies in the re-structuring of sense (Luhmann), both have become, at least in modern times, conditions for leadership. As such they will not leave the rest of society unaffected. Beyond that, there are a number of further similarities (and differences) between Adams and Luhmann which, in view of considerations to be taken up later, need to be inspected.

Let us first point out that both, Adams and Luhmann, share the notion of the relativity of truth. Yet, while Luhmann says that the truth of his modern kind of science is relative and that this is a statement relative to our day and age,[62] the re-definition of concepts of reality has been, for Adams, a human property all along. Adams also appreciates, in contrast to Luhmann, that re-definitions can ill afford to be incorrect, when it comes to the triggering of energetic processes, simply because real power cannot be had without them.

For Luhmann, the human subject is constituted, i.e. understands itself, in terms of its (temporarily valid) frame of reference. This allows Luhmann, the sense theorist, to understand that the individual was somebody else, e.g. in the religiosity of the European Middle Ages or in the kinship structure of a tribal society than it is today. For Adams, the anthropologist, the human individual has been the same at least since the Paleolithic and has always used, as a means to his end of power, whatever was around him, be it a religion or a technology. What Luhmann called instrumentalism, i.e., a means-ends thinking carried far beyond Max Weber's rationalism, is for him a recent emergent, while for Adams, though he does not use the term, instrumentalism has always been an intrinsic aspect of social, i.e. power relations. The only difference for Adams is that man, under less complex conditions, had access to fewer means than he has today. At his point, Adams position comes, in our view, into the danger of ignoring the significance of social form. To some extent in agreement with Luhmann, we would say that modernity does not just make more means available, but that also the identity or self-understanding of the human subject is, to say the least, not independent of the perception of these means. To the extent that man's self-understanding depends on where and how he/she places him/herself into that environment, qualitative differences and changes in man's subjectivity have accompanied his evolution.[63]

Under the conditions of modernity, environmental problems are, according to Luhmann, also primarily complex sets of information. Leadership in mastering these problems consists in proposing alternative ways of conceptualizing them. Pointing them out contributes to the continued leadership of a science of sense systems in its functionality for other social sub-systems. Thus, it can assist other agencies, like government departments, bureaucracies, technologies, environmental industries etc., as they have evolved into complex networks of communication with their intent to develop concepts capable of handling the environmental problems perceived to be at hand. While Luhmann is aware of the privileged status of working at that level, he does not conceptualize that that privilege is a consequence of an enormous energetic surplus taken from the environment and channeled into these vast networks. This, however, would be clear to Adams who sees that the activities of connoisseurs of sense mean little more than having another energy consuming agent in place. As such, this agent is merely a further threat to our survival in Adams' view. For Luhmann's theory of, as we might say, disembodied sense systems, such threat is again information only, to be dealt with most efficiently at that level. He would, of course, not deny that materially concrete problems underlie such information, but for the sake of cognitive efficiency, it would be better to deal with them only as sources of information. This is, for him, a result of the evolutionary process of increased levels in the division of labor.

Among the commonalities between Adams and Luhmann, there is one which would allow us to point out an important aspect in the ability of developing re-definitions.

Adams and Luhmann[64] share the view that the process of sense manipulation is beyond morals and/or ethics. They both do not deny that morals exist in social interaction, but they see them as being merely aspects of cultural systems which, like other such aspects, need not to be what they happen to be. This requires that one conceptualizes morals in a sufficiently detached way, in order to make them accessible for manipulation. This, however, could not be done, would the process of sense making accept moral limitations on itself. Disposing of moral limitations is, needless to say, a highly conditional activity. For Luhmann, the detachment from morals is constitutive for the ability of his kind of science to retain leadership; as such, this detachment is an advantage of increased differentiation in social evolution. For Adams, the manipulative detachment from morals requires power, i.e. is also based on a highly privileged position in social interaction; as such, it has always existed, but has increased along the lines of enhanced societal thermodynamics.

However differently conceived, for both Adams and Luhmann there is undoubtedly a vertical differentiation in contemporary society. By this, neither one means to suggest that today's society can still be characterized by traditional class distinctions à la Karl Marx. Stratification now is more a matter of gradation. Not everybody is equally successful in creating re-definitions and in making them accepted. While this matter would require a detailed examination - something we will deliver in chapter three - we would nonetheless suggest to express this distinction in terms of the concepts of instrumentalism on the part of the power elite and of adaptation rationality on the part of those having less power.[65] Both modes of thinking share the ability of re-defining, but instrumentalism manages to set the conditions (conceptually, normatively and evaluatively) to which others have to adapt. This adaptation rationality is practiced, e.g. when ego accepts alter's decisions and decides accordingly; or: when the applicant for a grant accepts the rules for the making of applications, instead of arguing with the granting body about these rules.[66] This indicates to us that, while instrumentalism and adaptation rationality reflect power differentials, they may also vary from one to the next case of interaction. In other words, differences in power are no longer necessarily institutionalized like classes were traditionally in capitalism.

At all levels of the system, growth in power and, thus, growth in constraints and frustration trigger, according to Adams, the interest in further growth. Among those who have substantial amounts of power, staying ahead of the pack implies a constant interest in obtaining means for getting more power; among those who have less or even little of it, the issue is to gain some of it, since having nothing that is valued by others could easily imply elimination from society. It is important to note, though, that even that danger can be used to exercise some power; e.g., totally destitute people can exploit the claim to the value of compassion by those more fortunate. This may very well trigger their help and the amount of that help is a measure of the power left to the destitute. Of course, this would only work where compassion happens to be valued.

The never ceasing interest in means indicates that instrumentalism and adaptation rationality have, as the modes of thinking implied in power systems, gone beyond traditional rationalism and some (though not all) of its previously existing limitations. On the one hand, the traditional rationalism as means-ends thinking has lost its ends in instrumentalism. We have reached a level in social evolution at which indeed anything, once accomplished, turns instantaneously into a means again; today, even one's own self can totally or in part be re-defined. Regardless of whether this has been the case since the Paleolithic or not, it is the case now. On the other hand, this process, while nearing universalization in modernity, has contributed to the transcendence-and-containment of all previously existing class divisions.[67] Furthermore, since means are all that is left and since they grant as little satisfaction to each of us as gold did to Midas, it is this Midas syndrome, as we like to call it, that implies permanent growth in the exploitation of Nature and also in the dumping of wasted (i.e. not usable for us) Nature back onto her. Increasingly excessive production and consumption necessitate the growing uninhabitability of Nature for us. If culture has to obey the Second Law of Thermodynamics, as Adams rightfully thinks it has, then the dissipation of unusable energy, i.e. waste, will eventually terminate man's evolution. This circumstance implies that instrumentalism cannot be without constraints. These constraints, however, are dealt with – instrumentalistically.[68]

At the same time, we should bear in mind that instrumentalism and adaptation rationality go hand in hand with an image of man of which it is by no means certain that it is *the* image of man. Certainly, under the circumstances that prevail, a different understanding of man and his/her relation to Nature appear illusory and a positive, i.e. non-suicidal synthesis with Nature seems indeed to be out of the question. By the same token, however, we wonder whether it is not precisely this circumstance which suggests that another kind of thinking and being could point the way out of the present impasse. Or, to phrase the matter differently: Does the absence of a positive synthesis with Nature not make it obvious that dealing with the problems that we have with Nature requires dealing with the problematic Nature that we have become, or, according to Adams, we have been all along? If this is close to the crucial point, then the enormity of the task to solve our problems with Nature comes to light as well; it would take us to the roots of our culture – and beyond. It would take us into a realm into which curative means, be they of a technological or "philosophical" kind, do not reach. Therefore, our own inspection of the problem at hand and our own attempt to indicate an alternative way of being and thinking cannot have the purpose of making a contribution to this undoable task. But, it may strike a chord in those among us who experience in themselves an evolvement of an alternative way of being and thinking. For those, our study of Goethe's view of Nature may very well be of interest.

At this point we would like to report an experience which we think is indicative of today's thinking. It may help to illustrate, however mundanely so, how difficult the proposal of an alternative to today's ways of being and thinking is.

After having given the first draft of this chapter to a few friends of ours with the invitation for critical suggestions, some of them told us that the chapter dealt too much with the human individual and society. This baffled us – particularly in view of the title given to the chapter - although we should have known better. This chapter seemingly has to look unbalanced to that majority of us that does not instantaneously see our species as an intrinsic and yet unique part of Nature. This reaction reinforced the desire in us to find out how it could be that such a way of thinking managed to gain dominance. This curiosity may also indicate that we, different from Adams, do not think that man has always been the way he is today.

Notes

[1] "Die Zeit", Overseas Edition, 1 Dec 1995, p. 9.
[2] Weizsäcker, 1994, p 6, see also "The Kingston Whig Standard", 24 Nov 1995, p 24, The "Guardian Weekly", 20 Aug 1995, p 13
[3] The "Guardian Weekly", 20 Aug 1995, p. 13 It is also reported there that the World Bank fears that the wars of the next century will be fought over water.

[4] Kloppenburg, 1990, pp. 118ff; Simmons, 1991, p 255ff; Weizsäcker, 1994, p. 6

[5] For an example from Philippine rice farming, see Shiva, 1991, pp. 2743.

[6] Seed producers increasingly offer seeds which require the use of only their own fertilizers; see "Society of Biodynamic Farming & Gardening", Newsletter Dec 1995, p 4 and Newsletter Summer 1999, pp. 1ff; see also Kloppenburg, 1990, pp 247ff.

[7] Simmons, 1991, chapters 5 & 6; Verbeek, 1994, pp. 1, 4

[8] This is a characteristic feature of modern science and its mode of thinking and yet it is totally unthinkable in Goethe's kind of science; see chapter 7 passim

[9] Weizsäcker, 1994, pp 6, 14

[10] The global warming together with the melting of the polar ice caps will lead to a rise in sea level of many meters The flooding of coastal lowlands and cities is an obvious consequence; see "Toronto Star", 30 Sept 1995, section B, p. 6.

[11] These are some of the consequences of large scale agribusiness as they are based largely on mono-cultures, see Kloppenburg, 1990, chapters 8 & 9, Weizsäcker, 1994, pp. 102, 107; see also Delouche, 1983, p. 8.

[12] Sixel, 1988, p. 19n13

[13] For suggestions of this kind, see Ayres & Nair, 1984, passim and also Guyol, 1971, p. 136.

[14] Simmons, 1995, chapters 5 & 6, Verbeek, 1994, pp 75, 205, Weizsäcker, 1994, pp 188ff

[15] Adams, 1975, pp 192ff

[16] The excessive growth in the demand for residential space is reflected, in the case of Germany, by the following figures $20 \ m^2$/person in 1960, 47 m^2/person expected in 2000; see Verbeek, 1994, pp 184, 272; see also Koch, 1987, pp 104ff

[17] The 80 million Germans have, statistically, 200 million car seats available to them. Most of these are driven around empty most of the time, see Verbeek, 1994, p. 191. The number of cars in operation has been steadily increasing there as in most other countries, see, e g., "Deutschland Nachrichten", 27 Oct 1995, p 4. The oil industry expects a doubling in the number of cars globally in the next 20 years, see "Der Spiegel", 23 Oct 1995, p. 214. Even only a brief look into the "Transportation Energy Data Book", 1998, pp 3/1 to 3/4, indicates that the emissions of transportation related gases have increased between 1990 and 1994 by about 5 – 10 % in North America, while they saw a slight decrease in the U K. and Germany.

[18] Tourism is a major contributor to environmental problems. Hotels built in so-called resorts seal the soil, close off seashores, remove natural vegetation etc., see Verbeek, 1994, pp. 182f. Hotels are also places of excessive consumption for which the use of water alone is a good example: 50 guests in a luxury hotel consume as much water in 55 days as 300 nomads and 450 cattle in 3 years, see "Guardian Weekly", 20 Aug 1995, p 13. Given the connection between tourism and air travel, it might be worth noting that the fuel consumption/passenger over a distance of 5000 km is equal to the use of a car for a whole year, this is the unanimous result of a telephone inquiry with several major airlines At the same

time, air travel is expected to grow annually four to five times over the next 15 to 20 years, see "Deutschland Nachrichten" 8 Dec 1995, p 5

[19] Energy consumption in the "First World" is still very much greater than in the "Third World" An average German, for example, uses more than 7 times the energy than an average Egyptian. This pattern holds for other kinds of consumption, see Weizsäcker, 1994, pp. 71, 204ff; see also Parikh, 1994, pp 2940f.

[20] Safe storage of nuclear waste requires a thinking in terms of tens of thousands of years. Our civilization is not prepared for that, see Weizsäcker, 1994, p 78; see also Simmons, 1991, pp. 346ff The safety standards applied in the operation of nuclear reactors today is one accident à la Chernobyl in 10 000 years. This, obviously, forbids the construction of those 10 000 reactors required in view of rising energy needs, see Verbeek, 1994, p 79.

[21] Deforestation per year at the global level occurs at a rate equal to the land area of Austria and Switzerland combined, see Weizsäcker, 1994, pp. 6, 59ff; see also World Resources Institute, 1989, pp. 69 – 88.

[22] For an example within the European context, see Weizsäcker, 1994, pp. 226f.

[23] See references in endnote 6

[24] For specific information, see Jha, 1995, p 492

[25] See Adams, 1975, pp 302f; Adams, 1988, pp. 57, 241, Simmons, 1991, pp 220, 234

[26] Adams, 1975, pp 302f; see also Frisken, 1973, p. 65, Summers, 1971, pp 105f.

[27] The bio-diversity of plants and animals, be it through traditional breeding or increasingly through gene technology, has been shrinking rapidly Vulnerability to diseases and infertility has grown accordingly. Recently, corn in the Southern US could only be immunized against certain diseases and thus be protected against possible extinction through cross-breeding with corn from a variety found in South Africa and extinct in the West While 3 000 year old seed from the Egyptian pyramids has been found to germinate, our gene technology has "succeeded" in keeping certain seeds, e g those of canola and soy, from germination; see Kloppenburg, 1990, chapters 4 – 9, see also Weizsäcker, 1994, pp 6, 102f, 130ff and "Society for Biodynamic Farming & Gardening", Newsletter, Dec 1995, pp 3f

[28] Verbeek, 1994, pp 71f.

[29] It has often been pointed out that people in modern society spend only one tenth of their life time working in the sense of making a living. This view ignores that the instrumentalism of late capitalism does not allow for "waste of time", since all activities are viewed as means to ends; for more on this, see below pp. 75-126. Not only are leisure activities in the strict sense of physics labor, they are even as forms of sheer consumption activities without which production, for instance, of sporting goods, would experience such a serious decline that industry would have to view that drop in consumption as catastrophic

[30] As is well known, Friedrich Engels described the same phenomenon for 19th century England

[31] In the last 10 years there has been a large decline in public assistance in all these areas, and yet a drop in population growth is not occurring, see Werner, 1995, pp. 149ff

[32] It is often claimed that it is the goal of "development aid" to globalize the Western "standard of living" This idea has for many decades been recognized as misleading The issue is to increase consumption potential and, therefore, buying power in the "developing" countries for the benefit of production and export sales by the "developed" countries. In this connection, see Adams, 1975, p 152. And yet, it should be stressed that even a stagnant world population, if it were to achieve the Western "standard of living", would make this earth uninhabitable It would take two to three globes to make such rise in the "standard of living" possible; see Weizsäcker, 1994, pp. 264, 270 The idea of limiting the population growth in the "developing" countries has also been associated with geo-political considerations, see Wilson, 1994, pp 203f

[33] See below pp 112, 116

[34] Verbeek, 1994, p 252 thinks that the "shadow of the future" is big enough to have some impact on us; see also Adams, 1975, p 315 who is, however, less optimistic about the impact of such shadow

[35] It is surprising to see how frequently concepts like "destroying the environment" or even "Nature" can be found in the public debate of environmental issues Even otherwise highly subtle minds are not immune against such misconceptions, see for instance, Schmied-Kowarzik, 1986, p 61. It goes to the credit of Hans Heinz Holz to have pointed out that speaking of the destruction of Nature can only make sense by relating our impact on Nature to the eradication of us as part of Nature; see Holz, 1975, passim and 1984, passim

[36] In most countries, an all out application of gene technology on humans is still legally forbidden, as Weizsäcker, 1994, pp. 137f points out However, human genetic material has been used in animals, see Sylvester & Klotz, 1983, p 28 The sale of human eggs for unknown purposes has occurred in England by using a loophole in the existing law, see CBC Evening News, 1 Nov 1995.

[37] Some experts know very well that solutions to existing environmental problems have to be much more fundamental and thus comprehensive than the ones that are politically feasible, see Verbeek, 1994, pp. 236ff and 251ff in particular, and Weizsäcker, 1994, explicitly on pp 168ff, 266ff

[38] Lotka, 1922, Litt, 1959, Odum, 1971, Summers, 1971

[39] Adams, 1975, pp. 97ff, 283, Adams, 1988, p. IX

[40] Adams, 1975, pp 9ff.

[41] Adams, 1988, p. 241; see also Sixel, 1991, p 206.

[42] Adams, 1975, p 315.

[43] ibid., pp. 9ff.

[44] ibid , pp. XI, 9ff

[45] Adams, 1988, pp 99, 177ff.

[46] ibid , pp. 41, 107f; Sixel, 1991, p 203

[47] Adams, 1988, passim

[48] Adams, 1975, pp 305ff

[49] Since norms are only secondary aspects in power structures, Adams does not pay much attention to norms The word "norm" is not even mentioned in the indexes of his major theoretical writings [Adams, 1975 and 1988] The closest he comes to the treatment of norms is in his considerations about the question of how power holders can use the "finer things of life", e.g., the humanities to channel people's interest. See e.g , Adams 1988, pp. 155, 177ff.

[50] Adams, 1975, pp. 13ff; ibid. p 278, he reminds the reader of Stalin's question regarding the Pope and multinational corporations, when asking. how many divisions do they have?

[51] Adams, 1988, pp 177ff

[52] ibid.: pp 10, 88

[53] Adams, 1975 pp 9, 75ff., for a critical analysis of this, see Sixel, 1988, pp. 63ff and Sixel, 1991, passim

[54] Adams, 1975, pp. 113f; Adams, 1988, p 170

[55] Adams, 1988, p. 11

[56] Adams, 1975, pp. 113f; Adams, 1988, pp. 41, 78ff.

[57] Roth, 1994, pp 250ff; Spitzer, 1996, pp 209ff

[58] Bateson, 1972, as quoted by Adams, 1975, pp. 113f

[59] Habermas & Luhmann, 1971; Luhmann, 1982, Luhmann, 1996, to name but a few of the publications relevant here.

[60] Habermas & Luhmann, 1971, pp 7ff, 25ff; see also Sixel, 1988, pp 80ff

[61] Habermas & Luhmann, 1971, pp. 25f, 29f, 59, 348, 359f; Luhmann, 1982, pp. 360ff

[62] Habermas & Luhmann, 1971, p. 86; Luhmann, 1978, p 41, Luhmann, 1981, pp 103ff, 127, Luhmann, 1982, p 305.

[63] It is perhaps worth noting that Marx was deeply aware of the significance of social form and individual self-perception ["consciousness"], see e g Marx, n d., pp. 5ff, 21ff Indeed, without this awareness, his thinking would not make the sense it has

[64] Regarding Adams, see endnote 49, regarding Luhmann, see Luhmann, 1978, pp 8ff; see also Sixel, 1983, passim; Sixel, 1988, pp 95ff.

[65] Sixel, 1988, pp. 103f; regarding powerlessness and adaptation rationality, see there pp. 134f.

[66] Luhmann's example, Luhmann, 1978, pp 65ff; see also Luhmann, 1983.

[67] Sixel, 1988, pp. 112ff, 126, see also below pp 73-74, 88.

[68] See below pp. 86, 90, 100.

Part II: The Evolution of Western Society

Introductory Note:
Evolution versus History

It has often and convincingly been argued (quite outstandingly so by Karl Marx, Max Weber and Talcott Parsons) that the evolution of Western society is rather unique. This uniqueness has demanded, and reinforced, features which have been identified by such key notions like individuation, abstraction, rationalism and, more recently, instrumentalism. It is our contention that re-visiting the evolution of the West could still shed additional light on the peculiar Nature of the modern individual, although this kind of individual was not foreseeable as a result of that evolution while that evolution was still under way.

Adopting this methodological stance implies projecting a modern point of view into the past. As we, different from Adams, acknowledge this, we are also aware of the circumstance that we add to already existing methodological problems. To understand the present social structure and mode of thinking by tracing their emergence into the past is an endeavor that can easily fall prey, among other problems, to the methodological dilemma of hindsight. In other words, we are in the danger to misunderstand our ancestors, because we know which decisions of theirs led into the future, i.e. our present, while our ancestors did not and could not know that.[1]

In this sense, one might say that the development of modernity, or of late capitalism, was a product of decisions which while not blindly made could not foresee much of their future implications. Therefore, while trying to avoid the projection of a rather dubious teleological wisdom into the past of Western parent societies of late capitalism, we are still entitled to raise the question of what developments and decisions led, however unintentionally so, to what is now the dominant culture on this earth: instrumentalism. In other words, it is not our intention to deliver a condensed *history* of Western Civilization, but to sketch the structural *evolution* of today's dominant culture. To put it differently and bluntly: we do not try to understand the past, but the present. Understanding past epochs, i.e. making *their* sense from within their horizon, may very well be the task of historians; it is not ours.

There is no doubt that the leading position of the culture of instrumentalism was attained through many centuries of developments permeated by conquest and loot, stunning successes, and great blunders. All these came in singular incidents hardly ever following a great vision beyond their immediate or easily obvious consequences. Thus, they changed their meaning through the changing constellations at the level of objective opportunities which, being seized upon, changed the subjective perceptions of those involved. Differently from Adams, we also try to be aware of these changes in subjective perceptions, while still attempting to explain shifts, i.e. losses and gains, of power among the major players involved. We do so, because we believe that even though power has objectively mattered in the emergence of instrumentalism, the social forms of power and the subjective understanding of social interaction were in the past quite distinct from what they are now.

Even though we would accept the widespread view that colonialism and capitalism figure prominently in the genealogy of late capitalism, it would still be advisable to note that not all forms of Western colonialism and capitalism have lead in a straight line to it. Inspecting cases that remained, at least until recently, outside of what turned out to be the mainstream of evolution so far, may still be informative about that mainstream and its peculiarity. It is necessary to emphasize this peculiarity, because in the spreading of late capitalism all over the world, the peculiarity of its mode of being and thinking is likely to be ignored or misunderstood.[2]

Notes

[1] This dilemma has been felt by Marx increasingly during his later years, see Marx, 1973, pp. 100ff, particularly pp 105f; see also Sixel, 1995, pp 19f, 91f

[2] Given that most of what we will present under "The Evolution of Western Society" is a knowledge common to those at least with a modest measure of education, we will not document or "endnote" the events discussed there However, the reader will find "Selected Readings" related to this part of the book at the end behind the "Bibliography"

Chapter 2

Absolutism, Early Capitalism and Their Forms of Colonialism

It was not only European powers who engaged in conquest and loot. Arabia, India, China, Inca-Peru, Aztec-Mexico and others conquered and looted as well. Yet, the forms that their conquests took differed widely from one another and from the European ones. Even among the European colonizing efforts, there existed considerable differences. This will come to light even when we limit our considerations to the main colonizing European powers like Spain (with Portugal), France and England (with Holland). Their colonies took on forms which bear the imprint of the fundamental differences in the social structures of these colonizing countries. And it is only out of one of these European colonial empires, namely the English and its North American offspring, the United States of America, that late capitalism evolved.

The European colonizing nations originated, more or less, in the collapse of the Mediterranean dominated civilization during the Peoples' Migration. This Migration which came to an end roughly around 500 A. D., helped to lay the foundations of the very different forms of feudalism in some parts of Europe and its absence in others.

The feudalism of France emerged when the conquering Franks replaced the heads of the many administrative units of the Roman province of Gallia by their own leaders. Being vastly outnumbered by the conquered, the Franks became soon absorbed ethnically and culturally into the christianized Roman tradition of language, law and belief. It was an important consequence of the division of what soon became

Charlemagne's Empire that its western part, roughly what is now France, separated from the eastern part, roughly what is now Germany. The latter was not romanized, barely christianized at that time, and was in the Middle Ages comprised of much larger feudal units than the West. In the western part, the many and relatively small feudal units adapted from the Romans enjoyed within and among themselves ethnic and cultural homogeneity. The gradual containment and unification of these units into a Paris based monarchy took a number of centuries, during which, in an interesting contrast, Germany with its Holy Roman Empire increasingly disintegrated, mainly because of the self-sufficiency of its constituent parts. In France, this centralization allowed for a much more effective flow of power to the monarchical top of the society than it did in Germany, as one would say using Adams' terminology.[1] The embryonic stages in the development of a power center in France benefited largely from the economic differentiation of its feudal constituents. The king became a protector of an increasingly unifying trade, while the Catholic religion was the idiom in which this integration was expressed. Already during the early stages in the unification of France around Paris, a Parliament of Jurists (1303) and a quite simple bureaucracy emerged within the court. It was the task of this kind of parliament to ascertain that the king's activities, both in their legislative and executive aspects, were consistent with the existing body of law. This, of course, implied an important difference to the English Parliament, which, as we shall see, was a legislative and deliberating body with considerably less concern about creating a coherent set of laws, let alone a constitution. Both, the Parliament and the bureaucracy of France, recruited their members from the Nobility. They laid down the foundation for a centralized administration in the slowly emerging absolutist sense. The noblemen, however, retained their roots in feudalism and their territories. When, in the Hundred Year War, the French Nobility began to draw upon the help of the peasants, i.e., those ones among their own people who were traditionally not supposed to carry weapons and to die in warfare, the unification of France advanced even further. After Jeanne d'Arc's (death at the stake in 1431; now a patron saint of France), the peasantry as the third estate developed yet a new sense of belonging; it became a political force in the sense of this particular political context. The basic framework of absolutist France was established around 1500.

In Spain, the conquering Germanic tribesmen were also soon absorbed ethnically and culturally by the carriers of the christianized Roman civilization. A feudalism, initially similar in structure to that of France, was soon squeezed by the Islamic conquest (700 A. D.) into the northern margin of the Iberian Peninsula. The Reconquista which started from here in 1063, was understood as a religious war and therefore solidified and strengthened the relationship between Crown and Church. This Reconquista did not lead to a return of the pre-existing feudal order. Instead, it was Castile with its vast (in European terms) territory and its socio-economic structure that gained the upper hand. With the final unification between Castile and Aragon (1465), the largely Muslim and Jewish controlled manufacture and trade located in the urban areas were destroyed. This solidified the Catholic absolutism of Spain further. Castile's production of merely raw materials, to a large extent sheep and wool, gained ascendance to the advantage of the rurally based Grandes and the King, who was one of them. Non-agricultural and non-pastoral production was largely ignored. From then on, all economically significant activities were under the immediate supervision of the Crown. In other words, economic relations were contained and channeled through the then evolving absolutist political structure. The absence of manufacture precluded technological innovations on any significant scale. Spain and its people thus lacked an important source of power. We also have to note that since the Reconquista this absolutism had its source of legitimation in the Catholic Church. Conquests without making converts implied that the Spanish Crown would stand to lose its legitimation.

Holland, yet another colonizing force in Europe, experienced an entirely different formation and, thus, had a distinct impact on the evolution of modernity. Rome hardly managed to exercise any power over it. Although loosely associated later with the Holy Roman Empire of the German Nation, feudalism was never fully established in the Netherlands, nor was Roman law and political order accepted, at least not north of the river Rhine. The organization of public works, like irrigation, drainage and, later, dykes, - necessities arising out of geographical conditions - , certainly went beyond private interests and yet were carried out in forms that did not transcend the level of an egalitarian, in many respects tribal, society. The ethnic homogeneity of the Dutch lent itself easily to task oriented mutual assistance organized on the basis of the Germanic concepts of "gouws" (geographical districts) and their assemblies of basically free and equal landholders, fishermen and seafarers. The success of this social structure in dealing with public problems helped to prevent the development of feudalism, at least in the French or the Spanish sense of the word. Christianity, along with ethnicity, soon served as a new unifying bond, though it did not change the social structure significantly.

The Dutch seafarers and free landholders did not establish a permanently effective centralized political power, and the "Stadhouder", a sort of lieutenant of the German Emperor, and later of the Spanish King, could not fulfill that function either. A containment of economic relations in political ones, as was the case in the absolutism of France and Spain, thus never occurred. Concentration of power among economically diversifying areas took place in the port city of Amsterdam. This concentration expressed itself more in economic than in political terms. Its resources, beside trade, were manufacture, centered on shipbuilding, and technical innovations mostly associated with it. Dutch ships, Dutch products and capital came soon to be in high demand over large parts of Europe and provided the basis for an enormous accumulation of financial power. The spirit of Amsterdam was to characterize the development of Dutch society and power for the next centuries.

Like the rest of western Europe, also what is now England experienced waves of Germanic invasions from the time of the Peoples' Migration. Although a large part of the island had previously been conquered by Rome, that conquest had not led to a lasting Romanization. The unconquered North (Scotland) remained ethnically homogeneous as did the indigenous and to some extent romanized people who were driven by the waves of Germanic barbarians into what is now the southwest of England. The waves of these invaders (e.g. Saxons, Angles and Danes) resulted in <u>layers of heterogeneous ethnicity</u> within political units. This made for the difference in the feudalism between England and the European continent. The Norman conquest (1066), essentially the last wave of invaders and thus the top ranking layer, integrated most of the English territories into one kingdom. This supersession by a monarch reaffirmed the peculiar form of English society. Henry I, the son of William the Conqueror, built on this emergent power structure by establishing alliances with the Anglo-Saxon barons and thereby managed to undercut the positions of other Norman overlords. The practice of forming alliances in an increasingly competitive power structures required, at least since the 13th century, the presence of noblemen, clergy and representatives of cities, principally London, at the court. These gatherings were the beginnings of the English parliamentary structure as a negotiating arena which strongly influenced the subsequent development of the English Monarchy. It was in this setting, i.e., one of ethnically distinct strata, that power became the only "unifying" societal bond. The ensuing power struggles led to numerous concessions by the monarch, usually formulated in "chartae", among which the "Magna Charta ad libertatem" (1215) was merely the most prominent one. Because of this societal peculiarity, the aspirations of the English Monarchy to absolutism never went fully beyond just that. The containment of economic relations within such kind of a political order remained problematic and religion was from the beginning little more than a mere means to power, i.e. an ideology, or as Adams would put it, it provided the "cultural potential" in the presence of which an all too frequent application of force could be avoided.

Turning now from our cursory inspection of the structural evolution of these nations to their colonizing efforts, we shall first concern ourselves with Spain (and Portugal), since theirs was the first one. As such, it also had a significant impact on several European countries in the 16th century.

The Spanish (and Portuguese) conquered and certainly looted what is now Latin America, but their extractions were made within a social structure characterized by the absence of a differentiation among economic, political and religious spheres. Moreover, the individual living in that system saw himself as being completely embedded in it and conceived of these spheres as one. Neither Vice-King nor "Encommendero" had a sense of privately owning land as a means of production. These people desired to lead the life of feudal lords. As "hidalgos", they had the honorific task to defend the native subjects of the Crown and to keep the peace among them. Surely, they supervised the productivity of these subjects as well, but this was done so that they themselves and their subjects could lead lives in accordance with Catholic teachings, although accompanied by vast differences in wealth and consumption. Tribute and the delivery of bullion, both rightful dues to the absolute monarch, were substantial tasks of the vice-kings, governors etc. from the very beginnings of the Conquista. Of course, these extractions, particularly the ones coming from mining, took a heavy toll of indigenous lives. This could not be prevented, no matter how strongly all servants of the Crown were supposed to avoid these casualties. After all, they wanted their subjects, baptized Catholics at least in name, to survive for two different and yet inseparable reasons. Iberian authority was contingent upon papal legitimation and, at the same time, the individual hidalgo, a role to which any Spaniard would aspire, had no inclination to do any work himself.

Certainly, the Spanish Colonial Empire as such was based on power. But, individuated ownership over significant means of production did not exist objectively and was, subjectively, not aspired to. Is this not to indicate that a social order and a way of self-understanding were in place that precluded forms of aspirations to an individuated power born later and somewhere else? We have to leave open the possibility that the Spanish subject identified wholeheartedly with the existing absolutist Catholic order, did not desire to change it and saw his self-expressions within it as his freedom. This state of affairs was not conducive to generating much power through internal competition and, thus, certainly contributed to a limitation of Spain's (and Portugal's) potential in the power struggle among the European nations.

Viewing colonization from within this social order, one may come to understand why Spain's colonies, for a long period of time, did not become settler colonies. In fact, access to the colonies was initially limited and open only to representatives of the Crown and the Clergy. Vast territories of the Spanish Empire took a long time to be populated by individuals from the homeland. It was not the Spaniards, at least not initially, who spread out in Latin America, but it was Spain that spread out Spanish (or Portuguese) culture. This culture with its administrative, economic, religious and artistic aspects had an impact that lasted for centuries and precluded the emergence of capitalism and democracy in many parts of that continent practically until today.

As is well known, the amount of bullion that flooded into Spain was enormous. And yet, Spain did not make "proper" use of it, if one thinks of use in the capitalist sense only. As we just saw, the culture of absolutist Spain (and Portugal) was not conducive to the build-up of manufactures and time/labor saving technologies. They had marginalized such activities in the homeland and, with their wealth in bullion, preferred to buy almost everything they needed, even grain, from the rest of the European continent and beyond. This, of course, meant that Iberia lost its wealth almost as fast as it came in, its citizens hardly ever thinking of turning it into capital. Needless to say though that other European countries, like France, England, not to a small degree, Holland, and even the shrinking principalities of the disintegrating Germany, benefited enormously from this constellation. In general, the dispersion of precious metal provided much of Europe with the much needed liquidity for its internal and, not to forget, Asian trade where goods could be had which Europeans could only dream of, but not produce themselves. While still spending its wealth, though with dwindling resources and significance, Spain (and Portugal) had eventually to admit to its inability to dominate the rest of the now partly Protestant Europe and to shape it in its Catholic image of a "Civitas Dei". Around 1600, it began to withdraw from the political and social developments of that continent. Therefore, Spanish absolutism remained largely unaffected by these developments, for instance by Protestantism and/or by the Enlightenment. It stagnated.

Absolutist France became a beneficiary of Spanish gold and silver, since it had a well established production base: its crafts. Tapestry, furniture, chandeliers, to name but a few, were gainfully sold by France and eagerly bought all over Europe, not the least by the Spanish. This influx supported the French lines of production and trade. The incoming bullion was seen as a means of investment in a state-mercantilistic and not in an individual-capitalist sense. This was the accepted social form of investment in a society in which production was almost exclusively organized in guilds. These guilds set intersubjectively accepted standards for the quality of work and the level of price. Strife for excellence, not competition for profit and individuated power mattered in French society. It provided the idiom for a person's free self-expression. Agricultural production remained feudal in essence, i.e., it was not entrepreneurial, be it at the level of the farmer or of the feudal lord. While economic activities were still embedded in political relations, religion and its organization, e.g. the appointment of bishops, had, in contrast to Spain, not been a privilege of the Crown since centuries.

With respect to the absolutist structures of Spain (Portugal) and France, it is certainly possible to speak of them, à la Adams, in terms of models of power structures and to see their internal subdivisions as "survival vehicles", but it is quite unlikely that such interpretation would come even close to an understanding of these societies from within. At the same time, we think that it cannot be denied that these glorious absolutist societies failed gradually to muster the power that eventually became available to other societies, primarily England. It should, however, be noted that regardless of the Spanish model, colonial expansion across the seas was not on the French (and the English) mind in a serious and lasting sense before the early 1600s.

Switching our attention away from France to Holland, we have first to note that the Dutch got increasingly involved in overseas trade. Shortages of grain, particularly in Spain and also in the other sheep farming country, namely England, provided them with an opportunity to buy grain, mainly in ports around the Baltic Sea, and to ship it to and sell it in these countries. This trade gave a boost not only to shipbuilding, ship outfitting and crafts, but more importantly, in the absence of feudal or absolutist structures, to the financial strength of enterprising individuals. All of these activities became concentrated in the port city of Amsterdam. By the beginning of the 17th century, the merchants of Amsterdam, having broadened the scope of their trade, became the wealthiest business oriented individuals in the Western world. They soon invented the stock market and thus made Amsterdam "the financial capital" of Europe. Since Holland still lacked a truly centralized political structure, its colonizing attempts in that era turned out to be quite vulnerable. Whatever limited feudal, monarchic or other forms of power centers emerged from within, they did so usually under external threats, first from Spain (16th century) and later (17th century) from France. While not having a lasting effect, they could nonetheless muster enough resources to prevail in these power struggles.

In the city of Amsterdam, practically owned by its richest merchants, "De Heren Zeventien" (the 17 gentlemen), the idea of capital as continuous investment for individuated profits had grown into common practice. This city called itself "the one and only liberty" in the world. Thus, it became ever more important to distinguish liberty from freedom. One had to have the liberty of pursuing one's own individuated interests in a basically entrepreneurial competitive setting which then provided the successful individual with a space for self-realization that other modes of production, e.g., that of absolutist France, could grant "first hand" through the elimination of such economic competition. And yet, this pacification through the containment of the economic in the political structure seriously limited the evolvement of an entrepreneurial spirit and, thus, the growth in "power content" of the absolutist states. In Holland, the successful practice of letting individuals exercise their liberty hardly encouraged the economically successful to reach out towards gaining political power specifically. This may help to explain the continued absence of centralized power in this prosperous country and thus the weakness of its colonizing attempts at that time. We admit that with this interpretation we cannot account for the internal peace of Dutch society. Whether ethnic homogeneity is sufficient to explain it, is not clear to us. Needless to say, though, that Calvinism was embraced in this setting as a form of religion. It was most suited to legitimize an otherwise unheard-of form of economic appropriation, the capitalist one, as Max Weber has explained to us quite convincingly. Whether, and if so how Calvinism substituted for the lack of political centralization are also unanswered questions for us.

As indicated above, the heterogeneity among the various layers of English society from top to bottom had provided a stage on which hardly any other means than negotiations, alliances, concessions and political maneuverings were available for sustaining social order. This situation gave the English Parliament its peculiarity and its significance. Participation in it, while being broadened over the centuries, remained a matter of privilege and egofocal interest for "Men of Substance", recruited first from the Nobility and then, later from the Gentry as well. At the end of the Hundred Year War, the Crown and the Nobility made additional concessions to those "below", culminating in the Lower House of the English Parliament. Thus an absolutist political order and its kind of intersubjectivity became an even more remote possibility. From quite early on, noblemen in England particularly those who had come from the outside as conquerors, understood their territories and its people as personal property. This perception found its practical expression most conspicuously in the "enclosures", a kind of measure that took place in other European countries centuries later, when absolutism had come to the end of its road there. Through these enclosures, land was largely cleared of peasants and mostly used for sheep farming. At times, remaining peasants were kept as tenants. This had two important consequences.

On the one hand, territorially and socially uprooted landless peasants began to flock to towns and cities. There they joined the ranks of craftsmen, who were initially organized in guilds, as was the case on the European continent. While guilds persisted on the continent in the form sketched above for France, they soon changed into associations of free craftsmen in England. As such, these craftsmen were allowed to pursue their own business. This led gradually to a vertical differentiation among them. In this increasingly competitive setting, those who lost out as well as those who were victims of enclosures, turned into an unskilled labor force, becoming precursors of the urban proletariat and/or emigrants to future colonies. Strange as it may seem, pauperization contributed to a significant growth in population. Political participation of these paupers was out of the question, although participating in the competition for power was the essence of the system. A new way of making these paupers exploitable again had yet to be developed. It eventually came in the form of industrial capitalism.

On the other hand, the Nobility turned into mere landlords developing an increasingly obvious monetary orientation. Together with the development of a Gentry, basically consisting of traders and merchants, they constituted, certainly since the mid 1500s, a class based on personal possessions and wealth. This class no longer saw itself, if it ever did, as being obliged to undertake the feudal duty of protecting the land and the people. On the European continent, such conversion of a formerly feudal nobility via an absolutist aristocracy into a money making upper class had to wait until the first half of the 18th century. Their "cousins" in England, however, were clearly and already competitors in a class structured society and participated as such in parliamentary politics, "legitimately" pursuing their interests through this avenue. Aspiration to absolutism by the monarchs, stemming from their external linkages, were dealt their final blow between 1650 and 1688. Through its "Glorious Revolution", England became a Constitutional Monarchy, while the Parliament became the center of English power.

A social system of such individuated power posed problems for retaining social integration. Such problems would have been quite hard to resolve in other socio-cultural settings. The parliamentary system, however, as it had evolved in England, provided a peculiar and simple mechanism for attaining integration among competitive forces: the rule of majority. A feature, perhaps surprising for outsiders, was (and still is) the perpetuated loyalty of those overruled in the system. Participation in it was not a matter of duty, but of "a well understood self interest" and that is what the overruled shared with the prevailing forces. Sticking it out under the domination by a majority and retaining membership in the evolving competitive groupings became instrumental for one's survival. One should note that in this setting, rational adaptation to newly created rules (laws) and circumstances and/or the manipulative creation of these rules influenced the mode of thinking early and deeply. Compromises in this system did not require changes in convictions or beliefs, since they were not grounded in them. A secular kind of civility evolved and softened the basically competitive social relations, while the state came to be looked upon as the Leviathan who enforced peace among individuals if required. Philosophical justification for this social order was provided by Hobbes, Locke and Hume, i.e. by thinkers who did not even contemplate a General Will as Rousseau proposed it about 100 years later in opposition to them. It was the General Will in which Rousseau saw, when the old absolutism began to crumble, a new foundation for intersubjectivity, i.e., a sharing of subjectivities without the demand for uniformity or even sameness.[2] England, instead, opted for the flexibility that only the combination of an individualistically competitive and yet deliberating system could grant. The flexibility of this system was primarily based on individuated economics. It took on a form which implied that its ascendancy had become, at least after 1688, only a matter of time. Crown and religion remained in place and served the purpose of being sources of unity at the sheerly ideological level. The first

"Constitutional King", William of Orange, brought over from Holland, symbolized, furthermore, an alliance between Dutch capital and a centralized political structure which was not even in his hands, but in the hands of the parliament. The importance of this union for future developments can hardly be overestimated. It is from within this marriage between individuated economic interests and a nevertheless centralized political order that capitalism began to flourish. To be sure, this capitalism was still merchant capitalism, but as such, it was a thorough preparation for the industrial capitalism yet to come.

In course of time, this structure has experienced a process of quantitative evolvement only, and not one of qualitative change, even though it has triggered vast qualitative changes wherever it spread. We are experiencing now the final stages of its expansion.

As indicated before, unleashing egofocality in the sphere of economics narrowed freedom to mere liberty. As Max Weber saw, rationalism, i.e., individuated means-ends thinking, began its growth and yet instantly required morals as a means of self-constraint. Spontaneity, that is the will or the drive, egofocal as it had become, had to be curbed from then on. The possibility of a General Will in which each could participate in equality (not sameness!) grew ever more inconceivable. Pleasure (thus aesthetics) and interaction (thus ethics) were no longer free but had to be regulated by a "Leviathan", i.e. by a morally repressive state, as it was required to prevent an otherwise chaotic war of one against another. Principles later spelled out by Darwin began to rule long before he was born. For today's mode of thinking, these principles were argued for by Richard Adams as having been universal since the Paleolithic. In our contextualization, however, they appear to have emerged in a quite peculiar social setting. While we still agree with Adams' view that culture is an elevation of Nature and of man as a part of her, we cannot help but note that Adams concept of culture, as it absolutizes just one form of social relations can at best account for interaction among individuated human individuals (in Marx's and Weber's sense), but it does not make any equivalent attempt to inspect what this does to the individual's will structure (drives, urges, spontaneity). We have to return to this later,[3] but this much should be clear already: The common bond of all Nature including the human being is conceived of by Adams as mainly implying competition among humans. This is, to say the least, a theoretically one sided option. This sets Adams quite apart from Rousseau and reveals his kinship to Hobbes. We are inclined to think that Adams simply articulates and projects backwards into all traditions what originated in the peculiar one of England. Staying within the latter tradition, it becomes indeed plausible that the concept of a General Will, i.e., the idea of a commonality among subjectively differentiated wills, had no chance to emerge. The absence of such a will not even as a foundation for a voluntaristic order, indeed, leaves no choice but the acceptance of parliamentary democracy as the political mechanism for curbing egofocal individuation.

It would be instructive for retaining a sense for the peculiarity of today's dominant mode of thinking, if we were to contrast what at that time shaped up in England with what France, though unsuccessfully, tried to avoid: the cutting lose of the individuated individual.

By the early 1500s, the socio-political structure of France had already begun to undergo a significant evolution in response to internal economic dynamics. Developments in the French mode of production were also triggered, like those in other countries, e.g., Holland and England, by the influx of Spanish bullion. The containment of productive activities in the social order of France had required modification of this order. In an increasingly differentiated production, social distancing and thus a measure of individuation had to occur. It is precisely for this reason that Calvinism as an individuated form of religion did find a considerable, even if short lived, response in France. Since about 1560, the Calvinist emphasis on the individual posed a serious threat to Catholicism, and to absolutism and the feudalism contained in it. Henry IV who wavered himself in this conflict decided finally to stay with Catholicism ("Paris is worth a Mass") keeping his crown with religious and legal legitimation. We have to concede that his return to Catholicism "smacks" of a rather self-centered understanding of his beliefs. Nonetheless, this maneuvering did not prevent absolutism and Catholicism from opening up to an increasingly abstracted philosophical reasoning. In their modernized form, they perpetuated their role as a social cement.

It was quite an important aspect of this modernization that the legitimation of the monarch could no longer be vested just in patrimony. The Crown as the embodiment of the state came to be understood as being above time, person and law. As the keeper of the traditional law, the Parliament of Jurists was considered as equally eternal as the nation. Absolutism required the Crown to be not only above the law, but also above the person of the King. While being independent and not entrepreneurially rooted in their feudal districts, this Parliament of noblemen still watched as a body of Jurists over the legitimacy of rulership over the land. Rule had to be consistent with the existing body of law and its Catholic foundation. This consistency, however, was increasingly expressed in terms of a philosophically enriched biblical idiom. Being a member of that kind of Parliament still remained a matter of duty and not a necessity of safeguarding one's own egofocal interests. In this connection, it may be important to emphasize that throughout French society ownership in means of production, for the most part in land, was still only minimally privatized. Hence, work was genuinely undertaken for the common good. It remained to be the case that an individual hoping to move upwards could only do so within that structure and its branches, such as the Church, the Law and the Court.

From the time of Henry IV, further centralization of power meant that production came to be increasingly monitored and controlled for quality by the Crown and its representatives. This unity of economic and political activities which is the characteristic feature of mercantilism implied the build-up of a large scale bureaucracy and with it the continued absence of individuated ownership in societally significant means of production. In this setting, it was the treasury of the Crown and not individuated entrepreneurs which appropriated the monetary surplus that was generated. The concept of taxation was hardly applicable to this mercantilistic system, let alone that of capital.

Changes in the meaning and function of the Crown, as indicated above, meant that serving the Crown required qualities increasingly different from those of a medieval nobleman. Here, the Jesuits played an important role. Under their guidance, the nobility's cultivation and, to some extent education, became increasingly refined. At the same time, the bureaucracy required more man power than the nobility could provide. This forced the Crown to create the "Noblesse de Robe", i.e., a nobility of office. Its appearance meant that an important channel for upward mobility came into being, and yet it was one in a state structure, not in an entrepreneurial system. At any rate, the status of being one of the "king's men" in France demanded now more than just being a carrier of weapons. The ideal that was born in this development was that of the courtier, a figure to be distinguished from the English Gentry and Nobility.

While the Crown was willing to maintain an ever growing bureaucracy, its sense for investment in means of production was poorly developed. The revenue of the French Crown was considerable. At times, it is reported to be more than double of what the English King received through taxation. And yet, bankruptcy was a phenomenon that the French Crown had to experience frequently. The expenses of the French Crown need to be understood from within its absolutism.

Centralization, bureaucracy and the display of grandeur and glory together with the cultivation of architecture, food, fashion, etiquette and the arts culminated in the royal court devouring incredibly huge sums of revenue. Towards the end of the 17th century, 900 secretaries surrounded Louis XIV in Versailles. At the same time, he was unable to man his fleet in wars against England (and Holland) and other European powers. To be sure, French ship building was second to none, and yet, the circumstance that the French fleet was laid up, at least in part, allowed the English (and Dutch) to bombard it into pieces (1697).

Between 1600 and the Revolution of 1789, France kept on facing increasing difficulties in its attempt at containing the individual and the economy in the overarching interest and self understanding of the state and the Crown. It was the Crown which retained an interest in accumulating surplus as a means of self-perpetuation in the confrontational setting among nations. Individual interests, economic or otherwise, were still not cut lose from society and state, although containment of the economic, in the context of an increasing division of labor, grew ever more problematic. The legitimation of power including the centralization of the economy had to be grounded in an ever more abstractly understood religion and an ever more abstract sense for the unity of the state in the Crown. French cardinals of the stature of, for instance, a Mazarin or a Richelieu who were both theologians and political thinkers, had a significant impact on re-defining the legitimation of the Crown. It needs to be noted, particularly in contrast to what happened in England, that the thoughtful attempts to retain legitimation for the existing order was carried out with an aim to maintain the still societally shared intersubjectivity. The voluntary, i.e. free, identification of the Frenchmen with "La Nation" was of vital concern for the Crown. This concern could, of course, be interpreted à la Adams as generating an ideology of nationhood serving mainly the power holders in France, but this would hardly be an attempt at understanding France from within itself. It would imply that the French people were unable to see that they were manipulated. It would also make it quite difficult to understand the widespread unwillingness among Frenchmen to leave their home country for the colonies, a phenomenon which, as we shall see, had serious consequences for French colonization, particularly in North America. The lack of emigrants stands in stark contrast to the Englishmen who left their homeland in large numbers; this difference certainly calls for an explanation. Undoubtedly, this much can be said already: We-ness and nationhood were differently expressed in France than they were in England.

However, the reason and ethics that kept France together became ever more secular in these attempts at re-defining absolutist legitimacy. This secularization paved the way for ideas that led to an overthrow of an increasingly tenuous and abstract integration. Absolutism grew fictitious during the 18th century, but this does not mean that it was like that from the beginning. With the simultaneous growth of differentiation and individuation, egofocality increased turning French noblemen eventually into merchants, e.g., by converting the tribute delivered to them by their peasants into entrepreneurial means. They simply responded to demands of the ever growing division of labor in the system and yet, these lords tried to hide such lowly involvement.

At this point in our considerations, we need to clarify a matter which could arouse a misunderstanding of what we have so far merely implied. There cannot be any doubt that feudalism and its transcendent, absolutism, did not just mean stratification; they meant a materially concrete exploitation of a historically worsening kind. In France, for instance, the culture of the Nobility, the High Clergy and the Court flourished more and more like an exotic orchid. The enormous refinement and elevation of this culture occurred on the backs of the people, the Third Estate. Its credibility and captivating power and hence its legitimation and wholehearted acceptance became ever more flimsy. Its abstraction meant alienation of the common people from a once-upon-a-time truly existing sense of unity. The times of "noblesse oblige", when only the nobleman had the right to carry weapons and to die for "La Nation", had slipped further and further away. The Nobility lived for itself and let others die for the state. The evolution of praxis had rendered the traditional belief, regardless of its adjustments, obsolete. The "nice illusions" (Marx) of freedom in feudal and absolutist stratification had come to be widely recognized as what they had not been before, namely fictitious.

While it may be clear by now that we see egofocal power and instrumentalistic re-definitions as emergents, we like to add that, in contrast to Adams and (differently) also to Luhmann, identification with the societally leading sense systems - religion and gradually philosophy - initially had a materially concrete grounding. Let us remember that being a member of the nobility once meant having the exclusive honor to live and to die for the commonwealth. Precisely because this meaning had been there once and was practically gone later, and precisely because it was retained as an increasingly hollow claim at the mental level in the late phases of absolutism, could the legitimation of crown and noblemen be seen as having grown problematic by the Frenchmen. At the same time, we would like to suggest that it is because of its collective memory that the French had difficulties for a long time to make capitalism work as effectively as it did in England.

Having retained a genuine sense for hypocrisy as it had crept into France's absolutism (in a different way from how it flourished in England's constitutionalism), French philosophers, like Montesquieu, Rousseau and others convinced the public of the need for revolutionizing a system that was less and less what it pretended to be. These thinkers tried to ground the political and social unity of France anew, now in the completely secular, i.e., philosophical, ideas of Reason and General Will. These philosophers developed their thoughts largely in contrast to Hobbes and Locke. Montesquieu's Reason is not an advocacy of the Leviathan and Rousseau's General Will is by no means the same as Locke's rule by majority. Reason and General Will were expected to tie individuals together in new and yet non-competitive and non-antagonistic ways. As is well known, this expectation was not at all realized by the Revolution of 1789.

There cannot be any doubt either that the increasing inability of France to compete with England was one of the main consequences of absolutist centralization and grandeur. It was, for quite some time, not seen in France that it was precisely this socio-cultural arrangement that was so counterproductive. The lack of individuated competition implied a politically insufficient growth of energy in the system, as Adams would put it. France (let alone Spain) could compete less and less with England and its fundamentally different social structure. Developmentally speaking, the significant battles between France and England (and their allies) were fought in Europe, however, the most consequential results of these battles occurred in the colonies, mainly in North America.

It is from within this absolutism that France, under Louis XIV and his predecessor, began to colonize in earnest. Besides minor activities in India and in the Caribbean, the thrust of its colonizing efforts focused on the St. Lawrence in North America. Similar to what Spain had attempted about 100 years earlier, France also set out to find precious metal and to christianize the people living where it hoped to find it. However, gold and silver could not be found in what was soon called New France. An attempt to make up for this disappointment was the use of the land as a source of agricultural produce. But this endeavor was not blessed by success either. This had two main reasons. First, the climate along the St. Lawrence was not, at least not in French eyes, terribly suitable for agriculture. Second, given their social structure, the Natives, although christianized to a small extent, were unwilling and unprepared to work for their colonizers. This was quite different from what was happening in major parts of Spanish South America particularly where the Native societies had been differentiated into those doing menial labor and others specializing in the "finer things of life". Recognizing this, France made an attempt to settle this colony with its own people, even though an already uprooted and individuated population did not exist in the homeland. Over many decades barely 15 000 settlers, usually only males, were brought over by the Crown which tried to settle them in a predesigned fashion by means of the so-called rang system. Under the supervision of Crown appointed intendants, seigneurs and clergymen, who saw this posting in the wilderness as a terrible exile, substantial gains for the Crown, needless to say the sole controller, did not materialize. This changed, to some extent, when the fur trade with the Natives began to flourish. It turned, however, a good many French settlers into "couriers du bois", thus threatening the significance of farming even further. This fur trade, as a monopoly of the Crown, hardly increased the wealth of the settlers in this colony.

Given the background of the settlers, the form of their income and their intimacy with the Natives, New France never became a market for French quality products. Nonetheless, in search for better climates, perhaps still bullion, and agriculturally more viable land, French exploration extended the sovereignty of the Crown via the Ohio (1669) to the Gulf of Mexico (1682). It must not be denied that this move took place increasingly for strategic military reasons as well. One should remember that in the meanwhile, colonization of the East Coast of the North American Continent to the South of the St. Lawrence had been successfully initiated by the English (and Dutch). French possession of the lands stretching from Lake Ontario, along the Ohio and Mississippi Rivers to the Gulf Coast, promised to contain a feared westward expansion of the English. Such competition had made itself felt on the banks of the St. Lawrence and the shores of Lake Ontario. Its impact on the French fur trade was appreciable, since the English exchange goods for furs, mainly rum from the Caribbean, were considerably cheaper than what the French used, e.g. their cognac.

Turning to England and its eventual ascendancy to being the world's dominant colonial power, we have to bear in mind its already modernizing social structure. The significance of individuated possession, first, mainly in real estate, and soon in other means of production, cannot be overemphasized. Being a "Man of Substance" meant little more than being a man of possessions. Without them, participation in public life was out of the question. This implied further emphasis on an egofocal profit motive and meant that one's social existence and relations were based in economic relations and not the other way around. Competition and an adaptive mode of thinking soon created a sense of sobriety. Matter, that is, control of it, was all that mattered and whatever was "above" it, was only material for manipulation. Ethics shrunk to a means for social control. This implies that ethics and economics differentiated from one another. Religion and art became social institutions beside and external to that of the economy, the latter being from then on the only "serious business". This "economistically" grounded system made nonetheless use of the institutions of religion and art for the pacification of wider society, i.e., of those with less power. Social order, otherwise an intersubjectively shared foundation for freedom, turned into a permanently required constraint on freedom which on that occasion turned into mere liberty of the individuated subject.[4] What socially emerged then could indeed be approached on Adams' terms. A system that allows for being understood in these terms originated there. It soon began to spread when England started to found colonies in a historically lasting way.

The English colonies on the East Coast of North America were not state colonies, at least not in the Spanish and the French sense. They were established either by individuals alone (e.g., William Penn, the Duke of York), by religious groups and/or by chartered companies (e.g. the Massachusetts Bay Company) in which individuals had stocks and the Crown had little if any say. Crown and Parliament granted a charter which provided military protection for economic activities. This was quite in keeping with the idea that politics could be made to serve the interests of enterprising individuals provided they had "substance". On the basis of the English Crown having granted control over sometimes huge pieces of land - which the Crown did not own (similarity to France and Spain!) - these individuals, groups or companies became proprietors of these lands (at least initially a difference from France and Spain!). In this capacity, they were free to run their territories any way they saw fit. All of them, however, had an interest in "planting" people on these lands. These people were given various amounts of land, either completely free of charge or at nominal prices. Some of these proprietors, e.g. the Duke of York, sought to exercise quasi-absolutist power over these lands (more or less the later New York State) and over the people beginning to live on them, but opposition from the settlers prevented that. The exercise of liberty was for these settlers the only way to get a sense of freedom. Self-government by elected representatives soon emerged, against which the English Crown and Parliament had little objection. Since these colonies enjoyed military protection by the homeland, primarily because of overlapping economic interests, taxation in the form of import and export duties had to be accepted. This military protection was granted against the French and the Natives. Attempts to incorporate the Natives in the emergent political order were hardly ever undertaken. The Native concept of land alone was already a hindrance to that since it was fundamentally foreign to the Anglo-Saxon concept of private property in land. To obtain such private property was, however, the main objective of these kinds of settlers.

The demographic differences between the settlement of the English colonies, on the one hand, and the Spanish and French colonies, on the other, are quite remarkable. For quite some time, Spain did not want to have its people settle in the colonies, and France always had great difficulties to find people to leave. This was not the case in England. Uprooted, individuated and impoverished people were available since centuries. This phenomenon evolved in other European countries only later, especially during the 19th century. In 1750, France had managed to populate New France with perhaps 30 000 French individuals. The English colonies, however, had grown to a population of more or less a million. By far most of them had come voluntarily in search of "making a living", some of them being united in shared (and persecuted) religious beliefs. These people hardly mingled or intermarried with the Natives; their interest was in getting possessions from the Natives, not in living with them. The French and Spanish intermarried with the Natives much more willingly. Thus, there is hardly an English equivalent to the French/Native "metis", or to the "ladino" in South America.

The immigration and the population growth in the English Colonies in North America were in themselves enough reason for a clash between the English and the French. While the clash in North America was of great significance for England, it was much less meaningful for the French of the time. Since the last decades of the 17th century, France saw itself at odds with England mainly on matters related to the European continent. An example for this would be the War over Spanish Succession (ending 1713/14). For France, this was mainly, though not exclusively, a matter of hegemonial strife among European nations. For England, the issue was the containment of France as a maritime competitor. By 1750, England's focus of attention was so firmly directed to the overseas colonies, be they in North America or also in India, that it needed an ally for the purpose of taking care of its still existing European interests. During the Seven Year War (1756-63), it found such an ally in Prussia. Under the guise of protecting the homeland of the English kings, namely Hannover, Prussia's main role was to serve the purpose of tying up French forces on the continent. The end of the Seven Year War brought a crushing defeat for France (and its ally Austria). In the Treaty of Fontainebleau (1762), the colonial issue was settled once and for all between England and France (the Treaty of Paris, 1763, settled the continental war in Europe). France lost its North American possessions in return for mainly Pondicherry and Chandarnagore in India, and Guadeloupe and Martinique in the Caribbean. The colonial empire of France's Ancien Regime was, to say the least, greatly truncated. While France sailed towards its Great Revolution, England "ruled the waves".

Of course, the victory in the Seven Year War was a costly one for everyone involved. As a way of retrieving these costs and meeting the increasing expenditures of maintaining the 13 North American Colonies, the English Parliament tried to impose tariffs and taxes on the North American Colonies. It needs to be noted that this was already the normal avenue available to the English political system for retrieving its expenditures. In the absolutist empires of France and also of Spain, this avenue was much less, if at all, viable. They could only have made funds available for military expenditures largely only by limiting the Crown's investments into palaces, cathedrals, opera houses, etc. In England, societally or politically significant matters had to be financed by the individually made profits of people who, however, otherwise felt entitled to care primarily for themselves and only secondarily for the "Common-Wealth". The peculiarity of this kind of politics and its financing will be lost, if one ignores that the original meaning of politics is the taking care of the common good, and within it, of the individual. It is problematic, no matter how common today, to see politics degraded to the mere taking care of a collectivity of individuals who retain their own segregated interests and join forces only as long as these interests, more or less accidentally, overlap. And yet, in hindsight it appears that both individuation and a politics that is in keeping with such individuation had to emerge by what appears to have been an evolutionary necessity, at least in the West. Accordingly, we should not ignore that an intersubjectivity was also crumbling where it once existed, e.g., in France. In this sense, the French Revolution "had to" come.

The now increasingly practiced promotion of private interests through politics is also illustrated, quite prominently so, by the English land development projects west of the Alleghanies. These were promoted, among others, by none less than Benjamin Franklin. His politics were determined by the perceived limitation of these interests by the intent of the English Parliament to grant, in 1774, colonial self rule to their newly acquired Quebec. Obviously, private interest and little else beyond that, was the driving force behind the politics pursued by Benjamin Franklin and his associates. At that time, the formerly French territory of Quebec, as mentioned before, reached well into the Ohio Valley and beyond. Colonial self rule of Quebec would have been a serious obstacle in the way of the westward expansion and, thus, of the economic growth of the American Colonies.

Conflicts of this kind between the Parliament and the Colonial Assemblies, flexibly and expediently united in the Continental Congresses, led to the "Declaration of Independence" adopted on the 4th of July 1776. The War of Independence was its immediate consequence. Militarily the war dragged on and was inconclusive, perhaps because of the involvement of France and Spain in it against England. The English Parliament grew tired of the war and conceded independence to the 13 Colonial States. The move was perhaps also motivated by the already far more profitable exploitation of India. In the Treaty of Paris (1783), England granted independence to the 13 Colonies and, in addition, gave up the territory south of the Great Lakes and east of the Mississippi. England retained what was to the north of these lakes, and the St. Lawrence River which later became Upper and Lower Canada. The Confederation of the 13 States had thus succeeded in removing serious obstacles to its westward expansion. The lands beyond the Mississippi did not arouse much interest at that time, but they were not viewed as being out of future reach. This view was not limited by a regard for those who controlled these lands nominally (Spain, for a while France) or really (the Natives).

The "Declaration of Independence" had laid down the principles soon to be incorporated in the United States' Constitution and the Bill of Rights. Work on these legal instruments was completed in 1788, although, indicatively enough, several amendments have been made since. The features of the constitutional groundwork most significant for modern culture were its emphasis on and understanding of the rights of the individual on the one hand, and the role of the state and the constitutional law, on the other. As far as the former is concerned, the "pursuit of happiness" became the most fundamental right of the individuatedly perceived individual. By taking this step, this colonial settler society took its own level of individuation for granted and assigned to the state and its policy the explicit obligation to protect the rights of that kind of an individual. Furthermore, this right was not simply understood as one entitling the individual to possessions. It was understood as giving the individual the right to *growth*, most importantly, to economic growth and, needless to say, to obtain it by competition. It is in keeping with this that the right to vote was extended to each individual provided he paid taxes. Women, as was a matter of course, were not included, simply because they had, like in England, no property right. Political participation thus was extended to almost all males. The right to being elected was broadened and yet was initially conditional on owning more than average property. Also, and different from England, the inheritance of political office and/or of a constituency was abolished. It needs to be noted that, while also the absolutist state and law was set up to protect the individual, it was now a new kind of individual that was being protected. He was not one that sought commonality with others, but one that sought competition with others. It is in this social context that the Constitution of the new 13 States specified the conditions for its own alterations and re-definitions. This did not introduce a new flexibility. This flexibility had already existed in England, where an explicit constitution had never existed. The novelty instead consisted in two circumstances: on the one hand, there were explications of both, the constitution and the conditions of its alteration (e.g. the required size of the majority) and on the other, there was a full acceptance that re-definitions of rules and reality was borne out of egofocal interests. The significance of these innovations is that they paved the way towards the modern notion that foundations of consensus and co-operation need not to remain what they happen to be at any given time. In this way, the young USA spearheaded a process that the Old Continent had started as well, for instance in the re-formulation of absolutist philosophy. There, however, it was still combined with the attempt to contain the individual non-antagonistically.

Having constituted itself this way, the United States could not help but embark, as Adams understands so well, on a course of expansion, be it in geographic, demographic, economic or political terms, although it would take the new country well over 100 years to become a world power (and soon after *the* world power).

It would be an interesting question, whether Johann Wolfgang von Goethe, the German poet and thinker, who was a distant "eye-witness" to these developments, had anticipated that kind of success of the new born country. He has expressed admiration for "Amerika", especially because of the freedom that it promised in his understanding to the individual. But we doubt that he foresaw the mutation of that freedom to mere liberty. His fear of future disaster was linked more to the widespread evolvement of industrialization as a form of production and as a knowing of Nature in which the sensuousness of work and of our relation to Nature is distorted. We are not sure whether Goethe fully understood the aspect of egofocal individuation as being inextricably part of industrial capitalism. This mode of production was at best just emerging in Germany.

The industrial form of the capitalist mode of production is, however, inseparable from the evolvement of the US. One can go that far to say that it permeates, like nothing else does, its collective memory.

Notes

[1] Adams 1975, pp. 68ff, 232ff.

[2] Equality, a motto of Rousseau, did not mean, as is often claimed, sameness; it meant the same degree of satisfaction for individually different needs; see Rousseau, 1950, passim)

[3] See below pp. 107-109.

[4] For the distinction between liberty and freedom, see chapter 5 passim, in particular pp. 111-112

Chapter 3

Industrial Capitalism and the New Colonialism

Even prior to the industrial form of capitalism, the leadership of individuated economics had turned out to be extremely beneficial for those who practiced it. The Seven Year War testified to this. The independence of the 13 Colonies only taught an important specific lesson to those abiding by this practice, but it did not change that practice. They learned that political interests were better served through safeguarding and promoting egofocal economic interests. By not grounding politics in political and/or philosophical convictions, the political was taken care of simultaneously. Great Britain could have learnt that lesson without going to war against its 13 Colonies.

At this point, however, we have to elaborate on an aspect in the development of capitalism that has been implied all along, but only becomes more obvious in our discussion of the industrial form of capitalism.

The now more advanced leadership of individuated economics still did not mean that other institutions like politics, the law, religion, the arts or education were of lesser importance than they had been before in early capitalist society. Instead, it meant that these institutions were increasingly being put to work for the egofocal interests where blatant egofocality encountered problems. This was particularly the case with regard to lending credence to norms and values. Honesty and trustworthiness, for instance, were still needed values in a social order that thrived otherwise on the basis of "flexibility". Thus, there remained a need for institutions that could generate values of this kind. For this purpose, religion (or other world views) had to be given space for survival and was not pushed out by an economics fundamentally antagonistic to its preachings.

Technologically, the industrial form of capitalism was rung in by the steam engine (1765). From then on the production process became increasingly machine driven. It not being the only distinct feature of industrial capitalism required an ever accelerating exploitation of fossil fuels and allowed for a proportional minimization of human labor cost in the production process. Around 1785, this fuel driven industrialization began to grow at increasing speed, first in England and North America. It started in the textile industry, required rapid growth of mining and metal industry which in turn required and implied vast growth in transportation by steamships and railroads. The consequences for further growth of other industries (chemistry, tool industry, etc.) are obvious. By 1850, major centers of this modern kind of industry had emerged in Scotland, Middle England, the Netherlands, Belgium, North East France, Northern Italy, Germany and the USA (mainly in the North-East). This similarity, however, did not abolish all social differences among these countries so that the common feature of individuation, which nonetheless evolved, became embedded in different social contexts.

Given the level of individuation already existing in England and the US, and emerging gradually in the rest of Europe, the economy became ever more sharply competitive. The individuated entrepreneur had from then on not just to secure a profit, but a growth in profit for the sake of his survival; stagnation easily meant bankruptcy. The growth of profit has to come ultimately at the expense of human labor, as most prominently pointed out by Karl Marx. Furthermore, this mechanization implies that the required growth of profit comes also at the expense of "natural resources". In other words, the fundamentally competitive increase in the productivity, meaning the shrinking of the wage portion (not necessarily of individual wages!) in production, pretty closely equals capitalist profit, that is the exploitation of labor and that of Nature out there, and the growth of all of these. In this context, the growth orientation already explicitly adopted by the socio-economic culture of the 13 North American Colonies takes on its particular significance. Today, the concept of growth has become so central a concept that it is undeletable from the theory and praxis of all modernized countries.

It is important to note at this point that industrial capitalism brought with it a drastic qualitative change in the man-fellowman-Nature-relationship. We feel compelled to emphasize that it is since then – and not since the Paleolithic, as Adams suggests – that the individuated individual is structurally allowed, even expected, to use "culture as his secret weapon in survival" and to do so not just against Nature but also against Nature in fellow human beings. In other words, the human individual had begun to act by treating himself as being different from all Nature around him. Prior to this drastic change with its vast social, economic and technological consequences, man accepted a social order and thus a self-understanding that precluded such predatorial existence.

For clarity's sake, let us bear in mind that the use of Nature by letting Nature work on Nature (breeding of plants and animals, the use of tools) has been all along and everywhere part of culture, and in that respect industrialization is not a qualitative novelty. Industrialization, i.e. the use of fuel powered tools, takes on the dimension of a qualitative change only, when it occurs in the context of full-fledged social individuation and egofocal competition. This development implies the increasing antagonism not only among humans, but also between humans and Nature. At the same time, this mode of thinking leaves it unacknowledged what allows for our interaction with Nature, namely, that we are Nature ourselves. This is to say that the primary status of the commonality of Nature is pushed aside, though not completely ignored, as we shall see.[1] On the basis of placing ourselves, consciously or not, outside or even above Nature,[2] industrial capitalism practices a synthesis with Nature that can only be negative (as we have put it above). The absurdity of this social order is that it has to constantly distort, in both praxis and theory, what it rests on, namely man's own Nature in its commonality with Nature out there including fellow man. This distortion lies at the root of what is little more than a vulgar "materialism". Let us hasten to add that we are not opposing industry per se or for that matter the making and using of tools. The question rather is: what is the form, socially and mentally, of our making and using tools, even of our understanding of the Nature of things and people? What seems to be required is a more encompassing elevation of Nature than the one advocated by Adams and practiced since quite some time now. Culture may then be more than the individual's "weapon in survival".

The circumstance that industrialization took place under capitalist social conditions was not merely coincidental to the birth of nationalism. The growth orientation of industrial capitalism forced capitalists to pursue more and more markets and to seek more and more territories for natural resources. This compelled them "to go abroad". Once there, they needed protection by those with whom they claimed "identity", now a nationalistic one. This claim was usually directed towards the masses of people in the capitalist's home country. Mobilizing them for the protection of their capitalist interests turned out to be a means for further exploitation of the have-nots (canon fodder!). This intention may not always have given birth to nationalism, but it is what it boiled down to.

The emphasis on the nation which until around 1800 was unheard of, assumed differing complexions in the various capitalist countries. Nationalism in England and the US, where it lacked an ethnic foundation, was bound to be different from the one that prevailed in Europe. The US was populated, to a considerable extent, by people that were individuated right from the beginning, while in England the ethnic heterogeneity had allowed for individuation to emerge since the late Middle Ages. On the European continent, nationalism was born in the presence of industrialization as well, yet there it had an ethnic foundation, e.g. in France, Spain, Italy, Germany and Russia, to name but a few examples. In these countries, romanticism, a movement with a strong tendency towards the glorification of the past, strengthened the ethnic foundation of their nationalism.[3] Therefore, capitalism, as it gradually evolved in these countries as well, took on different shapes in conjunction with their nationalism. And yet, it should not come as a surprise that capitalism in these countries reduced the sense for the nation more and more to an ideology as well. The new elites had to keep their societies ideologically together for their own benefit vis-à-vis increasing antagonistic division between classes at the objective level.

It is from within this broadly sketched context that Great Britain, after the loss of the 13 Colonies, entered into a second round of empire building. Without colonialism, the attainment of global dominance would have been unthinkable. However different England's first phase of colonialism had already been from that of Spain and France, the emergence of industrial capitalism added further reason to modernize its colonial activities.

England had felt that the loss of the 13 Colonies was a loss of "grace". The blow of losing it with the loss of control over the 13 Colonies was so severe in its own view that it took England some decades to evolve a strategy by which it could reorganize, re-define and then consolidate a new kind of empire. After having fought off external foes like Napoleon's France and internal threats like republicanism and jacobinism, the British Empire, roughly from 1840 onwards, remained unchallenged until early in the 20th century. This development is a story of amazing political flexibility, usually understood as exemplifying statesmanship. At any rate, it allowed Britain to establish its Second Colonial Empire.

India, a matter of great concern to Britain's colonialism since quite some time, now became the focus of its attention. This, of course, gave a boost to the importance of the already existing East India Company (founded in 1600). Right at the loss of its North American colonies, namely in 1784, the English Parliament passed the India Act, to be followed by similar ones in the 19th century. In this first Act, the Parliament assumed the right to appoint the Company's governors from then on, while the Company was left alone to follow economic pursuits. This did not mean that a clear segregation between the economic and political spheres was ever observed. It would require too much space to describe how the distinction between these two spheres was blurred. For several decades, Britain's influence on the Indian subcontinent was exercised militarily, i.e. through direct power, through indirect rule and/or by playing off indigenous power holders against one another, all of these, as the economic interests demanded.

Initially, the East India Company in Bengal only enjoyed the same trading privileges as in other areas of India. Against payments, the Company bought from Indian manufacturers, at that time world leaders in the production of textiles (cotton as well as silk), iron, salt, saltpeter, to mention a few. This trading activity had been profitable for the Company, not only because of its privilege to buy tax-free, but in particular because the East India Company sold, through its agents, this privilege to individuals not directly trading on behalf of the Company. In the case of Bengal, this trade undermined the ruler's revenue leading him to react militarily. Robert Clive, the military leader (!) of the East India Company (a trading company!) defeated the Nawab of Bengal in the so-called "Battle of Plassey" (1757). An actual battle hardly took place, since several of Nawab's officers, including the chief minister, had been bribed to switch sides on the battle field. From then on, the East India Company took over the revenue collecting and administering functions of the government of Bengal, and, needless to say, increased its loot. Thus a business company came to exercise political power directly and yet, it could hang on to the claim of dealing in business matters basically. Vast fortunes were made by individual agents of the Company, most prominently Clive himself. These individuals "naturally" understood this wealth as means of investment. Similarities notwithstanding, the difference in the understanding between this loot and the loot made by the Spanish in South America is obvious. Agents of the East India Company got into manufacturing and did that at a scale most Spaniards would never have thought of (had they thought in such terms at all). Parallel to this, the East India Company cornered the market for raw materials (for textiles mainly), introduced labor saving machinery and, in the event, undermined the traditional Indian manufacturers and artisans. This activity may well have contributed to the famine of 1770 in Bengal, which is well known for its mass starvation and death. Similar maneuverings were undertaken by the East India Company in other parts of India, e.g., Hyderabad, Mysore and around Bombay. Legitimacy was not seen as a problem.

The influx of funds from India and the obvious prospect of their future increases make it plausible that it was not too difficult for the English Parliament to part, in 1784, with the 13 relatively small and less profitable colonies in North America, while assuming a flexibly understood political control over the East India Company. This, of course, was the political power of a capitalist government over a trading company which must not be confused with the political power exercised by absolutist Spain over lands understood then as overseas extensions of the homeland. The control of the British Parliament over all the Company's territories acquired in India over and above Bengal was extended in 1813, 1833 and 1853 through subsequent India Acts. After the "mutiny" of 1857, which was the last attempt by some Indians to regain sovereignty, the Parliament took over the government of India completely. At that time, although this would change later, India was worth it. It was the "Jewel of the Crown" for England, because it served as a major source of raw material (cotton, gold, silver, saltpeter, etc.), as a vast territory of investments (railways, canals, mining, tea - plantations etc.) and, after the destruction of India's own manufacturing, as a highly populated, thus lucrative market for English industrial products (textiles, soon locomotives, railway stock, etc.). The industrially added value of these goods, implying an unheard of exploitation of labor at home, but also abroad, allowed for profits perhaps even exceeding the influx of bullion into the Spain of the 16th and 17th centuries.

It was yet another reaction to the loss of the 13 Colonies in North America that Australia was made a Crown colony in 1788 and populated as a settler colony from 1850 on. New Zealand was taken over in 1840 after the defeat of the Maori and became a settlement colony as well. The tribal peoples of these colonies were, like the ones in North and South America, of little use for the conquerors. Their egalitarian social structure precluded incorporation into the Western hierarchical social structure and its individuated economy. New Zealand soon engaged like Australia in wool production and, like other colonies, became geared to British capitalist interests. The task of securing the seaways grew in importance with the vast distances over which the parts of the Empire had spread. In connection with this task, but also in conjunction with territorial acquisitions by enterprising individuals (e.g. Cecil Rhodes), English colonies spread in Africa. Control was also established in Mediterranean Africa (the later significance of the Suez-Canal!) and the Middle East. At times, this was done by mere stationing of troops and establishing dominance (e.g. in parts of the Ottoman Empire) without formal annexation. All the while, England had retained control over those North American colonies that were soon to become Canada. These colonies, particularly Upper and Lower Canada, became sources of raw material (timber, furs, later wheat) and a dumping ground for English investments (canals, soon railroads) and for people who had become superfluous at home. As opposed to the 13 Colonies, industrialization was initially hardly permitted to take place, not even in settler colonies. It may certainly be assumed that at the time the idea behind this strategy was to avoid the mistake of granting a settler colony the right of economic self determination, as was inadvertently done in the 13 Colonies. As we shall see, political self-determination was soon a quite different matter.

After a period of uncertainty due to the loss of the 13 North American Colonies, it was the Durham Report (1837) that consolidated (among other measures taken in its wake) the peculiar structure of the Second British Empire. The integration of that Empire rested on materially grounded differences among its parts. It was an organic interdependence in the economic sense, and yet it was focused on England which in turn carefully maintained an image of cultural sophistication (education, parliamentary democracy, civil service and monarchy). Certainly, England also exercised centralized political power, but it was a flexible one over heterogeneous colonies. The social (e.g. settler v. non-settler colonies) and geographical characteristics of the various colonies, and the capitalist interests of the Parliament forbade any attempt at a politically homogeneous Empire. In view of a number of old and new competitors like France, Belgium, Germany and the expanding United States on the colonizing stage, and also of oppositional forces internal to the colonies (rebellious forces in Canada and India, and resistance by ethnically different people, e.g. the Boers), it became necessary for the capitalist British interests to devise locally specific systems of power. England and particularly London, no doubt, remained the center also in an economic sense. Political centralization oscillated between fluidity and rigidity depending on how conditions varied over space and time. Britain's flexibility, contradictory as it may seem, was fluid out of principle

Comparing, for a moment, the Spanish Empire with the Second British Empire, one can easily see that the Spanish Empire influenced by St. Augustine's idea of a "Civitas Dei" was primarily unified in the Crown and in its catholic belief without ever attaining a materially grounded organic interdependence among its colonies. In this sense, its unity remained basically a matter of mere cultural abstraction. This structure hardly stimulated any entrepreneurial activity, did not lead to individuated economic competition and, therefore, became increasingly powerless.

This, of course, was a major deficiency in a world that had begun to learn that nothing yields more surplus in power than a drive for individuated competition. Around 1800, when the Spanish Colonial Empire collapsed as a political unit, an economic cohesion of appreciable intensity among its parts was absent. The then politically independent countries which emerged largely in South America shared a similar culture, but were still not economically interdependent. Their internal differentiation had not advanced either and they were certainly not composed of capitalist competitive forces. These newly "independent" countries hence stagnated like the Spanish homeland, their former center.

England instead embarked on a gradual process of granting "responsible government" to its various colonies without ever losing power over them. A brief recapitulation of this process may very well grant an additional insight into the structure of the Second British Empire and also into what kinds of decisions it took to provide for the possibility of a powerful future.

It is astounding, for instance, to note the differences in time at which "responsible government" was granted to the various colonies. Leaving aside that externalization of costs (military protection, administration) was also on the minds of people at the British power center, we have to note that "responsible government" was only granted when capitalist interests, i.e. egofocal profit motives had permeated the society in question to a degree that opposition to it became negligible. The control of the French in Lower Canada, for example, who resisted the destruction of their communal life, could be managed in the form of "responsible government" after capitalist forces, hardly ever of French ethnicity, had gained dominance in Lower Canada in the first half of the 19th century. From then on, democratic forces could effectively keep the Quebecois from being masters in their own house. Although the Roman Catholic Church has usually not been understood as a friend by the British, its help continued to be used in this colony. At the other end of the continuum, India was given "responsible government" in the India Act as late as 1935. By that time, the capitalist system and parliamentary democracy had found sufficient support at least among the Indian elite. By contrast again, the Boers, protestant agricultural entrepreneurs, were given "responsible government" only a few years after their bitter defeat in the war against the British (1909). During all these developments, democracy was seen as a means of securing "legitimate" power for those in the homeland who knew that their interests were being taken care of by a sufficient number of individuals in the colonies who were equally inclined to pursue their own egofocal profits. Co-operation under the banner of liberty had become possible. In other words, democracy and good government did at best demand the appearance of identification, while the idea of "Civitas Dei" demanded the lived reality of identification. Now states and people could be united in antagonism.

As far as developments in the British homeland are concerned, it is particularly noteworthy how the acceptance of economic liberty as freedom had soon begun to undermine a socialist critique of capitalism. It did so by miraculously tying capitalist and working class interests together. Of course, such a miracle could only be accomplished by the further strengthening of nationalism and imperialism as overarching ideologies. This way, socialist politics had been neutralized (around 1850) in the English homeland and in the settler colonies alike. The circumstance that the right to vote was extended (1887) to practically all men (women, however, were still excluded) also helped to give them the sense of equal participation in a political system in which, however, "substance" was the only thing that still mattered. In these years, Britain's imperialism became wedded to another kind of ideology, namely that of racial superiority. While racism also emerged in other capitalist countries, e.g. in Germany and Japan, it had, like nationalism, a different complexion there as well. While not denying its ideological and practical significance, we have to leave out a treatment of this matter.

For the most part of the 19th century, i.e., during Britain's global dominance, the United States was absorbed in its own growth.

After the War of Independence, the strategy of the newborn country was determined by Hamilton's debate with Jefferson. Hamilton's emphasis on industrialization and political centralization prevailed (around 1790). The first task of the new country was to round itself off territorially. Politically serious obstacles against westward expansion no longer existed. What was then called Louisiana, i.e. the territory between the Mississippi - Delta and what is now Montana, was purchased from France in 1803. This purchase signaled the new meaning of land and the state: The state as a political entity emerged as a buyer of real estate, over which the state retained political control, while selling or giving pieces of it away to individuated interests. The Native inhabitants of these vast territories were never consulted. This way, enormous tracts of land became available to white settlers lured by the prospects of private ownership. Their number went up over the decades to tens of millions. Individuation among immigrants, not always present from the beginning was reinforced because of wide spread neo-locality arising from such factors as westward expansion and, later on, industrialization. Geographical mobility, unheard of until that time, soon evolved as a systemic requirement.

new way of new fcs
a life

Individuation and neo-locality meant a next to complete relegation of cultural tradition and identity. Individuals were "self made". This in turn implied that "making it" meant "making money" which was, in this setting, not only serious business, it was the *only* business. What one believed in, loved or enjoyed was acceptable as long as it was not made into an issue by some interested party. It did not take long for people to see that such idiosyncracies could get into one's way to "happiness". It is in this sense that the USA turned into a "melting pot". Individuals were reduced to mere producers and consumers. Production had become a mere means to further growth. In stark contrast to feudal and absolutist forms of production, working was no longer a source of sensuously and wholeheartedly accepted personal identity. Cultivation, and thus the quality of what was produced and consumed was no longer a matter of concern; quantity was all that mattered.

State and government became, ever more clearly, the "fostering hand" in individuated economic growth, as it was legitimized by the "Constitution" and the "Declaration of Independence". Unstoppable growth was felt as the "manifest destiny" of the USA and its "trusteeship under God". Acting out these notions made the growth orientation of each and all sacrosanct. It must be noted, though, that a complete laissez-faire economy was, from the beginning, limited by the "free" interaction and mutual constraints among all social institutions and actors. The degree of liberty attained by an individual depended on the "checks and balances" coming from others as they were collected in political parties, religious groups, businesses and other organizations. This means that the power that an individual could exercise often required "adaptation". Such adaptive ability required further disposal of personal identity as they were granted traditionally by convictions and overarching world views. Retaining these views would have made it more difficult to join ("the joiners"!) other passengers in the "survival vehicles". For this reason, the new society could not make allies among the Native nations, precisely because they were not smart or modernized enough to abandon their nationhood.

The penetration of Native land all the way to the West Coast has to be understood in terms of this new culture. Going West, one could escape the power of others and yet accumulate some sort of power base for oneself. The individuated search for gold, so different in its social form from the Spanish extraction of it, is a particularly good example of this ("gold rush"). The lack of title in land in Native cultures and the low density of the Native population, a requirement in hunting and gathering societies, meant to land hungry white people, an invitation to put this land to their kind of productive use. Given their cultural perspective, the settlers had no sense for making a serious attempt to understand the Natives. It was, for instance, totally alien for these settlers that the Native cultures had no concept of private ownership of land. The settlers did not see and did not care that such a concept was as alien to the Natives as a concept of private ownership of air would have been for them. Whenever settlers desired possession of land, the state protected them in this endeavor, often by incorporating the land in question into the United States. The Natives were then made to move, as has happened time and again, to "reservations" which even shrank over time.

Agriculture which was initially of a localized if not subsistence quality, grew already before 1850 into a market oriented and increasingly industrialized large scale production of agricultural produce. This trend was enhanced by the circumstance that land was a commodity and a matter of speculation leading to the agglomoration of vast farms and ranches by powerful individuals. In this process, the railroads played a significant role as well. Not only the size of the farms and ranches, but also the intent to save labor led to the necessity of acquiring industrially produced machinery and tools (plows, harvesters etc. for farmers, barbed wire for ranchers). This promoted the growth of industry, mainly in the East. It signified the birth of an interdependence between industry and an agriculture that was increasingly capital intensive itself. This kind of agriculture spread only much later in other parts of the world. Market orientation and an exclusive emphasis on commodity production in a competitive setting contributed to a yet growing intensity in the exploitation of land, fuels, water and other natural resources (including human beings), be it on the land or in the factory. The apparent overabundance of resources, compared with Europe at least, led to an incredible squander, which was strangely enough equated with "efficiency". In reality, this "efficiency" had come to mean mere replacement of human labor.

The settling of the West, the growth of circuits of exchange, and the growing need to overcome enormous distances accelerated the construction of railroads which greatly promoted heavy industry. The railroad companies also played an important role in luring both immigrants and capital, mostly from Europe to North America. The relative ease with which the immigrants could apparently cut their ties to the homeland and their sheer enormous number need to be understood from within the context of the industrialization that occurred on the European continent itself. As was the case before in England, people in countries like Belgium, France, Germany etc. were now uprooted, pauperized and pushed into individuation. Increasing poverty notwithstanding (or because of it?), the population growth was so dramatic that not even the "reserve armies of labor" could absorb it. The easily available way out for the surplus people was to follow the lure of US agents of immigration. The capital inflow from Europe to the United States briefly referred to above was, of course, also welcomed. Capital in the genuine sense of the word had come into being in large parts of Europe as well, mainly in the wake of industrialization.

This flow of individuated people and, needless to say, individuated capital from Europe to the US did not pose a political threat to the US. Its social form did in no way imply an influx of European powers. At least after 1850, it had become unnecessary to protect both North and South America against European states and their colonizing interests. This had been the initial intent and purpose of the Monroe-Doctrine (declared in 1823) and in that it was successful (a brief reign of a Habsburg Emperor in Mexico notwithstanding). Such interest was no longer of significance among European powers. Where it existed, like in Spain, it was not at par with the level of social evolution attained (in the USA and Britain). Before long, however, the Monroe-Doctrine could be used for foreign policy purposes by the US, although this required amazing changes in its definitions.

Before it came to that, the US had first to attend to a major internal crisis; the Civil War (1861-65).

In the US, industrialization was basically confined to the Northeast and the Northern parts of the West. The South was economically based on cotton and tobacco plantations where work was not mechanized, but was done by slaves. This meant that the South was not a lucrative market for Northern industry. The South had no interest in maintaining tariffs against industrial imports from Europe, mainly Britain, where the market was for its cotton and tobacco exports. This was not to the liking of the industrial North and this was the issue that was sorted out by the Civil War. Its result made little difference in the material circumstances of the, then, emancipated slaves. However, re-integration of the Old South into the Union remained a political issue for a long time to come, because the North failed, with a short lived exception, to soften the humiliation of the elite in the South. This kind of mistake was to be avoided later in the expansion of American capitalist interests, particularly after World War II.

The relatively free flow of capital between Europe and the US and, perhaps to a lesser extent, among European countries should not suggest that differences among the industrialized capitalist countries did not persist. The most significant differences were the following ones: Capitalism had either implied democracy right away (US) or had led to it quite rapidly (Britain). On the European continent, this development took place later and in a different form. There monarchs survived as political power centers, albeit with differences among them in the degree of centralization and in the granting of electoral privileges to the people. In this connection, one would think of France at one end of the spectrum, Russia at the other and Germany somewhere in between. Furthermore, the ethnic homogeneity of the various European states, with the obvious exception of the Austro-Hungarian Empire, implied that nationalism, regardless of its ideological abuse, had a more solid social foundation there than it ever had in England, let alone in the US. Besides nationalism triggering strong support in the working classes, particularly where national unity had not previously existed, for example, in Italy and Germany, it is of greater importance to point out that capitalists in Europe developed a different kind of self-understanding than they did in Britain and the US. Regardless of whether we think of Germany's Krupp and Siemens, France's Boigue and Marmont or the likes in other countries, in the absence of democracy, industrialists were readily willing to serve the interests of the political powers who, after all, paid only limited attention to the desires of their "underlings". In short, in large parts of Europe, non-democratic and nationalistic politics employed economic entrepreneurs for its political interests; the mirror opposite was the case in Great Britain and the US.

Returning to the evolvement of the US, we should first note that during the Civil War an economic boom led to the accumulation of vast capitals. These, in turn, stimulated, after the Civil War, the economic growth of "big business" to a considerable extent. And yet, periods of bust were quite frequent (e.g. in 1873/4, 1884 and 1893). While the specific reasons for these crises may be hard to determine in sufficient detail, it is important to note that the responses to them came primarily from business itself and only indirectly and ineffectively from politics (e.g. the banking act of 1864 and later, some anti-monopoly legislation). Business' reaction consisted largely in the formation of cartels and the integration, horizontal and/or vertical, of companies into ever growing corporations. Examples of such corporations would be Standard Oil, United Steel and Pennsylvania Railroad, to name but a few. These corporations integrated such diverse activities as railroads, mining, oil extraction, real estate, forestry, forging etc. Vertically, activities such as production, transportation, wholesaling and even retailing were integrated. At the same time, big corporations were less and less personally owned, but were run by executive managers who, as non-owners, had to prove success to the shareholders or other investors, that is to say, the true owners. This circumstance and the size of the operations required a much greater distance to the concrete activities of production, marketing, acquisition of raw materials, etc. Owing to the increasing variety of business related information, this new kind of business began to require the skill of cutting down to size the complexity of the incoming information (albeit in a still robust form), in order to facilitate decision making for the maximization of profits.

Needless to say that this development went hand in hand with increased capital intensity, i.e., further mechanization. This mechanization, as it saw its first culmination in Ford's assembly line was also inspired by information collection generated by Frederick Taylor's time-motion-studies. The significance of these studies lies with the circumstance that this information was gathered and viewed with what was claimed to be scientific detachment, i.e. with "objectivity". Here, two aspects need to be noted: 1.- "Objectivity" had already become a value among those scientists who were either non-informed philosophically or had adopted the position of analytical philosophy[4] as it prevailed in the Anglo-Saxon world any ways; 2.- The "elimination" of subjectivity in information gathering and knowledge construction reinforced the personal detachment as a requirement for finding "objective" information and knowledge. At the same time, we have to emphasize that non-detachment from profit interests, a highly subjective interest indeed, remained a matter that went without saying. Ignoring one's own entrepreneurial subjectivity while practicing it came to go hand-in-hand with another personal detachment, namely, that from the lives of individual human labor. Acknowledging the latter only as information data on a balance sheet made it easier to dispense with labor than it had been, e.g., in the relatively small shops of earlier industrial production. In other words: apparent, not real, elimination of subjectivity and its sensuous involvement became requirements in what had become a business that was increasingly claimed to be structured by "objective", if not "scientific" principles.

Gradually as all aspects in the running of a big corporation became matters of scientific inquiry, science became a *force* of production, in Marx's sense of the word. It was no longer just applied merely as a *means* of production, as for instance, when engineers made use of physics in the construction of railroads and locomotives. This evolutionary change took place already in the first decades of the 20th century. Karl Marx had anticipated this evolution,[5] but it is not certain that he, or other critical observers of the time, were aware of two important aspects of it. We do not think that it was seen that 1.- other institutions besides economics, namely politics, even religion, law, education and also art as entertainment became eventually permeated by this supposedly detached kind of thinking, and that 2.- this development led to a new concept of science altogether, one that eventually liberated itself in praxis from the notion of "objectivity" while still making claims to it publicly. This opened up new horizons for creativity in attempts to re-define reality. A more detailed exploration of this innovation will come later. At this point, we wish to briefly sketch how labor as a force of production adapted to the synthesis of capital and science, a synthesis in which capital, labor and science were transformed themselves.

As we have noted above, neo-locality, an outstanding feature of North American society, had not only led to the spreading of individuation, it had also implied the separation from cultural traditions. Without the evolvement of these new cultural trends, democratic flexibility would have been difficult. This had its consequences in the work life itself. Already by the 1800s, people had to be willing (spontaneously or not) to "apply themselves to everything",[6] no matter whether it was their apprenticed trade and whether they liked it or not. This meant that the "job" had begun to be separated from life as a whole. One was no longer a carpenter - let alone a life-long member of a guild - one did the job of a carpenter for a while, and something else later. The willingness to make such changes was also related to the permanently present threat of unemployment in the US. An "adaptation rationality" (Luhmann) thus came to permeate the thinking of the masses as thoroughly as the new type of science, namely "instrumentalism" (Luhmann), did in the thinking of the leaders, initially in business and politics, and later in everything.

It does not come as a surprise to us that "adaptation rationality" and "instrumentalism" precluded the formation of political parties that could deliver a critique, let alone a change, of the evolving politico-economic structure. Critique[7] as an unearthing of materially grounded contradictions in the praxis of society was undermined by a thinking that had begun to loose a sense for such foundation. This is not to say that material concerns did not matter to people. It meant that these concerns were understood exclusively in relation to one's own individuated advantages. Common wealth did not matter, what mattered was establishing partnerships in individuated pursuits. A materially grounded sense for the commonality with others, or whatever was left of it, evaporated. One made use of existing power constellations the best one could. Adaptation turned "survival vehicles" into (temporary) "homes". Challenging power as such was out of the question. The liberty of having the right to take care of oneself did, undoubtedly, not exclude excessive poverty in the US, notwithstanding high wages for some of those who had work and enormous profits for those who had capital. The practical absence of anti-capitalistic political forces soon became a remarkable difference to Europe, to a lesser extent than to Britain. In other words, in the US, labor was no longer, if it ever was, a working class in the "classical" Marxist sense. Labor saw itself, however erroneously so, as a partner of capital in a new corporate society. The idea of being one's own entrepreneur was (and still is) part of the "American Dream". It is only to be expected that in this setting social legislation did not only not exist, but that it was not even called for; it was widely rejected as "socialism". This is merely a concrete manifestation of a modernized mode of thinking in which labor, capital and science had taken on new meaning.

The mass production that evolved in the US economy required mass consumption. While abundance has probably always been the dream of us humans (many fairy tales attest to that), the modern mass consumption is a different matter. Jobs as mere means to consumption or other personal economic betterment have not even meant to be sources of satisfaction and identification in themselves anymore. Consumption had become, at the individual level, a substitute for such "old-fashioned" ideas. Consumption has probably always been used as a status symbol, as "conspicuous" consumption however, it turned into little else than a means for further growth. Thus, it too disappeared as an end in itself. The emergence of mass entertainment, i.e. radio and movies, began to increasingly substitute for a satisfaction that one had found previously in one's own actual play with words and music. At the same time, being seen as having a radio and as being able to go to the movies mattered, instrumentally. Satisfaction was no longer associated with one's own doing. Providing mass entertainment and soon also "high culture" came to be sensed as mere delivery of "shows". In this way, their consumption did not lead to a sense of community beyond the moment of their occurrence and, thus, diverted the masses from retaining a sense for truly social pleasure and satisfaction. Needless to say that the professionalization of sports (mainly of baseball and football), as it emerged early in the US, had the same function. Pseudo-satisfaction, supplied in abundance, contributed to political pacification; it kept people from asking challenging questions and, thus, from critique. In view of what art and thought had done in previous centuries, we would indeed see a novelty emerging in the use of the "finer things in life" (Adams). Contrary to Adams we suggest that only since recent times have these tools been used in the power games of society. Whether and how this precludes their revival as true expressions of human Nature is a question we have to leave aside for the time being.

All this is not to deny that similar developments emerged in Western Europe as well. However, mass production and mass consumption did not occur there to the same degree, since individuation and uprootedness was, and be it simply because of lesser geographic mobility of people, much lower than in the US These phenomena undoubtedly grew in Europe's industrial countries as well, but they were, however dubiously so, contained for quite some time yet in shared ideas, never mind that these soon evaporated into sheer ideologies as well.

Turning to the foreign policy of the US around the turn from the 19th to the 20th century, we would like to focus, not without reason, on the war between the US and Spain. We do so, since this gives us an additional opportunity to characterize the novelty of thinking that had emerged there. Let us look, in this connection, at the re-definitions of the Monroe-Doctrine, of imperialism (and colonialism) and even of geographic factuality, as they took place at that time.

The Monroe-Doctrine, initially intended to keep European colonial powers out of the Americas, was now re-defined as legitimizing military protection for American corporations which had entered Cuba and other Latin American countries. While this (and not Cuba's still nominal status of a Spanish colony) led to a military invasion by US troops in Cuba (and the war against Spain 1898), it did not lead to a traditional form of colonial take-over either. American corporations soon felt secure under a Cuban government as long as that government depended on US military might. Veiling its presence behind a locally recruited brutal government that was not even democratically elected, became part and parcel of this new kind of colonial imperialism, as it began to go beyond the colonialism of industrial capitalism. This imperialism was spearheaded by business corporations and not by the state. Wherever US corporations went in this new era, if they felt secure without direct US military interference, they practiced their intrusion without it; otherwise they used it. Imperialism was perhaps less obvious in such cases, but it was practiced nonetheless. Guatemala, Bolivia and Chile would be examples for this, while the taking of Panama resembled the Cuban case.

The fact that US business and military entered the Philippines, legitimizing even this by invoking the Monroe-Doctrine and the circumstance that this was not challenged on sheer geographic terms, demonstrated how powerful and acceptable the ability to re-define reality had become. Yet, this was only the beginning of this new mode of thinking. Much more was yet to come.

With these developments, industrial capitalism had arrived, at least in the USA, at the threshold of late capitalism. Capital, and science in a new form, were the new weapons in the power struggle available to the elite. Labor, as a force of production, underwent an equivalent change on its part; it had to develop adaptation rationality. Thus the previously existing divisions between the classes became blurred. Labor became practically co-opted into the new social system. Quite a few of them became stockholders in the corporate society. The difference between adaptation rationality and instrumentalism was, of course, only a matter of gradation, i.e., the less power one had the more one had to adapt. This is the setting in which "everybody is middle class", i.e., has some capital and some knowledge so that everybody can both exploit and be exploited, and yet as such can still contribute to the unstoppable growth of the system.

Notes

[1] See below pp 104, 108-110, 122

[2] Weizsäcker, 1994, p. 98 reminds us that God's mandate for man to subjugate the earth comes thousands of years after the introduction of agriculture and must therefore be understood as a late attempt at legitimizing such subjugation. Pointing this out, it does not seem to occur to Weizsäcker that agricultural land was also often and until quite recently in many parts of the Western world understood as being given into man's cultivating stewardship, thus preventing Nature from being ruthlessly exploited.

[3] The names of writers and poets that come to mind here are. Hugo, Musset, de Bonald, de Maistre for France; Schlegel, Arndt, the Grimm Brothers, Brentano for Germany; Byron, Shelley, Keates, Carlyle for England, to name but a few.

[4] Analytical philosophy does not assume that the human subject synthesizes its subjectivity, i.e its cognitive frame of reference, into its own statements Statements exist, i e , are "true", independent of human subjectivity.

[5] Marx, 1973, e g. pp. 699, 706.

[6] Marx, 1973, p. 105.

[7] Regarding the notion of critique, see pp. 104, 123, 124n6.

Chapter 4

Late Capitalism: "Liberation" and Global "Development"

Looking back for a brief moment at our sketch of the evolution of Western society, we would like to acknowledge that we have drawn this sketch under the guidance of the often used concepts of abstraction and individuation. This, however, is not a projection of a modern view into the past, since, different from Adams, we view the present including its individuation and abstractions as gradual emergents. It is in this sense that we claim that these concepts allow us to understand the present as a product of a long evolution. In view of this purpose, the concepts of abstraction and individuation require further inspection.

Since thousands of years, probably since the Paleolithic, our species has tried to organize its affairs in an amazing variety of social forms which on their part were manifestations of mental constructions about the meaning of our bodily existence. These constructs have evolved, more or less, along a line reaching from the justification of the incest taboo, to ancestor cults, high religions, and finally to ever more abstract philosophies. Each of these allowed for the organization of ever more complex societies and their ever more abstract understanding of life around them and in them. These "cultural potentials" have legitimized power in the sense that they helped, at times, to avoid the exercise of physical force. By no means, however, can we exclude the possibility that whole societies and also their leaders have, at least in the initial ascending phases of historical epochs, believed wholeheartedly in these cultural constructs. Therefore, we have no right to deny these cultures that they were sensed by members of society as idioms of self expression and thus as manifestations of freedom. It is a different matter whether we as outsiders might see forms of repression in them. Karl Marx speaks of these epochs, at least for the times of their ascendancy as "nice illusions". With the evolutionary increase in social differentiation, the cultural systems capable of keeping societies integrated had to grow in abstraction, more or less along the lines just mentioned. The increase in abstraction over the millennia was such that these symbolic constructs finally became so "thin" that they were blown away in major Revolutions (e.g. 1789, 1917). Also in the past, leaders may have turned into rulers by simply employing, in a self distancing fashion, beliefs venerated by their people. This does not only invalidate them for their times, but also for us. It is only since the evolution of capitalism that such beliefs must be understood as what they eventually came to be: "cultural potentials" in the exercise of egofocal power. Having been devalued once, old world views cannot be revived anymore. As we shall discuss later in more detail, new "philosophies" free of instrumentalistic use cannot be invented either anymore, since instrumentalism will instantaneously penetrate them like a cancer.

While abstractions served, once upon a time, to give meaning to man and Nature by tying the individual into great mental imageries of often astounding grace and beauty, the demands arising out of an increasingly complex division of labor made the circles of undoubted loyalty around the individual smaller and smaller. This is what sociological thinkers like Marx, Weber and Durkheim have conceptualized as the process of individuation. The circles of loyalty shrunk, roughly speaking, from clan to lineage, extended family, nuclear family to the single parent "family" of today. This, of course, went hand in hand with the process of abstraction in which culturally convincing reasons to sense loyalty beyond these shrinking arrangements lost their strength, time and again, but could be replaced until the recent past. Being completely individuated today, we now have ample reason to know that we have nothing cultural left to hang on to. We are left to our bodily existence, to other individuals like us and to Nature out there. Being however uniquely endowed by the ability to know all this, we have arrived at a point in evolution where it can also be known that there is indeed nothing else left than this insight to secure our survival. It appears as if it is now the central question whether we appreciate our own Nature or do not do so. This will determine whether glory or disaster lies ahead of us. Attempts at "muddling through" will only prolong the agony.

Our evolution towards late capitalism has brought us to this point of sobriety. Its current globalization could mean the globalization of this sobriety as well. Of course, the realization of this sobriety requires the overcoming of late capitalism and its abstractions of instrumentalism and adaptation rationality. Before we can deal with this matter, we have to clearly understand their emergence and further development.

Returning after this excursion to where we left matters in the previous chapter, we would like to reiterate that big corporations first emerged in the USA and influenced politics there directly. Soon they also came into being in other countries, as for instance in Great Britain, Belgium, France, the Netherlands and in Germany. In the Far East, Japan, after its forced opening in the middle of the 19th century, had also embarked on the path of industrial production. While the economic strength in each of these countries pushed corporations beyond their national boundaries, differences in social structure, regardless of economic similarities, gave very different forms to these expansions. As noted above, one could broadly distinguish between states in which the economy took leadership in this expansion enjoying, when the need arose, protection by political institutions, and others in which the economy served a primarily politically articulated interest in extending power. Thus, it was under different conditions that the economic sector could grow in these countries. The US and Great Britain are representatives of the first group, Germany and Japan of the second, while others like France fall somewhere in between.

During the first half of the 20th century, the countries representing the extremes, i.e. the US and Great Britain on the one hand, and Germany and Japan on the other, settled in two briefly separated World Wars the question of what kind of corporate capitalism would take dominance. The second half of the century completed the dominance of the Anglo-Saxon form of corporate capitalism. Their late capitalism succeeded in this by its Cold War victory over the USSR. The USSR had emerged as yet another social system in which the economy was meant to follow political interests. Indicatively, it was defeated on sheer economic terms. At the turn to the 21st century, a form of late capitalism had finally evolved that practically penetrated all social institutions in those societies that came to adhere to it.

Looking at this evolvement in a bit more detail, we would like to begin with the emergence of the rivalry between Great Britain and Germany. This rivalry quickly intensified after Germany's military victory over

France and its unification in a nation state (1871). One could approach the issue of this rivalry by raising the question: Why is it that the lesson that Great Britain had learned in the loss of the 13 North American Colonies could not be brought to bear on its competition with Germany? We think the answer lies in the following observation: the civility which the Anglo-Saxon forms of capitalism had developed for the resolution of conflicts was still alien to most European powers, certainly to Germany. This civility consisted in negotiating compromises in an astoundingly flexible, conviction-less way. Germany's nationalism under Kaiser Wilhelm II was not capable of that flexibility. The instrumentalistic employment of its nationalism by the elite there was far less developed and, thus, was far less visible to the common person in Germany than in the Anglo-Saxon countries. Germans were still more rightfully convinced of the validity and truthfulness of their national feelings. The same was the case in parts of the Austro-Hungarian Empire, and also to a considerable extent in France. In these countries, capitalist entrepreneurs followed and adapted to the demands of the national political leaders and pursued their profit interests by abiding by the political system and its ideology. There is no doubt that nationalism was strongly fostered in Great Britain as well, but it was only mobilized when economic expansion failed and came to require military protection. Germany ranked quite prominently among those countries on the European continent which, while having multi-headed economic systems, had no pluralist parliamentary democratic form of government, although the latter could not act without parliamentary approval. Measures aiming at gaining global supremacy and at establishing colonies were carried out more by the state and less by traders or corporate entrepreneurs. This allowed for a greater unity of action, but it also reduced the number of players acting on the international stage for Germany. Thus, for reasons internal to Germany, the channels and possibilities for negotiating compromises about Germany's expansion were fairly limited. As we shall see later, the same applies to Japan.

The leadership of politics in the case of Germany needs to be explained also in terms of its ethnic homogeneity. It was, in this sense, a nation state. The exclusion of the Austro-Hungarian Empire from the German unification in 1871 was explicitly reasoned on the grounds of its multi-ethnicity. Austria alone, of course, would, have been a different matter. Furthermore, it needs to be borne in mind that the initiative for the unification of Germany was taken by the clearly militaristic state of

Prussia and carried out largely by military action. To be sure, the political unification of the "Second German Reich" greatly facilitated the emerging industrial capitalist economy, but it implied that industrial capitalism in Germany would flourish from then on under the umbrella of a politics with a fundamentally militaristic, and not a business outlook.

Needless to say that the rapid growth of industrial capitalism in Germany in the last decades of the 19th century (including the emergence of large corporations) led to considerable poverty and individuation. Yet, this individuation differed from the one prevailing in the Anglo-Saxon countries, be it simply because of its recent emergence. The industrial labor force was recruited from among people who had just left strong rural and kinship ties. While having to fend for themselves individually through "selling" their labor force, members of the German working class still retained, for the most part, a vivid memory of loyalty and communal belonging. In this context, a level of geographical mobility as it existed in the US, or in Great Britain with its overseas colonies, was never attained. Given a widespread remembrance of social belonging, poverty led easily to socialist solidarity on the one hand, or was open to right-wing nationalist ideology, on the other.

This sense of national unity provided a favorable context for the political shrewdness of Chancellor Bismarck, when he introduced far reaching social security legislation which was unparalleled in the industrial world at that time. This legislation was accepted across all class lines. It has never been seen or even rejected as "socialism", as happened to similar measures in the US, e.g. later under Roosevelt. These new laws were, of course, intended to avoid social unrest which particularly in view of a strong socialist party was a very real threat. Yet, the political shrewdness involved here had more than one aspect. Health, old age and accident insurance, for instance, helped to avoid eventual social costs as well. The Bismarckian social legislation also helped to incorporate labor as a class into society and, thus, to reinforce an old pre-industrial stratification in a new way. In other words, the co-optation of labor in Germany did not contribute to the kind of individuation that had blurred class distinctions in the USA At the same time, Bismarck's social legislation also took, for a while, much wind out of the sails of the socialists and yet helped to make Germany's socialist working class permanently susceptible to nationalistic advances. This social legislation certainly did not strengthen the internationalism of the German working class. For this reason, it remained for decades to come an open question whether German working class solidarity would express itself in a right or a left wing form.

It is almost superfluous to explicate that the classes of capital and labor in Germany could easily indulge in a sense of identity. They lacked to a considerable degree the detached instrumentalism and adaptational flexibility that prevailed primarily in the US and also in Great Britain. In our view, this circumstance gave little reason for the pseudo-satisfaction of consumerism. In its absence, the profits of German industrial and soon corporate capitalism could only be derived from considerably lower wages than in the US Since this meant that profits had to be realized in an internal market that was less potent in Germany than the one of the US, it also implied that German industrial capitalism had soon to seek overseas markets. Obtaining raw materials cheaply was also a pressing issue in a country not heavily endowed by them. In this way, Germany came to challenge Britain as a leading trading nation.

Germany tried to back its economic aspirations by seeking naval parity with Great Britain. This political threat eventually called for war action, no matter which side officially declared war. While focusing on the British-German aspect of World War I, we do not mean to deny that other parties, like France, Italy, Russia, Austria, even the far away Japan were also involved in that war, each for their own different nationalistic reasons.

For the first two and a half years of the war, the US stayed neutral. Its entrepreneurs did not fail to profit from this conflict by supporting either side, albeit unequally so. It supplied primarily England and France with ammunition and other war equipment. In order to pay for the excessive costs of the war, Britain and also France floated bonds in the US This turned the US into a creditor country, while Britain suffered the most from losing that status.

The war remained inconclusive until 1917, when the US decided to intervene on the side of its main debtors. Undoubtedly, this decision could easily be legitimized by Germany's continued sub-marine warfare against US shipment of supplies to England. About the same time, Germany had made an attempt to ease its military situation by terminating the war on its Eastern front against Russia. Economic problems in Russia were exploited by the German leadership in what turned out to be a move of rather far reaching consequences. They transported Lenin from his Swiss exile to Russia in order to have him add to Russia's difficulties through revolutionary activities. This forced Russia to make peace with its enemies. However, this did not lead to Germany's victory on the Western front.

The German Armed Forces, undefeated on the battlefield, had to surrender because of the starvation and political upheaval among the German people. This aspect as well as the growing American involvement had put a victory out of reach for Germany. The peace treaty imposed on Germany (1919), mainly by France, Great Britain and the US, was seen by the Germans as an extraordinary humiliation. If the US had not exercised some moderating influence on France and Great Britain, the humiliation would have been worse. France wanted revenge for grievances against Germany stemming from the war of 1870/1 (Alsace-Lorraine) and was even more intent than Britain on breaking Germany's economic, political and military power. This was a consequence of the strong nationalistic antipathy between France and Germany. The US interest consisted only partly in getting reparations and, in fact, demanded much less than it could have done. At the same time, it looked upon Germany as a potential lucrative trading partner and thus had an interest in not inflicting too much damage on Germany's economy. According to the Dawes-Plan, the US lent money to Germany (in our view, an anticipation of the Marshall-Plan) for two purposes: to invest in German industry and to allow Germany to pay reparations to France and Great Britain who, in turn, had to make debt payments to the US In this manner, the source of interest payments to the US was made considerably safer.

In Germany, the Treaty of Versailles added to serious and wide-spread economic hardship, both directly (reparations, lack of capital) and indirectly (rapid devaluation of its currency, i.e. inflation). These factors intensified nationalistic feelings in all quarters of German society including the political left. The latter also suffered from the resentment of those political forces that blamed the abdication of the Kaiser on them. At any rate, the implementation of a parliamentary democracy was accepted with widespread mixed feelings. This is why the Weimar Republic got off to a shaky start and came to an early and easy demise. The civility of Anglo-Saxon politics and economics could not yet be embraced by Germany. In this setting, the German capitalist class could easily ally itself with the resurgent nationalism. Therefore, the circumstance that this class came to side eventually with Hitler must not be simplified as a mere placing of bets. The connections of German capitalists with their class brethren in the West remained comparatively feeble. It is evident that the German working class, like the working class in other countries, had fought enthusiastically in World War I and shared a strong sense of nationhood with the capitalists. An orientation toward a national form of socialism was still quite strong in Germany's working class. Its internationalism was still far from being universal. A strong link of that class with the intellectual and artistic elite of Germany was not established, although the latter had, for the most part, considerable left-wing leanings. This elite, possibly because of its greater international orientation, grew more and more isolated from the working class. In 1933, Hitler's "National Socialist German Workers Party" won the election. Thus, Hitler became the democratically elected Chancellor of Germany, although (or because) it was known that he was determined to destroy democracy. The elimination of all other political parties did not find a numerically strong resistance, because Hitler put Germany back on a path towards growth. This growth, however, was once again understood primarily in political and only then in economic terms. How Hitler and the Nazi-Party perverted the German sense for national self-respect into a barbaric racism needs no elaboration here.

Since 1917, the threat that the USSR posed to the Western capitalists arose out of the growth of a non-capitalist economy. The embeddedness of the economy in the state structure and, thus, the development of a concept of democracy entirely different from the one prevailing in Western Europe and the US, were viewed by these powers as a deadly challenge to their concepts of liberty and pluralist democracy. The strength of the Communist Parties in Western countries, including Germany up to 1933, added to the fears in the capitalist "free world". Hitler was for these forces more easily acceptable than communism, particularly because he soon eliminated all socialist ideas within the Nazi-Party. In this way, he came to spearhead, for a while, the opposition against the USSR.

In the USA, the First World War had provided an enormous opportunity for further growth of corporate business. The government fostered that growth by providing considerable subsidies to these businesses, primarily in connection with infra-structural measures like road, railway and naval construction. Not only the government, the corporations too came out of the war as winners. After the First World War, a decade of largely unbridled economic growth began and was supposed to ring in a "New Era". The big corporations were never asked to pay back the subsidies previously received by them. This was accepted as a matter of course. The veterans of that war, however, received the bonuses they were promised by law with great hesitation and did only as late as the mid-30s. Huge profits were made. This, of course, implied that consumption had to grow commensurately which it did. The unbridled growth on the side of capital, i.e. of mechanization, created a problem in so far as it paid little attention to the other side, namely, to the proportionate decline of labor, i.e. of buying power. At the same time, the costs of industrially produced goods were kept up (protected by high tariffs) leading to the increasing exploitation of Nature, besides that of the people employed as labor also to that of the raw materials extracted from Nature out there. It was increasingly because of the latter form of exploitation that the economic process could be reproduced. Those employed - by no means everybody - had to work and to consume hard. Time wasted in jobs not loved in themselves had to be compensated for. Making a living was not part of living. A good life came to mean an increasingly outrageous consumption. On the production side of the process, the squandering of raw materials, falsely considered to be inexhaustible in the US, expressed itself in low prices. Farm produce, for instance, became cheaper and cheaper.

At the same time, US society opted more and more for individual (what else under the prevailing social conditions?) modes of transportation than for the public ones. This stimulated road construction and the production of automobiles. Individuated mobility became ever more valued. "Decisions" of this kind helped to put society on an ecologically treacherous path, but consumption and corporations flourished.

With the growth of ever bigger corporations, their internal diversification grew as well. Diversification and growth implied the marginalization and often total disappearance of personal ownership. Executives took the place of owners in so far as they came to have the power over the corporation. Ownership now grew almost completely anonymous as it spread in the form of stock holdings. This added to the gradation system of the American form of stratification. "Class warfare" became less and less an issue in a society which retained, nonetheless, an enormous spread between rich and poor. Power in this social structure became more and more based on mental control over socially significant processes. The vertical gradation of people became ever more linked to instrumentalism, prevailing more at the top, and adaptation rationality more at the bottom. The mental flexibility required to constantly reproduce the social condition of next to total individuation, contributed enormously to the dynamics of US society. To the extent that these structural conditions have gained dominance today far beyond the US, they deserve our close attention. Paying this attention will hopefully help us to understand, on the one hand, the overpowering strength of late capitalism, as well as the kind of personality ("our problematic Nature"!) shaped by it, on the other.

We like to take off from the observation that senior executives of large corporations came to be less and less concerned with the specific and concrete activities of the corporation. The consumer demand for the products and the cost factors in production certainly remained matters of concern, but while keeping an eye on these, senior executives saw it increasingly as their main task to "cultivate" the company's environment. Attention is paid to, and manipulation is exercised on, political conditions, e.g. taxation, infrastructure, political movements etc., and on even broader social developments in areas like education, religion and others. Whatever is expedient on behalf of the corporation and in that sense meaningful, be it images including personal appearance of the higher ranking employees or the architecture of the corporate building, is viewed in terms of its exchange value. We could also put it this way: only means promising growth have meaning in this setting.

Since the sheer number of what is potentially meaningful grows so vastly, information about these matters has to be abstracted and condensed, i.e., strategically selected with an eye on its instrumental value. Concrete details do not usually matter to executives; they hardly even reach the desks of the junior executives. Top executives have to rely on the correctness of information fed to them, never mind that this correctness depends on selection criteria of the specialists below them (e.g. engineers, lab scientists, market researchers etc.) who have, like anybody else does, their own individuated (subjective) agenda. The senior executive must, therefore, be critical about his sources, since whatever he is being told must be understood and sensed (re-defined) in such a way that it leads to success for the corporation, and thus for him. Neither truth, nor even strictly speaking correctness,[1] is an issue in this interpretation. Instead, correct is what leads to success, that is to the growth in power of the corporation and the people in it. In this setting, the corporation becomes a "survival vehicle" for the executives and all the others working in it. While this mode of thinking soon permeates all organizations in late capitalism, it remains highly doubtful to us that one can claim that it had existed before that time. Certainly, as a structural requirement, it is a recent phenomenon.

The new skill of instrumentalistic understanding and re-defining has two aspects that need to be inspected. On the one hand, the activities of understanding and re-defining reality remain tied, in the final analysis to the issue of control over material goods (as Adams knows so well). On the other hand, the flexibility implied in re-defining reality has a fluidity with unpredictable changes to it. The reason for this is that definitions of reality take place in the context of other actors making their own, often unexpectable, definitions of the reality at hand. Thus, thought, i.e., the meaning of anything that has an existence, becomes "real" only when proving itself in whatever is seen as concrete success. While this forbids lasting convictions completely, it brings meaning "down-to-earth" but, sticking to this metaphor, only to that spot of the earth where the actor concerned happens to stand and wishes to make gains. Every participant in the "game" must know that meaning can neither be fully shared nor can its flexibility be taken lightly. This is obviously a consequence of the circumstance that individuated interests force us to change views at unpredictable intervals. This creates ever new problems. In this form, definitions once made may easily limit a corporation's, or for that matter, any other social actor's future ability to act. The reason is that putting one's understandings into practice may often imply commitments of some duration. And yet, even this situation is primarily viewed as merely posing a new challenge to one's ability to re-define. This challenge requires mental distancing from concrete reality, without, of course, its abolition. Contingency of truth and cognitive opportunism are obviously structural requirements for survival in the territories of unbridled competition. As such, these requirements may pose interesting problems for philosophers, but not for executives who have to face them at the level of daily praxis.

For clarification of this, one may look at the example of the requirements involved in the mobility and the eventual internationalization of big corporations. These imply, at least among the top executives, a way of thinking in which loyalty to the local community and even to the nation state may become, given certain circumstances, a means for the company's increase in power. Loyalty will then be displayed. Precisely for this reason, governments at all levels could be threatened by the company's (or any other organization, as the case may be) hint at the possibility of going away. Because the presence of a corporation may be valued by any number of agents in a social field, such as politicians, trade unionists, community or even church leaders, the corporation holds power over these agencies. Exercising such power implies commitments. Propagating nationalism at one point in time, for instance, may easily lead to the question of how to get out of it later, particularly at a time when going international appears as being gainful. As they exemplify the contingency of truth, such kinds of problems simply pose to men in praxis a new challenge to their re-defining abilities. The results of new re-definitions will require civility among all involved, since these dealings may not work too smoothly and yet nobody may wish to apply power in a somewhat raw form. As Adams says, often the "issue is to not let power show",[2] but to cover it under the mere "cultural potential" to exercise it. This, as a corollary of instrumentalism, is part and parcel of the cognitive opportunism, the practiced "philosophy" of late capitalism.

This does not at all mean that instrumentalism is a form of thought that has rid itself of limitations and constraints. They came along with liberty from the beginning and are far from disappearing now. Even though leading executives, for instance, have to be connoisseurs of capriciousness, daily interaction on the job also requires that they be "team players". In other words, measures of loyalty, honesty, reliability etc. have to be, and are indeed observed. Business companies themselves can in as little as individuals working in them afford to be seen as totally unreliable. Being plausibly unreliable, however, is a different issue. Rules and ethics play, therefore, their roles within big corporations (including the Mafia) and also, at least to some extent, outside of them. That is one of the reasons that institutions like religion, law, family and education do not get marginalized. Their input regarding ethics, values and sociality is still needed, in whatever modification. At the same time, the leaders in these fields had to acquire a style of thinking similar to that practiced by executives of business corporations. Activities in institutions like education and religion had to become business-like themselves, since it is believed that they function at their best that way. Thus, the corporate structure and its "philosophy" of instrumentalism could not help but penetrate fields like education, religion, the arts and the sciences. Accordingly, it is accepted that schools, universities, churches etc. have to compete for growth in their respective markets. These markets are not less competitive than that of economics proper. Growth is the issue where stagnation means death. This might help to explain that members of the societal elite could switch jobs and roles quite easily (and enhance their individual power that way). Loyalty to a new organization is easily displayed and switched. A move of a person from business to education and/or politics, for instance, merely indicates that this thinking "could apply itself anywhere" (Karl Marx). Those well versed in traditional scientific proof like physicists, chemists, etc. may encounter difficulties in this regard. They have first to unlearn a fair bit of what was ingrained in them at school. Accordingly, it is no surprise that those coming from disciplines stuck in positivistic notions of correctness, have not become a majority among corporate leaders. Lawyers or those with degrees in business administration or other social sciences are much better and more directly prepared for the exercise of cognitive opportunism. They are, therefore, over-represented in the elite of modern society.[3]

Much of this clearly illustrates that the new kind of knowledge required under the prevailing conditions focuses on social relations. This has rung in, at least according to Niklas Luhmann, the leadership of instrumentalism as a new mode of thinking, adequately backed nowadays by a cybernatically understood systems theory of sense. As discussed earlier[4] in our attempt to bring Luhmann's theory of sense systems and Adams' theory of power together, the power gradation among all actors involved in modern society is related to an uneven distribution in the ability of practicing this kind of thinking. Instrumentalism and adaptation rationality may be thought of as occurring in their pure form at opposite ends of the power structure.

Further aspects important in the functioning of the modern mode of thinking come to light when we cast an eye on how it impacts the praxis of the individual. For a number of reasons, the role of the scientist is a good example.

Provided a scientist "wants to make it" - and this, after all, is the issue -, he/she has to do that kind of research that is desired by others, be it, inter alia, a political agency, the military, a business corporation, or a church. Only where money for research is available, i.e. where power could be had, research will go. To be clear, the kind of science produced under this condition is not therefore incorrect, but a few questions about it do arise. Firstly, since knowledge is sought in areas which happen to be of interest to a society of an inherently capricious Nature, one has to wonder how a knowledge in areas rather capriciously selected could be adequate to the Nature of things? Secondly, if our knowledge of Nature around us is in the danger of being strangely piecemeal in character, is it then not plausible that this knowledge leads to a treatment of Nature that is unbecoming to parts of Nature, among them, to us? While we cannot go into a detailed treatment of these questions at the moment, we have to point out at this juncture that modern research on Nature may very well yield correct results, and yet we would have to wonder whether correctness of knowledge is enough of a criterion for its validity.[5] Claims for "objective correctness" of knowledge are, of course, bolstered by the denial of subjective involvement in scientific endeavors. This denial suffers from the serious oversight of the just mentioned subjectively motivated choice of research areas and of the interest of delivering desired results. The claim to "objective correctness" is also bolstered by the success in the application of scientific findings. We have to note here that "successful application" is reduced to limited purposes, such as when pain killers kill pain, while so-called side-effects are often ignored. Often only the appearance of success materializes, and yet "objective correctness" is treated as proven.

As for the scientist, the issue for everybody else in late capitalist society is to find others who value what one has to offer. The flexible ability to compete within this structure determines one's place in the gradation order of power. This form of stratification has transcended-and-contained (in the Hegel-Marx sense) the old capitalist class structure. While it needs to be borne in mind that this cognitive opportunism is a structural requirement in late capitalism, it does not follow that it is practiced by each individual. And yet, it must not be forgotten that versatility in this modern mode of thinking determines one's place in today's society.

For those willing to participate fully in this setting, everything and everybody have to become means for gaining further means. This is the same as saying that nothing can yield satisfaction anymore. It is under these conditions that the ancient myth of Midas to which we have made reference before, has become a lived reality. Its structural advantage is that it keeps individuals permanently "hungry". This way, it is largely guaranteed that permanent competition for growing levels of (still only pseudo-) satisfaction does not disappear. This creates permanent growth in consumption and thus production, making the plunder of Nature and the dumping of waste on her inevitable. At the same time, it is fashionable, or better to say, opportune, to join in the lament about our "environmental problems", and to suppress the insight that they reveal our own problematic Nature.

A society of this kind cannot help but have much power in it and even permanently increase it. This is of distinct advantage within the "community of nations" among which, like among individuals, nothing counts as much as power does. This competition, however, will accelerate the exploitative control over Nature and no end to this is in sight. Even if the nation state disappears, other competing units will evolve, because the egofocal interest in competitive growth will not cease to exist. As indicated above, the required disappearance of competitive growth would require of man, according to Adams, to cease being human. Instead, we wonder whether the problem is not simply our presently problematic Nature.

Returning from this excursion into the ground structure of late capitalism to our more detailed inspection of its emergence, we have first to look at that society that, in more recent times, contributed the most to that process, namely, the US In doing so, we have an opportunity to note a feature of instrumentalism that might surprise even a seasoned student of this capricious mode of thinking (but will only do so for a brief moment). If one notes that late capitalist societies also have the ability to learn from their mistakes, then one has to prepare oneself for encountering quite an absurdity. The absurdity is that late capitalist societies have an in-built tendency to correct their mistakes by applying to them what has led to these mistakes in the first place. On second thought, however, one comes to see that this is part and parcel of the "logic" of late capitalism and contributes to what we shall come to understand as its immunity. A remarkable example of this was the way in which the US handled what has come to be known as the "Crash" of 1929.

Throughout the 1920s, politicians in the US were voted into office because they held out the promise of providing a setting for increasing prosperity. The present day near universality of this habit of politicians may make it seem strange to find this political practice remarkable and yet, it is by now visible that this practice makes parliamentary democracy, given the growth orientation of today's culture, a problematic form of politics. We do not mean to advocate an abolition of democracy, but its transcendence-and-containment (in the Hegel-Marx sense). Anything else would ignore the level of individuation attained. We do believe that the individuation of the individual poses problems in democratic societies that need to be resolved, since the unavoidable growth orientation of modern society poses too much of a threat to our survival. It may very well be doubtful, however, that environmental obstacles to this growth orientation were as readily noticeable at the time of the 1920s as they are now. Yet, problems in the economic system forbidding such promises could have been noticed by the reflective observer and participant already at that time.

Had a political economy of the late 1920s in the US effectively been in existence, it could have identified the two significant factors that lead to the "Crash", namely the oversupply of commodities, on the one hand, and the increasingly speculative value of investments, on the other. This applies in particular to the trading of shares on the stock market. These problems, undoubtedly, could not be dealt with at the level of individuated cognitive opportunism. More was required, but this was not seen. Thus, as we shall see, the problems were solved in a typically instrumentalistic way. Their solution was simply based on the insight that it is instrumental for instrumentalism to restrict itself.

Oversupply existed to a significant degree in housing, cars, textiles and household gadgets, to name but a few. Since the wage portion in production did not keep pace with capital gains, the buying power dropped. Sales tricks like consumer credits helped, but, as mere re-definitions of debt, did so only in the short run. On the capital side, buying real estate and stocks on margins was the equivalent phenomenon to shopping on credit: both were based on the expectation of further growth. If this growth, however, does not materialize, then the "bubble" could easily burst. The oversupply led to a situation in which capital could no longer realize itself, i.e., its value shrunk. Holding shares, henceforth, meant loosing money. Early warnings notwithstanding (e.g., Florida's crash in land speculation, 1925/6), the system continued on its own course. When matters got obviously out of hand, measures such as the huge conspicuous buying on the part of business leaders to help to sustain the stock market, could not avert disaster. The trust in the economy had declined too much already. When the stock market crashed, production was soon reduced drastically and large scale unemployment resulted. After Hoover, who had presided over this development, Roosevelt was elected on the promise of restoring prosperity. Yet, restrictive measures, later known as the "New Deal" (1933), were not on his mind initially.

Roosevelt soon came to see, in accordance with his own words, that it was necessary "to save the bankers and businessmen from committing suicide". The first task was to put money back into the pockets of a large number of people so that at least some buying power was restored. Public work programs, housing projects, agricultural assistance, and prominently the foundation of the Tennessee-Valley-Project run by the Tennessee-Valley-Authority (TVA) aimed, inter alia, at that goal. These were government financed.

These measures gradually restored the confidence of individuals in the economy, but they earned Roosevelt the accusation of "socialism". It took the public a while to understand that Roosevelt's measures aimed at controlling laissez-fair capitalist interests in ways that were favorable for capitalism as such. The historical significance of these measures lay in the gradual public acceptance that the individuated pursuit of happiness needed public guidance. A saying like "what is good for General Motors is good for the country" was still valid, but it had become visible that if a corporation grew too much or was merely seen as having done that, then that growth could indeed pave the way to social disaster. Awareness for this danger is not intrinsic to an absolutely individuated interest in growth, but helpful for those fixated on it. This is what was learned from the "Crash" and the "New Deal". It became accepted wisdom that politics has to constantly negotiate with the economy and its leaders that which in appearance serves private *and* common interests. Civility now alluded to constraining the last "true conviction" that was around. It became accepted that the right to one's own individuated happiness had to be constrained. Freedom got further confused with its truncated mockery: liberty. Since instrumentalism had learned to be instrumentally restrictive towards itself and in that sense to be reflective, it could indeed further facilitate the growth dynamics of late capitalist society.

It should be remembered, though, that the economy of the US did not take off directly with the "New Deal". That only happened with the beginning of the Second World War. This war created a new huge market for the US, not only in war equipment but also in foodstuffs and raw materials. In fact, prior to its entry into the war (1941), the US economy had not achieved the level that it had lost in 1929.

While Great Britain and France, between the two World Wars carried on along their customary ways in economics and politics - not the least with the traditional exploitation of their colonies - countries like Japan, the USSR and Germany under Hitler tried to gain dominance each in their own ways.

Developments in Germany, after Hitler had come to power, aimed directly at military expansion. As a result, the German economy soon became geared to war preparations. The war economy boomed much sooner than in the US Here again a contrast between the US and the

German big business comes to light: In the US, politics was mandated to pave the way for economics (and thus for individuated interests) to flourish; in Germany, economics made the best of a political interest, namely, military expansion of power, while economic expansion came only along with it. The US way of doing things was the socially more advanced way, since it organized the pursuit of individuated interests, while in Germany, individuated economic interests accepted an interest of a society that still sensed itself as a whole, however ideologically perverted that sense had become.

Capital gains rose strongly in Germany and unemployment disappeared quickly. Also mass consumption could flourish quite soon and spread throughout the population. Similar in outward appearance to the US, owning a car and travelling became highly valued, but dissimilar to the US, even for these activities organizations of the Nazi-Party were set up. Prosperity, full employment and a strongly lingering sense of humiliation from the First World War made the Nazi ideology widely acceptable. This ideology, regardless of its conceptual poverty, spread by appealing to the people for the most part at the level of sensuous aesthetics and not at that of reasoned thought. It was not Hitler's writings ("Mein Kampf"), but Goebbel's parades and influence on the cultural industry (radio, movie, journals) that gained the enthusiastic, if not hysterical support of the German people. It has been guessed that 79.5 of the altogether 80 million Germans followed Hitler.[6] In a manner similar to the times of Wilhelm II, their re-awakened dream of greatness was carried out by the military invasion of Czechoslovakia and, later, Poland. This kind of expansion had to draw a military response, however poorly the Allies may have been prepared for it.

Japan too had embarked on empire building through military adventures. With interruptions, it had done so since 1905 (invasion into Russia). Heavily industrialized and multi-headed as its corporate economy had become, Japan sensed itself as an ethnically and religiously unified nation. The economy, in this case, followed a politically articulated national will which, similar to Germany, was fundamentally non-democratic. It too expressed itself in military conquest. Large scale individuated consumption was absent, indicated perhaps by the lack of a car industry, and also of an entertainment industry. Capital gains had to be made abroad, usually by trade in very cheap goods. Unemployment practically never existed, mainly due to the tight social networks in which each person lived. Access to raw materials, mainly in China and the

USSR, was the main incentive for Japan's military expansion. World War II was for it merely a continuation of previous military activities. Pearl Harbor simply added a new dimension to it.

The interest of the USSR in a communist world revolution was for the capitalist West only another expression of a growth orientation. Regardless of whether this interpretation was adequate or not, it imposed the role the USSR was to perform on the world stage in the 20th century. The hostility of the capitalist countries forced the Soviet Union to embark on a path of economic development that seemed to promise protection against this hostility. The economy emphasized the buildup of heavy industry resulting in the complete neglect of consumer oriented production. Gearing the whole economy to that end and ignoring the potential contribution that a consumer industry could have made to that purpose (as late capitalism and Adams know so well), led quickly to state organized central planning of every aspect of the economy, including agricultural production. It is, of course, not certain whether the introduction of consumerism would have increased the power of the USSR up to the level attained in the US. Such an attempt would probably have failed, since the level of individuation was too low. In this connection, we have to bear in mind that even today consumerism and a thoroughly entrepreneurial economy only have a slim chance in Russia.

And yet, central planning of economic activities annihilated almost all personal and local interests. This in turn rendered all socialist notions of democracy formalistic and implied a distortion, even vitiation of dialectical materialism. When World War II was forced upon the Soviet Union by Germany, it had to accept the offer of an alliance with the representatives of late capitalism, particularly due to the still dire state of its own economy. The socially backward structure of that economy could not allow for much power to be generated in it. There was little in it that could be directed to the outside.

The military result of World War II is well known; its political and social outcome, however, is a matter far reaching and requires further consideration.

The victory of the Allied Forces was not only a consequence of a so-called "material" supremacy in terms of natural resources and numerical man-power, it was, as we have tried to indicate, also a consequence of greater social advancement. Without the latter, i.e., greater individuation, greater flexibility of people and a more highly competitive productivity, such victory would have been more difficult. In short, the new form of capitalism that had been established in the US was the determining factor for the defeat of Germany and Japan.

The alliance between the Western Allies and the USSR could not and did not last beyond the end of World War II. The final struggle for global dominance between the USA and the USSR was a struggle between two systems with entirely different and mutually incomprehensible economic and political structures. Instead of exercising obvious military and political oppression of the vanquished, as the USSR did out of its mode of thinking, the US immediately began to propagate its liberty wherever it could. A repeat of Versailles became unthinkable. Attempts aiming in that direction and originating among its Allies, e.g. France, were stopped by the US The US had learned, at the latest after World War I, that assisting destroyed countries was more gainful than limiting their participation in "free" competition.

Perceptive people in East and West had anticipated the continuation of the conflict between capitalism and communism before World War II was over. In 1946, Bernard Baruch declared that the US was in a "Cold War" with the Soviet Union. At that time, Stalin had already begun to tighten the grip of the Red Army on most of the Eastern European countries.

Soon after the beginning of the Cold War, George Keenan inspired what came to be known as the "Marshall-Plan". Under Truman's presidency, $12 billion were sanctioned by the US Congress as an initial aid package to be offered to the European countries for reconstruction. This offer included the USSR and the countries under its influence. Similar assistance was offered to Japan and was accepted by it. The USSR, after a brief consideration, rejected the offer, because of its perceptions of the "strings attached". This is not to say that the USSR had begun to fully understand the capitalism that had evolved in the West. Until its demise almost 50 years later, it fought a capitalism that no longer existed in the form it had at Marx's or even at Lenin's times. Having dogmatized the writings of these thinkers, the Soviet leadership fought what was largely a figment of their imagination. We shall return to this in a moment.

Among the conditions for the acceptance of the Marshall-Plan, the introduction of parliamentary democracy ranked quite prominently. The impact of this condition differed between Germany and Japan. Japan, in contrast to Germany, was not divided and retained some of its political institutions (emperor, diet), although their new context changed their original meaning. Nevertheless, both countries initially had to accept restrictions which focused on eliminating all possibilities, economic, organizational and otherwise, for rebuilding militarism and military force. Thus, both countries exchanged their militarism for parliamentary democracy and soon for late capitalism.

At the political level, it could certainly be said that the system of parliamentary democracy had finally gained the upper hand in all capitalist countries. It soon proved to be the framework most suitable for implementing the kind of economic recovery and growth intended by the Marshall-Plan and desired by US economic interests. With some local variations, it triggered a phenomenal boom in the 1950s and 60s, particularly in West Germany. Strongly growth oriented production and consumption were embraced there to a greater extent than almost anywhere else. Its success strengthened the democratic spirit by turning political parties into organizations less and less guided by traditional convictions (or their historically adequate modifications). Parties became primarily suitable for conducting parliamentary elections and for the upwards mobility of ambitious politicians. Thus attempts at updating their traditional convictions were not made.[7] This way, political parties in Europe came to approximate their North American counterparts.

The Marshall-Plan completed the task of World War II in so far as late capitalism had a profound effect on the lives of individuals in the "Free World", that now included all of Western Europe and Japan. The just mentioned gradual transformation of political parties is only one of the many examples that reveals the significant shifts in the culture and thus in the self-perception of individuals. After overheated nationalistic ideologies had proven to be hollow by their defeat, particularly in Germany, identification with socially unifying ideas, be they Christianity or Marxism for instance, were soon rejected or, where possible, instrumentalistically turned into means for political success. The Midas syndrome penetrated quite fast next to all ways of making sense. Waves of consumerism, shifting their foci with increasing affluence from food to fashion, to tourism, luxurious housing, sex, etc., supported the growth orientation in the thinking even of wage earners. Needless to say that this fed into the growth orientation of business. The environmental consequences of a now overheated production and consumption soon became visible, though they only gradually turned into a social issue.[8]

There is no doubt that the Marshall-Plan and its economic consequences were highly desired by most people. They were seen as assistance allowing them to bring their lives back into order. The social consequences, however, came to light only later (never mind that they lived these consequences). What the Marshall-Plan had done to the identities of culturally distinct nations resembles that of the introduction of the Trojan Horse. While the American people may have not lost their identity since World War II, the one of the Europeans and beyond has become muddled. The persisting misunderstanding of North American life, now pervasive in many countries all over the world, is just one consequence of this. It expresses itself, for instance, in rather contrived, though locally colored imitations of US culture. But the problems related to the loss of social identity, to the growth of individuation and then ultimately also to environmental matters, have not led to a kind of soul searching that would be adequate to the task. Overcoming these problems can, of course, not mean a revival of the past, but a breakthrough into the future by containing the sociality of the past in a form adequate to the end of ideologies. Until then, late capitalism can celebrate its conquest of Western Europe and soon of the whole world.

Right after World War II, a wave of what was euphemistically called "de-colonization" or "liberation" came up and left behind what was then dubbed the "Third World". This process was greatly facilitated by the fact that in most colonies a Western educated elite (as junior partners of Western capitalists in their own countries) had become available to promote the capitalist "development". This way, two objectives were accomplished: the leading powers of the West could disemburden themselves of political and military responsibilities in their former colonies, while, at the same time, maintaining indirect political and direct economic control. Western corporations were under these political conditions able to maintain, even to extend, their economic influence. These changes provided the stage for what was soon called "development aid", a variation on the theme of the Marshall Plan.

From the beginning, "development aid" was meant to cater primarily to the economic needs of the "Free World" and, secondarily, in doing so, to help the "underdeveloped" new countries. Given the lead of their production/consumption systems, the capitalist West and Japan were in growing need of cheap raw materials and markets for their own products. The latter required that "Third World" countries become producers in order for them to create a buying power that allowed them to function as consumers. The elites in these countries were sufficiently integrated into the Western lifestyle to appreciate its economic advantages. They oftentimes managed to grossly inflate their personal buying power by either channeling considerable portions of the "aid" into their own pockets and/or by controlling whatever production went on in their countries. And yet, these nations have, for the most part, not been turned into large scale producers and consumers in the capitalist form. Vast numbers of people, e.g. in India up to 85% of the population, but also on the continents of Africa and South America, have not been drawn into the circuit of the modern economy, its social structure and its political system. This is not to deny that some progress has been made in this regard and to that extent one can say that "development aid" has aided the capitalist economy over the last decades to an appreciable degree. Further increases in production and consumption, in short, the never ending desire for a yet rising "standard of living", make the perpetuation of "development aid" a necessity. It has to remain the goal of the rich countries to shape all local economies and the social structures that go with them after the Western model. This spreading of individuation will make people susceptible to the consumerism of the West. The "perpetuum mobile" implied by the Midas syndrome will then run at a higher speed and with bigger wheels, never mind further losses in social and natural wealth. To be clear, we are not suggesting that traditional cultures should be retained in order to stem the flooding of the world with consumerism, but we are wondering whether the old cultures cannot be transcended-and-contained in a new one and its local variations. We will have to deal with this matter in the section "The Alternative to Today's Praxis".

While the returns stemming from this "aid" has far outstripped the "aid" itself, it has not done away with the problems of the capitalist countries, not to mention those of the "Third World". Unemployment, hunger and other forms of destitution like homelessness grow strongly everywhere, regardless of a significant growth in production and consumption at the global level. At the same time, the gap between unbelievable poverty and unbelievable affluence is widening worldwide. And yet, the fact that the growth in production and consumption is still slower than the one desired by the late capitalist countries, may very well be a blessing in disguise. Would the growth occur to the desired extent, our ecological problems would be even more serious than they are already. If the number of cars and refrigerators produced and consumed in China would only approximate the standard set by the West, the satisfaction of such kinds of needs would be close to deadly.

So-called "development aid" was not only granted by the "Free World", but also, though to a far lesser extent, by the socialist bloc. This suggests that, up until 1989, their "development aid" has also to be understood in the context of the until then ongoing Cold War. The issue of the Cold War was for both sides primarily the weakening and destruction of the other without letting the struggle erupt into another World War. This intent could easily be "sold" propagandistically in the West as defense of "freedom" and as "love for peace" in the East. The military threat on the Soviet Union and its allies was, however, clearly more powerful than the other way around, regardless of the vigorous attempt of the East to keep up with the West. The success of the West in the enormously expensive arms race was, needless to say, based on its far greater socio-economic power, particularly that of the US. Whatever ability the USSR had to resist this pressure was still based on an ideologically guided structuring of its own society and economy and went hand in hand with an antiquated understanding of its opponent: late capitalism. Confronting it as if it were the capitalism of Marx's and, at best, Lenin's times was in as much a grave mistake as was the failure to modernize its own society and economy as a credible alternative to what it did not even understand, namely, this new brand of capitalism. This way, the socialist countries grew more and more into being antiquated and unequal to the task of defending themselves. Its centrally planned and bureaucratized economy kept on suppressing individuated production and consumption instead of guiding their growth in a democratic yet socialist spirit. This made for less power in the Soviet system than what a late capitalist one could generate. It was not clear to the leadership in the socialist countries that the power of the Western countries was a consequence of a new social order in which the ruthless competition of one against another, driven by consumerism and its pseudo-satisfaction, had led to an unbelievable productivity and, thus, could pump unimaginable amounts of energy out of Nature into all of its social systems, including the military one. The East made only feeble and hesitant attempts to strengthen consumption among its people. It is doubtful that the East did that out of awareness for the kinds of power it could have obtained that way. It did certainly not see that the cutting lose of the individual for engagement in ruthlessly individuated competition had turned into a social order in which the class struggle of the past was transcended-and-contained and yielded the just mentioned surplus of energy and power.[9]

After the unconditional surrender of the East which put, in 1989, an end to the Cold War, the continuing enormous problems of the East testify to the fact that its people have great difficulties to develop a sense for the level of individuation that a modern economy requires. The differences between the East and the West in the united Germany attest to this in a glaring way.

While the Cold War was still on, the economic weakness of the socialist countries resulted in the inability to offer adequate aid to "Third World" countries. Consequently, the socialist countries were far less able to exploit and politically influence other countries. Accordingly, the USSR was relatively weak in international organizations such as the United Nations, Unesco, etc. However, these world organizations fulfilled the purpose of providing types of parliamentary arenas which functioned in the traditional Anglo Saxon ways of avoiding the breakout of open conflict by negotiations. These were carried out in front of a screen on which the "cultural potential" of enormous power was projected. In this manner, these international organizations were functional in promoting the idea of mutual constraint of self-interest. The educational influence of having avoided nuclear warfare this way, can hardly be over-estimated The practice of civility received an enormous boost, although localized wars have kept on occurring in different parts of the world almost constantly since 1945.

The outcome of the Cold War was such that it left late capitalism with no significant opponent. This is not to say that the social consequences of this victory are clear. We certainly do not claim to be able to predict the full magnitude of what lies ahead. And yet, it is our fear that as a consequence of this victory the negative synthesis between man and Nature about which we have spoken above[10] will make great strides. We would like to point out two indicators for what may lie ahead.

On the one hand, one can observe that the tendency to interpret anything instrumentalistically has become unstoppable. It does not shy away from employing and, thus, distorting the noblest causes. This instrumentalism has led to a situation in which causes such as feminist, aboriginal peoples and ecological movements have become little more than means for upwards mobility and for gaining public, needless to say, individuated profile. Anything, even the opposition to this very circumstance, is a means for individuated power. There is no question that this further weakens whatever consciousness of commonality is left among people.

On the other hand, what has become known as "globalization" and replaces, since 1989, more and more the traditional "development aid" is merely an attempt of the economy to liberate itself again from political constraints. The booming stock market, recently overheated mainly as a result of the emphasis on the "shareholder value" of corporations, and the growing capital intensity in production, may easily lead again to the shrinking of buying power. Instead of leading to solidarity among the empoverished, it further sharpens the competition in society everywhere. On closer inspection than we can engage in here, differences to what happened in the late 1920s may come to light, but frightening similarities can not be ignored either.

This instrumentalistic curtailment of the liberties that are left has become so pervasive that people confound the difference between liberty and freedom. We will have to deal with this distinction in more detail later, and yet, this much should be clear already: with the dominance of liberty there will be a proliferation of constraints.

These constraints, including the ones that regulate our impact on the environment, will only add, as they have so often done, to the frustration of people and will thus increase the desire to compensate for it. If "productivity flourishes on the soil of repression" (Herbert Marcuse), then consumption does so to exactly the same degree. After traditional philosophies and religions have now been ideologized and/or relegated to the private domain, they can be mobilized even more effectively at any level in society, from that of the individual up to that of the whole society. Even a modest measure of sobriety would suffice to see that "heaven is empty" and that our species has nothing left to work with than our own Nature and the Nature around us. Since this can be known, the ongoing "globalization" also holds the promise of globalizing this new sobriety throughout the world.

We think that we are confronted with an alternative in which there is no room for a compromise. Regardless, whether we speak of the Midas syndrome at the personal level or of "environmental problems" at the species level, the suffering from both makes us either willing to change ourselves or to face disaster. Much depends on whether we acknowledge that it is part of man's Nature to be part of Nature. Of course, we have always been part of Nature (as Adams knows so well), but we have expressed this for millennia and in a good many parts of the world in often beautiful and captivating images and ideas. It took us a while, historically speaking, to see that these past ideas were elevations of Nature in historically specific ways. It is the accomplishment of late capitalism that this has become visible to those willing to see. The issue now is to find out how we can elevate Nature in us and around us in ways adequate to the present state of human affairs. This task poses itself in such a way that attempts at "muddling through" with our problems appears to be out of the question. A compromise between a positive and a negative synthesis simply does not exist.

Our reason to think so requires a more thorough analysis of what modernity means at the perhaps not so obvious level.

Notes

[1] For the difference between them, see e.g. pp. 128, 147, 157, 164-165.

[2] Adams, 1975, p. 27.

[3] Sixel, 1988, p. 23n.

[4] See above pp 20ff.

[5] Further treatment of this is presented e g. on pp. 164-165, 209-211.

[6] This was noted, in frustration, in the diary of Victor Klemperer, one of the few, by now well known, Germans of a Jewish family who had survived in Germany, see Klemperer, 1998, p. XV.

[7] It is, of course, ludicrous to see the "Godesberg Programm" of the Social Democrats in Germany or the more recent "New Labour" platform of the Labour Party in England as an adequate updating of Marxism.

[8] A first warning came 1962 in Carson's book "Silent Spring", see Carson, 1962.

[9] The question of why the pollution problems in the East bloc countries were even more serious than in the West is an important one, but we cannot deal with it here We would suggest, however, that an erroneous concept of cost efficiency kept many industries in the East from using anti-pollution devices. It was not seen that their installation could have contributed, as in the West, to the GNP

[10] See pp. 12-13

Chapter 5

Modernity: The Culture of Power and Its Immunity

We think that the concept and praxis of "negative synthesis" provides a good departure point for embarking on a more thorough analysis of late capitalist culture. Since the concept of synthesis, negative or not, has rather far reaching implications, for example, in evolutionism and philosophy, we want to make it clear that we wish to limit our treatment of the "negative synthesis" to today's social praxis. We would not even consider making an attempt to go beyond that, since reasoning about how a negative synthesis with Nature threatens the survival of us in Nature is enough of a difficult task to handle.

For reasons stated earlier, we hold the view that culture is "only" an aspect of Nature, although an elevated one. This status of culture has rarely been appreciated, at least as far as the social sciences are concerned. Together with one of the few who have done that, namely Richard Adams, we can only speculate about their reason for this omission: it would, as Adams points out,[1] introduce a more disciplined and less subjectivistic thinking into these disciplines and, thus, reduce their share in the academic market.

Regardless of this and of Adams' own understanding of society and of academia as power structures, his own studies of man and society have nonetheless consistently adopted a materialist stance. While we would basically agree with the view that all that exists, is only different phases of energy and matter,[2] we still have a number of problems with Adams' kind of materialism. We have already pointed them out in the first chapter, but it may be helpful to repeat them here. 1.- Arguing for his materialist position primarily in terms of its investigative potency, i.e., of its instrumentality in research, comes, in an age of instrumentalism, not only close to a circular reasoning, but the claim that it has been like that "since the Paleolithic", is also dangerously close to an interpretation of all culture in terms of just one. Hence, it "smacks" of ethnocentrism. 2.- Not being able to sustain the theoretically adopted stance that all is matter at the methodological level while being forced at the latter level, as we saw above,[3] to act "as if" the mental and the material were different, signals yet another conceptual inconsistency. This argument of ours may not carry much weight for Adams, but the question remains, whether it is not his own conceptual set-up which creates this awkward problem. 3.- Being unable to propose a way to get off the "dangerous trajectory"[4] on which our civilization has embarked, and to believe that getting off that trajectory would require man "to cease being human",[5] imposes a one-sidedness on empirical perceptiveness. It precludes the conceptualization of, and even the empirical sensitivity for an alternative to the presently prevailing relation of man to Nature. To sum up our problems with Adams, we have to say that his problems arise with his failure to sustain his concept of the primacy of Nature when trying to understand culture, i.e., man's symbolizing ability. Trying to overcome this difficulty on our part, will hopefully bring to light that it is not Nature as such which precludes a future for us, but that it is the distortion of Nature in our culture which threatens the awareness for the commonality of all there is as Nature.

In view of Adams' accomplishments in pioneering a route to sobriety in the social sciences (and beyond), we expect that a carefully attentive critique[6] will allow us to see how Adams' position can be further developed beyond the point where the just mentioned inconsistencies in his theorizing emerge. We agree with Adams that it is part of human Nature to have the desire to know. This includes the desire to know how Nature is elevated and how it is contained in our culture. In other words, Richard Adams' project is ours as well, but we have to put it on a different footing.[7]

It is Adams' theoretical position that it is useful to treat everything as if it consisted of only one substance: "energy forms"; this is the basis of his materialistic monism. Energy and matter are only two different phases of one and the same entity.[8] This implies that "whatever it is that the social scientist may study, that thing must be of that world, or it cannot be studied".[9] With this call for sobriety and against the subjectivism so flagrant in the social,[10] and in our view in all sciences, Adams tries "to see whether human social evolution can be described ... in terms ... of energy process"[11]. He rejects the accusation that this would imply a reductionism; at best, so he points out,[12] can he be called an 'elevationist', since he understands certain energetic processes as being elevated into the human realm and thus into the mental.

This, of course, burdens Adams' materialism with the obligation to answer the question what kind of an energetic process the mental activity is. In response to this question, as we saw above,[13] Adams concerns himself with three concepts: information, meaning and value.

Information lies, for Adams, in the structuring, i.e. the form of energy.[14] Information that perturbs the human nervous system is in so far a special case of energetic flow, as it is received by the human nervous system in such a way that this receptor can self-organize it into meaning.[15] Meaning and images "pertain to the (human) nervous system", but "they give us no clues to their origin".[16] No doubt, what flows when information flows is not the meaning, only its material substrate.[17] Otherwise hearing, for instance, would be understanding. Meaning as such is of "zero-dimension".[18] We are, as Adams knows, not able to say how information is elevated to meaning in the "black box" of our mind.[19] This black box is, of course, the sole place where meaning has existence and does so only at those times when the black box is at work. How meaning is retained in it, e.g., as terms of reference for understanding information, is not clear either, recent findings in neuro-physiology notwithstanding.[20] In Adams' view, it is our inability to understand the elevation process which forces him to proceed at the methodological level in a manner, as if a dichotomy between the mental and the material existed.[21] But he does not subscribe to that dualism in theory. In passing, one might note that this constitutes, philosophically speaking, a classical case of taking a dogmatic stance; its assumption and its acceptance require a leap of faith of which one wonders how consistent this is with the materialist stance otherwise preferred by Adams. I suspect he justifies this mentalistic maneuver with its conceptual usefulness; it is instrumental. Furthermore, Adams does not share the optimism of those who believe that "a bridge will be constructed by future generations" between the "information processing psychology and neuro-physiology".[22] The "as-if-methodology", however opportunistically adopted, is not seen by Adams as posing any threat to his materialist monism, since meanings are only of interest to monism if they do something in this world,[23] i.e., influence the concrete behavior of human beings.

We agree with Adams that we will probably never come to know how the energetic is elevated to meaning inside the human brain, but we do know *that* this elevation takes place. This would imply that meaning in itself is outside the limits of study; as such it is a "limit concept", as philosophers would say.[24] We do not think, however, that this impasse forces an as-if-methodology and its implicit mind-matter-dichotomy on us. In our view, there is a way out of this impasse by placing the connections among energy forms, information, value and meaning within a more complex set of aspects. We will turn to this in a moment.

As indicated, we think that Richard Adams is right in saying that the human nervous system cannot possibly be understood as if it were a filing cabinet.[25] In order to get at the meaning of energy-information-flows, the electro-chemical apparatus of our brain has to be triggered to do something, i.e., to elevate some energetic flows to meaning. Studying this phenomenon, Adams has this to say[26]:

> The role of a trigger as a control over energy flow parallels that which has been argued for the disinhibition of neurons in the nervous system [Roberts, 1976]. The neuron is pictured as 'possessing an innate capacity for firing spontaneously', and it is inhibited from doing this by other neurons and cells 'Most neurons, in their normal environment, are members of neuronal circuits in intact organisms and have largely ceded their autonomy while becoming citizens of an integrated neuronal community' [Roberts.1976, p. 517]. In the same manner, the energy forms surrounding human beings are in different states of potential energy release or dissipation. By changing the equilibrium conditions they enjoy in the environment, they are triggered to release energy Some dissipative structures - presumably like the neuron - are so constructed to automatically fire or release energy unless inhibited. Their environment keeps them in a state of no dissipation, of equilibrium

The source that Adams uses here as supporting his position may be a bit outdated, but we are not aware that more recent studies (e.g. Damasio 1994, Roth 1994, Spitzer 1996) have gone much beyond Roberts' notion of the "innate capacity" of neurons. We think that it can still be said that the neurological phenomenon of spontaneity, or of "spontaneous firing", is assumed to rest on that "innate capacity". However, all this does not explain very much. Precisely because we agree with Adams that "a bridge between psychology and neurophysiology" can not be constructed, we have to say that reference to an "innate capacity" is only a cover-up. It keeps us from appreciating what we are up against, namely, yet another limit to what can be known.

In different contexts and following propositions that have not gained adequate attention in academia - see those of Duns Scotus (see Hoerres 1962), Martin Luther (see Luther 1954) and Friedrich Nietzsche (see Nietzsche 1954-56) – Friedrich Sixel has proposed[27] to call that spontaneity the will and to distinguish that will from decision; a decision, according to the thinkers referred to, is made consciously, while the emergence of the will is outside our conscious control. Conceiving of spontaneity as yet another limit-concept would not contradict Adams' concept of spontaneity, although he does not appreciate this status of spontaneity.

Adams could have studied the status of spontaneity more closely in his explorations of values. He could have explored the linkage as it reaches from the will to conscious ranking and finally to values. But, unfortunately, values receive less attention in Adams' more recent publications than in the earlier ones. In his 1975 work, Adams sees values as constitutive to power relations, as we have elaborated above, but later,[28] he comes close to dismissing their significance for social studies. And yet, it would be more important to note how Adams relates values to knowledge. He sees that what is being ranked has to be cognitively identified, i.e., it has to be part of a taxonomy.[29]

> This suggests that Adams defines these two aspects of the mental realm, namely knowledge and values in counter-distinction from each other and that he then relates .. them by establishing a connection which originates in knowledge (or a taxonomy) and reaches over to values in the sense that knowledge has a sort of logical priority.[30]

This advocacy of the priority of knowledge over values is not accompanied by an exploration of whether that what is known has to be "willed" to be known.

We would suggest that it is because of this lacuna and Adams' failure to appreciate spontaneity and meaning as limit-concepts, that the dualism between spontaneity and meaning remains unresolved. We would agree with Richard Adams that "the relationship between the two ... will simply never be understood so long as they are so separated".[31] In this sentence, however, we would place an emphasis on "*so* separated".

We think that the fundamental difficulty to resolve the mind-matter-dichotomy stems from the narrow treatment of the limit concepts of meaning and of spontaneity in particular. And yet, it is undoubtedly to Richard Adams' credit that he has not only brought their significance to the attention of the social sciences, but that he has also appreciated them as material phenomena. Clearly, the mental-in-itself is of "zero-dimension". Therefore, Adams is right in saying that the mental has only existence (for us) in energy forms. While some philosophers, quite prominently Immanuel Kant, but also Husserl with his concept of "intentionality", have postulated the significance of spontaneity for human cognition, they too have failed to investigate its way of being. Adams proposes to understand it as part of the energetic flow inside the human brain and thus inside the whole human body. That, however, makes it all the more surprising that he does not inspect, more closely, the relation between those energy forms that reach our brains from the outside to the energy flows that run spontaneously through our neurons. Therein lies a very important aspect of the commonality between our inner Nature and the Nature around us. As will be seen later,[32] the commonality between the will and Nature has not only been noted by Goethe, but by appreciating it, he can also propose a positive synthesis between Nature and man. Not exploring this commonality, makes it fundamentally impossible for Adams (and modern man) to see the feasibility of such a positive synthesis.

Taking off from Adams' views, we would suggest that the elevation of external energy-information-flows to mental constructs obviously requires two aspects of man's internal energetics: on the one hand, the spontaneous will to reach out into external energy-information-flows and, on the other, a compatible orderliness, i.e., a structure, of this internal energetic intent.[33] This conceptualization of the process of understanding as a process of elevating energetic flows to meaning does not dissolve the status of meaning and spontaneity as limit-concepts, nor does it collapse the dichotomy between mind and matter, but it opens up a way to contain these two limit-concepts and thus this dichotomy in a materialist dialectic.

It might help our understanding of this dialectic, if we first note that knowing does not derive from a sheerly mental relation of a frame of reference to an external energy, but from the kinship between the structured energetics of the human mind (which energetically thinks such frames of reference) and the energetics of the world out there. We will address the evolvement of frames of reference in the human mind later, when we try to enrich the inspection of a mere subject-object relation by that of the self-other relation. For the time being, we like to note that knowing and willing result from the activity of the same energetic agent, namely, the human body, and that this energetic agent appears to be able to dissolve the segregation between knowledge (taxonomy) and values (or ranking). In the dynamic relation between knowing and willing, knowing occurs as the antithesis to willing as the thesis. The dialectic between them runs this way, since knowing contains the will as the knowing manifests itself in willed energetic forms, e.g., in the production of thoughts, of speeches, of things or of whatever. One could also say that what is known has to be "willed" to be known. Energy, thus, remains the commonality ("die Vermittlung", or "das Übergreifende", i.e., the mediation in the Hegel-Marx sense) between thesis and antithesis in this dialectic, while the mental-in-itself (or matter without form) vanishes like the mind-matter dichotomy into realms strange to our species.[34]

Understanding the human body as the a-priori of all knowledge[35] places our species also "mentally" into this world in which it is materially at home anyway. This view implies Karl Marx's concept of the human being as the Transcending Other to Nature.[36] On other occasions,[37] it has been proposed to speak of the Nature–man–relation as the Nature–Other Nature–relation. However, let it be emphasized that even the mental Otherness in man to Nature, i.e., his thinking ability and its results, exists for us firmly and exclusively within this material world. The Otherness in us turns the human being into the only part of Nature that can give meaning to objects and can do so in a variety of forms depending on the inner Nature of the human being. And yet, even with this unique ability of defining and re-defining, we and all of our creations remain always part of the one and the only reality there is: Nature

If the will is the primary connection between Nature and the human being as Other Nature, then it is this will, this spontaneity, which we have to transcend-and-contain (In German: aufheben, used in the Hegel-Marx sense) in our knowing undistortedly. This transcendence-and-containment is the point where Nature is in the danger of becoming distorted. Every other distortion (e.g., the ones in the science, technology, social relations) is only a different and subsequent manifestation of our distorted relation to Nature. At the same time, Nature-in-itself cannot be distorted.

Acknowledging this embeddedness of each one of us in the flow of energy, i.e. in Nature, remains, although necessary, insufficient in accounting for our status as individually unique human subjects. We have seen above[38] how Adams accounts for this uniqueness and then immediately turns it into one of the important conditions for human relations to be nothing else but power relations. While this consideration of Adams' will be taken up briefly again in a moment, we like to think that this much should be clear from both Adams' thought and our critique of it, namely, that losing sight of the bodily, i.e. sensuous embeddedness of each individual's thinking in Nature's flow by not acknowledging it in praxis, is a severe limitation of our conscious awareness of ourselves; it is untrue to the Nature that we are.

We do not wish to leave it to doubt that we agree with Richard Adams that all there is and can be studied and dealt with is in and of this world. This includes all of culture which we as well understand as an elevation of Nature but as one that transcends her and yet never goes beyond her. It is in these often used classical philosophical terms, that we say that Nature is transcended-and-contained in culture in all of its forms. And yet, we obviously differ from Adams in ways which have, in our view, important implications.

Spontaneity and "categories" (Kant), or, if one prefers, the drive to know and the meaning of its frame of reference, are "in themselves" (Kant again) not accessible to us. Only after they have crossed the limit from 'God knows where' into this world can we deal with them. Before that, they have no existence for us. This relegation of a meta-physics into some sort of nowhere implies an immanent meta-physicality of culture; or, as we put it a moment ago, this meta-physics is a transcendence to Nature that remains within her. Different from Adams, we need not dogmatically postulate the primacy of all there is as being that of Nature and then practice "as if" there were a mind-matter dichotomy. For us, a thought not being thought by a human brain or a melody not being played have no existence.

This leads to yet another consideration hardly ever contemplated by Adams and yet of quite some importance. We would wonder how much of the Nature of things is contained without distortion in our concepts of them. For us, our thoughts, concepts, ideas, inventions and creations are an elevation of Nature (yet remaining within her). Human speech provides a good example for this: let's appreciate that the word "rose" is not a rose. And yet, the word "rose" is still of this world like the rose itself is. It is, therefore, still important to ask how the rose is transcended-and-contained in the word "rose". While it should be clear that without our peculiar status in Nature the word "rose" would not exist, we suspect that it is within our concept formation that dangers begin to loom for our bodily relation to Nature.

Understanding words, concepts, ideas etc., i.e. everything mentalistic, as firmly belonging to this world, places research on cultural phenomena into a different constellation than the one Adams proposes. For us, the main issue is whether or not thought is in keeping with the Nature that we ourselves are and that is around us. A body of thought, however, that leads to a negative synthesis between our inner elevated Nature and the Nature around us must be an outgrowth of a distorted inner Nature, i.e. of a distorted spontaneity; in this distortion, one part of Nature twists itself. A conceptualization of this as a distortion and of the causes of this distortion is hardly possible on Adams' grounds. Culture leads, according to him, to disaster at any rate. We think that Adams has to arrive at this problematic and hopeless conclusion since his concept of culture does not allow us to see that the commonality of all Nature potentially attains an entirely new level in the human being. There, this commonality can be cultivated to a life of being *for* one another thus elevating the commonality of all Nature to a positive synthesis of her with us. Leading such a life is, as we will argue, even one of man's primary urges. For Adams, however, culture is exclusively and one-sidedly an individuated weapon for survival to be used against Nature in all her manifestations. It does not matter whether we turn against the Nature in other human beings or against forms of Nature of lesser elevation. This problem only arises with individuation, yet not because individuation takes the individual out of Nature - it does not do that - but because individuation twists, that is, it distorts the flow of Nature inside the individual.

Postponing for the moment that Adams' position also implies a conceptualization of social relations in terms of usefulness, we wish, first, to underline that perceiving objects around us in terms of the Midas syndrome requires a guarded and, more importantly, a "second thought" type of conceptualization. In as much as a re-definition logically requires a previous definition, it also requires a re-directing of one's spontaneity. Such a "second thought" type of thinking is "cultivated" in the making of re-definitions; it has become habitual today, where all social relations are power relations. So we encounter in the Midas relation to objects a spontaneity that is not spontaneous. As a purposive and consciously twisted, i.e. a mind guided spontaneity, it turns against the primacy of Nature in the thinking process. As such the Midas syndrome is an expression of the twisted and, thus, distorted inner Nature of man. The second firing of spontaneity occurring under the guidance of a second thought misses the moment of its freedom right there. Instead it opts for a liberty that at best satisfies a second hand, "adopted" spontaneity, while the genuine spontaneity, i.e., the true inner Nature is repressed and goes without the satisfaction of connecting directly with what it is a part of, namely, Nature out there. Under this condition, man's inner Nature can only impose this distortion onto the Nature around the individual, be it that of things or of human beings.

We believe that the kind of urge to know fostered in today's sciences provides a good example for this kind of distortion. Above, we have briefly sketched the prevailing conditions of scientific research. It can hardly be maintained that this kind of research is encouraging a reaching out of man's untwisted inner Nature into outer Nature. At the point where inner and outer Nature touch one another, which is the decisive point of human sensuousness, a negative instrumentalistic synthesis has become inevitable in the praxis of today's science. In other words, our problems with Nature arise there because of the social construction of our inner Nature. Therefore, our environmental problems as arising in our conceptualization of Nature need to be resolved already within our ways of coming to know. Attempts to solve them at a later stage, be it by trying ethics, legal prescriptions, or technocratic measures, simply come too late.

Before raising our contemplations beyond the object – subject relation to the social level where the ego-alter relation or the Other Nature-alter Other Nature will be the focus, we should note that it is implied in the concept of elevation that known Nature is different from Nature as such. The German neuro-physiologist/philosopher Gerhard Roth distinguishes here between "Wirklichkeit" and "Realität". This distinction can perhaps be expressed by translating "Wirklichkeit" into "reality as it impacts our brain" and "Realität" into "reality as it is independent of our brain".[39] No matter what form of elevation we consider, a distorted or an undistorted one, whenever the human being as an Other Nature comes to know Nature, the whole of Nature is changed, for better or worse, beyond what it would be without that knowledge. In other words, our knowing of Nature adds to Nature what would not be in Nature without our knowing

Nature. This is to say that we agree with Adams that it is our species that continues the process of creation by adding "The Eighth Day" to it. Yet, we fail to see why "The Eighth Day" has to be our "doomsday".

At this point, we would like to insert a remark which is of no small significance for an understanding of the kind of natural science proposed and practiced by Goethe and to be inspected later in this essay. In our "reading" of Goethe as an advocate of Nature's primacy in the process of coming to know her, we believe to have discovered that there is hardly anything to which he objects more than to a "hypotheses guided research" into Nature. For him, even hypotheses are quite close to what we, in our critique of Adams, have referred to as "second thought" constructs. As we shall discuss later, it is, according to Goethe, of utmost importance for a proper understanding of Nature that the process of understanding remains adequate to both the Nature around us and the one in us. Goethe believes that this can be done by practicing the leadership of our senses in the process of coming to know and that we, in the elevation – a term even more central to Goethe than to Adams – of our sensuous experience be utterly careful not to distort the initial sensuous spontaneity. Without such undistorted spontaneity, an elevation of our encounters with her adequate to her would lead to problematic experiences of her. Goethe does not deny that knowledge about Nature is generated also in hypothesis guided research, but it is a distorted one for him. Such distortion, however, is intrinsic, even constitutive to what we call the Midas relation to objects.

There is no doubt on Goethe's part either that our knowledge of Nature adds a dynamic to her that goes far beyond anything Nature-in-itself could ever generate. But that dynamics takes on a perilous dimension if it is generated by a way of knowing her that is not grounded in undistorted sensuousness. As such, so Goethe saw, it cannot lead to a positive synthesis between man's inner Nature and the Nature around him. Goethe anticipated a spreading out of man's negative syntheses with Nature implying a dreadful future for our species. He saw it coming up with the growth of technology that had started in his life time (1749 – 1832). One needs only to remember the ending of his "Faust" or his "Wilhelm Meisters Wanderjahre". In our understanding of Goethe's views, he has, however, not fully anticipated what the Midas touch could contribute when it also enters the relation between man and his fellowman, i.e. when it enters the social relations. We believe - and in this regard we follow Adams, however critically so - that the understanding of outer Nature accelerated by a distorted understanding of fellowman, i.e. of alter Other Nature, attains an ever higher level of dubious successes. In them, we celebrate one pyhrric victory after the other.

As we have indicated above, Adams, like many others including ourselves, is of the view that culture is by necessity different among human individuals. This makes for the dynamic peculiarity of human communication, indeed of all human interaction. Surprises are even more frequent in social relations than in the ones we experience with non-symbolizing Nature. While human individuality lifts social relations, as dealt with before, onto a new level,[40] maintenance of expectability and of some cultural conformity turns into a difficult and costly task that needs to be worked at constantly from the level of person to person communication to that at the level of whole societies and beyond. Needless to say that these costs are energetic and that they are particularly high, where social relations are understood and practiced as power relations and where communication is, therefore, necessarily opportunistic and capricious. The avoidance of direct force in retaining some sort of cultural conformity by mere display of the cultural potential to use force eventually, hardly decreases the costs. Religious and/or educational activities supposedly aiming at that kind of pacification have always taken a disproportionately high level of energy. But this presupposes that some aspects of culture, e.g., religions, philosophies or other world views, had always and necessarily this instrumentalistic and no other purpose. As mentioned before, the possibility that they were wholeheartedly agreed upon symbolizations for both leader and those led remains outside Adams' conceptualization. This is, of course, a consequence of his one-sided assumption that social relations have always been power relations, since human beings, apparently per se, conceptualize one another as individuated competitors and/or as sources of power. No question, wholeheartedly agreed upon world views (religions, philosophies) and their celebration in often elaborate ceremonies have been costly as well, but they generated satisfaction in their practitioners and thus did not generate the rapidly cost increasing search for pseudo-satisfaction as is the case now.

What we find perplexing in Adams the materialist is that he attempts to ground what he calls a cultural conformity - which, strictly speaking, does not even exist for him but is a requirement for power, as we saw, - in the common Nature among humans. Instead of taking this commonality as a foundation for social co-operation, he opts immediately and without raising questions about it for the assumption that there is, regardless of the commonality or conformity, a mutual conceptualization among humans exclusively in antagonistic, competitive terms. This assumed antagonism is at best softened by some temporary truce among passengers of "survival vehicles". But, as is in keeping with Adams' lack of an inspection of spontaneity, he never wonders whether these mutual perceptions are directly grounded in man's inner Nature or whether they flow out of a "second thought" spontaneity. We, instead, suggest that the social praxis of power relations requires in as much the workings of the Midas syndrome as the instrumentalistic "second thought" perception of non-human parts of Nature does.

Inspecting the workings of spontaneity in human relations, we want to take off from our previous observation that, at the human level, 100%-feedback loops in communication are not just contained but also transcended in symbolizations (although not all of them are all the time). This implies that these symbolizations in different human beings are not by sheer material necessity what they happen to be. Since symbolizations are created on the basis of different frames of reference and since these are, as sedimentations of individual experiences (as G. H. Mead has described so well), by necessity individually unique, human communication, in fact all interaction, requires mutual understanding. This also implies that different groups of humans who lived and interacted together for millennia have organized their lives not just in terms of mere natural needs, i.e. at the 100%-feedback level, but also in terms of locally quite different cultures. In terms of these, people symbolically determine their realities, i.e., their needs, norms, values, etc, in fact all there is within reach of their perception. Cultures, thus, have led to pacification, personal identity and freedom for the human beings involved in them, since people "willed" these meanings throughout history, at times for quite long, historical epochs. These were, for Marx, the above mentioned "nice illusions". It is a widespread insight among social scientists (one which Adams obviously does not share) that along the lines of increasing individuation and abstraction, these nice illusions whithered away and ultimately led to modernity. It was only in the course of that process that the awareness evolved, and was functionalized, e.g. by Adams, Luhmann and today's praxis that culture helps enormously ("secret weapon"!) to secure the survival of the only entity that is directly material at the social level: the individual human body. This purpose has made members of modern society "willing" to accept, instrumentalize and if need be to re-define an enormous variety of meanings which then help to maintain social settings as power structures in ways described above. These structures, or "survival vehicles", range from friendships, to corporations, churches, whole political states and even beyond. The "willful" acceptance of constraints that have come along with the evolution of this modern culture is obviously of an instrumentalistic Nature. Beside the meaning given to objects, rules and values (including their "legitimation") are understood instrumentalistically as well. Man's Otherness to Nature is, however, now in the position to see that this way of thinking places our species on a deadly trajectory. But since the modern mode of thinking is unable to think the commonality of all human beings as a foundation for a non-antagonistic sociality, it has nothing to offer that would allow us to get off that trajectory. Any attempt to get off it is "naturally" looked for in terms of the present mode of thinking, i.e. instrumentalistically and is, thus, doomed. Questions for solutions have accordingly so far resulted in answers which urge more constraints and new technologies. As pointed out earlier, such reactions will at best allow our species "to muddle through" a little longer, but the threat of disaster will definitely increase with them. "Muddling through" would only imply a life of yet more pseudo-satisfaction and of yet more constrained liberty, but of no freedom.

In our view, only a different mode of thinking would allow for a change, but we like to stress (and unfold in a moment) that this mode of thinking cannot be created and disseminated instrumentalistically. If so, it would be an instrumentalism itself. Only a mode of thinking that willfully, i.e. in sensuous spontaneity, thinks and enacts its own insight into the primacy of Nature could make peace with what thinking is already a part of, namely, Nature. The crux of the matter is whether we bodily sense in our Otherness to Nature our kinship with her spontaneously. Such a mode of thinking would separate us from Adams and from the one dominant in today's praxis. It would put an end to the Midas syndrome through understanding and living our ability of culture as a peculiar and indeed higher form of Nature.

Adams and a few other theorists besides him who try to take man's Nature seriously, however, fail to contemplate the possibility of social relations being other than competitive, even antagonistic ones. Certainly, the rest of Nature is permeated by competitiveness and struggle for survival, but why should that hold for human Nature? We suggest that Adams arrives at this conclusion, because he understands what we call man's Otherness to Nature in a way that is limited to the mere cognitive, "categorical" dimension and does not include an elevation of the totality of man's inner Nature, i.e. also of his will, his inner energy flow. As we saw above, Adams does not inspect the Nature of values; he simply accepts their being there. Had he done so, he too might have seen, as we did, that the will is man's primary connection to outer Nature and as such is contained in his knowing. Ignoring this, he can acknowledge in as little as modern praxis does that the will too could be contained in man's elevation and that that would make man's elevation complete and undistorted. If so, little would be there to see, why man's Nature should not also elevate his relations to other human beings to a "willing" of the other, i.e., to be for and not to be against him or her. Under the other, and presently prevailing conditions, loving one's neighbor is a mistake, per se, so to speak. To the best of our knowledge, most social scientists do not contemplate that including man's will in man's elevation is at least a theoretically thinkable possibility. In our view, this omission is an indication of a serious conceptual limitation and as far as Adams is concerned, is a strangely truncated "materialism". We, instead, would go so far as to suggest that our thinking ability is grounded in Nature in such a way that it would be much more in keeping with our Nature that positive relations towards all there is would arise out of our Nature than negative ones. These relations would, of course, include the fellow human being. If everything is primarily Nature, why should it not at least be worth our contemplation whether acting out of our commonality with her would not set us on a somewhat higher road than the one that leads to the destruction of the Nature that we are?

While we argue that these thinkable possibilities were not explored by Adams due to a lack of theoretical thoughtfulness, we have to say that what we try to point out is more than just a philosophically grounded critique of his theoretical position. Certainly, we do subject Adams to such a critique, but we acknowledge that the merely mental exercise of such a critique, even if it points out the primacy of the will and, thus, of Nature may only think the primacy of Nature, but not practice, i.e., live that primacy itself. Critique cannot elevate itself to that level; it takes more than critique to do so. As indicated before, giving primacy to Nature takes sensing (not just thinking) the will, i.e., the flow of Nature in oneself and in the other. In doing so, also man's sociality, which is his positive recognition of the other, will become visible as resting on man's inner Nature.

Above, we have named a few of those thinkers who do not share the mode of thinking that has gained dominance in the West. Now we wish to focus briefly on one of them, namely on Jean-Jacques Rousseau who understands man's being as one that is primarily a being *for* one another.

Trying to briefly review the thought of Jean-Jacques Rousseau as it focuses on the social consequences of our Nature, we are faced with the problem that he, like others who do not stand in the dominant tradition of Western thought, has been largely misunderstood by those coming from that dominant mode of thinking. In order to understand Rousseau on his own terms, we would like to trace his concerns, step by step, as it moves from the Nature of the human being, to the cultivation of her, then, to the General Will and finally to the Nature of freedom. Obviously, we cannot possibly unfold Rousseau's thoughts on these ideas in full detail, but, hopefully, a plausible sketch of them may emerge here.

One of the most crucial points in understanding the Nature of the human being, or, as Rousseau put it, Natural Man, is to follow his reasoning for seeing "sympathy" as the socially most fundamental aspect of human Nature. He understood this concept in the original Greek sense of the word as "suffering with". Rousseau, in this one regard similar to Hobbes, thinks that scarcity led to suffering among human beings at a postulated pre-social level in man's evolution. As opposed to Hobbes' reasoning, this suffering brought individuals together, as they sensed the pain of the other as their own. In taking it for granted, Rousseau has rarely stated the degree to which the *sensuous* awareness of the state of the other, in this case that of being in pain, is a condition for the possibility of bodily grounded sympathy.[41] To the extent that it is part and parcel of man's urges ("spontancity") to symbolize, he elevates that pain up from his own sensuous feeling-with to an understanding of the other. Thus, this pain becomes part of a bodily grounded knowledge. Two directly related aspects in Rousseau's reasoning need to be noted here, especially because they stand in stark contrast to the accepted modern mode of thinking: Rousseau's assumption of spontaneous sympathy as a primary form of relating to fellow man is grounded in the consideration that without an initial (spontaneous) understanding of the other, a distortion of that understanding through distancing oneself from the other cannot occur. It is for this reason that culture as an individuated weapon for survival goes fundamentally against the Nature that we are, Hobbes' and Locke's theorizing notwithstanding.

If this way of being social is man's innate goodness and if this is as constitutive to human Nature, as Rousseau thinks it is,[42] then it has seemed to many of his critics that Rousseau would be hard pressed to account for the emergence of evil in society of which Rousseau is, of course, fully aware. After all, Rousseau himself has said: "man is borne free, but everywhere he is in chains". His alleged inability to account for evil is, however, for Rousseau and for anybody who understands him, a baffling misreading of his legacy. It can only arise out of the mode of thinking that is unable to appreciate the significance that Rousseau assigns to sensuousness. To know out of the sensuousness of experiencing is for Rousseau *the* condition for truly knowing, be it at the general or the social level. This becomes obvious when reading besides his "Social Contract" his work "On Education".[43] Here, Rousseau clearly points out that the distance and the detachment of our experiencing - incidentally, significant aspects of today's mode of knowing - , make us lose sight of the sensuousness as the foundation of our knowing. One should not ignore that Rousseau attributed the reason for the emergence of evil to the evolvement of social stratification.[44] It created the damaging social distance on the basis of which the pain inflicted by the Nobility on the Third Estate in Rousseau's France was no longer really sensed and known by the ones who were the culprits. Marie-Antoinette, as the story has it, could not even understand why the peasants, if without bread, did not eat cake.

In social relations based on nothing but power and the distancing ability of making re-definitions in cold blood, the inflicting of pain cannot help but become habitual. If we appreciate the competitiveness that power relations imply particularly when accompanied by the individuated segregation of people from one another, then this distortion of Nature in and among human beings demands a never ending interest in means and thus quite plausibly leads to an ever growing plunder of outer Nature as well. The Midas syndrome as a product of "second thought" spontaneity then enters all conceptualizations be they those of Nature, Nature inside oneself or in the fellow human beings. Yet, as we have said so often, these distortions are not detrimental to Nature as such, but to the Nature that we are; we could die of them, Nature will not.

Rousseau subsumes under the concept of will all human urges ranging from hunger and sex to talents like those for the crafts, the sciences, the arts, etc.[45] These Nature given talents, these gifts, which already imply individual uniqueness, need to be cultivated in "education", better translated into English as "socialization". This is to say that they must come to the awareness of the young person who has them, hidden at first, and of his "educators" in acts of practical, i.e. sensuous doing before they can be cultivated in the same sensuously concrete way. Thus, cultivation aims at helping the individual to retain his/her individual uniqueness by developing his/her natural gifts and by making them communicable. This is to say that in the practically life long process of personal cultivation and socialization, or as Goethe later puts it, one's life long elevation the human self, i.e. the individuality, moves through interaction to tendentially ever greater perfection. The "give and take" of that interaction socializes the needs and the abilities of givers and takers in all kinds of media, be they artistic, scientific, agricultural endeavors, etc. Appreciating how, for instance, human speech transcends-and-contains the 100% feedback process of sheer information exchange allows us to understand that sociality rests inside the ones involved in it and not just between them. We owe our sociality to the Nature of others, to the Nature of what we do with one another and to our own. An interaction that becomes distanced through a spontaneity that is guided by what we have above called "second thought" spontaneity, is deeply antagonistic to the Nature that we are and to her true elevation.

A socialization true to its Nature contributes to a build-up and strengthening of individuality. Accordingly, there is no room in Rousseau's views on "education" for the notion of "breaking-in" human individuality. Socialization is a helping to selfhood and that helping is meant to strengthen the already Nature given individuality of each human being. If learning and growing up are carried by "sympathy", they do not inflict pain in the struggle of personal growth. It is the opposite of the repression that would take place under "Leviathan's" rule. Having been brought up "à la Rousseau" should enable one to refine one's Nature by relating to the recognized Nature of the other. Cultivating one's inner Nature, i.e. knowing and fostering one's will in all its aspects as Rousseau understands it, is not a competition among those trying to get most suitably equipped for the struggle for liberties, but it is a development of one's freedom. In its very Nature, this freedom can only be one that is shared with others so that each one owns it uniquely in her or his way. The place of this freedom is the General Will as Rousseau understands it.

It has often been overlooked that Rousseau reasons about all this by emphasizing the idea of "progress". His well known motto "back to Nature" could certainly be seen as a methodological stance, but it does not just operate as a device to construct the ideal type of "Natural Man". Beyond that, it refers to the re-finding of one's inner Nature at whatever level of progress attained. In this context, Rousseau's advocacy of progress aimed at the evolvement of a society with such a high level of differentiation that human Nature in its multitude of variety would have ever more possibilities to unfold its individual uniqueness in it. Uniqueness understood this way must, of course, be contrasted to the ever greater individuation that in fact came along with capitalism and which has threatened individuality in increasingly serious ways. While we hope to have sufficiently elaborated on the process of individuation, it should not be denied that Rousseau also saw problems with a modernity in which the face-to-face contact so essential for sensuousness could be lost and where social relations aim at chaining others to one's purposes.

It is quite ironic to us that Rousseau's concept of "General Will" (i.e., the will in which the diverse individual wills are transcended-and-contained) and, by implication, his concepts of freedom and socialization have been considered as "utopian" (using this term in its vulgarized sense). Certainly, these concepts are far away from today's reality, but, what kind of a reality is this? Is it not a praxis and a theory that twist the Nature of things and of man through the Midas syndrome and, thus, leave no other route for our species than the one that ends up in disaster? If this is the one and only Last Judgement, then indeed "we and a God are thwarted ... and this is gruesome enough".

But there is also an undercurrent in Western culture which has never given up to envision the further elevation of man to higher forms of life; it has always dreamt of freedom as the manifestation of our undistorted Nature. It is a strange limitation in today's praxis and theory that they can, as expressed by Adams, relate elevation only to the process of conceptualization and not to that what has primacy in that process, namely the will, i.e. our inner Nature. After all, concepts cannot be without the will to create them. If the will, however, is left raw and left behind in the process of elevation, then the concepts co-produced by that will can hardly be fully elevated. Only an elevation of the human being in will and mind would deserve the full title of elevation; its occurrence is not only thinkable, it is also natural. Yet this can only be known and learned in the sensuous doing as it takes place together with other human beings.

Goethe, as we shall see, is one of the most outstanding representatives of this sensuous way of living, learning and thinking. Yet, besides Rousseau, Karl Marx and Friedrich Nietzsche were also eminent advocates of the elevation of Nature in man. For Karl Marx, the notion of communism was an expression of the General Will that practices the commonality of Nature by turning around the individuation of capital and, as he anticipated, of science into the freedom of truly social individuals. Also Nietzsche's "Übermensch" was envisioned as having transcended-and-contained the pitiful paltriness of the faceless masses that roam the overpopulated market places of this world. Those who point out what the teachings of these two have led to in the last 100 years, expose themselves to the counter question: is it not visible what happens to all teachings that late capitalism only partially understands, be it the ones by Jesus Christ or the ones contained in Vedic Wisdom?

The late capitalist human being by reducing anything to mere means in the exercise of power still practices the Nature given commonality among all there is, but while practicing this commonality in exploitation, it truncates that commonality, as we saw, inside the human body. Late capitalist man rarely acknowledges his own belonging to Nature. He only does so, if it is instrumental for him (and/or "after hours"). Both, the deceitful ignoring and the occasional, thus equally deceitful acknowledgement of man's being part of Nature remain, as instrumentalistic exercises, distortions of man's reality. As lies, they are ideologically constitutive aspects of modern praxis and, thus, an intrinsic aspect of it. The novelty of late capitalism to be understood here lies in the circumstance that praxis itself is an ideology. Today, goals are not goals and, like all accomplishments, are not really desired in themselves; one takes what one gets not yet knowing what it is good for. But: good for something, it has to be. Being related to the world around us through the distortions of instrumentalistic re-definitions, we place ourselves into a world which will always slip away from us, with which we cannot identify and in which we cannot be at home. This is to say that praxis itself becomes unreal today. Life is fictitious, ghostlike, a sequence of moments that are never one's own. Regardless of whether we speak of praxis being its own fictitious ideology or whether we speak of the modern individuated and egofocal mode of thinking, in either case we speak of a spreading cancer the unstoppable growth of which is immune against any cure. No religion, no world view, nor any philosophy can point a way out of this misery. All of them instantaneously lose their meaning under the Midas touch. Against traditional capitalism and its ideologies, one could at least think of starting a counter movement. Trying these now is not only unrealistic, it is at best a plot for a new version of Don Quixotte. In acting out such plots, only egofocal gains can be made and, thus, late capitalism is confirmed provided, of course, one finds someone valuing one's "new ideas". This is another way of saying, as we did above, that any cause, even the noblest one, cannot have any other function than serving one's own advantage. Obviously, this statement of ours could easily backfire at the authors of this essay, not because it precludes finding a following for us - something we don't want any way - but because we would get one. Whatever one does or thinks, an instrumentalistic purpose will be assigned to it. It cannot be understood any other way. This also applies to what we have tried to deliver here: a critique of today's mode of thinking. But, in this connection, we have to emphasize a point that is located at a deeper level than our argument: we know that a critique will not only not accomplish what needs to take place, it would if successful, only lead to false results. As we just said, the danger of a critique is that it would be seen as "useful". This, then, finally allows us to get to the point, but first in a negative way: we see here that the instrumentalism of late capitalism creates its own impenetrable immunity; like a cancer, it cannot be infected, it can only spread.

One might ask, why have we then delivered a critique at all? In response to this question, we would like to first identify our reason[46] for doing so and then make it clear what kind of transcendence we hope for. Our reason for writing what we wrote arose simply out of the desire to know as precisely as we possibly could what is false with today's mode of thinking. As sketched above, our critique revealed the reason for today's misery to us, but this clarification confirmed the long standing suspicion that had grown out of our experience, namely that a merely conceptual understanding and a "determinate negation" (in the Hegel-Marx sense) of what we take to be the problem was not enough; it did not even change our own lives, if at best our thinking. Certainly, attaining clarity was our purpose and also to communicate this to others, but we have known all along that it would reach only those who already have a *bodily felt* sense for today's misery in them. For those not sensing the misery of this day and age and/or not acknowledging their sense of it, our critique is fruitless; for them, it is at best an intellectual game.

While we do know that mentalistic exercises including a mere critique will lead nowhere at the practically-concrete level, and while we also know that a mere intellectual insight into the deadly Nature of today's praxis can at best initiate an instrumentalistic search for a way out of it,[47] we do not mean to say that there is nothing to be done. The question only is: where can the doing begin? And in what can it be grounded? Trying to answer these questions we hope to make our point now in a positive way.

However little may follow from our considerations, among them is at least the insight that the rectification of Nature in human beings has to be left to Nature. Maybe it is the pain suffered inside human beings which makes them acknowledge and then even enjoy what they really are part of: Nature. While we do not know whether Nature will care to rectify us and which forms and ways she might find to do so, we do know that this has to happen inside the bodily existence of the individual. At that level, the doing can start. We furthermore think that those that are being blessed by the grace of their rectification,[48] and those who have miraculously never lost their true Nature will obey their Nature also in so far as they join one another in order to let a new praxis grow that is on its part immune to ideology. In other words, our future lies in a new way of being, doing and thinking as it arises out of our inner Nature and reaches into Nature around us. This elevation of our being carries in it the knowledge that one cannot do much about the immunity of today's distorted praxis. Yet this new way of being and knowing will also be immune against that false praxis and its ideology.

Trying to anticipate how a return to Nature adequate to the level of our social evolution will affect our lives, is a matter of speculation. We will, therefore, not engage in it. Yet, this much could be hoped for: the birth of rich personalities in a rich society in which the tremendous waste of Nature in us and around us would be a matter of the past.[49]

Notes

[1] Adams, 1975, pp 17, 111
[2] Adams, 1988, e.g., pp 15, 17.
[3] See p. 18.
[4] Adams, 1988, p. 167
[5] Adams, 1975, p. 315
[6] We use this term to mean, like in the critical tradition of philosophy and sociology, an attempt at understanding a body of thought by bringing to one's awareness the conceptual connections made in it and to pinpoint where one fails to see them as being established. Failing to make the suggested connections will indicate a problem either on the part of the one who tries to understand, of the one who suggests and presents the mental connections or of both of them In any case, the presented thought requires revisions based on a

"determinate negation" of the point at which problems arise

[7] Our critique of Adams is presented here by summarizing and paraphrasing an essay previously published by F W. Sixel, see Sixel, 1991, pp 200ff.

[8] Adams, 1988, pp 15, 17

[9] Adams, 1975, p. 111

[10] ibid.: pp. 17, 111

[11] Adams, 1988, p IX

[12] ibid., p 196.

[13] See pp. 16-20.

[14] Adams, 1975, p. 113; 1988, pp. 78, 412.

[15] Adams, 1988, p 83

[16] ibid., p. 90.

[17] Adams, 1975, pp. 114; 1988, p. 77, 84.

[18] Adams, 1975, pp 113f.

[19] Adams, 1975, p. 107; 1988, p. 81.

[20] Spitzer, 1996, pp 125ff, 209ff.

[21] Adams, 1975, p 9

[22] Adams, 1988, p 10

[23] ibid., p 9.

[24] Martin 1974, Taylor, 1987.

[25] Adams, 1988, pp. 88.

[26] ibid., p. 50

[27] Sixel, 1981, pp. 247, 251f, 1988, pp. 67ff.

[28] Adams, 1988, pp 93.

[29] Adams, 1975, pp. 157ff.

[30] Sixel, 1988, pp. 66

[31] Adams, 1988, p 9.

[32] See p 207; regarding the consequences, see chapter 7 passim

[33] See in this regard also Spitzer, 1996, pp. 125ff, 209ff, 230ff.

[34] For an elaboration on this, see Sixel, 1988, pp 68f.

[35] See also Apel, 1963.

[36] Obviously, Marx's Theses on Feuerbach come to mind here, see also Habermas, 1973, pp 45

[37] For instance, Habermas, op cit , Sixel 1995, pp 12ff

[38] See pp. 14-15, 19-20.

[39] See Roth, 1994, pp 303ff.

[40] Adams, 1988, pp. 76ff, in particular 81f.

[41] Rousseau, 1950 [1762], pp. 222ff; 1986 [1762], p 69

[42] Rousseau, 1986, book V, passim

[43] Rousseau, 1986.

[44] Rousseau, 1950, pp 3, 272

[45] Rousseau, 1985, pp 160ff

[46] Not to be confused with purpose! See Sixel, 1988, pp 23-24.

[47] Among many others, Gadamer's thought on this matter is a good example for the thinking of those who are aware of the problems of this day and age and yet can only advocate a change in our life *in order to* avoid disaster Intellectually guided avoidance of the bad lying ahead of us does not carry within it the sensuous longing for practicing the good; see, for this view, Gadamer, 1983, e.g. pp. 20, 49, 75, 167

[48] Martin Luther makes the change of the inner will the crucial point in his theology of salvation. It is clear to him that the salvation from sin, i e , from "egofocality", to use our language, is not a matter of man's own doing but of God's grace; see Luther, 1954 passim

[49] This sentence simply paraphrases an idea that Rudolf Bahro once unfolded, see Bahro, 1977, pp. 484f specifically; see also Bahro, 1991. For decades, we have shared his hopes. Rudolf Bahro had initially thought that a true living could evolve from within the praxis of socialist East Germany When he left the "really existing socialism" of that country and came to the late capitalist West, it took him a while to understand what it takes to live in the "belly of the beast". After the unification of both parts of Germany, Rudolf Bahro believed that formerly East Germany carried in it more hope for living a new praxis. Needless to say then that Rudolf Bahro's premature death (1997) was sensed by us as a tremendous loss.

Part III: The Alternative to Today's Praxis: Goethe's Understanding of Nature

Introductory Note: Our Coming to Goethe

Since the ideology of egofocally distorting the common bond of Nature is to be considered as being constitutive to modern praxis, the question arises as to what practicing an acknowledgment of this insight would mean. We hope to have demonstrated that the most crucial point for practicing such an acknowledgement would have to be a change in the process of coming to know, i.e., in the process of understanding Nature in us and around us in its various layers from the merely mechanical up to the most elevated one.

Given that our concerns have originated in modern man's distorted synthesis with non-human Nature and given that we have come to see that this distortion is only one aspect of a whole distorted social praxis, we felt at first overwhelmed by the complexity of what needs to be sorted out. But then, after having traveled a few exploratory detours, we ended up studying Goethe's understanding of Nature and, as a consequence of these studies, came to see with new eyes that what had first appeared as an overwhelming complexity could be brought down to a quite simple and natural level. This is by no means to say that we would claim to have found the cure of modernity's ills in Goethe. This cannot be done by a mere reflexive study. However, a brief description of how we ended up with Goethe and how we derived a sense of simplicity from him may merit a brief description.

As we have tried to show, Western man's negative synthesis with Nature is not just a matter of his improper application of what is otherwise valid science. It is not even an issue whether or not modern science is correct. It may very well be that science is correct most of the time, regardless of whether we use the word science in its traditional (in English speaking countries) limitation to the natural sciences or in its late capitalist modern sense à la Luhmann.[1] In our view, the puzzling problem is that science may very well be correct, and at the same time not true. The difference between true and correct lies, simplifying matters a great deal,[2] in the circumstance that correctness is truth minus values. Today's supposedly value-free sciences have, since quite some time now, grounded their claims to correctness in so called "objectivity" which is, of course, as we saw above[3] merely a distortion of the circumstance that all knowledge, even the one distorted by claims to "objectivity", is grounded in the commonality of Nature between the inquiring human subject, i.e., the scientist, and the objects he studies. Without such commonality, i.e., without the objects and ourselves as subjects being parts of this world, such study would be impossible, no matter how egofocally distorted that commonality is and how little this distortion is acknowledged today.

While being quite aware of the peculiar evolutionary condition for this distortion, we had nevertheless contemplated the possibility of whether a grounding of human subjects in a shared world view, be it a resurrected old or a new one, could regain truth for science, and for knowledge in general. In other words, since we could not simply discard the notion that one had to ascribe the lack of a possibility for truth in today's praxis to the historical evaporation of commonly (i.e. non-antagonistically) shared values and overarching world-views, we began to look, however briefly so, into previously valid yet now outdated foundations for them. We abandoned this attempt in which we had looked at Aristotle, Leibniz, and Kant seeing quite soon that a resurrection of their thoughts would only repeat their historical overcoming. We looked then into non-Western cultures in order to find out what kinds of sciences existed there and what their truth value might be. We studied bits and pieces of East Asian sciences, particularly as they had been cultivated in pre-colonial India and China, we also turned to some of the Pre-Columbian societies of the American continent, particularly to those of what is now Mexico/Guatemala and Peru/Bolivia. But, for numerous reasons, we found them too far afield from what was and is happening in the West.[4] During these mental meanderings through alien horizons, we became increasingly uncomfortable and even embarrassed about ourselves. We felt that we were in the danger of falling prey to a distortion in Western thought that has been quite common, particularly since the days of romanticism. The discomfort about the culture in which we live seemed to make us, as it has been with others, seek comfort in cultures that do not readily speak to ours. Such comfort, however, is at best deceptive and can only be a matter of leisure time musings. Alien cultures are no remedies for the problems of today's praxis.

It was our discontent with our daily life experiences that reminded us, time and again, of where we were, what society we live in. We could not ignore how easily one could lose out to, and get confused by the fictitious, even ghostlike, reality all around us. We had to struggle for retaining our sobriety about this danger and did so by retaining our clarity on the question of where exactly, i.e. at which precise point, the distortions of modern thinking affected us. We had to acknowledge that this was mainly related to our bodily grounded desire not to be fooled by what we were told to be "the facts of life", "the way it is", what "sober" thinking would tell us, etc. It was in this regard that we came to understand how much we owed to the materialist teachings of Richard N. Adams. And yet, it was precisely the inconsistencies in his theorizing which made us see why he ended up being an ideologue of the status quo, i.e. of "the way it is". His kind of sobriety cannot offer a breakthrough into the future, since there is no clarity in it on the point where the elevation of human Nature gets truncated and distorted.

Retaining awareness for our own insight into this, we had to appreciate anew what was implied by what we have called a negative synthesis with Nature. In other words, we had to understand more thoroughly yet why this kind of a synthesis also meant an expansion of predatory exploitation beyond what Karl Marx, for instance, had analyzed once upon a time so thoroughly. And yet, we were unable to detect anyone among those to whom we felt akin in our views and mode of thinking whose teachings could be related to today's problems in ways that had more than just intellectual significance. So much of what these teachings had to offer was only theorizing, intellectually fascinating at times, but far away from concrete deeds, i.e., from a level where it really mattered.

It was more or less at that time that we noticed a resurgence in the debate on Goethe as a scientist. So we did what academics normally do when they try to understand something, we read books.[5] First, and this perhaps is also typical of academics, we read what others had written *about* Goethe's science. These readings, while for the most part of remarkable intellectual quality, left us with so many questions that we decided to read Goethe's own writings on science. It did not take much to make us see that many of these writings, particularly those on light and colors, were written against Isaac Newton, thus focusing on one of the central figures in the evolution of the modern natural sciences. But we eventually also noticed that even an awareness for what we took to be the methodological differences between the two was not enough to understand Goethe fully. It is again to our embarrassment that we have to admit that it took us a while yet to practically accept Goethe's often stated admonition to ground our understanding of what he was writing about in our own concrete experimental studies of these matters, be it with the help of a prism or without.[6] Given our claims to knowing the importance of materially grounded thinking, we should have done so from the beginning. Finally, we did not only read Goethe's "Teachings on Colors" and his earlier "Contributions to Optics", we also bought prisms and made a number of Goethe's experiments and observations ourselves. Making these experiments, we soon came to see how little a mere reading of the descriptions of his experiments and experiences did for a concrete understanding of Goethe's ways of thinking and coming to know. How seriously he takes it to do things with one's own hands is underlined by noting that he also describes how one could fabricate a prism for oneself given that they could not be bought easily anymore at the time.[7] In keeping with this, Goethe also made card board plates available for his readers so that the actual making of some of these experiments would become easier. All this was necessary in Goethe's view in order to enable the wider public to get what he considered to be a proper, and this is to say, a sensuously grounded understanding of what he had written about.

After having made quite a number of Goethe's observations and experiments on light and color ourselves and having also found out, though only by way of reading how he grounded all his other studies in concrete sensuous experience, we came to see that we needed to have at least some knowledge about how Goethe, the human being had evolved. What were the telling events in his life? How did he gain or retain his sense for the primacy of sensuousness in processes of coming to know? What allowed him to let his inner Nature reach out into the world around him so securely? Studying his life and a good many of his writings, we came to see that some of our questions were misplaced, i.e., came from a mode of thinking alien to him. Having gained a "feel" for his experiments during these studies, we came to understand how he unified in himself the incredibly great variety of his activities. After all, they ranged from being a poet, a novelist, a lawyer and a politician to that of a scientist. Obviously Goethe had, for himself, done away with the compartmentalization of life spheres as it already existed at his day and age. But this should not mislead us to seeing in Goethe a "Renaissance Man". He did not just know a lot of singular things, he knew them in an integrated way. Even the form of integration that kept his various endeavors together was quite different from what an already then dominant way of knowing had aimed for. His ability to tie all his activities together was a consequence of his way of being.

Taking off in his understanding of the world around him primarily from his own sense experiences, Goethe's knowledge of things came to be through what he called - in a striking similarity to Richard Adams - elevations ("Steigerungen") of these things to conceptualizations of them. As we have to unfold later, he considered this way of coming to know as arising out of the "Anschauende Urteilskraft", i.e., the "perceptively guided power of judgment". This concept was coined by Goethe in conscious counter distinction to Kant - an ardent admirer of Newton - and his "Kritik der Urteilskraft", i.e., his "Critique of the Power of Judgement".[8] To the extent that in Goethe's praxis, man's power or faculty to know involves the whole bodily self of a researcher, Goethe's understanding of the process of coming to know goes beyond what a merely philosophical or epistemological analysis à la Kant could fathom. To emphasize, Goethe's approach to the world around us does not just imply reflexive awareness for the student's total self in his/her relatedness to Nature, it practices the circumstance that man's own inner Nature is constitutive for all processes of coming to know. This materially reflexive way of practicing the coming to understand establishes kinds of syntheses with Nature which, because of their groundedness, generates a knowing of the world that retains its kinship to Nature in its own occurrence. In our own experimental studies on Goethe's work on colors, we developed a sense of what his way of coming to know concretely entails. As we grew in this way of understanding and its sensuously grounded certainty, the complexity of today's praxis lost much of its intimidating appearance. We came to see that this complexity is, because of its origin in the capricious re-definitions of all aspects of life by the late capitalist mode of thinking, merely a monstrous confusion about what is of an only ghostlike, though powerful existence. Having come to understand this does not, however, mean that overcoming today's confusing life-world turns into an easy task. Instead, it became ever clearer to us as we progressed in our studies that overcoming today's distortions requires a new praxis to be shared by those desiring to transcend-and-contain today's ways of knowing, doing and being. Such a new praxis is the only chance left to grow immune against the cancerous growth of today's fictitious mode of thinking. In other words, it is only in such a praxis that mere correctness can be elevated to truth, i.e., a truth then grounded not on artificially resurrected world views and their values, but in our willing acceptance of the commonality of all there is.

We hope that these remarks help to clarify why we feel that we have first to present a biography of Goethe in order to understand how he succeeded in keeping his senses undistorted. In this presentation, we also wish to bring out that Goethe takes on the appearance of an extraordinary human being only for those among us who are still stuck in today's dominant ways of being and thinking. The political scientist Ekkehart Krippendorff has remarked in his ground breaking study of Goethe as a politician that those who see in Goethe merely an object of admiration have not only misunderstood him, they also make life easy for themselves that way. They have an excuse then not to follow him as an example for what a normal - or natural - human being truly is.[9] The usual portrayals of Goethe as having been mainly a poet, playwright and novelist who, while being of world wide fame, could even enjoy himself in a few and rather unorthodox studies of science, have probably contributed to his image of a godlike rapture. This image has prevailed for quite some time. Particularly after Germany's unification in 1871, it was promoted by nationalistic interests. It had become useful to portray him as Germany's equivalent to England's Shakespeare, Italy's Dante and Spain's Cervantes etc.[10] The significance of his thinking was truncated by reducing his work to his artistic endeavors. However, at that time, there was no need for propagating the kind of being and thinking that the whole Goethe really represented. Today, other forces seem to be at work to suppress his kind of being and thinking and to hide or distort who he was and what he still stands for. We ourselves have been victims of this one-sided image of Goethe. This explains, in part, that it took us a while to turn our attention to his real existence and his whole work.[11]

Notes

[1] See pp 20-23

[2] For a more detailed elaboration, see Habermas & Luhmann, 1971, 228f, see also pp. 147, 157, 164-165, 207, 225.

[3] See e.g. pp 87-88

[4] It would require a treatise of its own to describe the differences between these conceptions of Nature and the ones of the West An attempt to understand non-Western forms of knowledge is also complicated by the circumstance that almost all pieces of the literature available on these matters are written from a Western perspective and, thus, are somewhat dubious regarding the adequacy of their understanding.

[5] This sentence paraphrases one of those admirably self-ironic passages of which Richard Adams is so capable. Since I could not find where he had said this, I asked him to help me in this bibliographic matter Here is his e-mail response of 13 Jan 2000: "I really don't know where I may have said this in print   . it is something that I say from time to time because my mind works that way. If you want to cite it, why not say, 'Articulo Fugitivo' .   Rick".

[6] See pp 158, also 206, 216, for references to passages where Goethe urges the reader to make the experiments See also Goethe 1988, II, pp. 60ff.

[7] Goethe, 1988, II, pp 60f

[8] For greater detail of Goethe's view on Kant see pp. 147-148, 160-161, 213-215, 265.

[9] Krippendorff, 1999, pp 36, 163

[10] Krippendorff, op cit, p. 19

[11] Also in former East Germany, attempts made by Bert Brecht and Volker Braun, for instance, to familiarize the wider public with Goethe's real significance, were not successful; see Brady, 1984, pp 31ff, 50f

Chapter 6

The Evolvement of the Phenomenon Goethe

> *"This book is titled 'Goethe', without any addition. - One can take it already from there what its intent is. the presentation of Goethe's whole being, the greatest entity in which the German mind has embodied itself" (Gundolf).*[1]

> *"Goethe – not a German event, but a European one   What he wanted was totality; he fought the falling apart of Reason, Sensuousness, Sensitivity and Will (preached in the most abhorrent scholasticism by Kant - the antipode of Goethe); he disciplined himself to totality, he created himself .   " (Nietzsche).*[2]

> *"Anybody can - at least can try to - appropriate his understanding of life, the universalism of his interests, the inner harmony   "* (Rosa Luxemburg)[3]

After we had started to read Goethe's writings on science and particularly after we had done a number of his experiments on colors, we came to see that focusing on Goethe's science while leaving out his other writings was inadequate even for a mere understanding of Goethe's ways of doing science. Goethe the poet and Goethe the scientist are one person and that person was by no means a schizophrenic. In fact, his poetry and his science, indeed his whole being has to be understood as pouring out of the same fountain: his Nature.

When one tries to trace Goethe's life through its various stages, one soon comes to notice that his growth was a continuous process of elevation itself; it was without drastic revolutionary changes. It was an unfolding in which there was no room for compartmentalization. It was important for Goethe to gain reflexive awareness of this and also to gain clarity on what it was that allowed him to retain unity among all his many activities. This was a process that did not only take Goethe quite some time, it was also an evolvement that did not come about without struggle. One could even say that his own evolvement would have been incomplete without this evolvement itself having become a matter of Goethe's own self inspection. This reflexivity adds, of course, to the appearance of complexity in the phenomenon that Goethe was. It was this self-conscious awareness for the dynamic growth in his own life and his responsiveness to that growth which defies the extraction of a philosophy, let alone of a systematic theory, from his work which a now dominant mode of thinking would like to obtain. This circumstance also explains why Goethe could not have disciples, at least not in the usual sense of the word. Those who hold this against him ignore that having disciples and spelling out a theory, a philosophy or a "Weltanschauung" would go against Goethe's Nature, and ultimately against the dynamics of all Nature. Nature was for Goethe always a totality which because of her flux defies logic. Ignoring Goethe's acceptance of his own Nature would also miss his own individuality. As we have pointed out above, human individuals are by materially grounded necessity different from one another. But Goethe's concept and praxis of individuality and its dynamics must not be confused with what late capitalist man has distorted into egofocality and capricious abstractions. Goethe stands above them. He transcends-and-contains these in his sense for the commonality of Nature. The way he led his life establishes paradigmatically, and in a new way, the uniqueness, the dynamics and the equality for each human being. And yet, while setting an example in this sense, his life and work is unsuitable for being distorted into a dogma. Instead, his life and work invite each one of us to be as uniquely him or her self as he was.

Goethe was aware that the writing of history like that of a personal biography can only be done out of the moment at which the writer has arrived in the flux of events. While accepting the dynamics of subjectivity this way, Goethe still refused to see in this a license to distort the materially concrete aspects of the past. He knew that events always appear in a different light as life goes on. This insight has expressed itself, for instance, in his own biography, aptly titled "Poetry and Truth" (in German: "Dichtung und Wahrheit").[4]

Having said this, we have to highlight another aspect in Goethe's concept of truth that will underlie much of what we have to unfold later. Truth itself was obviously a dynamic phenomenon for him. He could make statements that would sound amazingly modern and were yet not of the modern flexible kind. Once he has said, for instance, that what was perfect in 1800 could be a deficiency in 1850.[5] He could also allow for an astounding pluralism in the natural sciences, but he did so only, as we shall see, if a particular study had arisen out of the concrete sensuously mediated commonality between a researcher and his object of study. The dynamics of this view included his understanding of the dynamics of his own life. The concrete reality of his life and its description were for him manifestations both of Nature and of art. His life itself was consciously cultivated by him and so was its description. This is why one cannot simplistically trust Goethe's own biography. It is not an account accurate in a historicist sense. However for us, there is no doubt that his "Poetry and Truth" is a piece of literature from which one can truly learn a lot, certainly much more than from a so-called factually correct and all too often unconsciously subjective biography.

The way in which Goethe accepts himself, not only at times but in every moment, as being placed into the flow of Nature led to an intensity and scope in his activities which is beyond one's ability to believe. One certainly has to call Goethe excessively diligent, but his diligence was merely an expression of his obedience to the flow of Nature in him. While this manifests itself in the enormous volume of his writings as a poet, playwright and novelist, and also in the vast amount of his scientific studies in botany, zoology, meteorology, geology and on colors, his enormous energy also finds its expression in his rich social life. He knew and interacted with an incredible number of people, even during his "time of withdrawal" in his later years. As an indication, we would like to mention that there exist 50 volumes of Goethe's own letters in the so called "Sophien" (or "Weimar") edition of his works. These are, of course, merely those letters that have come upon us from a man who is known to have burned, ever so often, manuscripts and many of the letters that he wrote and not always mailed. At the same time, there exist 21 000 letters sent to Goethe from 3500 different senders, many, though not all of whom, got their replies.[6] His correspondence alone should make it clear that one has to understand Goethe's "diligence" in a way that is different from the widespread meaning it has today. When matters got his sensuous attention - and that happened nearly all the time - they instantly triggered his inner energy to explore them, to shape them, to write about them, etc. This is how he happily yielded to his inner drive. One can hardly overestimate the significance of the fact that it was his sense impressions that set his inner energy into motion. As we shall see, sensuous impressions, not abstract ideas or theories, led him in his scientific studies. This may be hard to understand for those of us who see so much of what they do as being guided by instrumentalistic "values", for instance by duty, but hardly by an "enticement to see", a "lust to know" or a "drive to give shape", in order to use a few of the terms by which Goethe characterized his motivations to act. Duty, alertness and diligence, thus, had like all other values, an entirely different meaning for him than the modern mode of thinking would assume. His values have already to be understood as expressions of a "re-evaluation of all values" long before Nietzsche coined this phrase.

In our now more detailed attempt to trace the unfolding of the phenomenon that Johann Wolfgang von Goethe was, we wish, first of all, to underline that our studies of him have not turned us into Goethe scholars. However, what we have read about Goethe's life, what we understood from re-reading some of his works and more so what we have learned from following his way of doing science by doing it with our own hands, has allowed us to get an idea of what kind of culture it would take, would we today also begin to live as enhancing parts of Nature, i.e., in a positive synthesis with her.

Johann Wolfgang Goethe[7] was born on 28 Aug 1749 into a wealthy and cultivated family in Frankfurt on Main, at that time a free Empirial City (Freie Reichsstadt). His father was a jurist and an "Imperial Council" ("Kaiserlicher Rat"). It would be inadequate to just say that the little boy received very good schooling and tutoring[8] in modern (English, French, Italian) and old (e.g. Latin and Greek) languages, in history, biblical readings, in studies of antiquity, and in art and poetry. These kinds of offerings were nothing unusual in a family of Goethe's status. Many other children of wealthy as well as of noble families enjoyed the same exposure, but did not become the kind of individual that Goethe turned out to be. We would like to consider two additional aspects that prepared the child for a later life of never ending enrichment and growth. We tend to think that these two aspects were, on the one hand, the culturally rich setting in which he grew up, both inside and outside his parental home, and, on the other, the freedom granted to a spontaneous curiosity, alive enough in the young child to reach out into these surroundings in all their diversity.

Goethe's parents and grandparents, but also other family members and friends did so many things in a fashion directly accessible to the young child that it was only natural for him to learn these things as well. The people around him enjoyed, for instance, to learn languages, to cook food and indulge in it, to enjoy paintings, tell stories and read poems (aloud!). Goethe's father was a person who, besides being professionally engaged in many matters, dreamed all the time about Italy, learned its language and admired its artistic richness so that little Goethe soon came to share these interests. He learned some Italian as well, came to love paintings and soon started writing, at which he was good, and also painting at which he was not so good.[9] At the same time, one cannot overestimate the influence that his mother had on him, particularly with regard to his poetry. This intelligent and sensuous woman told him story after story from his early days on to which the young child soon gave his own "spin", not liking it when his mother changed the plot on her volition.[10] Writing poetry, for momentary consumption or with greater substance, came naturally to him throughout his life. In short, Goethe's childhood was saturated with life in a multitude of ways so that knowledge and sensuousness could not help but grow rich and grow together.

When Johann Wolfgang was old enough, i.e., 7 or 8 years of age, he often roamed the neighborhood of his parental home and soon the whole city. Being given tickets for the (French speaking) theater by his grandfather, he went there eagerly, did not understand too much, yet improved his French gradually (Frankfurt was occupied by the French army during the Seven Year War). At that time, he developed the initial skills of writing and staging a drama. When he ran into people in the Jewish quarter of Frankfurt that he could not converse with, Johann Wolfgang wanted to learn Yiddish as well. When he wanted to get deeper into the stories of the Old Testament, he desired to learn Hebrew. His father thus hired an expert to tutor him.[11] At the age of 13 or 14, young Goethe grew tired of the exercise books for language studies (probably as dull as ours today) and instead set out to write a novel in the form of letters written to one another by siblings in the idioms of the different countries into which they were dispersed. Not many of Goethe's early writings have come upon us, yet it is certain that these literary attempts and his visits to the theater, let alone his roaming around the city must not be viewed as "educational measures" strategically imposed or allowed for by his parents. This is what we might think living at a time of estranged ideas on spending time and supervision. Young Goethe simply had the good fortune, perhaps rare today, that the adults around him were alive themselves, did things and spontaneously enjoyed what they did. This is what made his life rich. It would have been hard not to flourish under these circumstances.

Our glimpse into Goethe's childhood would be all too incomplete without telling the following story.[12] One day, Johann Wolfgang decided to bring Nature a sacrifice. The boy built an altar on his father's music desk and decorated it with items from his father's natural collection. He then lit candles with a burning lens dedicating the sacrifice to God whom he envisioned as being in direct connection with Nature. Whatever went wrong with this sacrifice - the smoke went up as hoped for, yet the candles left marks on his father's desk - this sacrifice is indicative of Goethe's already deep respect for Nature and God, or better, for God in Nature. After the shocking earthquake in Lisbon of 1755, which had left a deep mark on the child's mind, neither Nature nor God were seen as simply benign, as romanticists until now might do. God and Nature were overwhelming and inseparable forces for the young boy, too dangerous to toy with, and be it by making sacrificial offerings to them.

At the age of 16, Goethe took up his university studies in Leipzig.[13] When he came there, more mature and more knowledgeable than his age would suggest, he by no means focused his studies and interests on the field of law, as was expected of him by his father. In fact, he overextended himself in almost every thinkable direction: philology and horseback riding, art history and swimming, writing and reciting his own (usually love) poetry at festive occasions, trying his hand at etching, indulging in fine foods and yet trying to live up to what he and his friends understood by Rousseau's call "Back to Nature". Certainly, the financial support by his family was such that it allowed him to do practically anything he wanted. Thus, he lived out his curiosity and sensuousness in every regard imaginable. As a result of his over-extension, he returned home with a serious illness instead of a degree. Modern medical analysis of the available information on his illness makes it quite likely that the 18 year old Goethe suffered from tuberculosis.[14]

During the illness which lasted more than two years, the young man went through a struggle that affected him deeply. While it was a life threatening experience, it led in the end to a strengthening of his sense for the unity of all Nature.[15] Having become bodily aware of his own mortality, he knew much better than ever before that being human meant being part of the ebb and flow in Nature. In the elevation of this experience to a reflexively evaluated insight, Goethe enjoyed the thoughtful support by Susanne von Klettenberg, a noble lady who had been asked by Goethe's parents to take care of him in these difficult times. It was from this lady, in later writings referred to by Goethe many times[16] as "the beautiful soul" ("die schöne Seele"), that he came to understand the concept of "analogia entis", i.e., the common bond or the commonality of Nature in all there is.[17] The total inclusion of the human being in this "analogia" has been of utmost significance for Goethe ever since.

In our reading, the years after his recovery (1770) until his arrival in Weimar (1775), were still a period of restless fermentation. They were the years of "Sturm und Drang" ("Storm and Stress"), although the wildness of the Leipzig years was behind him. While we understand that Goethe had acquired a stronger sense for the wholeness of life, we have to confess that we have no indication that he tried to integrate, in his mind, the range of different interests that he pursued at that time. On the one hand, Goethe completed his studies in law in Straßburg,[18] took a clerkship in Wetzlar (1772)[19] and, with the help of his father, practiced law in Frankfurt.[20] On the other hand, and apart from continuing to write poetry at his usual amazing rate and from cultivating numerous friendships, e.g., with the theologian Herder,[21] he also wrote two of his most successful pieces: the drama "Götz" and the novel "Werther".[22] These works gained him enormous renown far beyond Germany. We would be at a loss, if we tried to integrate all these activities under a common theme, let alone when adding to this his strong interest in the world of Shakespeare. Perhaps, we have to assume that one of his statements made in those days, namely "Oh, if I would not write dramas now I would perish",[23] would simply suggest that the energy in him needed all kinds of outlets without caring too much to find a coherence among all of them.

Whatever experts on Goethe may say, these years of social glamour and literary flamboyance included a number of events which appear to us as having been of a decisive character for him. In his final year in Frankfurt, he traveled with some of his "Sturm und Drang" friends to Switzerland where he, among other experiences, met the then well known "Philosophical Farmer".[24] On his way back to Frankfurt, he got so inspired by the Gothic cathedral of Straßburg that he wrote a poem under the title of "Schaffenskraft", i.e. "The Force (Strength, Drive) to Create". This poem is a youthful celebration of man's creative strength as being unbound by externally imposed rules and being able to flourish as Nature herself does.[25] We wonder whether experiences seemingly as far apart from one another as these, namely, the concreteness Goethe came to see in a farmer's thoughtful and cultivating work in Nature and the gigantic and near perfect piece of Gothic architecture that he saw in Straßburg did not together strengthen the longing for greater dimensions and for more concreteness in his own life. He may very well have felt then that a more adequate outlet for his creative forces was not open to him as the young city dweller that he was at that time. This life was threatened to be cemented by marriage into the role of a son-in-law of a banker. Life with a banker's daughter was, however, not for him.[26] Whatever one may speculate here, one should remember that Goethe soon afterwards left such a life of merely verbal brilliance.

In 1774, Goethe had met the then 17 year old Duke Carl August von Sachsen-Weimar-Eisenach in Frankfurt. They had an intense discussion of ideas on proper governance which Justus Möser, a civil servant and political theorist, had published under the title of "Patriotic Phantasies".[27] This conversation led the Duke, when he traveled through Frankfurt again a year later, to invite the famous writer and poet who, after all was also a lawyer, to take a major role in the administration of his dukedom. Goethe accepted this invitation and arrived at the court in Weimar early in November 1775.

Goethe delved soon into a large number of administrative responsibilities ranging from mining, road construction, forestry, agricultural improvements, military budgeting and banking to education and theater management.[28] Without concrete experience in most of these tasks, he gained a great deal of knowledge in all of them rapidly. Proving his drive to learn and his increasing abilities, it is little wonder that he soon became a member of the Duke's Privy Council. Practically all of his learning in the areas under his responsibility took place by taking a "hands-on" approach in the literal sense of the word. In the course of these new learning experiences, he developed what he often called "anschauende Begriffe", i.e. "concepts arising in perception".[29] While this translation may sound awkward,[30] it does, to some extent, convey what became of increasing importance for him, namely that the perceiving act is the departure point and the guide in concept formation.

While we may be allowed to further unfold the meaning of this crucial concept later,[31] we have to emphasize yet another important, in this case social aspect in Goethe's praxis of understanding, particularly where it concerned technical and scientific matters. Accumulating knowledge in these areas always included, besides his keen and manifold observations, discussions between him and the people practically engaged in these activities, be they workers in mining, in forestry, road construction, agriculture, etc. Had we the space here to describe the nearly uncountable occasions on which he proceeded this way, we could convey how much Goethe's coming to understand scientific and technical matters was for him a task to be done together with others. Although we have occasion later to deal with his reasoning about proceeding this way[32] we would like to say here that, already in the context of his early "apprenticeship" in Weimar, his scientific studies almost always arose out of the concreteness of social interaction and out of that what we called a "hands-on" approach.

These were the foundations for elevating his understanding to a more general theoretical level. As Goethe has said more than once, from things and people he could learn, not from books.[33] It did not matter to him whether he had to talk on such occasions with learned people or workers. What mattered to him was the matter at hand and the sensuous alertness of people. Goethe's rather elevated status as a Privy Council (Geheimrat) with a salary that put him into the upper 2% of the income range in the Dukedom[34] did not get into his way of enjoying the experience of having "concepts arise in perception". His down to earth ways, but also his kind of diligence, literally appear before one's eyes, when one, for instance, sees that his studies in mineralogy led him to collect rocks which amounted at the time of his death to the unbelievable number of about 17 800 pieces,[35] a good many of them carried home on his own back.

In order to see Goethe's life in Weimar in its proper dimensions, one should also note that the Dukedom of Sachsen-Weimar-Eisenach had a population of only little over 100 000 individuals[36] of which just 7 500[37] lived in the court city of Weimar. This setting greatly facilitated his close contact to persons and their concrete activities throughout the Dukedom. Goethe could still easily travel to all sites of work, usually by horseback, be they mines, forests, sites of road construction, or the University of Jena, for all of which he had administrative responsibility; or he could simply walk over to the court theater in Weimar which he, the successful playwright, had under his direction as well. He worked on all these matters for many years and with such intensity that, at one point, he complained that it felt as if his whole existence was compressed between his eyes.[38] And yet, he regretted that he could do at best 1/100 of what he wanted to do.[39] His enormous efforts stemmed from his drive to turn the whole Dukedom into the flourishing community which he and the young Duke dreamed about since their first talk in Frankfurt. Under no circumstance, however, did Goethe regret having left Frankfurt where, as he has once said in a letter to his mother, he would have died of not having enough to do.[40] Let us bear in mind that this is being said by a person who could have enjoyed a life of leisure and even of glamour, either in Frankfurt or at the court in Weimar; so many others of his status did not more than just that. But – and this is an important point – this was not his sense of a life of fulfillment, or better, of an elevation that in its occurrence included his whole life. Without such elevation coming about, his life would not have been one of pleasure in his sense of the word. Pleasure meant for him obedience to his drives and senses. It is in this connection that we would like to repeat that Goethe should not be seen as an extraordinary human being that is out of reach for the rest of us mortals. Nature pulses in all of us, the issue only is to sense that and to live out of that sense. If there is anything extraordinary about Goethe, then it is the circumstance that he knew what he wanted and that he remained obedient to his inner Nature. He did not ignore, turn off or misdirect his inner energy like so many of us seem to do today, merely believing or persuading themselves that it is "fun" to do what they happen to do, or worse yet, are made to do.

One should not think, though, that Goethe's practical work had stopped him from writing. He worked in these years, inter alia, on the dramas "Egmont", "Torquato Tasso" and "Iphigenie" (prose version finished 1779),[41] started the novel "Wilhelm Meister's Apprenticeship" and wrote a vast number of poems, although not all of this got published at the time.[42] In view of all this, it becomes plausible that in a short and fervent prayer, he asked the gods for help in all these endeavors.[43] It may leave one in total disbelief that Goethe could still find the time to maintain an intense love relationship to a married court-lady by the name of Charlotte von Stein.[44] This relationship started within a few weeks after Goethe's arrival in Weimar and lasted well over 10 years. It contributed greatly to the cultivation and maturation of the "Sturm und Drang" poet that Goethe still was when he, just being 26 years of age, came to Weimar. His cultivation took shape through numerous conversations with her and an uncountable number of letters and notes exchanged on a daily basis. In his diaries, references to her are expressed not always by her name but very often by using the astronomic symbol of the sun for her.[45] The meaning of this symbol for Goethe can be better appreciated when one bears in mind, how much the sun as the sustaining source of all life meant to him.[46] Nevertheless and perhaps surprising, his relationship to Charlotte remained platonic.[47] Perhaps it is precisely for this reason that this relationship served the sublimation of Goethe's personality so much.

Regardless that his life set such an example of richness in so many ways, it did not stir many others to live to their full potential. Already in the first years after his arrival in Weimar, he had moments of strong disappointments in people around him including the young Duke on whom he had placed so much hope.[48] Goethe did not get very far with introducing reforms into the life of the Dukedom. He did not, for instance, even succeed in convincing the Duke of the damaging effects that his big hunting parties, a traditional yet, for Goethe, outdated custom of the Nobility, had on the fields and meadows of the farmers.[49] However, since not thinking highly of war as a means of politics, he did manage to reduce the Duke's little army by about 50%, making Goethe the perhaps only minister of war in history – nowadays euphemistically called ministers of defense – who reduced a country's armament costs.[50] But much more was not to be expected from the Duke and others in relation to the goal of building a truly new and flourishing society. This was what he had once thought would be possible in a small political unit as the Dukedom of Weimar. The new human being that Goethe had hoped for and with whom he himself had hoped to grow could hardly be found. There was next to nobody with whom he could share his sense for such values as diligence, clarity, sobriety, alertness, etc. Their re-evaluation as expressions of freedom was not shared.

This disappointment contributed to his long standing distrust in the possibility of changing society in a radical way, a belief that was quite widespread in Europe at that time and which soon led to the French Revolution. His negative reaction to this Revolution when it occurred needs to be understood in terms of his view that a non-hierarchical structure of society is impossible.[51] Instead, he expected leaders - at his time the nobility - to be exemplary for everybody through their deeds and to act out of care for the whole of society. To be clear, these expectations were not understood by Goethe as moral obligations, but as outpourings of a leader's true Nature. This finds a very clear expression in his poem "Ilmenau" (1783) written in celebration of the re-opening of an ore mine at a place with that name in the dukedom. His views on politics have, on several occasions, led him to severely reprimand the behavior of the Nobility. Throughout his life,[52] Goethe, long before Marx, had expressed his concern and anger about the exploitation of that sector of the population that represented for him the primary producers of everyone's livelihood. Among other pieces that could be cited in this connection, the fable "Reineke Fuchs" testifies to his views on late absolutism.[53] In this connection, one would have to wonder what he would have said, had he come to know the capitalist exploitation as it is so different from the feudal form of exploitation. After all, the latter was not yet geared to relentless growth in a completely individuated setting. Democracy, the political structure compatible to the capitalist setting, was not the kind of abstraction for him into which it has now been distorted. It was practiced by him at the moments of concrete interaction with persons of all stations in life. Trying to do justice to matters at hand required, in his view, that through attention, respect and justice be paid to people with whom one worked on these matters. Therefore concrete interaction demands that one has to be one among equals. This is what Goethe tried to do and this is what allowed him to take leadership in so many activities. For him, all those involved in solving concrete tasks had to "serve" the whole both in its social dimension and with respect to the materially concrete conditions at hand. His sense for co-operation among equals-in-difference will become clearer, when we turn later to his studies of colors. At any rate, work had to be a service whatever one did in one's position in life.

Goethe's understanding of leadership as being a service to the whole of society led Goethe to make "Politics against the 'Zeitgeist'", as Krippendorff indicates already in the title of his book on Goethe.[54] While Krippendorff notes that much more research is needed on Goethe as a politician, he makes it nonetheless clear that "service" was among Goethe's re-evaluated concepts. The meaning of it comes to light when one appreciates the following event: After one of his very frequent travels with the Duke on a practical-technical mission, Goethe says with an eye on the workers in a mine that "the lowest class is the closest to God".[55] Bearing in mind that Nature means for Goethe the concrete in which God lives and to which all of us owe our existence, one comes to understand that for Goethe the lowest class, i.e. the one that does the menial tasks, has the closest, namely, a bodily direct contact to Nature and thus to God. Goethe tried to serve that class by working with its members. Yet, with ideas like this, he found little response in Weimar.

This makes it plausible that the first ten years there were a time of growing disappointments for him. Goethe was often on the verge of withdrawing from public responsibilities. This has, at times, been misinterpreted, probably out of the intent to ideologize Goethe's image. His need for withdrawal, as it grew over the years, had emerged quite early after coming to Weimar. In our understanding, it arose out of the need for self-preservation against getting swallowed up by the aberrations that he saw coming up in politics, i.e., in the form of nationalism, in the di-lapse between science and art, and in the contradiction between mistreating Nature as a mere resource and glorifying her romantically. Furthermore, these aberrations tie in directly with his disappointment about hardly being able to find anybody with whom he could feel akin in his urge for a life as a new human being. It was a very happy circumstance for Goethe that the Duke at least understood the needs of his friend, although he himself failed to live up to many of Goethe's expectations. And yet, the Duke granted him the possibility to withdraw increasingly into his own studies and writings. This, however, was not done without the Duke's own political reasons: it was mainly Goethe who made Weimar internationally known.

Around 1780, Goethe allowed his curiosity, or if the reader prefers, his spontaneity to reach out increasingly into areas of Nature which he had neglected for a few years. Anatomy, for instance, had triggered his interest anew and so he investigated, in a comparative manner, the skeletal structure of the jaws of mammals. These investigations were related to an ongoing international debate on the evolution of mammals. In these studies, Goethe discovered that the "os intermaxillare" was also present in a residual form in humans, a matter that had been doubted at the time, not only by biblical dogmatics.[56] These findings and his further study of animal and human skulls reinforced his notion of the evolutionary connection among all aspects of life.[57] It is that dynamic connection among the parts of Nature which he termed from then on with increasing frequency "metamorphosis". With this notion, Goethe came to sense anew that every specific item in Nature is only "a shading of a great harmony".[58] While the notion of metamorphosis found, however gradually so, some acceptance in the sciences, Goethe remarked a few years before his death that it was at that time that he anticipated that he had to go his way alone in the pursuit of scientific studies.[59] Meanwhile, his insight into the metamorphoses of Nature brought his mind back to other studies he had done before on Linnaeus and Spinoza. Spinoza's notion of "Deus sive Natura" - meaning the unity of God revealing itself in each part of Nature - took on ever greater sensuously felt certainty for him.[60] This way, the "analogia entis" (Susanne von Klettenberg) was reformulated and contributed to the development of his "methodologically" important concept of "manifolding". This shall be explained later.[61]

In these years, Goethe also wrote his famous and often quoted poem "Das Göttliche", "The Divine".[62] This poem is of significance not only because it tells us that Goethe sees the human being as a part of the totality of Nature but also because it emphasizes the implications of man's elevated position in her. Here, he poetically expresses what we have remarked more than once so far, namely, that this elevated position, i.e., the Otherness of man to Nature implies man's reflexive awareness that each member of our species has a commonality with all of Nature and, thus, with each fellow human being. In his later writings, this awareness characterizes the human being as the crowning of Nature's unfolding. Acting in keeping with that awareness leads to what Goethe understood by truth and, inseparable from it, to freedom as it contains beauty and goodness within it.[63] As we demonstrated above, the absence of a practiced acknowledgement of man's place in Nature becomes, by way of contrast, clear as being fundamental to the late capitalist confusion about truth versus correctness, and freedom versus liberty.

It is quite plausible to us that a Goethe who sensed the universe the way he did had little interest in studying Kant's "Critique of Pure Reason", although it had a great impact on learned people when it was first published in 1781. Yet he studied this work, at least in part, quite carefully around 1790/91. It is important to note this, not only because it took place well before the start of his friendship with Schiller who is so often credited with having acquainted him with Kant, but also because these later studies of Kant coincide with his first intense investigations into light and colors.[64] But even in those later years, Kant's philosophy remained peripheral to his interests and his studies of Nature. Goethe needed not to be told that knowing the world around us is, in Kantian terms, a synthesis of our subjective categories with the world of objects. This went without saying for Goethe, since for him the synthesis between man and Nature, between subject and object, was more than a mere epistemological one; it was a sensuously grounded total experience of outer Nature in one's own inner Nature. This is one of the reasons[65] why Goethe, later in his life, could say that he "had no organ for philosophy in its specific sense".[66] Philosophy was for him too narrow for an understanding of our faculties to know Nature.[67] In his fairy tale "Die schöne Melusine", which saw its final draft in 1812 (but has been told by him since his childhood days), he ridicules the philosophers for creating ideals with which they only punish normal human beings in their natural abilities to make sense of life around them.[68]

During the first ten to eleven years at the court in Weimar, Goethe not only grew increasingly despaired about the circumstance that he could not find fully like-minded people around him, but was also uneasy about his own inability to fully understand the common bond among all his diverse activities. To simply accept, as he once did, that his artistic and scientific pursuits were pouring out of the same fountain, was not good enough for him anymore. He had to know how they concretely hung together. His inability to understand how he himself and his activities fitted into his otherwise deeply felt sense of the totality of all manifestations of life troubled him so intensely that death wishes were not absent from his mind.[69] Together with his sense of loneliness, it was also this discontent that was the driving force behind his sudden departure from Weimar's court and society to Italy in the early days of September 1786. This departure looked very much like a flight; he himself has said that "he stole away" from there.[70] While the idea of leaving had been on his mind for a few years, it was only the Duke to whom he had hinted about a temporary absence. Others, like even Charlotte von Stein, the adored lady of his heart, were completely surprised by his sudden disappearance. Few if anybody had noticed that Goethe had to sort out his own existence more fully yet.

We think that one could certainly say that Goethe hungrily reached out into everything that came his way in Italy. He mentioned in his diaries, in his later book "The Italian Journey" and in countless letters how much he was impressed not only by such things like architecture, sculptures, paintings, operas, landscapes and the customs of people, but also by the quality of the air, the vegetation, the light and the colors in Italy.[71] Associating himself mainly with artists in Rome, he nonetheless traveled extensively all over that country. On one of his journeys, while continuing his life long studies of plants, he came to see in full perceptive clarity what it is that makes a plant a plant and thus allows one to recognize any plant as such. At the same time, Goethe also recognized the way by which he had arrived at this insight. He made it clear to himself how he had allowed his careful and detailed visual perception to take the lead in forming concepts of what he saw. In this way, he arrived at the "anschauende Begriff" of the "Urpflanze", i.e., at the concept of the "original or archetypal plant" as one that had "arisen in perception". This was not accomplished in just one observation, but in a manifold variety of careful visual studies, captured in many drawings and then elevated to the synthetic concept of the "original plant". Under this concept constructed by a mind that willingly obeys the sense impressions, any plant is subsumed; or, putting it the other way around, the "original plant" manifests itself in any particular plant there is. It is in connection with this discovery that he stated later in his account on "The Italian Journey", what is also so significant for his way of understanding all other aspects of Nature, namely, that everything around us, in this case every plant, is "the sensuous form of the supra-sensuous".[72] The concept "supra-sensuous" can easily be misunderstood. For example: While the concept of the "original plant" is as such "supra-sensuous" for Goethe, it exists nowhere else than in every plant as it is viewed by the thoughtful human subject. The significance of this sensuously grounded way of arriving at highly generalized and abstracted concepts of objects can not be overvalued for an understanding of Goethe's praxis of science. It is from here that one can come to understand that even the most abstract ideas appear for Goethe always and only in a sensuous form. A "supra-sensuous" without sensuous manifestation does not exist for him. While this will hopefully become clearer yet in our later commentary on Goethe's essay "The Experiment as Mediator of Object and Subject", we should be prepared to see that this way of thinking separates Goethe fundamentally from his Kantian friend Friedrich Schiller, let alone from Kant himself and modern science. This difference remains irreconcilable, as we shall see.

While Goethe gained some recognition as a botanist with his essay "Die Metamorphose der Pflanzen", i.e. "The Metamorphosis of the Plants" (1790) (where he publicizes his concept of the "original or archetypal plant"),[73] his attempt at discovering the equivalent to the "Urpflanze" in the animal kingdom was never followed up by him, regardless of an enormous number of sceletal studies carried out in what he increasingly called his "way of seeing". But he remained convinced that the concept of the "Urtier", the "archetypal animal" could be arrived at.[74] He oftentimes expressed from then on how comfortably he felt with his way of studying things.[75] This, however, must not be misunderstood as if Goethe was from then on merely "applying" the one and only method uniformly to all there is. Among other reasons intrinsic in his method and to be discussed later,[76] the idea of proceeding uniformly in all kinds of scientific research was out of the question for Goethe, especially because he was aware of the hierarchy in the various manifestations of Nature. Goethe urged everyone to keep "crystallization (the mineral world), vegetation and the animal organization" distinct from one another while still seeing their relatedness as well.[77] It is in this sense, for instance, that he strongly objected against attempts, made at the time, which tried to see "crystallization" in the life of plants.[78] In other words, Goethe knew that different ways of being require different ways of study, although all studies have to be based in sensuous perceptions. We leave it up to the reader to compare this view with what is happening in this regard in today's sciences. It is all too obvious how poorly, for instance, the integration of mechanical, chemical, biological and mental aspects is understood in disciplines dealing with human beings.

Besides his studies of natural and artistic phenomena in Italy, he completed his dramas "Egmont" and "Iphigenie" there and continued his work on "Tasso", a drama he finished later.[79] In addition, he also captured the impressions of his approximately two years stay in Italy in about 850 drawings.[80] Consciously appropriating every moment of his living participation in the world around him, he felt a tremendous boost to his sense for the wholeness of Nature in him and around him.[81] As hoped for, he regained the purity of his senses and could "take interest again in the world"; his eyes had become "shiny, pure and bright" so that he could perceive of things again speedily, as he had disposed of "the wrinkles that … had been pressed on [his] mind".[82] And yet, he felt a lack of clarity in his understanding of the unity of all life forms around him and in him. He grew particularly restless about his inability to see the concrete connection between science and art, the two areas so central to his life.

Charged up, nonetheless, by his Italian experiences, Goethe returned to Weimar in the summer of 1788, eagerly longing to let others, at least a few of his friends and his co-workers, participate in what he had seen, deeply enjoyed and learned.[83] Needless to say, Goethe did not simply deliver methodological or theoretical speeches about the growth he had experienced in his artistic and scientific views. Instead, he tried to teach others by letting them participate in his ways of dealing with matters, as they, at least in part, arose out of daily practical tasks. Yet, Goethe's words and deeds now puzzled people around him even more than before. The responses he got were deeply disappointing for him. Much of this disappointment may have expressed itself poetically, though not biographically, in his "Torquato Tasso" (completed in 1789) in which he deals with a poet living at a princely court. Goethe soon started again to seek distance, now an even greater one, to those unable to share his sense of being and doing. Of course, Goethe kept his position as Privy Council, particularly because a connection to praxis was too important a life line for him. In fact, he retained public office until the end of his life.[84] While being regularly consulted by the Duke and others in government, he nonetheless reduced, over the years, his attendance at the cabinet meetings more and more. The Duke kept on supporting him generously. So he retained his extraordinarily high salary and other privileges.

In July 1788, a few weeks after his return to Weimar, Goethe, then almost 39 years of age, was approached, probably during a walk in a park, by the 23 year old Christiane Vulpius who at the time was working in a "factory" somewhere in the city.[85] She presented to him a request for help from her brother who was a young writer himself struggling to find his ways financially and otherwise. We think it is quite telling for how Goethe must have been known in Weimar that a young, uneducated working girl could dare to approach this very famous poet and top ranking politician so freely. We should, however, note that there had been previous contacts between her brother and Goethe. Given the unevenness in social, cultural and educational terms between him and Christiane, and given that it was so incomprehensible to most people - though not to Goethe's mother - we think that it is very important for an understanding of Goethe's way of being to at least characterize what tied him in love to this young woman. After all, this relation became a life long commitment and lasted until Christiane's death in 1816.

Christiane Vulpius and Johann Wolfgang von Goethe seem to have begun living together immediately after they first met, obviously without even considering to get married. Knowing the elite of Weimar, Goethe kept the relationship at first a secret. When it came to light, it was immediately met with the greatest resentment particularly by the ladies in and around the court. Charlotte von Stein was deeply hurt. Nobody would have paid attention to this relationship, had it just been an affair. For Goethe, however, it was much more. It was definitely never a question for him to either stick to Christiane (who in the meanwhile had become pregnant), or to regain the favor of Weimar's upper crust. Sticking to "his girl", as he often referred to her affectionately,[86] must have come from the bottom of his heart; it was his freedom, but while retaining it he was punished for it.

When it became clear that Goethe intended to live with Christiane in the stately mansion on the Frauenplan street, in close vicinity to the Ducal Palace, he had to leave this mansion which Duke August had provided him with in 1782. Goethe moved with Christiane into a small house initially built for forestry workers outside the city center. While this move gained Goethe privacy and made it easier for him to protect Christiane against the offensive behavior of Weimar's "society", it should not be hidden, though, that the Duke had his own plans with the mansion at the Frauenplan (which after all was still the Duke's possession). He wanted to use it as accommodation for a visitor from England whose daughter had become an object of the Duke's attention.[87] Goethe was hurt by how he was being treated, given that his sheer presence in Weimar, not to mention his continued work in the government, meant so much to the Dukedom. But he would not let Christiane go, and this was certainly not for some bourgeois moralistic notion of obligation; he loved her.

But this situation changed when, in 1792, Goethe after further important services to the Dukedom was given back the mansion at the Frauenplan by the Duke,[88] who after all had become the godfather of Goethe's son August. Christiane came to be in charge of a sizable household consisting of quite a few helpers including Goethe's personal secretaries. This household was also the gathering place for many visitors not only from inside the Dukedom but from far beyond. Having to admit here that Christiane only in later years participated in the social gatherings at the Frauenplan, one has also to note that Goethe himself was usually quite distanced to most of his visitors. Christiane took care of a large garden in which she kept a few animals like a pig and poultry for their own consumption.[89] She also maintained quite a correspondence,[90] mostly with Johann Wolfgang as he was quite often away, be it on official business with the Duke all over Germany, Switzerland, Venice, etc., or while spending time, e.g. often in Jena, the university town, to pursue his studies and writings. She also exchanged letters with Goethe's mother in Frankfurt with whom she shared, besides great personal warmth, an atrocious aptitude for grammar and spelling.[91] Christiane took quite some interest in Goethe's activities. It may be just one expression of the down to earth ways of her interest that Goethe took reason to summarize for her, the competent gardener, his "Metamorphosis of the Plants"; he put it into a poem.[92] Not caring anymore about the court ladies, Christiane often went to dances, sometimes without her lover[93] (which made Goethe somewhat jealous) and attended operas more frequently than Goethe did. It is said that she saw Mozart's "Magic Flute" at least 30 times in her life[94] which undoubtedly speaks for her musical taste. This is not to deny that Goethe too was very fond of Mozart's (and Bach's) music. The kind of relationship that Goethe and Christiane had is also well reflected, we think, by one of Christiane's letters to him. In it, she says that

> it is so nice with your kind of work· what you have done once, remains eternally. But it is totally different with what we poor devils do. I had the garden well in shape, planted and everything In one night, the snails have eaten up almost everything, my nice cucumbers are all gone and I have to start all over again.[95]

Christiane's ways of relating to the world around her made her the kind of person with whom Goethe could live.

As indicated above, Goethe usually kept quite some distance to most of his many official and intellectual contacts. The highly acclaimed poet, writer and playwright Friedrich Schiller, for instance, had to make a number of attempts to enter into a close relationship to him. He had always admired Goethe as a genius, yet at the same time thought of him as "cold", "too sensuous" and "too ego-centered".[96] Even after he had entered into a friendship with Goethe, the latter retained a certain distance to him. Bürger, another writer of that time, gave a quite similar description of Goethe[97] and so did Jean Paul, yet another literary figure in Germany.[98] Others, however, to whom Goethe felt akin in his way of thinking and being, were readily accepted by Goethe and had good reason to feel very close to him. In this connection, we can only mention Carl Friedrich Zelter here, a master bricklayer by trade and later professor and president of the Academy of Music in Berlin. Their friendship started in 1795 and lasted until Goethe's death. Zelter was among the relatively few individuals with whom Goethe was on a first name basis (this was not the case with Schiller even during their times of close co-operation between 1795 and 1805). Goethe never ceased to be impressed by Zelter's qualities of "solid capability" and "innerworldly vitality".[99] In the 1820s, Zelter discovered Felix Mendelssohn-Bartholdy and became his teacher. When

Goethe met Mendelssohn through Zelter, he took quite a liking to the then 12 year old boy. The straightforward musicality of this child prodigy seems to have captured Goethe's attention very soon, whereas Beethoven remained a distant figure in his life, even after they had met.[100]

During the early years with Christiane, Goethe's life long interest in colors turned, almost by accident, into a serious scientific endeavor never to be abandoned by him. Its beginnings were triggered by an observation which was based, initially, on Goethe's total misunderstanding of Newton's "Opticks". All Goethe had done so far to familiarize himself with Newton's studies, consisted in having read a little bit about it in some encyclopedia. It was part of his two misunderstandings that Goethe believed Newton's "Opticks" had exclusively focused on the emergence of colors. Goethe was unaware that Newton's interest was the field of optics proper and, thus, the avoidance of colors in telescopes. There they could easily emerge as a nuisance because the prisms with which these instruments were equipped easily "created" colors. Their avoidance required of Newton an understanding of the conditions of their emergence. Goethe's misunderstandings of Newton's work led him to focus on the emergence of colors realizing only later what Newton's actual project had been. And yet a major disagreement between Newton and Goethe on the form of scientific research came to Goethe's awareness through his own studies on light and colors.

While it is certainly important to note that Goethe's "Farbenlehre", i.e. his "Teachings on Colors"[101] turned out to become Goethe's most voluminous work among all of his writings, it is not primarily its size (5 volumes) which makes it the center of our explorations of Goethe's concept of science. We draw upon it, because the "Farbenlehre" provides the main background for an essay which on its part is the best and most economic way to bring Goethe's kind of science and its method into the open. While we think that presenting and commenting on this essay will further clarify Goethe's scientific method, we would also like to recommend to our readers that they take a close look at Goethe's writings on colors and even make at least a few of the experiments described there themselves. As mentioned above, we, on our part, have benefited very much from having done so.

An understanding of Goethe's "Teachings on Colors" would not only be incomplete without telling the story of how Goethe came to undo his misunderstanding of Newton's work, but the widespread misinterpretation of Goethe's initial misunderstanding provides us additionally with a good opportunity to become aware of a fundamental aspect of Goethe's scientific method.

In January of 1790, incidentally only a few weeks after his son August was born in the small house to which Goethe and Christiane had been relegated, a messenger showed up at his door to retrieve a prism that Goethe had borrowed for intended studies on Newton's "Opticks". Goethe had failed to return the prism despite a number of requests by the owner. Goethe hurrying downstairs to hand over the prism to the messenger quickly cast an eye through the prism onto a plain white wall expecting to see the wall covered with bright colors. It seems obvious that Goethe had not worked with that prism before. Misinformed about all details of Newton's sophisticated experiments, Goethe was quite surprised not to notice any color before his eyes.[102] Only at points where the light hit upon spots on the wall, his eyes perceived colors through the prism. When he turned the prism towards the window, no colors appeared in the sky. He saw colors, however, near the wooden partitions between the glass panes. Upon recognizing this, he said "… loudly that the Newtonian Teachings are false".[103] This was the so-called aperçu which the literature on Goethe's studies on colors, and also Goethe himself, often refer to. He quite clearly admits how important this event was for him.[104] It is seen as demarcating the point at which Newton's and Goethe's views on science begin to differ radically. But, how exactly this aperçu demarcates their difference is often left vague in the literature so that a central aspect of Goethe's science is lost. In fact, we have not come across any publication which, dealing with this brief incident, treats it adequately, i.e., by appreciating it on Goethe's own terms. The most blatant case of misinterpreting Goethe's conclusion drawn from his "experiment" that we have come across is the one presented by Albrecht Schöne in his book "Goethes Farbentheologie", i.e. "Goethe's Theology of Colors". Its brief inspection is, in our view, informative.

Schöne speaks of the moment when Goethe calls Newton's teachings false as Goethe's second religious conversion; the first one having occurred when he as a young man suffered from tuberculosis.[105] We consider this a dubious interpretation, although we agree that this event remained indeed the cornerstone in Goethe's objection against Newton. Schöne argues that this aperçu was a suddenly taken theoretical position which, once taken, Goethe stuck to faithfully in complete intransigence. We reject this interpretation, although widely shared in the literature, because it runs counter to Goethe's whole emphasis on sensuousness as the primary mediation of the world to the human being. Goethe, at that moment of looking through the prism did not leap to a mental (or spiritual) position adopting it as a frame of reference for further research. What happened, instead, was that his eyes saw colors and this made him instantaneously notice that colors emerge when something happens to the flow of light. This was Goethe's insight arising from his eyesight.[106] This aperçu is completely in line with his sense for the common bond of all Nature as he had felt it since his childhood sacrifice to Nature and as he had come to understand it much better during his two years of illness as a young man. Over many years, in Weimar and in Italy, he had grown in awareness for the significance of that common bond for the process of coming to know.

Certainly, also according to Newton, colors would not have shown on the wall in Goethe's mere glance through a prism. Furthermore, Newton could have easily explained with his theory that colors reveal themselves at the spots on the wall and at the window frames. That Newton could have done that was even unknown to Goethe at that time. Instead, it was something different that was decisive for Goethe, namely, the emergence of colors where something happened to light and where that affected his own natural, i.e. sensuous perception. For Goethe, it was not a theory, but his own senses that told him what the phenomena out there were for him as a part of Nature himself. This, the primacy of one's own Nature in understanding is the point where Newton's and Goethe's views begin to differ. To the extent that Goethe had always derived his knowledge from his sensuous experience and had always thought, as we shall see,[107] that everybody proceeded that way, it came "naturally" to him to deliver his judgement on Newton the way he did: the ... "Newtonian Teachings are false". Later and after having made many experiments, Goethe comes to know that colors are "deeds and sufferings of light",[108] in the sense that colors emerge for the eye where the flow of light, its "deed", is kept from flowing straight, i.e. where it "suffers". His understanding of light and colors found its more refined formulation later in what he called the "Urphänomen" i.e., the "ground phenomenon", of colors.[109]

It was between this first, certainly misguided "experiment" with the prism on that January day of 1790 and the spring of 1792 that Goethe's whole understanding of science and with it his self-awareness took yet a decisive leap forward in its bodily grounded certainty. Goethe had, initially, been quite disturbed by his differences with Newton, the famous physicist. Growing skeptical about the encyclopedias and their indeed mistaken presentation of Newton's studies, Goethe started to read Newton's "Opticks" itself and, as was typical for him as a person who normally "could not learn from books", delved immediately into numerous experiments. Goethe then combined these experiments with old and new observations of his own and published his findings as "Beiträge zur Optik", i.e. "Contributions to Optics". He also wrote, at that time, an essay outlining his method in scientific research later published under the title "The Experiment as Mediator between Object and Subject". It is this essay on which we wish to comment later on in quite some detail, since it is so important for an understanding of Goethe's views. Given, however, that what is presented there took on significance already at this point in Goethe's evolvement is so important, we find it justifiable to briefly sketch its results now.

His reading of Newton and his own experiments led Goethe soon to recognize with greater precision what constitutes the fundamental difference between his "way of seeing" and Newton's. Newton's theory of light and colors is grounded in his "experimentum crucis", i.e. his crucial experiment[110] by which he proves his hypothesis that pure white light is a composite of all rays that stir color sensations in our eye. Goethe remained definitely mistaken about his doubt regarding the correctness of Newton's experimental result, although he had, like most people at his time, noted that white color does not materialize when one mixes paints of all colors. The result of such mixing is, in fact, at best a dirty gray. Also for this reason, Goethe concluded that Newton's theory on colors was wrong. However, as is known now, if one mixes all of previously separated light rays again (instead of all colors), the white light is obtained indeed. While this clearly establishes that Newton's theory on light is correct, it is still not true for Goethe, and that is to say it is not true for us as parts of Nature. What Newton deals with is not the Nature of light as it is mediated primarily to our own Nature, but as it is mediated to a sense - the sense of vision - that has given up the status of being our primary connection to Nature and has accepted to be influenced by a mentally constructed theory on light. Proceeding in line with this, one ignores that our senses have, as our inner Nature, logical primacy in all conceptualizations since they are the condition for our mind to have concepts at all. This brings us yet closer to the crux of the matter disputed by Goethe with regard to Newton's views on color.

Goethe most vehemently opposes Newton's crucial experiment, because it is grounded in a mentally pre-conceived hypothesis which originates in one absolutized sensuous perception. In order to avoid such absolutization, Goethe wishes to arrive at concepts of light and colors by making as many observations and experiments as possible in order to arrive at an insight into how these aspects of Nature out there relate to our own Nature. For Goethe, Newton comes to perceive what Newton's mind thinks should be perceived and takes that *con*ception of color as being *the per*ception of color. This takes the primacy away from man's inner Nature and gives it to man's mind. In other words, in Newton's experiment light is forced to appear to man as what man *thinks* the Nature of light is. Therefore, by using a play on words, Goethe calls Newton's crucial experiment[111] i.e., his "experimentum crucis" a "crucifixion of light by experiment". Studying Nature by giving the lead in it to man's mental abilities is from then on for Goethe ever more consciously understood as inflicting torture on Nature. Its result is not just a distorted understanding and consequently a distorted treatment of Nature (leading to today's "environmental problems"), but also the erroneous belief that Nature would then still remain friendly with us. Harming Nature, and thus ourselves as part of her, is a fundamental, in fact the original sin in Goethe's view.[112]

Just a year after his first glance through the prism, Goethe had assembled enough material from his own experiments that he could publish, in 1791, Part I of the "Contributions to Optics". Part II appeared in the spring of 1792.[113] The latter is indicatively accompanied by the above mentioned card board plates and a description of how the reader could build a prism. To his disappointment, Goethe got such little response that he terminated publishing his findings and thoughts. But this does not at all mean that he terminated his experiments and observations on the relationship between light and color. In fact, he intensified them and ended up doing an "uncountable number" of them until his death in 1832.[114] Goethe took the lack of interest in his approach to colors (and beyond) as an indication that Newton's kind of studying Nature had conquered the world of science and its methodology. The primarily mind guided construction of theories and the formulation of hypotheses had firmly taken over the whole field of scientific research. For Goethe, this way of proceeding further estranged the natural sciences and its practitioners from Nature.

In the spring of 1792, Goethe, as mentioned above, summarized his views on how to study Nature, and colors in particular, in the essay "The Experiment as Mediator of Object and Subject". We should note, though, that he had initially given the title "Kautelen des Beobachters" to it. This title simply meant something like "Cautions to be taken by the Observer" (of Nature).[115] There, he presented, on the one hand, his arguments for giving one's own inner Nature the lead in the study of Nature, and he describes, on the other hand, how one goes about doing this and what role the mind has to play in studies carried out this way. It is quite typical for Goethe's non-philosophical stance, particularly at that time, that he gave this essay such a clearly non-philosophical title. He only changed it decades later, possibly as late as 1823,[116] when he finally published it. From then on this essay is known under the title "The Experiment as

Mediator of Object and Subject". This wording is, of course, quite reminiscent of Kantian-Hegelian philosophy, although not too much of it can be found in the text of the essay itself.

In the next years, activities other than scientific studies seemed to have kept Goethe busy. But this was only in appearance. His scientific studies and reflections on them went on unabatedly. We would like to narrate these other activities, since they, too, are important for an understanding of Goethe, the human being.

In mid-1792, when Goethe, together with Christiane and their son, had just moved back into the mansion at the Frauenplan, he was asked by the Duke to join him into a war of the allied forces of Austria and Prussia against the French Revolutionary Army. His writings on that war, among them his "Campaign in France" and "The Siege of Mainz" written decades later,[117] allow one to see how negative Goethe was about this whole event and how much his views contradict the ideologically distorted image created about him since around the turn from the 18th to the 19th century. Reading these pieces makes it clear that he was in as little a nationalist then as he was later after the collapse of the "Holy Roman Empire of the German Nation"; neither was he a "Fürstenknecht", i.e. a "Serf of the Noblemen", as some so-called democrats called him. Instead, he was as critical of the nobility in general as he was, since quite some time, of his Duke. He saw in the nobility mainly exploiters and oppressors of their own people.[118] Thus, Goethe went quite reluctantly into that "Campaign". He felt that it mainly furnished the nobility with an opportunity to enjoy their destructive pleasure of waging a war which they, like other power holders on so many occasions before and after, portrayed as being carried out for reasons of justice. The claim was that Austria and Prussia wanted to come to the help of those who had been dispossessed in the French Revolution. Those dispossessed were, in most cases, the French "cousins" of the Prussian and Austrian nobility. Certainly, Goethe was an opponent of the French Revolution, but he took that stance because he saw in it the emergence of a form of economics and politics which worried him. He has expressed his views on this in a few minor ad-hoc plays like "Die Natürliche Tochter" or "Die Aufgeregten" and also in his much weightier "Hermann und Dorothea".[119]

His objections against the French Revolution could easily be seen as contradicting his objections against the nobility's exploitation of the productive masses, be it in France, in the little Dukedom of Weimar or wherever.[120] But this is not so. It was more than understandable to him that the masses in France had finally risen. In this sense, he blamed the Revolution solely on the French Nobility and the French King. Their exploitation of the masses had grown hand in hand with the distance to their own people. At the same time, Goethe was indeed skeptical about mass participation in government mainly because the masses, in his view, had been kept incapacitated to govern themselves.[121] One could say that, for him, their treatment had precluded their potential elevation. There was simply no humane interaction among people, e.g., among the educated ones and the uneducated and potentially knowledgeable. Thus, it is all the more plausible, how sarcastically Goethe treated, in his "Campaign", the awkwardness and inefficiency of the communication between the ranks of the (noble) officers and the soldiers in the army of the allied forces. The officers and soldiers of the French Revolutionary Army, of whom he had not seen too many, were instead described in almost glowing terms.[122]

When this brief war had finally ended in a settlement between the army leaders, which basically allowed the allied forces to withdraw from France without having accomplished much, this whole episode was all the more seen by Goethe as a waste of time and people. During this war, Goethe on his part spent as much time as possible on studies and observations both of people and natural phenomena, particularly on matters related to light and colors.[123] Distancing himself increasingly this way from a political reality that grew in his view ever more fictitious, did of course little for his acceptability among those rejecting or applauding the French Revolution Later, after the Napoleonic Wars and the War of Liberation (1813 – 15), his anti-nationalism and his advocacy of small political units made him hardly any friends either. His politics had become even more a "Politics against the Zeitgeist" (Krippendorff).

During the next few years up to about 1795, Goethe traveled a lot on behalf of the Duke, e.g. to Venice and to Silesia, wrote on the evolution of the animal skull, attempted to write a comic opera[124] of which no trace is left, published the "Roman Elegies", previously titled the "Erotica Romana",[125] while all along expressing the desire to devote himself to science only,[126] as we know, a promise Goethe, the poet, could not keep.

The growing lack of response, also to his poetic work - not even an edition of his Collected Works sold well[127] - did not diminish the intensity of his pursuits. While officially retaining his position on the Privy Council, Goethe could keep an open eye for social, political and, of course, cultural matters even though they disturbed him quite a bit. He at last read Kant's three "Critiques",[128] starting in 1790/1 with the "Critique of Pure Reason" (published in 1781), then his "Critique of Practical Reason" (published in 1786) and finally his "Critique of Judgment" (published in 1790, better translated as "Critique of the Faculty of Judgement"). Kant's concept of "epigenesis", as presented in his last

Critique, caught Goethe's particular attention.[129] Kant had subsumed, under this term, his views on the evolution of Nature including the one of the human mind. These studies certainly did not turn Goethe into a philosopher, and yet he began to anticipate that these considerations on the "epigenesis" of all aspects of Nature would speak to his concerns about the growth and unity not only in Nature out there but also in us and in our pursuits of science and art. In other words, even prior to meeting Schiller (and Schelling) who certainly reinforced his philosophical contemplations later, the concept of epigenesis had already caught Goethe's attention. This had expressed itself in his brief essay "Anschauende Urteilskraft", i.e. "The Perceptively guided Faculty of Judgement", which, published 1820, was written in obvious opposition to Kant.[130] In it, his earlier idea of "anschauende Begriffe", i.e., "concepts arising in perception"[131] found considerable refinement.

It was in 1794 that Friedrich Schiller, himself a highly acclaimed poet, playwright and writer, finally came to have a first extended conversation with Goethe. The two had briefly met before on occasion, but Goethe had kept his distance from Schiller. Goethe did so, because Schiller, the younger of the two, was still too much involved in "Sturm und Drang" forms of expressions and remained, on the whole, too philosophically oriented for Goethe. Schiller, on his part, admired Goethe's genius, but disliked the sensuousness in Goethe that seemed not even to need philosophy.[132] In this connection, a remark about Goethe's friends made by Schiller after visiting Goethe's house during Goethe's stay in Italy may be quite telling: "There (in Goethe's house) one sooner collects herbs or does mineralogy than gets lost in hollow demonstrations".[133]

One evening, after Goethe and Schiller had attended a session of the "Naturforschende Gesellschaft" ("Society for the Study of Nature") in Jena, Schiller is supposed to have commented on that session - according to Goethe's much later recollection[134] - that "such a piecemeal way of treating Nature" could hardly have pleased the audience. Goethe remembers to have responded by saying that it is certainly possible to consider "Nature as not sundered and singularized, but to present her as working and living, as reaching from the whole into the parts". Schiller asked for an elaboration on this. Goethe responded by summarizing his "Metamorphosis of the Plants" and by explaining his concept of the "Urpflanze", i.e., the "original plant". Schiller's reaction to it was that he shook his head and exclaimed: "This (the "original plant") is not an experience, it is an idea".[135] Goethe was, to some considerable extent, irked by this. Old resentments against Schiller came up in him again. Yet Goethe swallowed his anger and, with obvious irony replied: "It suits me very much that I have ideas without knowing it and can even see them with my eyes".[136] Goethe then notes[137] that this comment by Schiller had marked, with utmost precision, the point at which their views parted from one another: what was an idea for Schiller was, for Goethe, an experience "of the higher kind", i.e., one that was elevated through numerous sensuously guided observations, but still expressed itself, even had its existence only in concrete phenomena.[138] Although neither one convinced the other of his argument, this conversation initiated over 10 years of close co-operation and friendship between the two men.

It seems to be a matter of agreement among Goethe scholars that Schiller, through this conversation and what followed it, had rescued Goethe from his growing isolation.[139] However, there are also other voices, e.g. Friedrich Gundolf's,[140] which suggest that, besides supportive influences, this co-operation also had dimensions which slowed down Goethe's coming to find his true self and his true message.

At any rate, the differences between Goethe and Schiller persisted and perhaps because of this circumstance their association helped Goethe to sharpen his own way of seeing and studying. He who had developed what he called his "perceptively guided faculty of judgement" was too happy with his "manner of seeing" to ever give it up. This too must not be understood as an indication of Goethe's stubbornness, but of his sense of commonality - since then also understood by Goethe as his transubstantiating appropriation (in German: Anverwandlung) of Kant's "identity" - between his self and the objects out there. It was nonetheless Schiller[141] who, with an eye on Goethe's scientific studies, convinced him to keep apart and yet relate better to one another light and colors and also subject and object. While this led Goethe already in early sketches of his "Teachings on Colors" to treat the physiological (i.e. exclusively subjective) colors first (where they remained in the published version), it had also given Goethe reason to send his 1792 essay "The Experiment", then still titled "Kautelen", to Schiller in early 1798. A few weeks later, Goethe wrote, as a reaction to Schiller's response, another sketch of his "Teachings on Colors" that reveals his now more philosophical concerns even in its title: "Phenomena [of colors] ordered according to Kantian Categories".[142] While this in itself makes it obvious that Goethe's appreciation of Kant had grown under Schiller's influence, it must not be overlooked either that Goethe tried to keep the poet Schiller away from too much exposure to Kant. For Goethe, as he beautifully expressed it in "Das Märchen" ("The Fairy Tale") of 1795, the poet is like the sun himself and can do more than simply reflect, as Schiller did in Goethe's view, the enlightening "rays of another reason", in this case those of Kant.[143]

It is not our intent to diminish the role that Schiller had begun to play in Goethe's life, but we have to underline that Goethe found his way to a full understanding of the commonality-in-difference between science and art more in counter-distinction to his Kantian friend Schiller than in agreement with him. We also have to note that quite a few of their joint projects in these years failed miserably and that their co-operation did not keep Goethe, in 1797, from seriously considering to leave Weimar and move to Rome again.[144] We will now take a closer look at these developments starting with Goethe's reflections on the connections and distinctions between science and art.

In this pursuit, Goethe does not seem to have found enough of a philosophical companion in Schiller. This makes it plausible that Goethe in his capacity of overseeing educational matters in the Dukedom called, in 1798, Friedrich Schelling, the increasingly renowned philosopher of Nature, to teach at the University of Jena. In frequent discussions with him, Goethe attained a yet clearer understanding of the originally Kantean idea of "epigenesis" to which Schelling had given a new interpretation.[145] It was through this innovative appropriation of Kant's ideas that Goethe finally, around 1800, came to fully see the commonality, though in diversity, between Nature and art which as such implied the commonality between the study of Nature, i.e. science, and the creation of art.[146]

Goethe now sees that the human mind is capable of creating thought which, in the case of science, elevates the sheer being of Nature to a known reality and, in the case of art, creates phenomena, i.e. products of art, which add to the world of being what would not be there either without the human mind or, as he called it later, without "Der Bildungstrieb", i.e. "The Drive to Give Shape (or Form)".[147] This "Drive" is in a way close to what we call awkwardly today "the energetic flow of matter". Also the modern way of thinking knows that it triggers our neurons to elevate sense notions to symbolizations. But today, we know this in a way that does not acknowledge the primacy and commonality of Nature in real praxis, including scientific praxis, as Goethe did. This primacy manifests itself, our modern denial notwithstanding, in the circumstance that Nature is the "conditio sine qua non" for all and each moments of being, thinking and doing. This is what we, according to Goethe, need to acknowledge willfully. To be sure, not doing so would not abolish the primacy of Nature, but it would distort Nature in her flow through our mind. For Goethe, this flow of energy, or in his words, this "Drive", is the dynamic commonality of all Nature which finds its distinct culmination in man's thinking ability, as it is at work, both in the creative processes of the sciences and in those of the arts. In his view, these culminations have the potential of being positive syntheses between man and Nature. Such positive elevations of Nature have conditions which rest with the highest form of the driving force in Nature, namely the human mind. This must not be understood as if Goethe would advocate man as the master or ruler over Nature. This precisely would preclude a friendship between Nature and man. Instead, it means that man was given his position in Nature as her care-taker.[148]

In our attempt to identify these conditions, the focus of our essay is more on the conditions that turn, according to Goethe, science into positive syntheses with Nature than on the ones that do that in art. This is a consequence of the departure point of our concerns, namely the circumstance that it is the instrumentalism of modern science which contributes so much to today's problems. The role art plays under these conditions requires, of course, a whole treatise by itself. With our focus on science, we obviously proceed somewhat one-sidedly as far as Goethe is concerned. He kept these two areas of human self-expression much more closely related to one another than we can. We hope to compensate for that onesidedeness to the extent that Goethe does in the essay "The Experiment".

In his understanding, it is in science that we appropriate Nature mentally as our home so that we then do not merely happen to live in her, but also understand and willingly accept her as the locality of our freedom. In art, we celebrate our sensuousness as the fertile ground for the elevation of Nature to beauty. Knowing Nature and celebrating Nature are since then known by Goethe as manifestations that Nature can find in us, provided - and this is the main condition - we retain our sense for her primacy in these two spheres, act out of that sense consciously and retain that conscious knowledge willingly, i.e. not by intellectually guided decision, but out of that very drive that unites all of Nature. This is how Nature truly comes to know herself in what she culminates in, namely, the human being. The truth of our knowledge of Nature comes to rest on the freedom to acknowledge the Nature that we ourselves are. When Goethe got this clear in his mind, he knew the point at which we establish, time and again, our identity with Nature in us, around us and in our fellow human beings. At that point, truth and beauty reveal that they are only different expressions of the freedom which enacts itself in the cultivation of Nature in us and by us. Having finally and in all clarity gained this insight, Goethe knew how science and art turn into that elevation of man and Nature without which, as he also knew, our species and Nature will be doomed.

It may be appropriate, at this point, to briefly return to our simplified statement made above, where we say that correctness is truth minus values. Goethe arrives at a concept of truth since he senses, in the process of finding it, his "drive" towards it as an enjoyable, i.e., as a sensuously satisfying moment potentially common to all human beings. He knows of the possibility that this drive can become distorted in egofocal purposiveness,[149] but he also knows, as we ourselves have argued,[150] that this distortion cannot have the status of primacy. This means that our understanding, if truthful, is grounded in a shared, though not uniform sensuousness that turns into a multiplicity of socially shareable desires, i.e. values. As we said above, obedience, diligence, clarity, alertness, etc., were Goethe's undoubtedly shareable values. These are then obviously not ideologically prescribed values that need the backing of grand theories or philosophies as in the past, but they are values that are, in a historically new way, constitutive to the discovery of truth. For us today, they may very well appear as "re-evaluations of values", but while practicing them we may notice that they bless us more with a sense grounded knowledge of our kinship to Nature than with such a philosophical concept of them. They allow us to know the circumstance and the way in which we share, in our elevation of natural phenomena to knowledge, what Kant once called, in a much more lifeless way than Goethe, our "identity" with the objects around us.

It obviously has taken Goethe a major effort to arrive at this clarity. Appreciating Goethe's effort, one wonders how the rest of us mortals can share in his insight? Is Goethe's accomplishment so extraordinary that not everybody can live it at an equivalent level of clarity? Above,[151] we have quite explicitly denied Goethe the status of being extraordinary and we still do so now. Goethe remains exemplary in our view, although his insight is not normal in a statistical sense. We have to agree that the vast majority of people seems unprepared to share his insights. We have even to note that not many people around him were prepared for his insights in his life time. His isolation clearly indicates this.

If we have to accept that nothing is more natural than to obey the Nature of which our own individuality is a part any ways, then we have also to point out that we, who live right here in the purgatory of late capitalism, have even more reason to sense this commonality than Goethe did.[152] All we have to do in this "materialist" age is to openly acknowledge what we all tacitly know. Nothing would bring us closer to Goethe's own insight. This acknowledgement was probably more difficult prior to the arrival of capitalism (e.g. at Goethe's time), when people still had some reason, at least in large parts of the European continent, to believe in philosophies, traditions and other mind guided insights. For us today, acknowledging the role of Nature should be easier. All it takes is the will to know it, i.e. to ac-know-ledge it. But therein lies the problem. It is precisely this will, the drive of our inner Nature, which, though it cannot be aborted, is constantly distorted, in so many people today. Strong mechanisms about which we have spoken above are in place to make sure that they stay in place. Television, tourism, the internet, etc., in short, today's life threatening consumerism, do wonders in this regard. These mechanisms increase the pain of the Midas syndrome. The number of people longing for ever more distortions seems to grow still, but so does the small number and yet determinate strength of those who try to live out of the acknowledgement of the common bond of Nature. Increasing use of alternatives in medicine, education, food production and consumption, for instance, attest to that.[153]

Goethe, as we saw, had always lived out of his sensuous Nature. It took him a while until he also gained conceptual clarity on this. He then came to see also how little it takes and how normal it is that Nature be acknowledged as the undistorted source of all cultural productivity. While this clarity had finally and fully materialized in his numerous discussions with Friedrich Schelling between 1798 and 1800, he also sensed that the greater the clarity he had, the less it was shareable with people that got more and more absorbed in a "Zeitgeist" which drifted into a different direction. This was yet another lesson he had to learn in the final years of an apprenticeship, so to speak, that had begun before he went to Italy and had come to an end during the time of his discussions with Schelling.

This is not to deny that Schiller has also been a source of stimulation for Goethe in more ways than one. Like Goethe, Schiller had also dealt with the concepts of "beauty" and "freedom" in his philosophic-aesthetic writings, e.g. in his "Über Anmut und Würde" ("On Grace and Dignity") and "Über naïve und sentimentalische Dichtung" ("On Naïve and Sentimental Poetry").[154] These considerations struck a cord in Goethe, although his concept of the elevation of Nature as her transcendence-and-containment into the symbolic realm goes beyond Schiller's concept of a balance between the untamed wildness of Nature and the purity of reason. And yet, the way Schiller understood that balance and how he saw it as leading to "beauty" and "freedom" made Schiller's concerns important for Goethe as well. Goethe found enough commonality with Schiller to enter with him, time and again, the arena of public literary debate. They jointly developed an aesthetic, artistic and educational program which they tried to propagate in a number of publications, inviting others to make their contributions on these issues. Their publications mainly projected the idea that the tradition of Ancient Classical Greece should be renewed, since in that distant epoch, as the two of them thought, the balance between Nature and mind had been attained in a culture saturated with beauty. This balance had to be regained, under obviously new and different conditions.

With this program, Schiller and Goethe found themselves increasingly, if not from the beginning, in opposition to the romanticist/nationalist movements in Germany and beyond. These movements, not Schiller and Goethe, gathered momentum at that time. While the Holy Roman Empire of the German Nation, an entity at best surviving in name, approached its collapse under the impact of Napoleon's imperialism, young German intellectuals who had never thought much about the Holy Roman Empire while it was still around, unexpectedly developed a longing for a national identity. Later, after Napoleon's defeat, this wave of sentiment even grew stronger. This new national identity, however, was more grounded in a mystified historical past than in concrete reality. Similar nationalistic developments had emerged, as we saw above, in other European countries and had their own merely ideological foundations there. In Germany, unlike a few other countries, there was some grounding in an ethnic unity, but little of a concrete economic basis for it. The longing for a national identity found its expression in Germany not only in the artistic creations of the romanticists as they focused on the past, but also in those that derived their topics from Nature and landscape. In these creations, Nature was hardly understood as what it was in real life praxis, namely, the source of our life. Instead, she was understood as a mystified place be it of peace or raw ferocity. This mystification was for Schiller and Goethe a strange, if only partial flight from reality; it indicated to them a problematic state of mind.[155] It was for this reason that Goethe and Schiller joined forces in their literary attempts to avoid the di-lapse of the artistically sublime and the materially concrete in Germany. For a short period of time, perhaps ending already in 1800, Goethe, like Schiller, believed that they could influence the public on these and related issues via the written word.

Through journals and publications like "Die Horen" and "Der Musenalmanach", Goethe and Schiller came to be seen as trying to take on the role of a spiritual institution. However, their statements, particularly their epigrams ("Die Xenien"), were all too often either too sarcastic or too overbearing for an audience that had begun to turn its interest away from classical antiquity. The response Schiller and Goethe got was very limited so that the publication of "Die Horen" was terminated after having

been in the market for roughly a year.[156] Goethe's later attempt (1798 -
1800) to invite submissions of dramatic and other works by way of the
journal "Propyläen" remained also unsuccessful.[157] The standards for
selection of the material submitted were sensed by the public as highly
artificial, even academic. In our view, it is quite telling that Goethe, during
this time period, gave the advice to the young poet Friedrich Hölderlin, the
writer of large scale odes: "...to take more narrowly defined
subjects...".[158] Concreteness not grand ideas should be the subject of
poetry. This suggestion shows how much Goethe missed the genius of this
young man. Goethe's attempt to keep Hölderlin in a down to earth state of
mind may very well have been carried by Goethe's own good reasons, but
we wonder whether this kind of a suggestion was not a sign of a
dogmatism to which Goethe had fallen prey, however temporarily so.

There are clear indications that Goethe, even during these years of
their closest co-operation, kept his distance to Schiller. We think it is a
telling sign for the distance and difference between the two, when we
come to see how little Schiller had come to know about Goethe's ways of
working, writing and thinking. As an example of this, one could use the
case of Goethe's work on his drama "Hermann und Dorothea". First of
all, Schiller did not know, for quite some time, that Goethe was writing
that drama (finished 1797); secondly, he was later astounded to hear that it
had been on Goethe's mind for several years already; and finally the point
that, when Goethe wrote it down, the text kept pouring out of him at a rate
of about 150 hexameters per day, a rate of writing about which Schiller
who had to struggle for every line, could not even dream.[159] Schiller did
not know that Goethe always took a long time to allow matters to mature
in him, before he gave them their final form on paper. Schiller also
remained unaware of the circumstance that Goethe had cultivated that way
of proceeding almost throughout his life. Goethe has characterized this,
for instance, in his "Confession of the Author" (of the "Teaching on
Colors") written 1810[160] Although this piece was written a few years after
Schiller's death, it still strikes us as if a real closeness to Goethe, had it
existed, would have made this way of working more obvious to Schiller.
As mentioned above, Goethe even considered to settle with Christiane and
his son August in Rome. Schiller certainly came to notice the perpetuated
differences in their ways of thinking, but it is not certain that he ever came
to understand Goethe's ways very well. Schiller tried to conceptualize
these differences by portraying himself as a speculative mind, while he
thought of Goethe as having an intuitive one.[161] Such a characterization,
however, ignores how hard Goethe worked on everything he laid his
hands on, how much he demanded of himself not only in terms of

precision but also in terms of endurance, regardless of whether it was in his studies of Nature or in his unfolding of literary characters and events. We would even doubt that "intuition" captures Goethe's understanding of "perceptively guided judgement", of "exact sensuous fantasy."[162] and of diligence, to name but a few aspects that characterize Goethe's mode of working. His "Faust" and his "Teachings on Colors" are only two of the many examples of pieces on which he had worked for decades with utmost precision of thought and observation. Only when matters were fully thought through, did he give them their final form. Goethe himself has written about the requirement of a "power of imagination (in German: Einbildungskraft) which never goes into vagueness, but ... is always on the grounds of ... the real ...".[163] If one wishes to speak of Goethe's "intuition" at all, one has undoubtedly to understand it in the context of such a statement. We do not doubt that the friendship between Schiller and Goethe was a working alliance that was of great significance for both of them. However, in this relationship it was perhaps Goethe who deviated the most from his true self, i.e. from the "daemon" in him, as the Goethe scholar Friedrich Gundolf put it, when he evaluated this period in Goethe's life.[164]

From their inability to influence political and cultural events in Germany, Goethe seems to have learned that verbal or other attempts at making converts were doomed. When Ekkehard Krippendorff remarks that Goethe never tried to teach others "by raising his pointing finger",[165] then we have to say that this is not true for the period between 1795 and 1800, although it was true for most of Goethe's life. Certainly, Goethe kept resenting the romanticists as subjectivistic, even as characterless and formless,[166] but he fought them with decreasing effort. He also accepted the modernization rung in by the French Revolution albeit with growing misgivings about its consequences. He related these negative consequences to man's distorted sense for his own Nature. Originating there, he saw man as having increasing difficulties to relate properly to Nature "out there" and in fellow human beings. The confluence of these difficulties in late capitalism would probably have frightened him even more. The romanticists were increasingly seen by him as making a merely wishful attempt at providing a contrast to the upcoming modernity, but not as representing a solution to its problems. And yet, to the best of our knowledge, Goethe did not notice that they did fulfill the function of ideological usefulness for the evolving capitalism. Not seeing this may be related to the circumstance that his understanding of that mode of production remained rather limited. Sarcasm and polemics, though, largely disappeared from his agenda with the striking exception of his

"Polemics" against Newton, to which he dedicated one of the five volumes of his "Teachings on Colors".[167] It was only very late in his life that he distanced himself, to some extent, from his often intemperate attack on this famous opponent of his. He advised his secretary Eckermann not to insist on the inclusion of the "Polemics" into his post-humus Collected Works, should the publisher hesitate.[168]

It is quite important for an understanding of Goethe's way of thinking to take to heart that he retained his longest lasting hostility against an opponent with whom he disagreed on matters of science, i.e., of man's relation to Nature. He was more easily willing to relax vis-à-vis disliked social movements like the nationalists and the romanticists. This is not to say that he ever approved of these, but that he saw man's social relations as secondary ones, which could be corrected out of proper relations to Nature. Once man's relations to Nature are in order, then his social relations will be in order too.[169] In 1808, i.e., during his editorial work on his "Teachings on Colors", he wrote that

> ..since almost a century, the Humaniora [i e. the Humanities] have no impact anymore on the human soul [in German· das Gemüt] and it is a happy circumstance that Nature has interfered, has drawn [man's] interest on her and points us, on her part, the way to humaneness [in German   zur Humanität] [170]

In other words, while the modernization of social thought and social relations may have, in our modern view, contributed to an understanding of Nature that distorts Nature and, thus, endangers man himself, it is for Goethe Nature and a knowledge adequate to her that will be the primary agent in setting man's mind and life straight again.[171] After Marx, it was particularly the political Left that had focused on social relations as the culprit for modernity's misery; now, after science in its contemporary version has become visibly an exploitative force as well, we have ample and additional reason to listen to Goethe's views on science as a part of our relations to Nature.

In the years between 1800 and 1806/7, Goethe returned to what was more central to his own interests. At the same time, re-centering himself meant keeping an even more determined distance to processes and events of which he could not approve and which were beyond his ability of changing. We are inclined to subsume under these processes and events besides cultural, scientific and political ones, also the occurrences of death among people more or less close to him. Strange as it may seem, given that death is part of life and its flow, we have to note that Goethe has always tried to avoid all manifestations of death. And yet, we should still try to understand his reason for doing so. In this connection, it needs to be noted that for him everything that was not contributing to one's elevation were phenomena one should stay away from. The occurrence of death or all that what had deadly influences, belonged into that category.[172] Therefore, he fled those phenomena, usually seeking refuge in particularly intense work. He has always viewed work as a fruit bearing activity and, thus, as a counter force to the deadly. This explains his way of reacting to the deaths of Schiller (1805), of Herder (1807) - to whom he had been close since 1770 - and, most remarkably, of Christiane in 1816. Yet, such self-preserving withdrawal was also mixed with fears regarding his own mortality and the real threats to his own personal life. The displacement of his fear through activity and of his own awareness of this circumstance may very well be another feature that Goethe shares with modern man. He had perhaps mastered it only in his own last few hours. Then he seems to have accepted that aspect in the flow of Nature as well.[173]

In connection with Goethe's reaction to the unavoidable, as it is often inherent in life threatening events, we have also to mention a few of his experiences as they came along with Napoleon's conquest and occupation of Weimar (and the rest of Germany and Austria) in 1806. The conquest of Weimar and the looting and partial burning of the city by combat soldiers of what was, incidentally, the first truly modern and nationalistic people's army in history[174] threatened Goethe's house, work and life directly and shook him up profoundly. He had come to see what a modern machinery, in this case a war machinery, could do and how it, literally and figuratively, was turning everything upside down. Goethe feared the burning and looting of his mansion, because all his notes, his sketches, drafts, abstracts, letters, books, in short, so much of his whole life was in there. He also became aware that his ownership of the mansion was quite tenuous. It rested on a mere agreement with the Duke who, on top of it all, was away from Weimar at the time, fleeing eastwards with the Prussian army. Goethe probably saw, at that moment, a whole traditional social order collapse and go up in flames. Miraculously, Christiane kept the looting and burning French soldiers at bay and, thus, saved Goethe, if not his life, then certainly his refugium. Goethe now saw that his life had to be based on new foundations. It could no longer be rested on a benevolent, personalized and patrimonial aristocratic order. Therefore, he got legal title to his mansion as fast as he could, and he also put his relation to Christiane swiftly on a legal foundation by marrying her.[175] Although his ownership of the mansion at the Frauenplan had been put in writing in 1801, Goethe now felt that even a personal piece of paper trying to formalize what was essentially still a feudal relation between a lord and one of his men was not good enough anymore. He saw that social relations had changed radically. His possession of the mansion at the Frauenplan had to become a sheerly economic one. Therefore, this possession had to be commuted through legal title into private ownership; this is what he did.[176]

Looking at the war time year of 1806 alone, we get a feel for the degree to which destructive and yet uncontrollable circumstances led him to seek elevation in intense work. He invested almost all his attention into the following tasks: he finished "Faust I", a revision of his "Urfaust" of decades ago,[177] he started to write up his "Teachings on Colors"[178] which he completed in 1810 and he delved into meteorology, an old area of observation for him which he now begun to systematize.[179] At the same time, he brings to bear ideas on his "Teachings on Colors" that he had expressed in his famous "Winckelmann Essay" of 1805 in which, reminiscing on ideas of Schiller's aesthetic writings, he celebrated "the beauty of the human being as the last product of a Nature which permanently seeks to elevate herself".[180] While war rages around him, Goethe celebrates the sun-like Nature of the human eye as an organ that the evolution of Nature, i.e. her "epigenesis", had selected for the creation of colors in it. From here, so he enjoys to contemplate, our species can reach an even higher level in evolution: we can work towards a scientific understanding of the phenomenon of colors and, needless to say, towards a use of them as elements in our artistic expressions.

In 1808, during Weimar's occupation by the French Army, Goethe met Napoleon; he did so on the young Emperor's initiative.[181] The contents of their conversation has not been reported in detail, but this much is clear: there was a great deal of mutual respect between the two men; they saw each other as equals though living in different domains. In these domains, each sensed the other as being driven by a higher force. Goethe spoke, with unconcealed admiration, of the daemonic qualities of Napoleon. He saw in him the force that promised to unite all of Europe, to create a new forward looking social and legal order (abolition of serfdom!) and yet granted and guaranteed the survival of such small political units as the Dukedom of Weimar.[182] It was only there that politics could be protected against anonymity and abstraction. Goethe accepted the "Medal of the Legion of Honor" from Napoleon, but he turned down an invitation to live in Paris. After Napoleon's defeat, Goethe came to acknowledge that peace and unity could not be grounded in military victories.[183] This insight of Goethe's makes us wonder today whether global peace and unity-in-diversity could be grounded in "globalization" and instrumentalism, two of the monstrous strategies of the modern human mind.

Goethe also resigned himself to the insight that the publication of his "Teachings on Colors" would only have minimal public impact, and yet until his death considered it as one of his greatest accomplishments: "...what would it have mattered had I written a few more dramas instead...", he rhetorically asked in his old age.[184] Goethe had to publish this piece as a demonstration of what truth and true science are all about. After having stated this publicly, he could (while still keenly observing what he considered to be the growing madness in politics, science and art around him) devote his time though largely in loneliness to his own further growth as a human being.[185] Goethe's life remained very active after his struggle for self-clarification. His still enormous literary output notwithstanding, our characterization of Goethe's further pursuits and insights can now be limited to relatively few major examples.

Accordingly, we may just mention that Goethe worked in this decade on quite a number of projects of which some saw completion later. He began, for instance, to write his biography "Poetry and Truth"[186] in which he describes his life as having grown in a process that was a metamorphosis itself. He also started to write "Wilhelm Meister's Wanderings" at that time[187] and published his "Elective Affinities".[188] Just mentioning all this, we also have to add Wilhelm von Humboldt's observation of 1812[189] that Goethe hardly ever left the triangle of Weimar, Jena and Karlsbad anymore, with a few important exceptions (one brought him to the Rhineland and others to Marienbad which, however, is close to Karlsbad). He certainly still received many people and he also engaged in much correspondence, but he only allowed very few individuals to be close to him.[190] This certainly helped him to maintain the usual intensity and variety of his work. Besides his official duties, he kept on studying meteorology, mineralogy, geology, needless to say, colors and, of course, he kept on writing poetry, dramas and novels. Among the most remarkable examples for not only new and yet close relationships, but also new fields of interest, we wish to briefly inspect those related to Sulpiz Boisseree, Marianne von Willemer and Felix Mendelssohn-Bartholdy.

In 1811, Goethe, at that time 62 years of age, came to meet and respect the then 28 years old Boisseree.[191] This young man succeeded in drawing Goethe's attention to medieval art, even though this art had become a topic monopolized by the much disliked romanticists. Up to that point, Goethe never had much interest in the Middle Ages, his earlier poem on Straßburg's Gothic cathedral notwithstanding. To be sure, Goethe's new interest in the art of that era did not mean that he abandoned his deeply rooted preference for classical antiquity. But Boisseree's measured and self-confident appreciation for the art of the times prior to 1500 stirred Goethe's interest in it as well. It led him to read, for instance, an early medieval epic like "Die Nibelungen". This tragic piece impressed him deeply, but did so more because of its heathen mode of thinking than because of the foreshadowing of Christianity that the romanticists saw in it.[192] At any rate, Goethe's initially hesitant relationship to Sulpiz Boisseree tells us that Goethe's resentment with much of what happened at that time did not make him blind to new experiences provided they struck his senses. While Goethe certainly misjudged some of his contemporaries,[193] young Boisseree gained Goethe's respect and kept close contact with him for the rest of Goethe's life.

Around 1815, when Goethe was once again confronted with death (Christiane died in 1816 after suffering painfully for several months) and with political turmoil (the Liberation Wars led to the defeat of Napoleon and fired the madness of romanticist nationalism), Goethe fled into the creation of perhaps his greatest cycle of poems, namely, "Der west-östliche Divan" i.e., the "West-East Divan". This flight was again a withdrawal from events over which he had no control and which did not contribute to an elevation of life.[194]

During this time of turmoil, Goethe turned to the works of the Persian poet Mohammed Schemsed-din Hafiz which stimulated his "West-East Divan".[195] Goethe's interest in Hafiz came out of his hope to retain his own balance by studying and poetically re-creating Hafiz's poetry as an example of a balanced way of being. Goethe had to make an enormous yet tremendously driven effort to understand a world that was initially alien to him. This is reflected in the circumstance that about half of the several hundred pages of the complete edition of the "Divan" are devoted to the study of the 14th century Persian context in which Hafiz lived. Needless to say that Goethe took it for granted that readers of the poems would put in their own effort to understand that background. As he grew more acquainted with this alien world, Goethe became increasingly fascinated by this poetry (which he read in translation).[196] What impressed Goethe the most was that the whole oeuvre of this Islamic figure is one glorious symphony on the theme of elevating the sensuous to the sublime. This theme is played out in 1001 variations. Goethe recreated Hafiz's sensuous mysticism in his adaptations of many of Hafiz's poems to the German language and, of course, wrote hundreds of poems in the same vein himself. While the themes of elevation and sublimation already make Goethe's interest in Hafiz's work plausible, a third reason, to be taken note of, lies with the circumstance that Goethe did not just read and write about this theme, he practiced and experienced in a whole new way the sublimation of his own sensuousness. In these years, Goethe carried on an emotionally intense relationship with a young former actress by the name of Marianne von Willemer. The love poems he exchanged with her re-created the sensuous mysticism of Hafiz and, thus, allowed them to sublimate their own love into poetry. All these poems, Goethe's and Marianne's, and the ones adapted directly from Hafiz, were included in the collection of the "West-East Divan".[197]

During this politically as well as personally difficult time period, Goethe also wrote that portion of "Poetry and Truth" which deals with the "Italian Journey", one of the most pleasant memories of his life. Being absorbed in these writings, also in his travel to the Rhineland, where Marianne and her husband lived (where he also saw young Boisseree's collection on medieval art), he kept not only the dreadful public events away from his mind, but also the painful dying of his beloved Christiane. While avoiding the sight of her death bed most of the time, he wrote one of his most beautiful, playful and yet serious love poems for her.[198] This poem was not at all a compensation for petty guilt over neglect; instead, it was a celebration of a human being and a lover that he adored and yet could not help. It was, incidentally, also out of the same sense of helplessness that he had not attended the funerals of his friends Schiller and Herder. Charlotte von Stein who knew him so well even ordered that her funeral procession should not pass by Goethe's house, the shortest route to the burial site.[199]

Yet another example for Goethe's selective sociality would be his appreciation of Felix Mendelssohn-Bartholdy, whom he first met in 1821 (as a twelve year old) while still a student of Goethe's friend Zelter. Goethe took an immediate liking to him and his piano playing. Later, in 1830, when Mendelssohn played again for Goethe, their discussions turned into lessons on music for the then 81 year old Goethe, regardless of Mendelssohn playing, inter alii, Beethoven whom Goethe basically rejected as too "grandiose". But this did not threaten the relationship between the octogenarian Goethe and the 20 year old and already celebrated composer.[200] Given Goethe's resentment of Beethoven's music, it may perhaps be plausible that he was not favorably disposed to Beethoven's attempt to write music for his tragedy "Egmont". Also their encounter in Teplitz did not bring them closer to one another.[201] We find it, however, hard to understand that Goethe never reacted to Schubert's attempted correspondence with him, let alone that he ignored the beautiful music that this young genius had written to quite a few of Goethe's poems. We must admit that we have no explanation for that except that

Goethe had become so cautious about people in this time of "Restoration" that finding "Elective Affinities" had become an unlikely proposition for him.[202] Developments in science and technology also made him increasingly concerned in these years.

As a counter-statement against these processes, Goethe published, in the years between 1817 and 1824, two parallel series of scientific writings, one under the title of "Zur Naturwissenschaft überhaupt" ("On Natural Science in General") and the other under the title of "Zur Morphologie" ("On Morphology"). These series mainly served as a means to edit and publish both older and more recent ones of his manuscripts. This seems to suggest that Goethe had not completely given up hope to find an audience for his views on the study of Nature. In the series "Zur Naturwissenschaft überhaupt", he publishes, in 1823, the above mentioned essay "Kautelen des Beobachters" then under the new title of "Das Experiment als Vermittler von Objekt und Subjekt", i.e, "The Experiment as Mediator of Object and Subject". This philosophically sounding title may easily mislead the reader to expect a theoretically "grounded" methodological treatise on science. This, however, is not what Goethe delivers there.[203] While a detailed explication of what he in fact delivers will have to wait until we come to our commentary on this piece, the following may be briefly pointed out: Man's understanding of Nature is, for Goethe, Nature's way of coming to know herself through man and, thus, to arrive at levels of elevation at which she herself changes. Above[204] we noted that known Nature is different from an unknown one. This gives our knowledge an intrinsically dynamic form, regardless of this being acknowledged or not. Since coming to know changes the one who has come to know, the process of coming to know could never be carried out in terms of finite and thus static categories. For this reason alone, Goethe must not be expected to present a fixed methodology, i.e., an operationalization of a mentalistic theory. He knows that nobody has a final say on any matter, as he says in "The Experiment".[205]

In his last years, while finishing such giant pieces as "Wilhelm Meister's Wanderings" and "Faust II" - the latter not too many months before his death - Goethe also came to see, with growing clarity and pain, that all ways of coming to know have their limitations. He came to suffer from the circumstance that our knowledge will always be limited to the specificity of the concretely known. Totality can only be approached through the manifolding of our experiences of phenomena of which each will remain specific. In the very moment of knowing, there will always appear something unknown.[206] In other words, there will always remain a "not yet" (Ernst Bloch) in every arrival at a new insight. Certainly, this awareness had always been with Goethe; it had always formed the polarity to his hopeful concept of elevation but, at least since around 1800, it had also led him to what he called "Entsagung" i.e. to renunciation (to be distinguished from withdrawal as a social act). Now he knew, yet with sadness, that the whole story will never be told and the final word can never be spoken. On our part, we must admit that Goethe's suffering from the "not yet" that we find in all knowing and being, puzzles us to some degree. We tend to think that this "not yet" is an essential aspect of the dynamics of Nature, a Nature which Goethe otherwise so wholeheartedly embraces. It is not clear to us what it is that we are missing here in Goethe's sense of renunciation. At any rate, we do understand that renunciation and elevation have a polar relation to one another in the sense that one cannot be without the other. Accordingly, renunciation did not keep Goethe from still trying to seek elevation in every aspect of his life. In a letter to Wilhelm von Humboldt written just five days before his death (on 22 March 1832), Goethe celebrated his friendship with Humboldt by pointing out that striving for ever more clarity and growth of the mind had always been a commonality between the two of them.[207]

In as little as there can be an identity between the cognizing subject and its object, can there be a "generally" valid system of thought for Goethe, let alone of a "general theory" (or philosophy). The question of how this relates to his praxis and concept of "pluralism" in the sciences will concern us later.[208] For the same reason, having disciples in the traditional sense of the word, could not even be thought of by Goethe. Yet for decades, Goethe had been keen to find likemindedness in other human beings. At times, he found it in even unlikely social constellations. However, the mode of thinking that he saw evolving not only with science, but also with nationalism and romanticism, struck Goethe as a threat to true individuality and freedom. It is well known how much he viewed the future with deep pessimism. This found its most explicit expression in "Faust II", particularly towards its ending where technologically distorted efforts destroy the idyllic life of Philemon and Baucis. In the other great piece of his old age, in his "Wilhelm Meister's Wanderings", he lets a female principal of a cotton processing factory say: "The world of machines (in German: das Maschinenwesen), as it takes over, frightens me, it rolls nearer like a thunderstorm, slowly, slowly, but it has taken aim, it will come and hit".[209] It is the abstraction in modern knowledge, i.e. its loss of a foundation in undistorted sensuousness which Goethe so much resented. And yet, this was seen by him as going to win the day and create a Nature uninhabitable for our so gloriously endowed species.

As often indicated, we do not think that Goethe fully saw how deadly the otherwise clearly anticipated abstractions in the modern mode of thinking would become. We believe he could not see this, since he had only limited experience with capitalism and its inherent legitimation of egofocal strife.[210] On the few occasions where he made reference to the United States of America, as in the poem "Den Vereinigten Staaten", i.e. "To the United States", he praised that country as a land of the future where true individuality (not egofocal individuation), could blossom without the baggage of dead traditions.[211] There, people would be able to relate to one another in complete tolerance. As an example for this, Goethe notes in his "Maximen und Reflexionen", i.e., his "Maxims and Reflections", that 90 different Christian "confessions" (i.e. denominations) existed in New York City. This indicated to him that people did not just preach tolerance, but practiced it as well.[212] He obviously did not think that a society would come into being in which convictions, grounded or not, had become superfluous, and where only egofocal "growth" would matter. He seemingly did not anticipate that next to nothing of what he had hoped for vis-à-vis "Amerika" would come to flourish. What in fact evolved and what is now spreading globally is something we have come to experience as instrumentalism, i.e., the deadly penetration of all life by a mode of thinking in which only egofocal strife and deceptive abstractions matter. It is in view of this that we have to fundamentally rethink Goethe's hope that Nature may grant us salvation. For Goethe, this hope arises out of what he called, very prominently towards the ending of "Faust II", the "eternally-feminine" in Nature.[213] While an attempt at clarifying the meaning of Goethe's view of the "eternally-feminine" would take a study all of its own, we do wish to say that this concept must certainly not be equated with what is propagated nowadays as "feminism". Regarding the idea of the "eternally - feminine", we may be permitted to say at least this much: this idea implies a move away from the hardening of the mind as it carries with it the belief or, worse yet nowadays, the only pretended belief in "hard facts", "solid objectivity" and "valid theories" while having, in reality, an eye on little more than taking away from fellow human beings whatever power can be obtained from them. It is our view that only where life is experienced as being constantly perverted by the Midas syndrome, can the pain of that feeling open our senses for the "not yet" of positive syntheses with Nature. While the social phenomenon of capitalism in its late form has contributed to bringing out our problematic Nature (and thus our problems with Nature), it is the change in our relation to Nature that implies changes in our relations to Nature in ourselves and in the other. Sensing that change in our being as parts of the "analogia entis" has primacy, i.e., is conditional for changing the relations among ourselves. It will not happen the other way around, as so many of us have believed for too long.

Notes

[1] Gundolf, 1918, first sentence; my translation.

[2] Nietzsche, 1955, II, pp. 1 024f; my translation.

[3] Rosa Luxemburg on Goethe in a letter of January 26, 1917 to Luise Kautsky. Quoted according to Krippendorff, 1999, p 7; my translation

[4] See Goethe, in Trunz, 1948ff IX. Regardless of its specifically autobiographical intent, it would still be an interesting undertaking to compare this piece of Goethe's with Gadamer's "Wahrheit und Methode", i e. "Truth and Method", Gadamer, 1976.

[5] Conrady, 1993, II, p. 40.

[6] Conrady, 1993, II, pp 573f.

[7] *von* Goethe since 1782, when he was ennobled by the Emperor of the Holy Roman Empire of the German Nation

[8] See for Goethe's early childhood and learning Conrady, 1992, I, pp. 25 - 46; see also Gundolf, 1918, pp 31ff.

[9] Goethe, 1988, III, pp. 240ff

[10] Mommsen, 1984, pp 107ff.

[11] Conrady, 1992, I, pp. 34f

[12] See Conrady, 1992, I. pp. 38f.

[13] For these years, see Conrady, 1992, I, pp. 49ff; see also Gundolf, 1918, pp. 53ff

[14] Conrady, 1992, I, p. 84

[15] Regarding this time, see Conrady, 1992, I, pp 83ff

[16] See, e.g Goethe, "Dichtung und Wahrheit" ("Poetry and Truth"), Second Part, Book 8; Goethe, in Trunz, 1948ff, IX, pp. 338f.

[17] Conrady, 1992, I, p. 87; see also Schöne 1987 pp 11ff Schöne is among those who have interpreted this result of Goethe's illness as one of the two religious conversions in Goethe's life, the second one being the 'chromatic conversion of 1790'. We hesitate to accept this interpretation, see pp. 155-158

[18] Conrady, 1992, I, pp 136ff; Gundolf, 1918, p. 85

[19] Conrady, 1992, I, pp. 177ff

[20] ibid., pp. 193ff.

[21] ibid., pp. 105ff, 110ff; Gundolf, 1918, pp. 88ff.

[22] Conrady, 1992, I, pp 151ff, 210ff.

[23] ibid., p. 280, our translation.

[24] ibid., pp 266ff.

[25] ibid., p 273.

[26] ibid.; see also Gundolf, 1918, pp 202ff

[27] Conrady, 1992, I, pp 250f

[28] Conrady, 1992, I, pp 340, 415ff.; Fairley, 1947, p 73, Pausch & Pausch, 1996, pp. 176f.

[29] Conrady, 1992, I, pp 368, 377, 417.

[30] We have yet to find an adequate translation for this term. When, e g., Vietor, 1950, p. 63, circumscribes this notion by writing about it as "contemplative thinking" in "a detachment from the sensual world", he misses Goethe's position fundamentally.

[31] See pp 149, 161-162, 211-212, 221-222, 246-247

[32] See pp. 200-201, 233-235, 270-271, 290

[33] Conrady, 1992, I, p. 417

[34] Conrady, 1992, I, p 323, see also Pausch & Pausch, 1996, pp 174ff.

[35] Conrady, 1992, I, p 420

[36] Conrady, 1992, I, p 300

[37] Conrad, 1993, II, p 299.

[38] Conrady, 1992, I, p 347

[39] Conrady, 1992, I, p 349.

[40] See e g. Conrady, 1992, I, p 299

[41] Fairley, 1947, p. 108f.

[42] Conrady, 1992, I , pp 208ff, 299, 504, Fairley, 1947, p 109ff

[43] Conrady, 1992, I, p. 348.

[44] Conrady, 1992, I, pp. 331ff; Fairley, 1947, pp. 102ff

[45] Conrady, 1992, I, p. 347.

[46] See pp. 242-243; in this connection, see also pp. 258, 271-272

[47] This comes clearly to light in a letter sent by Goethe to her after their separation, see Conrady, 1992, I, p 492.

[48] Conrady, I, 1992, pp 347, 349, 357.

[49] Krippendorff, 1999, pp. 74ff.

[50] ibid , p. 82.

[51] See e.g., Conrady, 1992, I, p. 342

[52] For instance, in 1785 and 1805, see Conrady, 1992, I, p 342, 1993, II, p. 41

[53] See, as a very explicit example, Goethe, in Trunz, 1948ff, II, book VIII, verses 109 – 138, pp 369f. A translation of a few of these verses would be "The king (in this fable portrayed as the lion) himself steals as well as anybody can, we know it / What he does not take he leaves to the bears and the wolves/ And believes this to happen with justice There is nobody to be found, no confessor, no chaplain/ Who dares to tell him the truth, so far evil has gone./ They remain silent. Why that? They too benefit from it, even if only a coat could be gained " [verses 109 – 113] Or: " ..For what is gone is gone,/ and what a powerful takes away from you, you had possessed once. Little attention/ Is paid to a complaint which finally tires out./ Our Lord is the lion, and to grab all for himself/ He views as in keeping with his dignity. He usually calls/ Us his people. Indeed even that, so it appears, belongs to him." [verses 117 – 122] And finally·"…wolf and bear sit on the council. ./ They steal and rob, and the king loves them / Everybody sees it and shuts up, hoping to get his turn/ .. if a poor devil, like Reineke Fox, takes a small chicken/ They all

will be after him/ . and condemn him to death loudly and all like with one voice" [verses 126 – 133] My translation

[54] For an elaboration on this, see Krippendorff, 1999, pp 10ff

[55] Quoted according to Conrady, 1992, I, p. 416, our translation

[56] See, for Goethe's studies on this matter, Conrady, 1992, I, pp 423f; Fairley, 1947, pp. 87ff

[57] In 1784, Goethe managed to get an elephant skull which he had hidden in a backroom of his house in order to avoid increasing the puzzlement about him among the people in Weimar; see Conrady, 1992, I, p 424

[58] Quoted according to Conrady, 1992, I, p 423, our translation, see also Fairley, 1947, p. 94.

[59] Goethe, in Trunz, 1948ff, XIII, pp. 48f.

[60] Troll, o.J , pp 15ff.

[61] See pp. 201, 203, 257-258, 286-287, 289, 293.

[62] For a beautiful discussion of it, see Conrady, 1992, I, pp 411ff, 418

[63] See, in this regard, also Conrady, 1993, II, p. 230.

[64] Conrady, 1993, II, p. 230; Schieren, 1998, pp 43ff

[65] The other one relates to his rejection of the philosophical systematization of knowledge, see pp. 199, 203, 265-266, 272, 303

[66] Goethe, in Troll, o.J., p. 285, my translation

[67] Sixel, 1999, passim.

[68] Mommsen, 1984, pp 57, 146

[69] Conrady, 1992, I, pp 428, 435.

[70] Conrady, 1992, I, p. 428.

[71] Regarding Goethe's Italian journey and its implications, see Conrady, 1992, I, mainly pp 431ff, 487ff; see also Fairley, 1947, pp 121ff

[72] Quoted according to a passage in Conrady, 1992, I, pp 517ff; our translation.

[73] See Goethe, in Troll, o J , pp 127ff, 455ff

[74] See Stephenson, 1995, p 5 on this matter.

[75] See e.g. pp. 210, 244, 268 and also 288-289, 300, 305

[76] See pp. 200-201, 287-288.

[77] Conrady, 1992, I, p. 517.

[78] See, in this regard, his essay "Kristallisation und Vegetation", i e. "Crystallization and Vegetation" of 1789, see also Fairly, 1947, pp. 203ff. on this matter.

[79] Conrady, 1992, I, pp. 463, 472.

[80] Conrady, 1992, I, p 449

[81] Fairley, 1947, p. 137

[82] Quoted according to Conrady, 1992, I, pp 442f; our translation.

[83] Fairley, 1947, pp. 92, 156f.

[84] Krippendorf, 1999, p. 187.

[85] Regarding Goethe's relation to Christiane, see Conrady, 1992, I, pp. 489ff and, of course, Damm, 1998, passim

[86] See Conrady, 1992, I, e.g. p 493

[87] Damm, 1998, 132f

[88] Damm, 1998, p. 158

[89] Damm, 1998, pp 129, 279, 281

[90] Of these letters "only" 600 are still preserved, see Conrady, 1992, I, p. 496.

[91] ibid

[92] ibid., p. 519

[93] ibid., p. 496.

[94] Conrady, 1993, II, p 249

[95] Quoted according to Conrady, 1992, I, p 496; our translation

[96] Conrady, 1992, I, pp. 491f; 1993, II, p. 90.

[97] Conrady, 1992, I, pp 498f.

[98] Conrady, 1993, II, p 281.

[99] Conrady, 1993, II, pp 305ff

[100] See p. 175

[101] The title "Theory of Colors" used in Charles Lock Eastlake's otherwise excellent translation – first published 1840 and oftentimes since – is somewhat misleading given today's meaning of "theory" Goethe's own use of the word "theory" will hopefully become clear in chapter 7

[102] Goethe, 1988, III, p 244.

[103] Goethe, 1988, III, p. 246

[104] ibid.

[105] See Schöne, 1987, pp 19f

[106] It was not an "intuition" either as some others say; see e.g pp 229-230

[107] See p. 292.

[108] Goethe, 1988, I, p. 45.

[109] See pp. 246-247, 261, 272, 293.

[110] For a detailed description of this, see p 256

[111] See pp. 257

[112] See p. 258. It is quite surprising that Schöne, in his study "Goethe's Theology of Colors", comes only occasionally close to explicitly stating that a torture of Nature was a serious sin for Goethe; see Schöne 1987, pp 17, 40, 63 ("torture"), 88, 90, 139.

[113] Goethe, 1988, II, pp. 15, 60 Later, Goethe admitted that he should not have titled his "Beiträge zur Optik", i e , his "Contributions to Optics", that way, but had better called it "Beiträge zur Farbenlehre", i e "Contributions to Teachings on Colors"; see Goethe, 1988, II, p. 14.

[114] According to Schöne, 1987, p 22. Goethe did so in his zealous endeavor to prove his point of view to the world. We instead think that Goethe had, possibly as early as 1810 given up on this

[115] Trunz, 1948ff, XIII, p. 563.

[116] See p. 191.

[117] See Krippendorff, 1999, pp 98ff; see also Conrady, 1993, II, pp 63ff

[118] See also our brief reference to "Reineke Fuchs" on p. 145.

[119] See Gundolf, 1919, p. 484, Conrady, 1993, II, pp 67f, 259, 463

[120] See Conrady, 1992, I, p.371 and 1993, II, pp. 26, 38ff; see also Krippendorff, 1999, p. 27 and Mommsen 1984, pp. 159f See here e g pp 142, 144-146

[121] Conrady, 1993, II, p 26

[122] Krippendorff, 1999, p 103

[123] Conrady, 1993, II, p 71

[124] Conrady, 1993, II, p 50f

[125] Conrady, 1992, I, pp 520f

[126] Conrady, 1992, II, p. 107

[127] Conrady, 1993, II, pp. 116f.

[128] See Schieren, 1998, pp 43ff.

[129] Conrady, 1993. II, p. 104.

[130] See Troll, o J., pp. 289f, notes on p 471, see also Trunz, 1948ff, XIII, p 566, our translation.

[131] See p 149

[132] Conrady, 1993, II, pp. 89ff; see also Fairley, 1947, p 93

[133] ibid.

[134] Goethe wrote about this event as a "Glückliches Ereignis", i.e. a "Happy Incident"; see Goethe, in Troll, o J., p. 265ff, notes on p 470, see also Conrady, 1993, II, especially pp 91f.

[135] See Goethe, in Troll, o J., p 267, our translation.

[136] Ibid.

[137] See also Conrady 1993, II, p. 91.

[138] Regarding the notion of "experiences of the higher kind", see Goethe's essay "The Experiment" on our pp. 201-203, and our commentary on them

[139] See Conrady, 1993, II, pp 105f

[140] See p. 169

[141] See Trunz, 1948ff XIII, notes on pp 607, 563

[142] Trunz, 1948ff, XIII, notes on p. 607.

[143] Mommsen, 1984, pp. 213f.

[144] Mommsen, 1984, p. 159.

[145] Regarding the relation between Kant and Schelling, see Schmied-Kowarzik, 1996, pp. 37 – 65

[146] See also Conrady, 1993, II, pp. 287f, 340

[147] This is a term increasingly used by Goethe particularly from 1818 on, see Goethe, in Trunz, 1948ff, XIII, pp 32ff, also notes on pp 567f

[148] See also Krippendorff, 1999, p 167.

[149] See pp. 200, 202, 278ff, 298ff.

[150] ibid.

[151] See p. 136.

[152] See in this regard also Krippendorff, 1999, p 171.

[153] For a few examples, we would just like to point out the following observations. The number of farmers attending organic and bio-dynamic workshops and sales shows has grown by the factor of ten since 1995 in the province of Ontario, as Uli Hack, director of the "Society for Biodynamic Farming and Gardening in Ontario" told me in conversation on 12 Jan 2000. Macleans's, 7 Feb 2000, pp 44ff reports that organic food is a $ 1 billion business in Canada having grown from an acreage of 50,000 hectares in 1985 to that of 404,000 hectares in 1998 This, however, is

still only 6 % of Canada's farmland The number of people seeing practitioners of alternative medicine seems to be growing rapidly on both sides of the Atlantic Reliable quantitative information on this, however, is not available according to Shayne Vipond, see also Vipond, 1999, passim. Regarding European data on this, see McGreogor & Peay, 1996 and Furnhman & Smith, 1988 Furthermore, the number of Waldorf Schools, i.e., schools who teach the arts and the sciences in a way that acknowledges Goethe's way of pursuing these fields, have grown in number and attendance markedly Now there are, for instance, three Waldorf Schools in the Toronto, Ontario area, where there has been only one until ten years ago. Another Waldorf School has been opened quite recently in Barrie, Ontario. This is information obtained from the administrative office of the Waldorf School at Bathurst Street, Toronto, on 20 Jan 2000 In Europe, Waldorf Schools are quite numerous.

[154] The translations of these titles are at best approximations to the complex meaning that is unfolded in these essays; for more see Wiese, 1959, pp. 446–564

[155] Conrady, 1993, II, pp 213, 325

[156] Conrady, 1993, II, pp. 118ff.

[157] Conrady, 1993, II, pp 221f

[158] Quoted according to Conrady, 1993, II, pp. 195f; our translation

[159] Conrady, 1993, II, pp 90, 163; see also Fairley, 1947, p 157

[160] See Goethe, 1988, III, p. 239, see also Conrady, 1993, II, pp 102f and Fairley, 1947, pp. 168ff

[161] Conrady, ibid

[162] See p. 289.

[163] Quoted according to Schmied-Kowarzik, 1986, p 70, my translation.

[164] See Gundolf, 1918, p 484

[165] Krippendorff, 1999, p 99

[166] Conrady, 1993, II, pp. 213, 280, 325.

[167] Goethe, 1988, vol. III.

[168] See Eckermann, 1984, p. 430 (dated 15 May 1831), see also Goethe, 1988, III, p 12

[169] By contrast, Carl-Friedrich von Weizsäcker has once said "No peace with Nature without peace among human kind", quoted in Scheffran & Vogt, 1998, p 7, our translation In our view, this statement is turning matters upside down, as is typical for philosophers

[170] Quoted according to Krippendorff, 1999, p. 171, my translation.

[171] See also pp. 195, 218ff.

[172] See pp. 277-278

[173] Conrady, 1993 II, p 569

[174] This was no longer an army of mercenaries who were usually unwilling to fight and quite prone to deserting their commanders. Instead, it was a people's army which believed to fight for a cause, never mind that this belief is usually a matter of ideological deception, see regarding the new type of army, Wehler, 1989, pp 463ff.

[175] See on these events Damm, 1998, pp. 158f

[176] How much Goethe had still thought in feudal terms is indicated by the circumstance that he had delivered an oath of fealty when he had taken possession of a farm at Oberroßla in 1799 Although he had acquired it through payment of money, i.e., on modern terms as a piece of real estate, he treated that farm as a feudal grant; see Conrady, 1993, II, p 237

[177] Conrady, 1993, II, p. 309.

[178] Trunz, 1948ff, XIII, p. 608

[179] Conrady, 1993, II, p 275.

[180] Quoted according to Conrady, 1993, II, p. 230, our translation.

[181] Regarding this encounter, see Conrady, 1993, II, pp. 332ff; and also Gundolf, 1918, pp. 536ff

[182] Krippendorff, 1999, pp 215, 221

[183] ibid , p 220.

[184] Eckermann, 1984, noted under 19 Feb 1829

[185] This growth, incidentally, aimed at a goal that was vastly different from what a Benjamin Franklin was so keen to accomplish in a social structure that had begun to evolve in North America

[186] Conrady, 1993, II, pp 382ff

[187] Conrady, 1993, II, p 514

[188] Conrady, 1993, II, p 127

[189] Conrady, 1993, II, pp. 286f

[190] Conrady, 1993, II, pp. 286ff.

[191] Regarding their relationship, see Conrady, 1993, II, 378ff

[192] Conrady, 1993, II, p. 381.

[193] For instance Hölderlin and later Schubert, see pp 168, 175 respectively

[194] After Napoleon's defeat and the re-structuring of the German principalities at the Congress of Vienna, Goethe was again appointed by the Duke to the post of minister of education, see Conrady, 1993, II, pp 412f.

[195] Conrady, 1993, II, pp 390ff, 400ff

[196] Conrady, 1993, II, p 390

[197] The circumstance that Goethe published this collection under his name alone could be interpreted as some sort of plagiarism This, however, would be a misconception for more than one reason. First, it would ignore that Marianne and Goethe wanted to keep their relationship a secret. Marianne who incidentally married Herrn von Willemer during that time, kept it that way until many years after Goethe's death. Second, and perhaps more importantly, we have to note that, while all of Marianne's poems were stimulated by Goethe, most experts seem to agree that Marianne could not have written them without him. Marianne has, to the best of our knowledge, never objected to Goethe's publishing them under his name. Regarding this issue see, in particular, Unseld, 1988, pp. 51ff, 63, 82ff. Incidentally, a similar controversy regarding Goethe's authorship surrounds his "wisdom literature" in which he collected folk wisdom and put it into his own words. Some consider these collections as genuine reflections of his thought, others see it as unoriginal in which he hides his sources Nobody, however, seems

to have denied that his "wisdom literature" represents masterly rhetorical re-formulations of traditional thought, see Stephenson, 1983, pp. 14f, 257.

[198] See Conrady, 1993, II, p. 423f.

[199] Conrady, 1993, II, pp. 477.

[200] Conrady, 1993, II, pp 565f

[201] Conrady, 1993, II, pp 378f

[202] Conrady, 1993, II, pp 472, 492

[203] This is also noted by Conrady, 1993, II. pp 446ff and by Gundolf, 1918, pp. 414ff.

[204] See p. 112.

[205] By the same token, he had to reject the Kant of the "First Critique" and the Kantian notion of "identity" The Kant of the "epigenesis" was a somewhat different matter. See also Sixel, 1999, passim.

[206] Fairley, 1947, p. 265; Gundolf, 1918, pp. 415ff.

[207] Conrady, 1993, II, p. 287.

[208] See pp. 304-310.

[209] Wilhelm Meister's Wanderings, book 3, chapter 13; our translation.

[210] This is not to say that Goethe had no sense at all for that mode of production There are passages in "Faust" which indicate that he did have some sense for it, see e.g. verses 5447ff, in this regard see also Conrady, 1993, pp. 543f But contrary to the highly interesting reading of "Faust" presented by the economist Hans Christoph Binswanger, we doubt that all the many ramifications of today's capitalism have been clear to Goethe, see Binswanger, 1991, pp. 57ff.

[211] Goethe has sent this poem in 1827 to Zelter; see: Goethe, 1902ff, vol 4, p. 127.

[212] Goethe, 1984, XVIII, p. 648, no. 881

[213] See also Conrady, 1993, II, pp 551f

Chapter 7

Goethe's Praxis and Concept of Science

A. Introductory Note: Past Context and Present Significance*

Before presenting and discussing Goethe's essay "The Experiment as Mediator of Object and Subject", we always felt that we had to remind the reader of the context within which we plan to discuss this piece. In doing so one runs into what may appear to be a contradiction. On the one hand, we claim that Goethe hardly had any experience with traditional capitalism, let alone late capitalism, on the other hand, we suggest that he can still speak to late capitalism and its intrinsic problems. Addressing this apparent contradiction allows one to come close to the crux of the matter regarding the not too obvious relation between the late capitalist fabrication of distorted reality and Goethe's wholehearted obedience to the real Nature of things.

---

* On the day we had planned to start writing the first draft of this section of the book, namely on the 10th of April 1998, my good friend and co-author Baldev Luther passed away. My return to our joint work was not an easy one. I hope that the rest of the book and the revisions made throughout the whole text would meet with his agreement.

Late capitalism and Goethe have in common that they both give primacy to Nature. Their difference, however, is that the former does not acknowledge this, while the latter admits to it happily. This commonality-in-difference places the two into a dialectical relationship which, our philosophical characterization notwithstanding, is a fundamentally practical one. Goethe who has never laid claim to being a philosopher, has, this circumstance notwithstanding, advocated the primacy of Nature, has in a peculiar way reasoned about it and has described in detail the way in which he practices the primacy of Nature in scientific research. This description has been delivered by Goethe most explicitly in his essay "The Experiment as Mediator of Object and Subject" and this is what makes this essay speak to us today with particular weight.

Nothing would be gained, however, if this essay would only *speak* to us. It is not even enough that we hear Goethe speak in "The Experiment" – essay to the distinction between a concrete phenomenon itself and the concept of it. Furthermore, it is also insufficient, if we only hear him point out, how problematic it is to "...enjoy(s) ... more the conceptualization than the thing itself..." (See paragraph 2 on p. 199 of "The Experiment".) [*]

Goethe loved Nature as such, i.e., he loved all the things that make her up. Since he also sensed himself as being part of her, he wished to come to know her by accepting the Nature in himself as a guide in the process of coming to understand her. While the way by which he did that requires quite some additional explanation, it must also be pointed out that Goethe's way of proceeding in scientific studies cannot be grasped fully when one only *reads* Goethe and does so in a merely philosophical way. One has to bodily feel what his way of studying means by practicing it. He expects, as we have mentioned above, that his experiments and experiences are being made with one's own hands and eyes. This way one may come to know what a process of coming to understand means which in its concrete occurrence transcends-and-contains the distorted sensuousness and abstraction of late capitalism.

---

[*] References to passages in Goethe's essay are from here onwards indicated by inserting brackets in our text containing the page number and paragraph number of the passage concerned. Accordingly the present reference is to 203,2.

After we ourselves had made quite a few of Goethe's experiments and observations, it became almost incomprehensible to us how so many students of his writings could simply dismiss Goethe's own frequent statements on the limitations of philosophy and his equally frequent invitations to his readers to make the experiments and experiences for themselves. Goethe has reiterated in many variations: "I had no organ for philosophy in its specific sense".[1] Kant's somewhat contemptuous phrase of "the bustle of the senses" could never have been coined by him, while he has more than once made remarks such as "Natural system, a contradictory expression".[2] Goethe has always thought that Nature is too great for our systematic comprehension, but he has known at the same time that we are totally part of her. Since Goethe is so clear on this, including his rejection of a merely mind guided science, it is a riddle for us that so many writers, philosophers and scientists alike, from Robert Bloch to Gernot Böhme, Karl Jaspers, Jost Schieren, Dennis Sepper, Karl Vorländer, Werner Heisenberg, Walter Heitler, Carl Friedrich von Weizsäcker, to name but a few, have treated Goethe as if he had never said what he did about philosophy and a systematic science. We have next to no indication that these, usually very thoughtful writers, have made any substantial number of Goethe's experiments. This makes us wonder: did they enjoy the conceptualization of things more than the things themselves?

One must certainly admit that Goethe himself has, in a way, misled his audience to a philosophical reading of his often studied essay "The Experiment as Mediator of Object and Subject". This is particularly due to the philosophically sounding title that he eventually gave to this essay. A brief look, however, at the essay itself makes it clear that this piece is by no means a merely philosophical treatise, or for that matter a methodological essay in the tradition of the theory of science.

Turning to the bibliographical context of this essay, we would first like to note that this essay exists today in different versions. For our purposes, we have chosen the earliest manuscript version available. It has been published by Erich Trunz in his "Hamburg Edition" of Goethe's Works.[3] This earliest version has been dated by Goethe 28 April 1792. Since we found it helpful for a thorough understanding of this essay, we have contrasted this 1792 version with the latest one, i.e. the published version of 1823.[4] In other words, the text which we present is the manuscript version of 1792 in which those passages that have been eliminated or altered in the published version have been retained but have been put in italics. The passages omitted in the published text (but included here) make, in our view, the organization of the essay more plausible. They also indicate shifts in Goethe's views, however minor these may be.

On January 10, 1798, Goethe had sent a manuscript version of this text to Schiller whom, as will be recalled, he had befriended just a few years earlier. We do not know with certainty whether this version is identical with the version bearing the date of 1792. A copy of it has not come upon us. Schiller's reaction to this essay is not known in detail, but in a note to Goethe, dated January 19, 1798 (and still available), Schiller calls Goethe's way of proceeding in scientific matters a "rational empirical one" (in German: rationale Empirie). This may sound philosophical, but it leaves it ambiguous how one can obey empirical reality and yet accept the guidance of the mind. This certainly points at a major epistemological problem, but it finds in Goethe's research a surprisingly simple solution. Goethe basically advocates in the essay how to follow one's sensuousness in scientific research and to do so by being mindfully careful in avoiding conclusions drawn in "rashness" (paragraph 198,3/199,1). Yet, following one's sensuousness trustingly is alien to Schiller (as it is to so many of us today). This is what Schiller, as a Kantian, has apparently never fully understood or agreed with. This is manifested, when Schiller adds in his reply to Goethe that the latter's "trust in the regulatory use of philosophy in matters of experience would grow", if he would compare his way of judging experiences with that of Kant. Goethe responded by mildly pointing to the differences between him and Kant. One has to acknowledge, however, that Goethe, as indicated above,[5] does order his studies on colors in accordance with Kantian categories, but he does so only to the extent that, even in this most philosophically oriented period in his life, his own way of studying is not compromised.

At the time of first writing this essay, Goethe was still heavily involved in the publication of the first parts of his "Beiträge zur Optik" ("Contributions to Optics"). He seems to have written the essay with the intent of clarifying his own views on how to proceed in scientific matters and, thus, to demarcate his differences to what had become mainstream thought in science and philosophy. While it is quite certain that Goethe had studied Kant's "Critique of Pure Reason" (publ. in 1781) around that time and had resented it as a static theory of cognition and knowledge, and while it is also clear that he had read Kant's "Critique of Practical Reason" (publ. 1786) and, with more sympathy, his "Critique of Judgment" (publ. 1790),[6] a line that could unequivocally be related to Kant in an agreeable way can hardly be found in "The Experiment". Instead, he retained his own fundamentally non-Kantian and non-idealist views, mainly because he saw it as highly problematic to replace the primacy of Nature in the process of coming to know, and be it by a "Table of Categories" or any other construct merely located in our mind. It is in this connection that it should be remembered that Goethe had initially given to the essay a title that in no way reflected the philosophical vocabulary that was gradually becoming en vogue at the time. As mentioned, he had called it "Kautelen des Beobachters", meaning "Cautions to be taken by the Observer" (of Nature).

It was in 1823, i.e. more than 30 years after having written the essay, that Goethe published it in his periodical "Zur Naturwissenschaft überhaupt", i.e. "On Natural Science in General". He had found an apparently undated manuscript version of it while sifting through his correspondence with his old (and by then since long deceased) friend Schiller. At that time, Goethe seems to have changed the title of the manuscript to its classically philosophical wording: "The Experiment as Mediator of Object and Subject". We do not know whether this was done out of reverence for Schiller, the Kantian, or whether this choice indicates how Goethe tries anew to target the audience of philosophers and scientists. Given the state of affairs in the sciences and philosophy, such an attempt - by merely changing the title - had turned even more into wishful thinking than before.[7] While the text remained basically unchanged and essentially non-philosophical, the new title describes, surprisingly enough, the contents still adequately, provided the words "object", "subject" and "mediator" are understood as referring to what are primarily aspects of Nature and not as mere concepts of parts of Nature. If so, a full and that is to say a sensuously rich understanding of the contents of the essay materializes leading to much more than a merely thoughtful contemplation of "ideas".

We also would like to caution the reader against expecting a treatment of the object-subject-relation "in general". For doing that, "The Experiment" is undoubtedly too focused on the study of light and colors. It is only occasionally that Goethe makes references to what points beyond that focus, for instance, when treating light and color in the context of "the more common forces and elements" (paragraph 200,7/201,1) in Nature. Goethe, thus, implies that Nature contains other and more complex aspects than these. Given his awareness for the hierarchy among entities in living Nature, the human subject has to relate in more elevated ways to these more elevated kinds of objects. This proposition, already referred to above,[8] indicates that the study of Nature beyond the level of light and colors requires more than Goethe can deal with in this relatively short essay. He has practiced sensitivity to this complexity in those studies of his that relate to anatomy and plants in particular. Unfortunately, we are not aware of contemplations that expand on the study of such kinds of objects to the extent as "The Experiment" does this with its focus on light and colors.

We present this text in an English translation. We made our own translation, and we wish to gratefully acknowledge the co-operation of our friend Hans Kummer, a physicist and mathematician at our university, in this endeavor. We did not use other available translations, because they suffer, in our view, from serious inaccuracies.[9] We do not assume, however, that our translation is perfect. At times, our wording may very well be problematic. Therefore, we have, on numerous occasions provided the reader with the German wording and phrasing, particularly where we could not find a satisfying equivalent in English. On the whole, however, we feel more comfortable with our own translation. This judgement is, needless to say, prejudiced by the circumstance that two of us share the mother tongue with Goethe, while all three of us translators are bilingual, to some extent.

Let us now turn to the text.

Notes

[1] Quoted according to Troll, o J , p 285; our translation
[2] See Goethe, in Trunz, 1948ff, XIII, p. 35, our translation; see in this connection also Sixel, 1999, passim.

[3] For our bibliographic remarks on Goethe's essay, see Trunz, 1948ff, XIII, pp. 563f.

[4] See Goethe, 1988, II, pp. 119ff.

[5] See p. 162.

[6] Trunz, 1948ff, XIII, p. 607.

[7] Goethe's acceptance among philosophers and scientists was already quite limited during his life time. How much less his science was appreciated not too long after his death becomes glaringly clear when one reads Helmholtz' lecture of 1853 "On Goethe's Scientific Research". Helmholtz tries to be quite understanding of Goethe and how he approaches Nature. Yet, after referring to Goethe's "principle (!), that Nature must reveal her secrets of her own free will", he continues by saying that "we are compelled in every explanation of natural phenomena to leave the sphere of sense, and to pass to things which are not objects of sense, and are defined only by abstract conceptions" See Helmholtz, 1962 [1853], p. 15.

[8] See pp. 200-201, 287-288

[9] The best translation we have come across is the one made by Douglas Miller. It is included in Goethe's "Scientific Studies", as edited by Douglas Miller, 1988, pp. 11-17. Yet even this translation did not appear to us as being always accurate enough, because it apparently aims to enhance readability rather than precision. Limiting ourselves to merely a few examples taken just from the first page of Miller's translation, we have to point at the following ones: Miller translates the title of Goethe's published version, namely, " Das Experiment als Vermittler *von* Objekt und Subjekt" by saying "The Experiment as Mediator *between* Object and Subject" This misleads the reader to think that what mediates between object and subject is not also something that is *inside* object and subject Goethe, however, wishes to speak about the experiment that shares with object and subject the commonality that permeates all of Nature, is *in* all there is and not just *between* all there is. Beyond that we would like to mention the following cases of somewhat problematic translations: German: "...Gegenstände um sich herum. ."; Miller: "...objects in his environment..."; ours: "...objects around him..."; German: ". Trieb nach Kenntnis .."; Miller. "...thirst for knowledge. "; ours: "...drive for knowledge ."; German: "...als Menschen..."; Miller: "... from the human standpoint "; ours· "...as human beings..."; German: " einen Gegenstand in Beziehung zu sich selbst .."; Miller: " an object in its own context. ", ours ". an object in relation to itself ...".

B. Goethe, Johann Wolfgang v.: The Experiment as Mediator of Object and Subject

N.B. At the end of each paragraph of this essay the reader will find a reference to the pages where the commentary on that particular paragraph can be found. For my commentary on the title, see pp. 204ff.

As soon as the human being (in German: der Mensch) becomes aware of the objects around him, he considers them in relation to himself, and rightly so (in German: und mit Recht). For his whole fate depends on whether they please or displease him, whether they attract or repel him, whether they benefit or harm him. This entirely natural way of looking at and judging things seems to be as easy as it is necessary, and yet, in it the human being is exposed to a thousand errors, which often times put him to shame and embitter his life. (commentary on pp.208ff.)

Those ones take on a far heavier task (in German: Tagewerk) who, fired by their drive for knowledge, strive to observe the objects of Nature in themselves and in their relation among themselves; for one thing, they no longer have the yardstick, which came to their help, so long as they as human beings considered things in relation to their own selves. It is precisely the yardstick of pleasure and displeasure, of attraction and repulsion, of benefit and harm, that they have to renounce totally; they should, like indifferent and, as it were, godlike beings, search and study what there is and not what pleases. Thus, neither the beauty nor the usefulness of a plant should move the true botanist. He is supposed to study the plant's formation and its relation with the rest of the plant kingdom; and as they are all lured out and shone upon by the sun, he too, should look upon and survey them with the same calm gaze, and he should take the yardstick for such coming to know, the data for judging not out of himself but out of the sphere of the things which he observes. (commentary on pp. 213ff)

The history of the sciences teaches us how difficult this abnegation (in German: Entäußerung) is for any human being. How he in this manner arrives and must arrive at hypotheses, theories, systems and whatever other kinds of representations (in German: Vorstellungsarten) there might be through which he tries to grasp the infinite, will concern us in the second section of this small essay. I devote the first part of it to the consideration of how a human being proceeds when he strives to know the forces of Nature. History of physics, which at present I have reason to

study more carefully, provides me often with the opportunity to think
about this matter, and so this little essay originates, in which I strive to
visualize for myself in a general way the manner in which distinguished
men (in German: Männer) have advanced (in German: genutzt) and
harmed the teachings on Nature (This italicized section of the text is not
included in the published version of 1823). As soon as we consider an
object in relation to itself and in connection with other objects (in German:
mit andern) and not immediately desire or detest it, then with a calm
attention we shall soon be able to create a fairly distinct concept of it, its
parts and its connections. The further we continue these observations (in
German: Betrachtungen), the more we connect these objects with one
another, the more we practice the gift of observation (in German:
Beobachtungsgabe) which is within us. If we know, in our actions, to
relate these insights to ourselves, then we deserve to be called smart.
Smartness is not a difficult matter for any well organized person (in
German: für einen wohlorganisierten Menschen) who either is moderate
by Nature or has been rendered moderate by circumstances: for life sets us
right at every step. However, if the observer is expected to apply this keen
power of judgment to the examination of hidden (in German: geheimer)
natural connections, to watch his own paces and steps in a world in which,
as it were, he is alone to guard against rashness, to constantly keep his
purpose in sight, without letting pass unnoticed on his way any useful or
harmful assistance, if he is further expected to be his own most strict
observer where he cannot be controlled so easily by anybody, and if, in
the course of his most zealous endeavors he is expected to be always
distrustful of himself: then probably everybody can see how strict these
requirements are and how little one can hope to see them totally satisfied,
whether one poses them to others or to oneself. Yet these difficulties, one
can even say, this hypothetical impossibility, must not prevent us from
doing the utmost possible, and we at least get the furthest if we try to bring
to our awareness the means in general by which distinguished persons (in
German: Menschen) have been known to expand the sciences, if we point
out precisely the false routes on which they went astray, and on which a
great number of students (in German: Schüler) have followed them
sometimes for centuries until later experiences have guided the observer
back again onto the right path. (com. on pp. 218ff)

As little as anybody can deny that experience has and should have the
greatest influence in the teachings on Nature, about which I speak at
present in particular, as well as in everything which the human being
undertakes, can one gainsay the high, and, as it were, creatively

independent power of the forces of the soul, by which these experiences are grasped, drawn together, ordered and given shape. However, it cannot be generally known, or appreciated, how to make and to use these experiences, how to form and to employ these forces. (com. on pp. 226ff)

As soon as sharp-minded people (in German. Menschen) (These italicized words are not contained in the published version which would read, instead: "As soon as people of sharp, fresh senses...") of whom there are, by a moderate use of the word, many more than one thinks, have their attention directed to objects, then one finds them as inclined to, as adroit at, observation. I have been able to notice this often, since I have been concerning myself zealously with the teachings of light and colors, and, as usually happens, have conversed with (This word is missing in the handwritten version, but it is included in the published one) persons to whom such considerations are otherwise alien, about that what interests me so much. As soon as their attentiveness was lively, they noticed phenomena, which in part I had not known, in part had overlooked, and through that they corrected quite often a too hastily conceived idea; indeed they gave me cause to take faster steps to emerge from the confinement in which a laborious investigation often holds us captive. (com. on pp. 228ff)

Thus what is valid in so many other human undertakings is valid here as well: that the interest of several people directed towards *one* (Goethe's emphasis) point is capable of bringing forth something outstanding. Here it becomes obvious that the envy, which likes so much to exclude others from the honor of a discovery, that the intemperate desire to treat and to develop something one has discovered only in one's own manner, are the greatest obstacle for the investigator himself. (com. on pp. 230f)

I have been feeling too good so far with the method of working together with several other people to not want to continue this way. I know exactly to whom I, on my way, have become indebted for this and that, and it shall be my pleasure to make this known publicly in the future. (com. on pp. 231f)

If, already, even unaffected attentive people (in German: natürliche aufmerksame Menschen) are capable of being so beneficial, how more far reaching (in German: allgemeiner) must be the benefit if educated people (in German: unterrichtete Menschen) work hand in hand with each other. A science is already in and for itself so huge a mass, that it carries many human beings, while no human being is able to carry it. One may notice that knowledge, like a contained but living water, rises gradually to a certain level, that the most beautiful discoveries are not made so much by human beings as by the times; as for instance, very important things have been accomplished by two or even more experienced thinkers at the same time. If even in the first case we become so much indebted to society and to friends, then all the more we become indebted in this case to the world and to the century; and in both cases we cannot sufficiently acknowledge how necessary communication, assistance, reminding and objection are in order to keep, and to advance us on the right way. (com. on pp. 232ff)

Thus, in scientific matters one has to proceed in a manner just the opposite to the one in which one has to do it in works of art. For an artist does well not to let his piece of work be seen in public until he has completed it, because one can neither easily advise nor give help; however, if the work of art is completed then he has to think over and to take to heart the reproach or the praise, to integrate this with his experience, and in this way to cultivate (in German: auszubilden) and prepare himself for a new work. In scientific matters however, it is indeed useful to publicly communicate each single experience, even conjecture, it is indeed most highly advisable not to erect a scientific edifice before the plan, and the materials for it, are generally known, assessed and selected. (com. on pp. 235ff)

Now I turn to a point which deserves all attention, namely to the method of how one proceeds most advantageously and most securely (The italicized text is not included in the published version of 1823). (com. on pp. 239f)

If we intentionally repeat the experiences which have been made prior to us, which we make ourselves or others simultaneously with us, and if we again present the phenomena, which in part accidentally, in part artificially emerged, then we call that an experiment. (com. on pp. 240ff)

The value of an experiment, be it simple or be it composite, primarily consists in that it can be carried out at any time again under certain conditions with the help of a known apparatus and with the required skill, as often as the required conditions can be brought together. If we were to even only superficially (in German: obenhin) consider the combinations which have been created, and the machines which have been invented, and one can safely say, are being invented every day for this purpose, we can rightfully admire human ingenuity (in German: Verstand). (com. on pp. 245ff)

Regardless of how valuable any experiment, considered individually, may be, yet it acquires its value only through unification (in German: Vereinigung) and connection (in German: Verbindung) with others. However to unite and to connect two experiments, which have some resemblance with each other, takes more rigor and attention than even astute observers often have demanded of themselves. Two phenomena may be akin to one another but by far not as closely as we believe. Two experiments may appear to follow one from the other, even when between them a large series [of connections] has to be inserted in order to bring them into an adequately natural connection. (com. on pp. 252ff)

Therefore, one cannot be careful enough in neither drawing conclusions too soon from experiments, nor proving something immediately by experiments, nor wanting to confirm some theory by experiments; for it is here at this pass (The published version reads here, in English: "like at a pass", and moves this phrase to a later part of this sentence, namely, between "where" ... and "...his inner enemies") at this transition from experience to judgment, from the known to the application, where all his inner enemies lie in wait for man (in German: dem Menschen): the power of imagination which already at this point lifts him up on its wings while he believes that he still touches the ground, impatience, rashness, self contentedness, rigidity, mode of thinking, preconceived opinion, indolence, frivolity, fickleness, or whatever else this whole horde with its entourage may be called, all of them lie here in ambush and overpower unexpectedly the actively engaged observer, as well as the quiet observer who seemingly is unassailed by all passions. (com. on pp. 259ff)

As a warning against this danger, which is greater and closer at hand than one thinks, I should like to put forward a kind of paradox, in order to stimulate a livelier attention. Namely, I dare to assert, that *one* (Goethe's emphasis) experiment, even several experiments viewed as interconnected (in German: mehrere Versuche in Verbindung) prove nothing, indeed that nothing is more dangerous than to want to prove some proposition immediately by experiments, and that the greatest errors have arisen precisely because one has not recognized the danger and inadequacy of this method. I must explain myself more clearly in order to avoid the suspicion that I wanted to open the floodgates (in German: Tor und Tür öffnen) to doubt. (The published version would read, in translation "... that I wanted to say something peculiar" and ends the paragraph with these words.). Each experience which we make, each experiment by which we repeat this experience, is really an isolated element of our knowledge; by frequent repetition we turn this isolated element of knowledge into a certainty. Two experiences within the same discipline can become known to us, they may be closely akin to each other, but they may appear even more closely akin, and we usually are inclined to consider them more closely akin to each other than they are. This is in keeping with the Nature of the human being, history of the human mind provides us with a thousand examples, and I have noticed in myself that I commit this mistake almost daily. (com. on pp. 263ff)

This mistake is closely akin to another one from which, for the most part, it also arises. Man (in German: der Mensch) enjoys, as it were, more the conceptualization [of a thing] than the thing itself, or, rather we must say: man (in German: der Mensch) enjoys something only in so far as he conceives of it, it has to fit into his kind of sense (in German: Sinnesart) and howsoever high he might elevate his way of making sense (in German: Vorstellungsart) above the ordinary way, howsoever he purifies it, it usually remains still only a way of making sense: that is to say, an attempt to bring several objects into a specific intelligible (in German: faßliche) relationship with one another which they strictly speaking, do not have; hence the inclination towards hypotheses, theories, terminologies and systems which we cannot disapprove of since these must necessarily spring from the organization of our essence (in German: Wesens). (com. on pp. 267ff)

If, on the one hand, every single experience, every single experiment must be viewed as isolated by their very Nature, and if, on the other hand, the power of the human mind strives with tremendous force to tie together all which is external to it and comes to be known by it, then one easily comes to acknowledge the danger to which one is exposed, if one wishes to connect a single experience with a preconceived idea or if one wishes to prove through singular experiments some connection which is not entirely sensuous, but which the creative power of the mind has already formulated. (com. on pp. 269ff)

Through such an effort, most of the time, theories and systems arise which do honor to the sharp-mindedness of the authors, which, however, if they find more acclaim than is appropriate, if they survive longer than is right, immediately (in German: sogleich) slow down again and harm the progress of the human mind which they in a certain sense advance. (com. on pp. 273ff)

One will be able to notice that a good mind applies all the more artfulness, the fewer the data lying before him; that he, in order to show his sovereignty, as it were, even selects from the available data only a few favoring ones (in German: Günstlinge) which flatter him; that he knows to organize the remaining ones in such a way that they do not contradict him directly; and that he, in the end, knows to confuse, to entangle and to push aside the opposing ones so that then the whole does not really resemble anymore a freely functioning republic but a despotic court. (com. on pp. 275ff)

For a man (in German: Mann) who has so much merit there cannot be a lack of admirers and pupils (in German: Schüler) who, in the course of time (in German: historisch), come to know and admire such a fabric and, as far as it is possible, appropriate their master's imagery (in German: Vorstellungsart). Oftentimes, such a teaching gains the upper hand in such a manner that one would be considered defiant and bold, if one would dare to cast doubt on it. Only later centuries would dare to approach such a sacred relic, submit the matter under consideration again to common human sense (in German: gemeinen Menschensinn), and take the matter a bit more lightly, and repeat about the founder of a sect what a witty mind has once said about a great scientist: he would have been a great man, had he not invented so much. (com. on pp. 278ff)

But it may not be enough to point out the danger and to warn against it. It is fair that at least one makes one's opinion public and makes it known how one believes to be able to avoid such an error (in German: Abweg), or whether one has found out how someone else before us has avoided it. (com. on pp. 281f)

Earlier, I have said that I hold as harmful the immediate bringing to bear of an experiment to the proof of any hypothesis, and have thereby given to understand that I hold a mediated bringing to bear of it (in German: derselben) as fruitful, and since all depends on this point, it is necessary to explain oneself clearly. (com. on pp. 282ff)

In living Nature, nothing happens which does not stand in connection with the whole, and if the experiences appear to us as being isolated, if we have to view the experiments as isolated facts (in German: Fakta), it is not thereby said that they are isolated, the question only is: how do we find the connection among these phenomena, of this occurrence. (com. on pp. 284ff)

We have seen above that those who sought to connect an isolated fact (in German: Faktum) immediately to their power of thought and of judgement were subjected (in German: unterworfen) to error from the very beginning. Contrary to that, we shall find that those have achieved the most, who do not desist from exploring and working through all aspects and modifications of a single experience, of a single experiment, in accordance with every possibility. (com. on pp. 286f)

It merits a future consideration of its own, how the intellect could come to our help in this endeavor. Only this much may be said here (The italicized text is not included in the published version of 1823). Since all things in Nature, but especially the more common forces and elements, have an eternal effect and countereffect, one can say of each phenomenon that it stands in connection with countless others, as we say of a free floating glowing point that it sends out rays in all directions (in German: auf allen Seiten). Having made such an experiment, having made such an experience, we cannot investigate carefully enough what immediately borders on it, what immediately follows from it; that is what we have to pay more attention to than to what relates to it. The manifolding (in German: Vermannigfaltigung) of each single experiment is, therefore, the proper duty of a student of Nature (in German: Naturforscher). He has the exact opposite duty to that of a writer who wants to entertain. The latter will make for boredom, if he does not leave anything to be imagined (in German: zu denken), the former must work restlessly, as if he wanted to leave nothing for his followers to do, although the disproportion between our intellect and the Nature of things would soon enough remind him that no human being has enough abilities to have a conclusive say on any matter (in German: in irgendeiner Sache abzuschließen). (com. on pp. 287ff)

In the first two parts of my Contributions to Optics, I have sought to establish such a sequence of experiments which directly (in German: zunächst) border on each other and immediately touch (in German: berühren) each other, which, indeed, if one knows and oversees them all exactly, constitute *one* (Goethe's emphasis) experiment, as it were, represent just *one* (Goethe's emphasis) experience under the most manifold perspectives. (com. on pp. 291ff)

Such an experience which consists of several others is evidently of a higher kind. It represents the formula through which innumerable single cases (in German: Rechnungsexempel) are being expressed. To work towards such experiences of the higher kind, I hold to be the duty of the scientist (in German: Naturforscher) and the example of the most eminent men (in German: Männer) who have worked in this discipline points us in this direction (At this point, a paragraph has been made by Goethe in the published version of 1823), moreover the thoughtfulness (in German: Bedächtlichkeit) in joining the next only to the next or rather, in deducing the next from its immediate antecedent (in German: aus dem Nächsten), we have to learn from the mathematicians, and even there where we do not dare to calculate, we always have to go to work as if we were accountable to the most demanding geometrician (in German: Geometer). (com. on pp. 293ff)

For, properly speaking, it is the mathematical method which, because of its thoughtfulness and purity, reveals at once each leap in an assertion; and its proofs are really only detailed (in German: umständliche) explications, that what is presented in connection was already there in its simple (in German: einfachen) parts and in its whole sequence, that it has been surveyed in its entirety and found to be correct and irrefutable under all conditions. And thus its demonstrations are always rather presentations, recapitulations than arguments. Since I make this distinction here, I may be permitted to take a look back. (com. on pp. 296ff)

One sees the great difference between a mathematical demonstration which takes the first elements through so many connections and the proof which a clever speaker could bring forth through arguments. Arguments can contain quite isolated interrelations and yet they can be brought together into *one* (Goethe's emphasis) point through wit and power of imagination, and, surprisingly enough, the appearance of a right (in German: eines Rechts) or a wrong (in German: Unrechts), of a true or a false is fabricated (in German: hervorgebracht). The same way one can, in support of a hypothesis or theory, compile singular experiments like arguments and deliver a proof which is more or less dazzling. (com. on pp. 298ff)

The one, however, to whom it matters to proceed in his work in honesty (in German: redlich) to himself and to others, will try to develop the experiences of the higher kind through the most careful arrangement of singular experiments. These allow themselves to be articulated through brief and comprehensible statements, to be put side by side to one another, and the more of them are generated, the more they can be put into an order and into such a relation that they can stand unshakably alone or together as well as mathematical statements do. The elements of these experiences of the higher kind, which are many single experiments, can then be investigated and tested by anyone, and it is not difficult to determine whether the many singular pieces can be expressed through a general statement, for here there is no room for capriciousness. (com. on pp. 300ff)

With the other method, however, by which we wish to prove something that we assert through isolated experiments in the same way as through arguments, the judgement is often deviously obtained, if it is not entirely mired in doubt. If one, however, has compiled a series of experiences of the higher kind, then one may exercise one's intellect, one's power of imagination and one's wit on them, as one wishes. This will not be harmful, indeed, it will be beneficial. That first endeavor cannot be undertaken carefully, diligently, vigorously, indeed pedantically enough, for it is undertaken for the world and the posterity. But these materials must be ordered and presented in sequence, not be put together in a hypothetical manner, not be used for forming systems (in German: nicht zu einer systematischen Form verwendet). Then it sets everybody free to connect them according to his way and to form a whole from it which in general will be more or less comfortable and pleasant to the human way of making representations (in German: der menschlichen Vorstellungsart). This way, what is to be distinguished is distinguished, and one can enrich the collection of experiences much more speedily and purely than if one has to put the later experiments aside unused like stones which have been gathered after a building has been completed. (com. on pp. 302ff)

The view of the most eminent men and their example let me hope that I am on the right path, and I wish that my friends may be satisfied with this explanation, who ask me sometimes: what actually my intent is in my optical endeavors? My intent is: to collect all experiences in this discipline, to perform all experiments myself and to conduct them in their most manifold variety (in German: Mannigfaltigkeit) so that they can easily be repeated and not be removed from the horizon (in German: Gesichtskreis) of so many human beings (in German: Menschen). And then to put forward (in German: aufzustellen) statements through which the experiences of the higher kind can be expressed, and to wait and see in what way these too can be subsumed under a still higher principle. If, however, the power of imagination and the wit sometimes run ahead impatiently, then the mode of proceeding itself specifies the bearings of the point to which they have to return. (com. on pp. 311ff)

Date: 28 April 1792

C. Commentary on Goethe's Essay "The Experiment as Mediator of Object and Subject"

N.B. This set of commentaries is not meant to be read like a chapter in a book. Since each commentary focuses on a single paragraph of Goethe's essay, it should be read in conjunction with that paragraph. In order to make this somewhat easier, I have placed each paragraph of Goethe's essay in fine print at the top of its commentary. Each of these tries to clarify the thoughts presented by Goethe in that particular paragraph by also pointing out aspects in Goethe's thinking that are not explicitly discussed there and yet are part of the context within which a given paragraph needs to be understood. This leads to cross-references and repetitions which I regret, but of which I hope that enduring them will ease access to Goethe's rather condensed presentation of his scientific method.

The Title: A Surprising Inversion

This philosophically sounding title may have easily misled many of Goethe's interpreters towards thinking that he had dealt here with a "Philosophie in systematischer Absicht", i.e. a "Philosophy carried out in Systematic Intent".[1] This however, was not what Goethe intended to do. If one bears in mind, though, that Goethe has always been deeply permeated by the sense that the unity of all there is rests primarily with Nature and not with philosophical constructs, then one will still benefit greatly from this new title.[2] In other words, a somewhat paradoxical situation arises: on the one hand, a traditional philosophical reading of this admittedly philosophically titled essay is misleading, while on the other, the title is fully adequate, if one reads it out of having made Goethe's experiences and experiments oneself. This paradox arises, since Goethe has, philosophers might say, materialistically transcended-and-contained an idealist understanding of the subject-object-relationship. This transcendence also expresses itself in the inversion of the traditionally idealist wording of this relationship; the title implies an object-subject-relation, not a subject-object-relation. For Goethe, the object, i.e. the thing out there ranks first, since it represents in pure form what the subject in an elevated form shares with the object: Nature. Awareness of this helps Goethe to avoid seeing the relationship between objects and human beings as static. In this way, this new title captures a practically never ending dynamics that at best arrives momentarily at more durable statements. The subject changes in the moment of better understanding the object and thus him/herself.

Contextualizing this essay (and its title) only a bit into Goethe's whole work and life, the philosophical wording of the title accentuates, paradoxically, the primarily non-mentalistic status of the experiment as the mediator of object and subject. This mediator of object and subject is for Goethe not a frame of reference, a set of Kantian categories or some other mentalistic construct, but a practical, materially concrete doing, namely, that of setting up and executing an experiment.[3] The experiment, while undoubtedly having mentalistic aspects, is itself not primarily of a conceptual kind. The claim that this understanding of the experiment is in keeping with that of Goethe's is backed up not only by the whole argument of the essay, but in particular by the passages of paragraph 200,4ff of his essay. Nowhere else, except where the essay makes reference to notions like "immediate" and "mediated", does the essay appear to come close to a classical philosophical language. More importantly, and as we shall see later in greater detail, these paragraphs, regardless of their somewhat more philosophical language, emphasize the primarily material status of the experiment as a mediator. As such, the experiment is primarily a materially grounded relation to Nature, while its meaning has to arise as an elevation from that level in a cautious, still Nature guided, process. The primary role of Nature in that process has usually been overlooked in the literature. Walter Heitler, for example, one of the eminent physicists who have studied Goethe so carefully, misses this point completely. Yet, he misses this point in a most informative fashion, when he wonders how a great man like Goethe could contradict himself so badly, when he, in his objections against Newton, conceives of the experiment as a torture of Nature, and yet, "does not always live up to his own views by having made experiments himself" (very many of them indeed!).[4] What Heitler, like others, ignores here is that, for Goethe, it was only the "immediate bringing to bear of an experiment" (paragraph 200,4) on theorizing, as done in the Newtonian tradition, which was problematic. Heitler fails to see that this is not being done in those experiments that practice awareness for the primacy of the material mediation of object and subject. Awareness for this status of experiments is, however, quintessential for Goethe.

It may be helpful for an understanding of the all pervasiveness with which Goethe gave primacy to the materially concrete, when one remembers how he also appropriates artistic creations. His own enjoyment of art, for instance of poetry, was a truly active one, and as such had its own materially concrete aspects. With reference to his readings of Mohammed Schemsed-din Hafiz's "The Diwan",[5] he writes in May of 1815, to his publisher Cotta

> I have concerned myself…since quite some time with oriental literature, and in order to acquaint myself with it more intimately, I have written several pieces of poetry in the feeling and manner of the Orient.[6]

Understanding something, be it in the arts or in Nature out there, requires, in Goethe's mind, that the matter to be understood has to go through one's own hands, speaking figuratively and concretely. Thus, the understanding of poetry required the doing, i.e. the creating of poetry, particularly when confronted with unfamiliar poetic material or when trying to understand uncharted territories of Nature so to speak. This, incidentally, is why we, during our research, came to see that we had to do a number of Goethe's experiments ourselves, in order to understand Goethe's descriptive and theoretical writings on colors.

If the experiment materially constitutes the mediation, or commonality, between the material object and the material side of the human subject, then this is not to deny the distinction between the world of things and the human subject. Without a distinction in which this commonality ranks first, the object-subject-relationship would indeed implode into a mere identity. It is through this distinction, however, i.e. through the mental Otherness that the Nature of the human being has vis-à-vis Nature around him that the human being can create what Nature without the human mind would never create: knowledge. In this sense, the human being is both elevated Nature and can elevate Nature around him. As Goethe says on more than one occasion in this essay, it is part and parcel of the Nature of our mind that it, on the basis of its materially concrete workings, tendentially elevates any object we sense, i.e. see, hear, smell etc., to a concept of it. But in these elevations, be they scientific or poetic ones, done out of our Otherness to Nature, lie also serious problems.

The commonality that Goethe sees between object and subject should make it obvious that his mode of thinking and being precludes the Cartesian split between object and subject, or between "res extensa" and "res cogitans".[7] This way of coming to know also eliminates a segregation between supposedly subjective and objective areas of knowledge. This segregation was once projected by Werner Heisenberg into Goethe, when he saw fit to undertake what he as a physicist took to be a rescue mission for Goethe's views of Nature.[8] Ignoring the circumstance that Goethe's research transcends the Cartesian split by containing it in man's Otherness to Nature indicates that one does not follow Goethe's thought. This is Heisenberg's problem.

This common bond of all of Nature, i.e. the "analogia entis", cannot become a matter of systematic philosophy and yet remain truthful to Nature at the same time. This is related to the Nature of knowledge. Kant has already spoken about spontaneity as a constitutive element in our cognizing activities, but he has never explored its Nature.[9] Today, "spontaneity" may be replaced by the "firing of our neurons", as Adams among others puts it, and we may be aware of the circumstance that without such "firing" no thinking could take place, but this only helps us in our problems regarding the relationship between thinking and matter, if we appreciate that the drive of spontaneity, or the turnover of energy in us, is part of the whole flow of Nature in us and around us. Distorting that flow by not acknowledging its primacy distorts our relation to Nature at the level of knowledge and, thus, perverts the dynamics of Nature without abolishing it. Goethe knew this and has expressed this in a multitude of ways. Once he says "...our will belongs to Nature and relates us to external Nature".[10] In the process of coming to understand Nature, we change Nature in us and around us. As we have put it above[11]: known Nature is different from the one not known, let alone the Nature on which we work out of our knowledge of her. Only if these changes benefit the Nature in us and around us, would Goethe speak of elevation. Needless to say that this elevation implies an understanding of fellow man in the same materially grounded way, i.e., by appreciating the material commonality among people. Indeed, without Goethe's sense for what Karl Marx later called the "double dialectic" between Nature and man and between man and fellow man, the depths and the dynamics of what Goethe understands by elevation cannot be grasped. Thus, man's relation to Nature must not be understood statically. But this is precisely what Erich Trunz, the highly respected Goethe scholar, has done. He thinks that the assumption of an "identity" being seen by Goethe between "external stimulus and our preparedness for it" is characteristic of Goethe's thinking.[12] Putting matters this way indicates, in our view, that one reads Goethe with Kantian eyes, and that is to say, inadequately.

2. The Heavy Task of Abnegation
(Commentaries on paragraphs 194,1 to 197,2)

Paragraph 194,1

As soon as the human being (in German der Mensch) becomes aware of the objects around him, he considers them in relation to himself, and rightly so (in German und mit Recht) For his whole fate depends on whether they please or displease him, whether they attract or repel him, whether they benefit or harm him This entirely natural way of looking at and judging things seems to be as easy as it is necessary, and yet, in it the human being is exposed to a thousand errors, which often times put him to shame and embitter his life

Goethe delivers, in the very first sentence, an acknowledgement of the subjectivity of awareness. While awareness, as an initial perception of objects, must not be confused with knowledge, it is the departure point on the road to true knowledge. As the first sensuous connection between objects and the human subject, the initial perception is by no means lost, but transcended-and-contained in the laborious process that leads to knowledge. The containment of subjectivity in its bodily rawness is the beginning of that process by which we enact the primacy of Nature in our coming to understand her, since it is at that level where our subjectivity materially meets with the objects of Nature. I just wish to note in passing that the awareness for the containment of subjectivity in knowledge precludes an advocacy of an unalterable subject-object identity only, if reflexivity is appreciated as an aspect of subjectivity. It appears doubtful to me that the assumption of subjective involvement in all knowledge formation as proposed by at least some branches of contemporary neuro-physiology and neuro-philosophy allows for such reflexivity. To that extent, these schools of thought have to face the following question: If Nature is for us what our neurons suggest it is (Roth: "Wirklichkeit"), then our learning from mistakes would only be explainable by adducing the notion of a physiological mutation. Understanding man this way means to understand him as a participant in nothing more than the 100%-feedback communication that permeates all of Nature at the pre-human, non-symbolic level. Leaving matters at that level would preclude any possibility to account for our ability to re-define, let alone to have a historically variable truth. We shall return to this issue later, when we discuss how the bodily grounded reflexivity of the human subject can transcend the level of 100%-feedback loops in Nature and yet arrive at historically and individually flexible truth.[13]

At this point, it is more important to underline that the subjectivity in our awareness for and in our knowledge of Nature has, for Goethe, more than just a sheer epistemological dimension; it clearly has an aesthetic and utilitarian one as well. This must be underscored here for three reasons: First, Goethe hardly ever comes back in "The Experiment" to the unity of the epistemological and utilitarian aspects in our relation to the world around us, obviously because he takes it for granted. Secondly, Goethe emphasizes the importance of our aesthetic relation to objects for the process of coming to know explicitly only once more in this essay, albeit strongly so (paragraph 199,2).[14] Thirdly, the inclusion and sustained practical awareness for the utilitarian and aesthetic dimensions give his scientific studies a truly holistic form. This holism, however, has been truncated, if not even ignored in much of the literature that concerns itself with Goethe. This is a consequence of the almost exclusively epistemological concerns with Goethe's science. Relating objects "rightfully" to oneself, as the second sentence of this first paragraph does, is a materially concrete issue not just a philosophical one for Goethe; our "whole fate depends" on it.[15] When Goethe briefly unpacks this dependency by relating it to notions like "please or displease him", "attract or repel him" and "benefit or harm him", he makes it abundantly clear that he keeps together the aesthetic, the utilitarian and the epistemological aspects of our relation to the world.

After Goethe had eventually succeeded in elevating his sense for the commonality between art and science to the level of conceptual clarity, this elevation contained his sense for practical usefulness in it. Let us remember that he had come to scientific matters from his practical tasks as a minister at the Court of Weimar. Therefore, it should be clear that it is quite inadequate to read Goethe by narrowing down one's focus of attention to a specifically epistemological set of questions. Being aware of this, we were puzzled by how much of the literature on Goethe does just that.[16] While I am prepared to concede that our treatment of Goethe could also be understood as having an epistemological emphasis, I would like to keep it clear how essential it is to view the epistemological dimension of his science in conjunction with his artistic and also utilitarian sense of life.

We have wondered, nonetheless, how the widespread disregard for the utility of Nature could be explained. With this in mind, I would like to inspect just a few examples more closely.

Albrecht Schöne, for instance, is strangely ambivalent about this matter. On the one hand, he suggests that Goethe did his science undisturbed by any considerations for the usefulness of knowledge,[17] but only a few pages later, he claims that Goethe did not allow for the separation between research and its application.[18] Jost Schieren in his quite subtle philosophical study of Goethe's scientific methods, titled by Schieren as "Anschauende Urteilskraft", i.e. "Perceptively guided Faculty of Judgement", quotes the first sentence of "The Experiment" presently before us, but only in order to support his views of Goethe's epistemological position. In his quote, he leaves out the second sentence of that paragraph where Goethe speaks of the importance of Nature as being of "benefit or harm" to man.[19] Examples like these to which I could easily add others, make one wonder why people shy away from truly dealing with Goethe's sense for the usefulness and benefits coming to us from Nature. Could it be that they, living under conditions of late capitalism, have lost a sense for appropriately making use of Nature? Is use always abuse? Could they not sense anymore that something would be at the same time gainful and beneficial without being egofocal? One must not forget that Goethe's "Teachings on Colors", although reaching onto quite abstract theoretical levels, still contains passages, even chapters, with clearly practical contents, e.g. the section titled "Relation to the Techniques of Dyers".[20] It is all too often ignored that Goethe's interest in highly refined contemplations, even abstractions, go easily hand in hand with down to earth practical concerns.

Sensuous pleasure and scientific rigor were also intimately related for Goethe. His scientific writings oftentimes express how his sensuous pleasure stirs his curiosity and brings him to enormous precision in his studies of Nature. Even a cursory reading of the "Teachings on Colors" would make anybody aware of his frequent references to the sensuous enjoyment of his rigorously made observations and experiments. In fact, the very first words of this voluminous opus are "The lust to know".[21]

Instead of simply opposing the segmentation of the merely philosophical interest in Goethe's science by an advocacy of holism – which as such would remain unfounded - I would suggest to take note what it is that allows Goethe to unite pleasure, attraction and benefits in man's relation to Nature. At this point, one can hardly overemphasize that it is the enjoyment of Nature (see paragraph 199,2) and not the concept of her upon which Goethe's science flourishes. Being attracted to her, trying to come to know her and receiving from her – materially – are only different manifestations of his relation to Nature. It is indeed the question which our understanding of Nature has to face, namely, whether it is the sensuously felt kinship to her or a sheer greediness which permeates our interest in her. Where the sense for kinship is absent, a splintering of our relation to Nature is unavoidable so that our distinction from her threatens the "analogia entis" and turns the taking from Nature into acts that leave at best a bad conscience in the egofocal individual.

However, Goethe's appreciation of man's wholesome subjectivity as it combines all aspects of our being does not keep him from seeing that "(T)his entirely natural way of looking at and judging things..." exposes the human being "...to a thousand errors..." and "...put him to shame and embitter his life". It needs to be noted that Goethe, on the one hand, obviously blames the subjectivity of man for these errors, but he does, on the other, in no way propose to eliminate subjectivity from the processes of awareness and of knowledge creation. While Goethe does not have the problems that objectivistic scientists have with subjectivity, he also knows that a lot needs to be done by man about his subjectivity, in order to not let it "embitter his life". Obviously, Goethe highly values avoidance of such embitterment, but it needs to be clarified how he avoids "a thousand errors".

On one occasion while discussing the process of scientific work and expressing his hopes to not ignore the beneficial results of that research, he says: [22]

> Our whole attention has to ... be directed towards carefully listening to Nature's ways so that we do not make her recalcitrant through forceful prescriptions to her, yet, on the contrary, not allow her to remove us through her arbitrariness from purpose.

Obviously, Goethe does not at all deny that man wants something from Nature, but this desire of ours must not get into our way of understanding her willingly on her terms which, after all, are our terms as well. Having an understanding of her keeps our love for her from turning into raping her.

Before we turn to an inspection of the second paragraph of "The Experiment", we should further note that Goethe speaks in this paragraph of "(T)his entirely natural way of looking at and judging things...".The combination of observing and passing judgement on "things", usually rejected by so-called "value-free" science, is obviously quite acceptable to Goethe. Without awareness of this, one is bound to misunderstand one of Goethe's central concepts, namely that of "Anschauende Urteilskraft", i.e. of "Perceptively guided Faculty of Judgement". Goethe certainly knows about the instantaneity and simultaneity of the processes of conceptualization and of evaluation.[23] After having elaborated on how much pleasure is involved for him in studying Nature by "carefully listening" to her, we do not think it needs to be emphasized how much the selection of what we "look at and judge" is already a matter of evaluation. This should make it clear that the inclusion of evaluation into our conceptualizations of Nature is, for Goethe, not what leads to the problems involved in subjectivity. Instead, Goethe thinks that we are prone to "a thousand errors", precisely because we do not pay sufficient attention to what truly attracts us to Nature and provokes us to practice the accuracy of our sensuously grounded gifts for observation and knowledge. To say the opposite would obviously be absurd. It would be a sign of weirdness, would one avoid knowing someone whom one loves. This must be related to what Goethe elaborates on later in the essay,[24] when he points out that all too often preconceived concepts, if not interests, get between our selves and the Nature that we wish to understand. These interests and projections distort our knowledge of her and keep our concepts of Nature from being true elevations of internal and external Nature. Being joyfully attracted by Nature and exercising "perseverance in work"[25] would in this combination allow us to avoid the "thousand errors" in our understanding of the world to which we are otherwise prone.

Finally, it is quite important, in my view, to at least take issue with the question at which point precisely in the elevation from the sensuous to the conceptual/evaluative level the "thousand errors" arise. For the time being, I would like to merely point out that for Goethe an error cannot occur at the level of a sheer response to a stimulus, i.e. at the level of our senses. In Nature, an error can not occur; it can only occur at the level of our Otherness to Nature. On one occasion among many others, Goethe says: "The senses do not cheat, the judgement does".[26] At yet another time, when Lord Rumford speaks about optical illusions, Goethe angrily replies: "It is blasphemy to say there is such a thing as an optical illusion".[27] In other words, Nature cannot go wrong within Nature herself of which our senses are a part. However, Goethe also knows that our senses are constantly under the influence of our conceptualizations. It is in terms of previous and not fully sense grounded elevations, i.e. of dubious concepts to which our senses may have become so accustomed that they can seduce us to "thousand errors". This is to say that it is our constant task to keep our senses as "shiny, pure and bright" as Goethe had regained them on his Italian journey.[28] If this task, however, is sensed as a moral prescription, then there is still something at work in us that has gone wrong in our love for Nature. Love out of morality is a love estranged from the object of its (pretended) affection. In other words, there is more than one way in which false, mentally misguided elevations can rob the status of primacy of our senses. This is what makes the elevation of Nature to symbolic Nature so risky. Falling prey to that risk creates our environmental problems. These are, as we noted above, not caused by an incorrect science, but by a correct one that is not truthful to Nature.

Paragraph 194,2

Those ones take on a far heavier task (in German Tagewerk) who, fired by their drive for knowledge, strive to observe the objects of Nature in themselves and in their relation among themselves, for one thing, they no longer have the yardstick, which came to their help, so long as they as human beings considered things in relation to their own selves It is precisely the yardstick of pleasure and displeasure, of attraction and repulsion, of benefit and harm, that they have to renounce totally, they should, like indifferent and, as it were, godlike beings, search and study what there is and not what pleases Thus, neither the beauty nor the usefulness of a plant should move the true botanist He is supposed to study the plant's formation and its relation with the rest of the plant kingdom, and as they are all lured out and shone upon by the sun, he too, should look upon and survey them with the same calm gaze, and he should take the yardstick for such coming to know, the data for judging not out of himself but out of the sphere of the things which he observes

Goethe speaks in this paragraph about those students of Nature who, instead of engaging in their work by considering "...things in relation to their own selves...", "...strive to observe the objects in Nature in themselves and in their relation to themselves". It needs to be noted, first of all, that no trace of a moralistic objection on Goethe's part against that approach can be found here. But for those who study Goethe mainly with a philosophical interest, another observation may be of significance.

I think it is quite telling that Goethe uses the term "objects in themselves" in a way that seems to reveal a lack of Kantian influence on him. It needs to be remembered that Kant had rigorously denounced the feasibility of coming to know "things in themselves". This meant for Goethe that Kant had reduced the human being to a sheerly cognizing subject and the world of objects to one of mere appearances ("Erscheinungen"). For Goethe, however, this world, this Nature, is the one and only world and reality. It is God's creation and through it he reveals himself.[29] In it we live as real human beings of flesh and blood and not just as "cognizing subjects". Accordingly, Goethe speaks here simply of human subjects who aim at cognizing objects in detachment from their own subjectivity and in that sense of objects "in themselves". To the extent that Kant does not hold an analytical position and to the extent that Goethe knows Kant's position[30] and yet prefers to inspect the position of those who claim to study "things in themselves", this paragraph could be read as demonstrating Goethe's, at that time, quite limited regard for Kant's epistemology. It was only later, through Schiller and Schelling, that Goethe appropriates, in modification, some aspects of Kantian thought.

Staying away from such philosophical concerns (in 1792 and in 1823!), Goethe simply inspects here how those proceed in their research who truncate their subjectivity to a mere "drive for knowledge", a drive that is supposedly free from all other interests (and without questioning the origin of that drive). Goethe inspects this position not only for the sake of argument, but also because it has yielded scientific results which he cannot deny.[31] That kind of subjectivity can speak, though differently from Kant, of its objects as "things in themselves" to the extent that that subjectivity is, or at least claims to be, detached from them. For Goethe, by contrast, the "drive for knowledge" *and* the "yardstick for coming to know" are part of human Nature. Therefore, things are in his view simultaneously "things in themselves" and "things for us". There is nothing "behind" or "above" them, as we will hear him emphasize later.[32] It is for this reason that Goethe, as mentioned above, could even see "ideas"; not even ideas are outside of this world for him, but are sensuous elevations of Nature's multiple manifestations. We have come across numerous cases[33] of strictly philosophical interpretations of Goethe's "methodology" which miss this point, i.e., the point of Goethe's sustained "innerworldliness". As far as we can tell there are only very few assessments of Goethe's science[34] which try to clarify the issue of Goethe's naïve trust in Nature and in man's senses.

A remarkable and informative example of missing this innerworldliness is represented in Jost Schieren's aforementioned book "Anschauende Urteilskraft", subtitled, in English translation, "Methodical and Philosophical Foundations of Goethe's Scientific Ways of Coming to Know" (in German: "Methodische und philosophische Grundlagen von Goethes naturwissenschaftlichem Erkennen"). In Part II of his considerations,[35] Schieren's philosophically excellent treatment of the reception of Kant by Goethe seems, in my view, to miss the decisive point of their difference in a total and yet telling way. It is not the issue, as suggested by Schieren, whether Goethe saw in contrast to Kant an identity between mind and matter,[36] or whether Goethe's study of Nature was of a qualitative and not of a quantitative kind.[37] The issue, instead, is that Goethe *sensed* the kinship between Nature and man, elevated that sense to his knowledge and studied Nature out of that self knowledge. One could, of course, argue that this was not yet fully clear to Goethe and that Goethe had not yet fully appropriated Kant's concept of epigenesis, when he wrote the "Kautelen" in 1792,[38] however, he had understood and overcome the limitations of Kantian philosophy when he published "The Experiment" in 1823! After having published, in 1820, his "Anschauende Urteilskraft", i.e., his "Perceptively guided Faculty of Judgement", it is quite clear how he distances himself from Kant. Yet, at either points in time, Goethe knew, as expressed in the paragraph before us (unchanged between 1792 and 1823!), that the "drive for knowledge" alone without a more far reaching appreciation of the material commonality between object and subject makes the "task" of studying Nature a "heavier" one than it would be with such appreciation.

The elimination of personal "pleasure", "attraction", "benefit" and their opposites and, thus the denial of a full fledged material commonality-in-distinction between object and subject imply that students of Nature "...should, like indifferent and, as it were, godlike beings, search and study what there is and not what pleases." This diminishes the significance of man's subjectivity also in so far as it forces the student of Nature to "...take the yardstick for...coming to know, the data for judging ... out of the sphere of the things which he observes". Human subjectivity then has lost, if we may still put it in Kantian terminology, its categories but not its spontaneity. This implies a serious problem which Goethe, however, does not contemplate at this point. For us the problem is: how could one at all "...take the yardstick for...coming to know, the data for judging ... out of the sphere of things ...", if there is no correspondence to them, no commonality with them, in the human subject beyond the "drive for knowledge"? Or, in view of modern scientific research, we wonder how could a subjectivity reduced to a "drive for knowledge" account for more than "pure research" done by "godlike beings", namely, for an interest in the application of research? Furthermore, if application of research is not accounted for, not even by an interest in "benefits", does this, then, not help to explain why it is looked down upon, though usually only in appearance, by the "pure researcher"? Finally, if other forces motivating research like beauty and pleasure are relegated to another segregated area, namely, that of art, how could a pure "drive for knowledge" then even account for itself? In other words, Goethe's (temporary) acceptance of truncated subjectivity in science reveals to him that it rests on a rather shaky foundation. This comes out much clearer later in "The Experiment".[39] Here Goethe writes that "… neither the beauty nor the usefulness of a plant should move the true botanist". This way, scientists make themselves look like priests of knowledge, while artists as connoisseurs of beauty turn into dreamers who, like the romanticists in Goethe's times, easily adhere to fictitious and merely sentimental "common bonds" with Nature. But Goethe does not discuss such fictitious notions in this essay. Instead, he inspects research based primarily on "hypotheses, theories, systems and …other kinds of representations" (paragraph 194,3/195,1). At that point, the "drive for knowledge", here linked to "… indifferent and, as it were, godlike beings …", finds a somewhat sober explanation not far from egofocal ambitions (e.g. in paragraphs 198,2; 199,5/200,1; 202,2).

At any rate, a science without full fledged human subjects leads to what Goethe called, - in a letter written to Zelter in 1808, - the "greatest mishap of the more recent Physics", namely "…that one has segregated the experiments from the human being".[40] Of course, when taking the stance of an "indifferent and, as it were, godlike being" towards "what there is", then the modern idea of a subject-less, i.e., presumably a totally objective understanding of Nature, is only a thought carried to its logical conclusion. Less than 200 years after Goethe, it has been seriously noted, albeit with a measure of concern and yet without even a hint at an alternative, that the human subject has been replaced in the sciences by methodologically reasoned procedures and/or apparatuses that do the actual observing of Nature.[41] Only a few among contemporary philosophers, among them the above mentioned Gerhard Roth[42] have pointed out that these measuring machines have still to be read (and understood) by human subjects. Moreoever, these apparatuses still need to be built and calibrated by people, without which they obviously would not even exist. They have also to be set in motion by humans who, by accepting their distance to Nature, get only that understanding of objects that exists for these apparatuses. This situation was anticipated by Goethe, as one can see upon reading only a little further in the just mentioned letter of Goethe to his friend Zelter. He says there that the mishap of the segregation between experiment and human being implies that "…one wishes to come to know Nature merely through what artificial instruments show, even to limit and to prove that way what she is capable of doing".[43] We will have occasion later in our discussion of the "The Experiment"[44] to inspect Goethe's views on the use and misuse of instruments in scientific research. After all, he used instruments as well.

With this quote from Goethe's letter, we obviously reach beyond the paragraph of Goethe's essay that is presently under our consideration. And yet, there is something important coming to light here which we cannot let pass unnoticed. Goethe sees that a study of Nature which only narrows and yet does not eliminate the role of the human subject, limits itself also with regard to seeing "what she is capable of doing". In saying this, Goethe does more than just point out that a distanced knowledge of Nature makes her, through the application of that knowledge, "recalcitrant" and, thus, less and less inhabitable by real human beings. This has been pointed out today by many others as well.[45] But beyond that, we come to understand, together with Goethe, that those scientists (and environmentalists, for that matter), who proceed that way, simply lose a sense for what Nature could deliver to those truly living with her. As a consequence, they have little more to offer than moralistic warnings and/or technocratic placebos against our abuse of Nature.

A tendentially subjectless study of Nature does not only have limitations as far as its results are concerned, it itself as a form of research was seen by Goethe as a "far heavier task" than the one that those students have who act out of an awareness of their own being part of Nature. The consequence of having eliminated one's full bodied interest in Nature carries inevitably with it the burden of ethical surveillance not only in the application of science, as many suggest today ("constraints"), but also in the research activity itself. Where the yardstick for judgement is no longer experienced and acknowledged as being within our own Nature, moralism has to reign in our inner Nature. If it is only the "drive for knowledge" that is left of human subjectivity, then a drive for goodness has to be added somehow and somewhere. While a determination of the point at which ethics should be brought in is already an uncertain undertaking, a yet more difficult question to answer is: where should goodness come from? On what could it be grounded? On another occasion, when dealing with Newton's personality, Goethe states this problem quite clearly. He says that Newton and the tradition he has co-founded imply that man is " the more moralistic, the more rationalistic [he] is,...". He then adds that the more rationalistic and moralistic man gets, "... the more untrue he becomes...".[46] This statement implies a concept of truth that goes, of course, beyond sheer correctness. Later on in the essay (e.g. paragraphs 198,2;199,4;199,5/200,1), Goethe deals with the estranging requirement of moralism more closely and characterizes it as being faced by serious temptations.

Today, a few attempts have been made to indicate that the ethical problems involved in modern kind of scientific research can hardly be resolved by staying at the level of ethical prescriptions. E.U. v. Weizsäcker[47] is one of the few who think that there are, at a deeper level, "methodological problems" that modern science has to resolve. And yet, not even when making reference to Goethe in this connection,[48] does Weizsäcker clarify what exactly he means by solving "methodological problems". His advocacy of a unification between the natural sciences and the humanities[49] does not help either in this regard, not the least since it remains unclear what such a unification could possibly mean. Others, though, go far in the opposite direction by saying that "…we have to impose ethical expectations more distanced from Nature on us,…if we do not wish to sacrifice us and our earth to the age old Darwinian race of the fittest".[50] This latter position is widely shared and expresses itself in the growing bulk of laws, legal measures and control agencies the main commonality of which is that they all struggle to be seen as less futile than they are.[51] We, on our part, have explicated above why we think that attempts at tackling environmental problems from within the late capitalist mode of thinking are futile. Something quite different and beyond solving "methodological problems" is required. Goethe exemplifies it.

Paragraph 194,3/195,1

The history of the sciences teaches us how difficult this abnegation (in German Entäußerung) is for any human being How he in this manner arrives and must arrive at hypotheses, theories, systems and whatever other kinds of representations (in German Vorstellungsarten) there might be through which he tries to grasp the infinite, will concern us in the second section of this small essay I devote the first part of it to the consideration of how a human being proceeds when he strives to know the forces of Nature History of physics, which at present I have reason to study more carefully, provides me often with the opportunity to think about this matter, and so this little essay originates, in which I strive to visualize for myself in a general way the manner in which distinguished men (in German Männer) have advanced (in German genutzt) and harmed the teachings on Nature (This italicized section of the text is not included in the published version of 1823) As soon as we consider an object in relation to itself and in connection with other objects (in German mit andern) and not immediately desire or detest it, then with a calm attention we shall soon be able to create a fairly distinct concept of it, its parts and its connections The further we continue these observations (in German Betrachtungen), the more we connect these objects with one another, the more we practice the gift of observation (in German

Beobachtungsgabe) which is within us If we know, in our actions, to relate these insights to ourselves, then we deserve to be called smart Smartness is not a difficult matter for any well organized person (in German für einen wohlorganisierten Menschen) who either is moderate by Nature or has been rendered moderate by circumstances for life sets us right at every step However, if the observer is expected to apply this keen power of judgment to the examination of hidden (in German geheimer) natural connections, to watch his own paces and steps in a world in which, as it were, he is alone to guard against rashness, to constantly keep his purpose in sight, without letting pass unnoticed on his way any useful or harmful assistance, if he is further expected to be his own most strict observer where he cannot be controlled so easily by anybody, and if, in the course of his most zealous endeavors he is expected to be always distrustful of himself then probably everybody can see how strict these requirements are and how little one can hope to see them totally satisfied, whether one poses them to others or to oneself Yet these difficulties, one can even say, this hypothetical impossibility, must not prevent us from doing the utmost possible, and we at least get the furthest if we try to bring to our awareness the means in general by which distinguished persons (in German Menschen) have been known to expand the sciences, if we point out precisely the false routes on which they went astray, and on which a great number of students (in German Schüler) have followed them sometimes for centuries until later experiences have guided the observer back again onto the right path

The italicized section of this paragraph is the longest section of the manuscript version that has not been included in the published text. We are not sure why Goethe has omitted it. Erich Trunz, the editor of the Hamburg Edition of Goethe's works, thinks that dropping it "served the greater precision...whereby however, the structure [of this essay] got blurred".[52] This may very well be the case, but this omission also eliminates a first hint at Goethe's views on theorizing. If read from within the context of this whole essay (and beyond), this paragraph already allows one to anticipate that Goethe is not per se negative or resentful about "theorizing" in the sciences.

In this paragraph, Goethe sets out to explore a kind of scientific research in which the researcher acts as if he could set aside his own relations to objects. For Goethe, doing so is an "abnegation". *"The history of the sciences teaches us how difficult this abnegation (in German· Entäußerung) is for any human being"*, never mind that it can only be a partial one, as we saw reading paragraph 194,2; the "drive for knowledge" is a property of the human subject that cannot be set aside in research. Researchers proceeding in such partial abnegation *"... must arrive at hypotheses, theories, systems and whatever kinds of representations ..."*. Stating matters this way, Goethe already indicates that he is not readily willing to accept that way of studying, but he does not flatly *"... disapprove of ... hypotheses, theories,... and systems ... since these must necessarily spring from the organization of our essence"* (paragraph 199,2). Certainly, Goethe sees problems with this approach, yet we have first of all to note that he does not ethicalize his opposition against it. After all, Goethe himself theorized, but he did so in a different way, as we shall see. Goethe rejected this dominant way of theorizing simply because it distorts the elevation of natural phenomena to knowledge and, in doing so, the Nature of the human being. While those who do adhere to that dominant way of proceeding have, as in the past, "advanced", they have also "harmed the teachings on Nature". Since "abnegation" cannot be total, the question arises for Goethe: how is subjectivity to be treated? His question is not how much or how little of subjectivity is admissible. I like to underline here that Goethe does not take the ambiguous, if not contradictory status of abnegation of subjectivity as a departure point for a critique. Instead, he demonstrates, step by step in this essay, how a student of Nature can remain faithful to Nature precisely by fully retaining his subjective Otherness to her.[53]

Later on in this essay, Goethe speaks of theorizing as being part of our "essence". Only one paragraph prior to this characterization, namely in paragraph 198,3/199,1, he talks about how researchers directly correlate phenomena in their minds, even though it is not clear yet, whether these phenomena are directly related to one another in reality. To do this, so Goethe thinks "…is in keeping with the Nature of the human being …" (paragraph 198,/199,1). But, in the same sentence with reference to our haste in making premature mental connections, he adds: "I commit this mistake almost daily". So the question arises: what is it in our essence, even in our Nature, that makes premature theorizing, i.e. the hasty creation of mental connections among phenomena a mistake, even one, at which one "must arrive", if one approaches objects without an inner yardstick?

I think, an attempt at answering this question is aided by listening to an often quoted[54] passage from Goethe's "Preface" to his "Teachings on Colors". There he says:[55]

> Each looking-at changes (in German· geht über) to considering, each considering to thinking-over, each thinking to connecting, and thus one can say that we already theorize with each attentive glance into the world. However, to do and to enact this with consciousness, with knowledge of oneself, with freedom and with irony - in order to make use of a daring concept - requires such a dexterity, if the abstraction of which we are afraid, should

become innocuous and if the result of the experience that
we hope for should become really vivid and useful

We do not suggest to make an attempt, at this point, at fully exhausting
the meaning of this passage, but it seems to be clear that Goethe
certainly does not object here to the activity of theorizing, provided it is
done with caution, i.e. "...with consciousness, ... with knowledge of
oneself, with freedom and with irony, ...". It is only then that our
abstractions have a chance to become "... innocuous, ... vivid and
useful". This "consciousness" and this "knowledge of oneself" refer to
the awareness of one's place in Nature, a question with which Goethe
had struggled for quite some time. With clarity on man's place in
Nature, the human subject can carry out his research by not only not
abnegating his self but by cautiously and ironically watching his way of
conceptualizing the objects around him. "Ironically watching" focuses
here on the question of whether or not one distorts one's own Nature in
"theorizing". Goethe's suggestion of how to avoid such distortion
should come out in proper detail in our inspection of the second part of
"The Experiment".

This much, however, can already be anticipated.

In paragraph 200,4, Goethe says that an "... immediate bringing to
bear of an experiment on the proof of any hypothesis ..." is "harmful",
while a "mediated" one is "fruitful". This passage brings us a step
closer to an understanding of Goethe's vehement objection to Newton's
conceptualization of light and colors. For Goethe, Newton brings one
crucial experiment, his "experimentum crucis", to bear on his whole
theorizing on color. Newton takes a "yardstick" out of Nature by taking
off from the observation that light when refracted yields different color
impressions in the human eye. He then generalizes this to the theory
that all colors are contained in light. Newton finally proves this to be
the case in a rather complicated and skillfully arranged experiment (to
be discussed later).[56] Having proven the composite Nature of light,
Newton turns this yardstick into a guiding principle for all of his
studies of light and colors. Without giving primacy to this mental
construct, the further study of light and colors would have been
unfounded in theory and thus would have been problematic for
Newton. In this sense, theory becomes the primary basis for Newton's
research. Having abnegated every other mental relation to the objects of
light and colors by having absolutized a small set of sensuous
observations (those related to refracted light), Newton gives us an
example for scientific research that "... *must arrive at hypotheses,*

theories ... " etc. Proceeding in this manner turns mental constructs into instruments in terms of which we fabricate interpretations of Nature, but not an understanding of her that does justice to her (and to us as parts of her). I leave aside here, as Goethe does, that Newton's yardstick is not, at least not in its origin, a primarily mentalistic yardstick. In fact, it is initially a sensuous one as well, but this circumstance is pushed aside, when a sensuous yet spurious experience gets mentally absolutized and takes as such primacy in subsequent experiments. Newton's teachings become for Goethe as "unclean" as those of the alchemists, since they took "... leap[s] from the idea ... to reality ... to mendacious assemblages".[57] And yet, Goethe concedes that insights gained this way temporarily "advance" the teachings on Nature like Newton's did for almost hundred years. But they also "harm" our arriving at truth in the long run, as he says not only here, but also later on in this essay (paragraphs 199,4; 199,5/200,1; 200,2) and elsewhere in his writings.[58]

For the sake of clarity on this important point, I would like to approach it from yet another angle.

In the second part of the essay, and as announced in the paragraph before us, Goethe says: *"It merits a future consideration of its own, how the intellect could come to our help in this endeavor"* (paragraph 200,7/201,1). I am not aware that such a consideration has ever been delivered by Goethe, yet I believe that the text of the essay before us allows one to understand how Goethe conceives of this help. In view of Goethe's reference to "consciousness" and "knowledge of oneself", I wish to emphasize that the help of the intellect in this endeavor must not be interpreted, as if Goethe himself gives, in the final analysis, primacy to the mind and not to Nature in scientific investigations. Knowledge of oneself, i.e. of one's place in Nature, could be interpreted as if Goethe had seen it as a matter of "smartness" to grant primacy to Nature in dealing with her, because doing so promises success in controlling her truly. Phrasing this issue in terms of our discussion of Adams' materialist concept of culture,[59] we could say that Goethe was conscious of the primacy of the spontaneous will in the act of coming to know and that knowing this could have made him bow to Nature in a merely instrumentalistic way. After all, doing so would guarantee success in attaining truth and well being in the long run. The decisive question - decisive also for an understanding of Goethe's concept of "elevation" - is however, whether our conceptualization of things in Nature arise out of an interest in controlling her mentally (and otherwise) or out of sensuous enjoyment of her beauty. It should be clear that the driving force in Goethe's science is this sensuous enjoyment (see paragraph 199,2) and not a "second thought" type of "smartness". This enjoyment is a primarily bodily grounded relation to Nature and can as such not be manipulated. For Goethe, this is man's primary connection to Nature,[60] it is in this enjoyment where the human being *is* Nature. This being one with Nature triggers, in our species, the "lust to know" her better and better. The process of coming to know then turns the doing of science in as much into a satisfying activity as other forms of our communion with her do, regardless of whether they take place in art or in the making of things, i.e. in production, or in consumption. It is ultimately this Nature grounded, and certainly not strategically chosen, sensuousness which keeps Goethe's essay "The Experiment" from being a treatise on research techniques and their reasonability. In short, it is wrong to see Goethe's science as grounded in a philosophically reasoned methodology, as has been suggested so often.[61] The doing of science is, for Goethe, a thoughtful celebration of our kinship with Nature.

In my reading of that part of the paragraph which has been retained in the published version of "The Experiment", I find Goethe writing about two different subtypes of the representatives for hypothesis guided research. Both share that they are in their studies "... soon able to create a fairly distinct concept ..." of the objects they investigate, as this is in keeping with "human essence". The two types of researchers begin to differ, when it comes to the depth of their studies and the just discussed "smartness" of relating their insights to themselves, i.e., to their own status as human subjects.

On the one hand, practicing the subjective "... gift of observation, which is within us ...", one kind of researcher begins "... in [his] actions to relate these insights to [himself]". This "... deserve(s) to be called smart". Such smartness is considered by Goethe to be a property of a human being "...who is either moderate by Nature or has been rendered moderate by circumstance: for life sets us right at every step", i.e. it corrects us. Moderation and smartness, so it seems to be suggested here, arise out of Nature, because Nature – "life" – brings us back to the insight that we cannot go against her. Yet, saying that such correction is "... not a difficult matter for any well organized human being..." implies that the criterion for being judged as "well organized" rests obviously with the willingness to accept being set right by life. In other words, those not willing to accept the lessons taught by Nature are not "well organized": a beautifully clear value-judgement on us today vis-à-vis our continued distortion of outer and inner Nature.

On the other hand, there is the observer of Nature who will "... apply his keen power of judgement to the examination of hidden (in German: geheimer) natural connections ...". The German word "geheimer" could also be translated by the English word "secret". In view of what Goethe says in later paragraphs in this essay about this kind of research work (e.g. paragraphs 198,3/199,1; 199,2; 200,6; 202,4/203,1) and on other occasions about the technical tools ("apparatuses") necessary for it,[62] we think that he refers here to research on aspects of Nature less readily accessible to our senses. This research, therefore, requires tools which go, qualitatively, beyond what our senses can do. At any rate, the further the researcher moves into such "hidden" territories, the more "... he is alone..." and "... cannot be controlled so easily by anybody ...". Today, we have reason to understand better than Goethe could, how uncontrollable research is, particularly where it claims to be "on the cutting edge". Goethe accumulates numerous examples for the kind of caution this supposedly "calm" (paragraph 194,2) researcher has to impose on himself. The most striking aspect of these cautions is that they are close to being mutually exclusive yet strict, and that they apply to the researcher's own status as subject. His has to be a "...most zealous endeavor..." (and yet "calm"), while being "... distrustful of himself ..."; he has "... to guard against rashness ...", and yet "... must keep his purpose in sight ...". This self-focused skepticism culminates in that he is "... expected to be his own strict observer where he cannot be controlled so easily by anybody ...", i.e. he has to police himself. These conditions are indeed strict, as Goethe expresses this by using the word "strict" twice within only a few lines so that "... probably everybody can see ... how little one can hope to see them totally satisfied ...". Calling this heavy task a "hypothetical impossibility", one has additional reason to see how self estranging (yet self serving) the priesthood of "pure science" was and still is today. Not even a trace of "lust" or of a drive which, for Goethe, is the connection between object and subject[63] can be found here. How then can a "drive for knowledge" be cultivated, when it is policed? Here, we come across the problems of "abnegation" again. Abnegation while ambiguous is also far away from sensuousness, its elevation and its cultivated satisfaction.

In the closing sentence of this paragraph, Goethe suggests that it could be fruitful "... to bring to our awareness the means in general by which distinguished persons ...", obviously those working in this "impossible" manner, "... have been known to expand the sciences ...". Clearly, Goethe again admits that that kind of research has made its contributions, i.e., it has " advanced" (though also "harmed") "... the teachings on Nature". In the same sense, we have acknowledged above that modern science has delivered enormous results which one cannot simply dismiss, let alone treat as incorrect. Yet, we called them false. Goethe implies here that our studies of the accomplishments of distinguished men "... at least get the furthest, ... if we ... point out precisely the false routes on which they went astray ...". This is what Goethe tries to do later in this essay, when he identifies the point where "false routes" are taken up by hypothesis guided research.

In closing my commentary on this paragraph, it may be in order to point out an important difference between Goethe's way of thinking and that of a particular tradition in philosophy evolving at his life time.

Philosophically oriented people will remember how much "critique", i.e. the conceptual inquiry into systems of thoughts, was traditionally expected to lead through the discovery of "contradictions" to true insight. The "critical tradition" from Kant, Hegel via Marx up to "critical theory" is full of examples for this. But one should notice here that Goethe expects "... experiences ..." to guide "... the observer back again onto the right path". Goethe hopes to find truth by following and making the experiments of distinguished men who went astray in their research and not by "critique". He puts his trust in his own studies, i.e. in his own finding out by concrete experiences and experiments. If truth is claimed to have been revealed but cannot be found in one's own experiences and experiments, one has to "... point out precisely the false routes ..." taken by previous research. Materially concrete experiences and experiments, and not just a mental "critique", will guide one much more solidly "...back again onto the right path". Critique may allow one to arrive at the "determinate negation" of "contradictions" and then to establish mentally valid "determinate affirmations", to use the terms of that "tradition", but these, not grounded in concrete experiences, remain non-committal. At least, they have done so all too often in the past. Truth, however, (not just "value-free" correctness), can only be found where object and subject are experienced as mediated by experiments that appreciate the primary status of Nature in object and subject alike.

Paragraph 195,2/196,1

As little as anybody can deny that experience has and should have the greatest influence in the teachings on Nature, about which I speak at present in particular, as well as in everything which the human being undertakes, can one gainsay the high, and, as it were, creatively independent power of the forces of the soul, by which these experiences are grasped, drawn together, ordered and given shape However, it cannot be generally known, or appreciated, how to make and to use these experiences, how to form and to employ these forces

In this short paragraph, Goethe admits that "… it cannot be generally known … how to make and to use … experiences, how to form and to employ these forces", i.e. the forces "of the soul" - Goethe's much richer term for what we call "subjectivity". Yet, Goethe also knows that nobody "… can deny that experience has and should have the greatest influence in the teachings on Nature, … as well as in everything the human being undertakes …". It is from experiences, i.e., from our sensuously concrete connections with objects, that one learns primarily (and "not from books" i.e. from previously created thoughts frozen in print). The elevation of these experiences to understanding requires that they have to be "… grasped, drawn together, ordered and given shape" by the "… creatively independent power of the forces of the soul …". While Nature and bodily grounded experience deserve the status of primacy in these processes, one must not overlook that the "forces of the soul" are understood by Goethe as having a "creatively independent power". In view of later paragraphs (paragraphs 198,2ff) as well as in view of Newton's subjective absolutizing of a single observation based hypothesis, we are entitled to see here an awareness for the possibility that our "soul" makes itself "creatively independent" from experiences. Liberating one's soul from experience does not mean to act as if experiences did not exist or were not made at all – then the soul would have nothing to work with - , but it means to "grasp, "order" and "shape" experiences by not retaining the sense for their dependence on Nature out there and in us. A creatively independent soul in this sense would not come to a truthful elevation of Nature, only to her distortion. And yet, there is more to true elevation than concrete experiences and the soul, i.e. static objects and subjects. At the end of this paragraph, Goethe indicates that we have also "… to form … these forces", meaning the forces of the soul. To form one's subjectivity, to elevate it in the process of experiencing, means to cultivate one's mind in every moment of making sensuous observations to the growing awareness of how varied Nature around us presents herself to our senses. Educating our senses means the growth of Nature in us, but not the forcing of our "soul", i.e. of our power of judgement to bow to her. Instead, it would entail following our own senses in their contact with her joyfully, a contact without which no Nature would exist for us any ways.

It is at this point where we can return to the differences between Schiller and Goethe as they came to light in their first extended conversation in 1794 and which remained irreconcilable.

It was an important aspect of the differences between Schiller and Goethe that the latter had no desire for the freedom that Schiller had found in Kant's concept of freedom.[64] Kantian freedom arises out of the acceptance of the categorical, i.e. mental identity between subject and object. Schiller thinks that man finds freedom in following the Kantian Twelve Categories, i.e. the structure of the mind. Accordingly, Schiller's freedom is the freedom arising out of insight into what we cannot help but think, i.e. have to think by "necessity". Therefore, Schiller cannot help but understand Goethe's "Urpflanze", i.e. the "original plant" as anything else than a primarily mental construct, "purified" from empirical, experiential singularity, i.e. as an "idea" in that sense. For Goethe, the "original plant" was a revelation of the commonality that each plant represents to the senses and the minds of subjects who experience it through the "perceptively guided force of judgement" common to all human beings. Goethe has joyfully and keenly watched thousands of different plants and has made numerous drawings of them so that he knows in detail how their commonality comes across to our senses. Goethe brought their common Nature through his own Nature to his pleasure seeking attention. In this sense, the idea of the "Urpflanze" was for Goethe a product of his whole inner Nature and not just of his mind. Each plant was a bodily experience and thus elevated to a bodily desired manifestation of what plants-in-themselves are all about. Knowing "the plant" this way, was Goethe's freedom, while for Schiller, freedom meant to accept the result of the order creating Kantian "power of judgement". Schiller's kind of freedom could only be, if the human subject mentally rises above the concreteness of singular manifestations of Nature to conceptually "generalizing ideas". This may open up our mind to a world beyond the one we live in, i.e., to a "cyberspace" of the philosophical kind. However, the cost of that freedom is, for Goethe, the loss of the sense for our kinship with Nature, the only reality there is. The cultivation of

our bodily grounded kinship with Nature is, therefore, a happily
accepted task; it is work, but not labor. The kind of work required is
explained by Goethe later in this essay starting with the next paragraph.

Paragraph 196,2

As soon as sharp-minded people (in German Menschen) (These italicized words are not
contained in the published version which would read, instead "As soon as people of sharp,
fresh senses ") of whom there are, by a moderate use of the word, many more than one
thinks, have their attention directed to objects, then one finds them as inclined to, as adroit at,
observation I have been able to notice this often, since I have been concerning myself
zealously with the teachings of light and colors, and, as usually happens, have conversed with
(This word is missing in the handwritten version, but it is included in the published one)
persons to whom such considerations are otherwise alien, about that what interests me so
much As soon as their attentiveness was lively, they noticed phenomena, which in part I had
not known, in part had overlooked, and through that they corrected quite often a too hastily
conceived idea, indeed they gave me cause to take faster steps to emerge from the
confinement in which a laborious investigation often holds us captive

Right at the beginning of this paragraph, we come across a change
between the hand written and the published version of "The
Experiment" which, I think, is quite telling. Instead of referring to
"sharp-minded people", as he had done in 1792, Goethe now wants the
reader of the publication to know that he is speaking of "people with
sharp, fresh senses". As we have mentioned before and as we shall see
again later in our commentary,[65] it is quite important for Goethe that
mere sharp-mindedness without "fresh senses" only leads to problems
in scientific research. It is almost impossible to count, let alone to quote
here, how often Goethe speaks of the importance of "sharp, fresh
senses" in his writings and how often he advocates to practice and
improve their sharpness. Let us again remember how much Goethe, this
"Augenmensch" (i.e. this "eye oriented person"), celebrated that his
eyes had become "shiny, pure and bright" again in Italy so that he
could perceive of things like before, namely, without the distortions
coming from "wrinkles" in his mind.[66] Without pure senses, little if
anything of what is right can be accomplished in life, whatever the
sensuous intake is mentally elevated to.

Of "… people with sharp, fresh senses … there are, by a moderate
use of the word, many more than one thinks …" and they are, with a
little help, i.e. with "… their attention directed to objects … as inclined
to, as adroit at, observation". This combination of a willingness and a
capability to observe has been "… notice[d] … often …" by Goethe,
even in "… persons to whom such considerations [of light and colors]

are otherwise alien...." Finding in others an inclination to and adroitness at "... what interests [him] so much ..." was reason enough for Goethe to converse with them, "... as usually happens ...". Sensuous interest and not a high social status or even learnedness, triggers his desire to talk, listen to and interact with people. This is how Goethe understands and practices what otherwise would remain an abstraction: namely, the commonality of Nature among things, man and fellow man.

This commonality also helps to "notice phenomena" of which Goethe admits freely that "... in part I had not known, in part I had overlooked ...". Experiencing this kind of help, he succeeds in getting out of "... a too hastily conceived idea ..." and he could then "... take faster steps to emerge from the confinement in which a laborious investigation often holds us captive", at times for centuries (paragraph 198,2) and like in " a despotic court" (paragraph 199,5/200,1). This enjoyable sociality was the way "... to use ... experiences .... and to employ ... forces" (paragraph 195,2/196,1) of the soul to arrive at true knowledge. Along these lines, one breaks out of "confinement" in "laborious investigations" in which one is held captive by conceptualizations which, as we put it above, are dubious, since they are not fully grounded in our senses and yet influence them.[67] Neither instrumentalistic reasons nor ethical concerns let Goethe work that way. Instead, he pursues his studies in social openness, because he has "... been feeling too good so far with the method of working together with other people to not want to continue this way" (paragraph 196,4).

Socially shared sensuous pleasure, not rigid abnegation and not an individuated "drive for knowledge" go for Goethe hand in hand in the search for truth. In this sense, Carl-Friedrich von Weizsäcker is right, when he writes that "truth is" - for Goethe – "a way of being human".[68] Truth found in such a way has overcome the separation of correctness from truth, of which Heisenberg knows.[69] It is a separation to which Goethe was as vehemently opposed as Heisenberg himself. Yet, while being concerned about sheer correctness, Heisenberg misses, regardless of Goethe's frequent reference to it, the significance that sensuousness has for the coming to truth. This comes to light, when Heisenberg claims that concepts like the double helix of nuclear acid or the elementary particles of nuclear physics are in as much cognitive ideas as Goethe's "idea". Heisenberg admits that these modern constructs can no longer be "intuited" the same way as Goethe's "idea" could be,[70] but he fails to explore and tell us what his notion of "Goethe's intuition" concretely means. When, on occasion, Heisenberg comes to speak of Goethe's sensuousness, he ignores its importance for "intuition" and, mistakenly, suggests that Goethe was at times willing to part with sensuousness. Heisenberg argues[71] that Goethe had eventually even to accept Copernicus' concept of the solar system although, presumably, one cannot sensuously experience the heliocentric structure of that system. I have to confess that I have no indication to believe that the Copernican concept of the solar system has ever been a problem for Goethe. The passage from Goethe's "Teachings on Colors" quoted by Heisenberg in order to support him in this regard seems to merely indicate that Goethe was aware of how difficult the acceptance of Copernicus' concept was for people who had just barely learned that the earth was round.[72] At any rate, I would like to point out, as Baldev Luther had emphasized so often, that for life on earth and for an understanding of it, e.g. for that of plants, it is sufficient to see, feel, enjoy and comprehend how important it is that the sun "comes up" and "goes down". Our knowledge of a heliocentric system may matter under other circumstances, perhaps in space flights, but not for us here and now, let alone for Goethe's day and age.

Paragraph 196,3

Thus what is valid in so many other human undertakings is valid here as well that the interest of several people directed towards *one* (Goethe's emphasis) point is capable of bringing forth something outstanding Here it becomes obvious that the envy, which likes so much to exclude others from the honor of a discovery, that the intemperate desire to treat and to develop something one has discovered only in one's own manner, are the greatest obstacle for the investigator himself

"Envy", i.e. an egofocally distorted social relation, in connection with an "intemperate desire", is an aspect of man's distorted inner Nature or his "soul", identified here as "... the greatest obstacle for the investigator himself". While "something outstanding" can be brought forth, if the "... interest of several people ..." is "... directed towards *one* (Goethe's emphasis) point ...", egofocal individuation does not only harm all of us, it does not even serve the individual investigator himself in his pursuit truly. This is not to say that it does not serve such an egoist in the short run, as we noted above,[73] but Goethe did not engage in short term considerations here; scientific research was "... for the world and the posterity" (paragraph 202,4/203,1).

This paragraph opposes social isolation in research for yet another reason. It is part and parcel of one's "intemperate desire", "... to treat and to develop something one has discovered only in one's own manner ...". This is to say that an "intemperate desire" is certainly understood as being capable of making discoveries, but this success, gained in social isolation, is in the danger of turning "one's own manner" of viewing and understanding into a habitual way of doing research. Thus, it may turn into an obstacle for an understanding of Nature adequate to her by placing primacy on a way of seeing which conceptually absolutizes a socially isolated and thus sensuously distorted way of viewing. Goethe seems to argue here against the emergence of an individuated "tradition" so to speak, which, like any "Great Tradition", turns qua being easily reduced to a mental inheritance, into giving primacy to thought. Today, after the death of all "Traditions", we are in the historically advantageous position to see that it is only our sociality, if grounded in Nature, that can save each one and all of us from getting individualistically distorted. Truth cannot be found alone.

This is not to deny that sociality is also appreciated in late capitalism as an important condition for learning and creating new knowledge.[74] Nowadays, we are also aware that norms backed by traditions are sensed not only as outdated, but more importantly, as limiting cognitive flexibility. In this way, Niklas Luhmann has argued that norms and traditions limit communication and, thus, the growth of cognitive control.[75] In view of the falsely appearing similarities between this view and that of Goethe, it is hopefully enough to point out that Luhmann, so obviously different from Goethe, assumes an instrumentalistic kind of sociality with the problematic consequences dealt with above and fearfully anticipated by Goethe.

I should not make it appear, as though a comment on this one paragraph would exhaust Goethe's views on the relations among individuality, individuation, co-operation and tradition. We will have occasion to return to these issues.[76]

Paragraph 196,4

I have been feeling too good so far with the method of working together with several other people to not want to continue this way I know exactly to whom I, on my way, have become indebted for this and that, and it shall be my pleasure to make this known publicly in the future

As far as this very short paragraph is concerned, I wish to comment on only one aspect of it. Goethe promises that "... it shall be my pleasure to make known publicly in the future ... exactly to whom I ... have become indebted for this and for that ..." (in his work). On this promise, however, Goethe has not always made good.

From his poetic work, we know that he has not always done that, e.g. with regard to Marianne v. Willemer's contributions to the "West-East Divan".[77] When it comes to his numerous letters, a fact well known among Goethe scholars needs to be mentioned, namely, that his long time secretary Dr. Riemer wrote very many of them, being instructed only in general terms by Goethe regarding what he wanted to say. These letters were then written by Riemer immaculately imitating Goethe's style. Goethe simply signed them without any mention of Riemer's name.[78]

Among those who have studied Goethe at least to some extent, it is also widely known that he encouraged all sorts of people ranging from acquaintances to his own son August to report to him in writing about their travels, their observations of Nature and numerous other topics.[79] Goethe used these pieces of information freely, but the sources of much of it were never made "known publicly". This neglect could conceivably rest with the circumstance that Goethe saw himself as having put together into a larger picture what anybody else could have done but did not do. After all, many artists from Rembrandt to Picasso, from old Greek playwrights to Bertolt Brecht[80] had co-workers who took care of details in the pieces produced and yet were never mentioned. Let us also remember that many of those who share Goethe's peculiar mode of "working together with other people" easily forget what their own contribution and that of others really are. After all, how much of what we are aware of, conceptualize and publish, is originally ours? In addition, we should ask: since when and under what social conditions has individual "mental property" become a consideration? Whatever the answers to these questions may suggest, the fact remains that Goethe did not always live up to the promise he made in this paragraph.

Paragraph 196,5/197,1

If, already, even unaffected attentive people (in German natürliche aufmerksame Menschen) are capable of being so beneficial, how more far reaching (in German allgemeiner) must be the benefit if educated people (in German unterrichtete Menschen) work hand in hand with each other A science is already in and for itself so huge a mass, that it carries many human beings, while no human being is able to carry it One may notice that knowledge, like a contained but living water, rises gradually to a certain level, that the most beautiful discoveries are not made so much by human beings as by the times, as for instance, very important things have been accomplished by two or even more experienced thinkers at the same time If even in the first case we become so much indebted to society and to friends, then all the more we become indebted in this case to the world and to the century, and in both cases we cannot sufficiently acknowledge how necessary communication, assistance, reminding and objection are in order to keep, and to advance us on the right way

The thrust of this paragraph is once again on emphasizing the communicative and co-operative sociality of scientific research, but now with the particular bent on its socio-historical dimension.

While Goethe first acknowledges that "... even unaffected attentive people are capable of being ... beneficial ..." for the furthering of the sciences, he takes that acknowledgment as a reason to point out "... how more far reaching ... the benefit ..." would be "... if educated people work hand in hand ...". This sounds quite plausible, but it needs to be emphasized that "educated people" did not mean for Goethe what it has come to mean now, namely people full of abstracted knowledge. Goethe, I think, means to speak here of people that are educated - shall we say "affected"? - in the sense of having learned and having been taught in a "hands-on" way. This is not only in line with the thrust of the whole argument of Goethe's essay (and beyond), but also with his prior reference to "unaffected *attentive* people" (my emphasis). "Educated" people in his understanding have, first of all, retained their attentive senses and have cultivated them through their studies. Do I have to say that "elevation" is on Goethe's mind when he speaks of people as being "educated"?

Goethe notes that the body of scientific knowledge is so voluminous that no individual could ever hope to accumulate all of it. Science "... carries many human beings, while no human being is able to carry it". The growth of knowledge is, then, described as a gradual process in which "... the most beautiful [but not therefore useless!] discoveries are not made so much by human beings as by the times ...", i.e., as occurring as simultaneously as water rises equally in connected tubes.[81] Even if "... two or ... more experienced thinkers ..." do not directly communicate with one another, they may make the same discovery within more or less the same epoch. The history of the natural sciences provides us with quite a few examples for this up to today.[82] This circumstance indicates to Goethe that individual discoveries are owed "... to the world and to the century ...", i.e., they are social products, no matter whether individuals involved in these discoveries acknowledge their social connectedness or not. It follows, and this is how Goethe ends this contemplation, that "... we cannot sufficiently acknowledge how necessary communication, assistance, reminding and objection are in order to keep and to advance us on the right way".

Speaking of the sociality and historicity of scientific discoveries may remind us of the circumstance that Goethe nonetheless implies that knowledge advances even under conditions of an individuated sociality and of sensuous distance from the objects of study. Such studies may "harm" the progress of science, but they also "advance" it (paragraph 194,3/195,1). In other words, it would not appear to be possible to derive from Goethe's thinking a justification for the suggestion that today's science should be abolished or ignored simply because it is merely correct. Furthermore, we have to note that there is still a sociality at work in the merely correct sciences, no matter how distorted this sociality is under today's conditions. Therefore, the question vis-à-vis today's dominant sciences must not focus on their abolition, but on the undoing of their distortion. To the extent that solving this problem involves a social praxis, as suggested above,[83] an answer to it can only be developed at the practically-concrete level. Attempts at solving this whole issue by just thinking and writing about it, are bound to fail.

At the same time, we must not forget that individuals and societies suffer under the dominant mode of thinking. So did Goethe. He suffered under the circumstance that the Newtonian mode of thinking was so strongly established at his time that an audience for his writings on science, let alone co-workers in its pursuits, could hardly be found. And yet, this did not make him change his ways of being, doing and thinking. Like what so many scientists and other academics do today, he could have gone along with the general flow and also join the "scientific guilds", as Goethe called them. He became aware, however, that those guilds were not so much interested in real phenomena than in their particular ways of conceptualizing them.[84] Joining them would have meant that he would have lost his own self and with it his joy and freedom. This was, indeed, a price that Goethe was not willing to pay. When he said that he had "... been feeling too good ... with the method of working together with ... other people ..." (paragraph 196,4), he meant a form of working together in which one could keep one's own subjectivity grounded in a sensuousness that granted both individuality and commonality. The refusal to join the "scientific guilds" by following his spontaneous rejection of them may make Goethe appear as an unusual human being, but as before, we have to say[85] that it does so only in a statistical sense.

Modern science, since around 1800, has endangered the human subject even more in its relation to its primary object, Nature. Theodor Litt, who approached the distortion of science in those terms almost 50 years ago, sees that this went hand in hand with "... the most radical drainage of meaning from this world".[86] As a solution to this disaster, Litt contemplates a synthesis between Newton's and Goethe's science. Meanwhile, science has evolved in late capitalism into a force far beyond what Litt had known while writing in Germany around the 1950s. Science, in the form of instrumentalism, has given egofocality a form of sociality and has given abstraction a form of "materialism" which has created a ghostlike yet deadly reality in every regard. It is clearer today than it could have been at Theodor Litt's time that this presently even weirder "drainage of meaning" cannot be stopped by theoretical contemplations on a synthesis of these two lines of thinking.[87] Stopping the "drainage of meaning" can only be dealt with by those living a new praxis.[88]

Paragraph 197,2

Thus, in scientific matters one has to proceed in a manner just the opposite to the one in which one has to do it in works of art For an artist does well not to let his piece of work be seen in public until he has completed it, because one can neither easily advise nor give help, however, if the work of art is completed then he has to think over and to take to heart the reproach or the praise, to integrate this with his experience, and in this way to cultivate (in German auszubilden) and prepare himself for a new work In scientific matters however, it is indeed useful to publicly communicate each single experience, even conjecture, it is indeed most highly advisable not to erect a scientific edifice before the plan, and the materials for it, are generally known, assessed and selected

This paragraph compares the task of the artist with that of the scientist. This comparison is, in Goethe's case, again not a sheer theoretical exercise of an academic or of a philosopher, it is a reflexion on his own activities, on his own real life.

In the first sentence, we read that, in science, "... one has to proceed in a manner just opposite to the one ... in works of art". Creating a piece of art is seen as a lonely process in which one has to proceed without advice or help from others. It is only when the piece of art is completed and released to the public, that the artist should open up to the reaction from others, be that reaction "reproach" or "praise". This is what he "... has to take to heart ..." and "... to integrate this with his experience, and in this way to cultivate and prepare himself for a new work". The reaction by others to his product is what the artist has to incorporate into his existence - "take to heart" – in order to allow his inner creative force, thus enriched, to work again on a piece of art hopefully enriching the lives of others in a renewed way. In this particular paragraph, we are not told more about the production of art in comparison to that of science.

The scientist, on his part, better conveys to the public "... each single experience, even conjecture ...", with an eye on jointly building up with others a body of adequate knowledge of Nature. It "... is indeed most highly advisable not to erect a scientific edifice, before ... the materials for it are generally ... selected". As we shall see later (e.g. in paragraph 202,4/203,1), there is no such notion in Goethe's mind that a scientific edifice would not require modification or extension at some later time, but scientific research, as it constructs images in the mind on how phenomena "out there" relate to one another, has to work in gradual stages towards "experiences of the higher kind" (e.g. paragraphs 202,1; 202,4/203,1). In other words, science while a creative process itself, has to be a different kind of endeavor from the beginning, since "... no human being is able to carry it" alone (paragraph 196,5/197,1). Even as a joint effort, it remains, like art, a gradual process.

Later on in this essay, Goethe briefly returns to the praxes of producing art and of working in the sciences. Regarding the latter, he says that the scientist has to work "... restlessly, as if he wanted to leave nothing for his followers to do ..." (paragraph 200,7/201,1) and "... as if [he] were accountable to the most demanding geometrician" (paragraph 201,3) who expects no detail to be left out. We also read (paragraph 200,7/201,1) that this is the "... exact opposite duty of a writer who wants to entertain. The latter will make for boredom, if he does not leave anything to be imagined". In this sense, science and art are differently related to one and the same force, that of Nature. Art is an enactment of the artist's imagination and as such it stimulates the same inner force of Nature in fellow man, i.e. his/her imagination, and allows it to elevate itself following the artist's imagination. Science is, of course, also a human creation,[89] but one in which the force of Nature inside man is stimulated to meticulously create an understanding of the forces of Nature out there. Thus, science in comparison to art draws upon another aspect of the will or the spontaneity, i.e. the material force inside the mind. It is that aspect of her in us which desires to follow Nature's ways and connections faithfully. As such, it is primarily drawn to the forces of Nature out there to which it feels akin and which it enjoys. While it naturally enjoys them more than their conceptualizations (paragraph 199,2), it is this enjoyment which as a part of our inner Nature is the primary driving force that pushes us forward to the conceptualization of Nature, i.e. to science. To do so is part of our "essence" (paragraph 199,2). In art, this enjoyment makes us celebrate Nature in song, poem, novel, painting, etc.

Goethe saw a "Bildungstrieb", a "formative force", at work in all manifestations of Nature including the human being. As he says in the short essay written under the title "Bildungstrieb" - above also translated by us as "Drive to Give Shape" - this "formative force" is not only at work in each individual manifestation of Nature, e.g. in each of the plants, animals and human beings, but also in the evolution of Nature, as she has elevated herself from "the more common forces and elements" (paragraph 200,7/201,1) to the highest life form, namely that of the human being as an "Other Nature".[90] Within man's mind, this force manifests itself as a "teleological force of judgement" as Schelling puts it.[91] This force of judgement in man enables the scientist not only to understand Nature fully, i.e. in terms of the dynamics proper to her, but also to experience himself on that occasion as the highest form of, and as a contributing force to, these dynamics. It is in this sense that Goethe's science knows itself as a part of the "epigenesis" of Nature herself, using this term in Schelling's sense. Therefore, it would lead to untrue knowledge of Nature, if one would not follow her with one's own inner Nature, i.e. by granting one's senses the lead in knowledge creation. Only by giving primacy to our inner Nature, i.e. to our senses and their drive to elevate themselves, can the process of research hope to transcend-and-contain Nature in us and around us. Having our mind follow Nature meticulously and faithfully by noting both how our senses connect us with her and how our senses follow the connections in Nature out there, we are entitled to hope that we meet *the* conditions for our knowledge to be true.

In this way, science and art, while both being different forms of elevations of Nature, could carry on Nature's creation as a potentially never ending process and could overcome the disaster that Richard N. Adams sees as inevitably coming along on the "Eighth Day" of creation. Both, science and art, can only do that if they contain, undistortedly in themselves, the Nature they elevate. In other words, the issue is, whether our science is beautifully true and our art truly beautiful.

Goethe combined work in both areas, at least since his arrival in Weimar. This combination has been a riddle for many people since then. Yet, it will only remain a riddle as long as his art and his science are not understood, each on their own terms and then, also together in terms of their distinction-in-commonality. Goethe had to fight off the suggestion that his investigations on colors were alien to his life as a poet. He objected to that in a quite determined way in his "Confession of the Author" (of the "Teachings on Colors"), where he makes the point that both interests are harmonious parts of his life.[92] He had already made this point quite a few years earlier, in 1794. In a letter written to his friend Jacobi,[93] he reacts to those who assumed that he had given up his "optical studies" (probably since he had discontinued the publication of his "Beiträge" in 1792) by saying angrily: "He who told you that ... knows nothing about me". He continues in the same letter by saying: "This matter [of color] is ... such an exercise of the mind which perhaps would have happened to me in no other form". At the same time, his writing of poetry and plays goes on without its flow being ever interrupted. Scientific studies and poetic creativity were harmonious parts of his life. His poetry could not have been without his knowledge of Nature and his knowledge of Nature could not have been without what Schmied-Kowarzik has so aptly termed his "leidenschaftliche Aufmerksamkeit", i.e. his "passionate attentiveness",[94] a mere consequence of his "drive to give shape".

3. Not Proof, but Secure Knowledge

3a.- Dazzled by Proof
(Commentaries on paragraphs 197,3 to 200,2)

Paragraph 197,3

Now I turn to a point which deserves all attention, namely to the method of how one proceeds most advantageously and most securely (The italicized text is not included in the published version of 1823)

This very short, one sentence paragraph appears only in the hand written version, not in the published one. It prepares one, as the editor Trunz rightfully says,[95] for a better understanding of the rest of the essay.

As announced by Goethe - also only in a hand written portion of this essay, namely in a section of paragraph 194,3/195,1 - the second part of the essay begins with this paragraph. In it, Goethe first inspects the "mistake" of what he later calls "the other method" (paragraph 202,4/203,1) and then presents a description of his own way of proceeding. This is to say that this second part itself is divided into two sections. The second section of this second part begins in paragraph 200,3 where Goethe agrees that "(I)t is fair that at least one makes one's own opinion public ...".

Regarding his "own opinion", the short paragraph before us announces an astounding degree of confidence. Goethe calls his method quite unashamedly "most advantageous" and "most secure". The combination of these characterizations form, in our view, an aspect of Goethe's science that is both left largely unexplored and yet is of greatest importance. As paragraph 194,1 states clearly, the doing of scientific research is seen by Goethe as "advantageous" not only for pure scientific interests, but also as useful for man's whole life. The claim of his science to yield "secure" knowledge is thus connected in as much to the harvest of lasting "benefits" from Nature, as it is to the yielding of reliable truth. Goethe, in fact, condemns in this last part of the essay all methods as false that do not give primacy to Nature; in this regard, no tolerance can be found in Goethe's words. But this is not to say that he opposes pluralism in the sciences. To the contrary, his way of understanding Nature "advantageously and securely" *implies* pluralism. For him, the truth of our knowledge does not preclude the subjectivity, or better, the subjectiv*ies* of the researchers, as we shall see.[96] Individual subjectivity is explicitly respected as an expression of the difference-in-commonality among those aware of their belonging to the "analogia entis" of all there is.

Paragraph 197,4

> If we intentionally repeat the experiences which have been made prior to us, which we make ourselves or others simultaneously with us, and if we again present the phenomena, which in part accidentally, in part artificially emerged, then we call that an experiment

In this paragraph, which is almost as short as the previous one, Goethe presents an initial definition of the experiment. By calling it an initial definition, we mean to indicate that Goethe's understanding of experiments and, for that matter, of experiences, has a complexity for the modern mind which requires a gradual explanation based on careful reading of the later paragraphs as well.

To begin with, we could say that Goethe makes only a slight distinction between experience and experiment.[97] They differ in that experiments are "... intentionally repeat[ed] ... experiences ...", regardless of whether these experiments repeat one's own experiences or those made by others, and also regardless of whether they "... again present phenomena, which in part accidentally, in part artificially emerged ...". Therefore, phenomena no matter whether these phenomena had been observed accidentally, i.e. in mere experiences, or had emerged "artificially", i.e. in previous intended experiments, have the status of being experiments if presented again, i.e. if intentionally repeated. To the extent that experiments repeat phenomena, they are "artificial", or, in order to use a phrase from the "Teachings on Colors", they are "elevated experiences".[98] This is to say that experiments are experiences as well, simply because they are experienced in their process and in their result. In paragraph 201,2 of "The Experiment", Goethe says that all the experiences and experiments described in the "Beiträge" "... constitute *one* (Goethe's emphasis) experiment ... represent just *one* (Goethe's emphasis) experience ...". This is to say that definitions of the two must not segregate the two, since they have a commonality in their distinctiveness which Goethe expresses by referring to experiments as "elevated experiences".

Furthermore, the circumstance that both, experience and experiment are *made*, clearly indicates that the difference between the two is not related to presence or absence of activity. They both require the actively experiencing subject without which neither one would exist.

Let us first note that there are experiences that can only be repeated by manipulating the human subject, so to speak, but not the objects involved. This also eliminates intentional repeatability as the difference between experience and experiments. Most astronomical observations, for instance, may remain experiences, but others can be elevated to experiments, since they can be repeated, at least to a degree, by placing our own bodies or apparatuses into geographical positions where we can observe constellations in which the time/place co-ordinates of the objects are outside our control. In other words, experiments transcend-and-contain experiences in so far as experiments require manipulation of subject and/or object (but occasionally only of the human subject). While this may stretch the common meaning of experiment somewhat, the important issue is that both have in common the requirement that the human subject has to actively and sensuously experience them. In other words, we must guard ourselves against losing sight of the circumstance that Goethe understands the conscious making of an experience in a completely non-idealist way in so far as the making of an experience does not only require activity on the part of our minds, but also and already activity at the pre-conceptual, sensuous level. As in the case of an experiment in which we are also involved at the manual level, experience and experiment require our materially concrete involvement primarily; this is the condition for their elevation. Without that mediation, neither one would exist.[99]

This contrast between Goethe and the dominant way of practicing science can be brought out very well when one begins by comparing the following statement of Newton with one that Goethe made. At first glance, both statements appear to be quite similar. Newton says in his "Opticks"[100]:

> And if at any time I speak of Light and Rays as coloured or endued with Colours, I would be understood to speak not philosophically and properly, but grossly, and accordingly to such Conceptions as vulgar People in seeing all these Experiments would be apt to frame. For the Rays to speak properly are not coloured. In them there is nothing else than a certain Power and Disposition to stir up a Sensation of this or that Colour

Newton continues there by making reference to sound waves and what *they do* in the human "Sensorium", in the same way to what light waves *do* in the eye, namely "stir up a Sensation". Goethe, instead, after having called colors "deeds of light, deeds and sufferings" (of light),[101] continues by saying that an[102]

> ... immediate kinship of light and eye can be denied by nobody; yet, at the same time, to conceive of both as being one and the same, contains greater difficulties It becomes more plausible, however, when one asserts that a quiet light resides in the eye which can be stirred by the slightest stimulation *from within* (my emphasis) and from without. We can evoke, on command of imagination, the brightest images for us in complete darkness.

The kinship, or if one wishes, the commonality-in-difference between light and eye and the active involvement of the latter as a sheerly natural organ in the *creation* of color is *the* point of difference between Newton and Goethe. Certainly, light itself has to do something ("deeds"), i.e. it has to radiate and something has to happen to it ("suffering"). It has to go, for instance, through darkening media for color to emerge, but that is not all it takes for color to show. For color to emerge, the human eye also has to *do* something. In other words, color is not only a consequence of the eye being passively involved in the emergence of colors, i.e., being merely "stirred up" is not enough; the eye has to be *actively* involved. This active involvement of the eye in the emergence of colors is then studied at length in the first part of Goethe's "Teachings on Colors" titled, "Physiological Colors". The difference, in this particular regard, between Newton (together with mainstream science and philosophy) and Goethe is the following: Newton still acknowledges the role of the human senses in the creation of color phenomena (though analytical traditions in science and philosophy do not do that), but the senses need to be stirred to act; this means that their contribution to the creation of knowledge is reduced by Newton to a mere passivity. Goethe, instead, appreciates and retains awareness for the active role of the senses in so far as they can not only create colors by themselves, but also act as the primary linkages between outer and inner Nature. In this way, the senses are understood as constituting not just the only link but also as the active link of the mind to Nature. That link, furthermore, is itself natural. This circumstance, according to Goethe, is better willingly remembered by the mind as the departure point for the mind's workings, i.e. when it elevates sensuous experiences to concepts. In other words, via the senses, Nature is transcended-and-contained in thought, in culture. Let us listen to a well known four line poem which goes back to the mystic Jakob Böhme and is inserted into the Introduction of the "Teachings on Colors"[103]:

> Were the eye not like the sun,
> How could we see her light ?
> Would God's own force not live in us,
> How could the Divine strike a cord in us ?

> (in German:
> Wär' nicht das Auge sonnenhaft,
> Wie könnten wir das Licht erblicken?
> Lebt' nicht in uns Gottes eigne Kraft,
> Wie könnt' uns Göttliches entzücken?)

It is obviously Goethe's view that our participation in Nature is at all levels, from the physical up to the mental, an interaction among partners in kinship. The issue then is whether or not we appreciate that it is primarily our sense organs which relate us to the world out there and that our mind, as an elevated organ, in the enjoyment of that kinship carefully follows the lead of our senses.

At this level of our considerations, it may be helpful to approach the difference between Goethe and the dominant way of thinking in yet a different way. Let us note that Newton, Goethe, modern neuro-physiology and neuro-philosophy, all agree that colors do not simply exist as things-in-themselves. They all agree that colors exist as co-products of the human eye; would our eyes be different from what they are, e.g. like those of a cow, colors would be different for us as well. For Goethe,[104] it is as clear as it is for modern biologists and neuro-physiologists[105] that sunlight, in the process of evolution (or elevation) of Nature, has selected and developed the eye as the organ to create the beautiful miracle of colors for us. Coming from there, Goethe and modern neuro-philosophy also agree that our conceptualizations of Nature arise primarily from this, our sensuous reception. The world of knowledge ("Wirklichkeit", according to Roth) and the world of Nature ("Realität", according to Roth) are different yet related entities.[106] From this point on, however, i.e. when it comes to questions regarding the relationship between the things out there and their conceptualizations in us, Goethe branches off from the dominant line of thinking, as it also prevails in modern neuro-physiology. Goethe does not just propose, in a merely theorizing fashion, to see our conceptual world as an elevation of Nature, he is aware that the sensuousness of our experiences better be as broad as possible and better be retained in its elevation to knowledge. Certainly, Newton's (and the mainstream sciences') experiments also have some sort of sensuous basis, but this basis is almost always limited to very few sensuous experiences which then are absolutized as being sufficient for the construction of far reaching hypotheses and theories. This is exemplified in Newton's "experimentum crucis". It must further be conceded that modern evolutionists, neuro-physiologists and neuro-philosophers theoretically appreciate the physiological foundations of our conceptual reality ("Wirklichkeit"). There is, however, no advocacy in their suggestions that knowledge creation should be based on as broad a basis of sensuous experiences as is possible and that that creative process should accept such sensuousness as a primary and sustained guidance, as Goethe does. There is, in other words, no point in Goethe's ways of coming to know where the material-sensuous changes into something that is different from Nature and is segregated from her in the same way as the mental is segregated from matter in Adams' theory. Let us remember, Goethe *saw* the "Urpflanze"; it was not just an "idea". Goethe's concepts as elevations of Nature do not, therefore, carry the domineering intent in them as is clearly the case with a knowledge that is unaware of its being part of Nature. Goethe's drive to know is carried through as an activity of Nature even when leading to the highest abstractions possible. It is for the reason of this containment that his way of knowing can be simultaneously scientific-theoretical, praxis oriented and aesthetic. Since these aspects do not fall apart in Goethe's science, his science can flourish without requiring ethical control.

Coming to know Nature is just one of our communions with her. Other communions with her would be such "mundane" activities like breathing, smelling, eating etc. It is part of man's elevated "essence" that he also desires to know her and to understand our material connections with her. On this basis, Nature "pleases", "attracts" and "benefits" us (paragraph 194,1). Our experiences and experiments simply enact our natural will to follow her ways and not primarily the ways of a mind erroneously claiming to be totally distinct from her and entitled to dominate her. The urge to follow and understand Nature finds its satisfaction in every moment of wondrous discovery and, thus, has in it as little a sense for the Midas syndrome as does a whole life that lives out of free obedience to the Nature that our life itself is.

Therefore, both, experiments and experiences, need to be experienced consciously as primarily sensuous acts. Regardless of this commonality between experience and experiment, the difference between them is that experiments are made artificially and intentionally. The experiment as a mediator between object and subject cannot, therefore, be carried out with apparatuses which threaten the sensuousness of that mediation. This issue is among those attended to in the next paragraph of "The Experiment".

Paragraph 197,5

The value of an experiment, be it simple or be it composite, primarily consists in that it can be carried out at any time again under certain conditions with the help of a known apparatus and with the required skill, as often as the required conditions can be brought together If we were to even only superficially (in German obenhin) consider the combinations which have been created, and the machines which have been invented, and one can safely say, are being invented every day for this purpose, we can rightfully admire human ingenuity (in German Verstand)

Let us first of all note that Goethe writes here quite positively not only about the repeatability of experiments but also about the employment of apparatuses and machines in them. These imply, respectively, that he had a positive view on the reliability, if not lawlike predictability, of Nature as well as on the issue of progress through the invention of apparatuses and machines. This, however, is not the way Goethe has always been understood.

The circumstance that an experiment "... can be carried out at any time again ...", i.e. the fact that it can be repeated "... as often as the required conditions can be brought together" by an experimenter who has "the required skills", is clearly spoken of as being the value of an experiment. This implies that Goethe expects a regularity to reveal itself in the interaction between experimenter and the natural phenomena involved. Given that Goethe has formulated a wealth of statements on his experiments (and experiences) which primarily express the regularity of natural phenomena, we think that it is beyond doubt that his trust in Nature assumes a concept of "law of Nature". Of course, it has yet to be determined whether and if so to what extent this concept differs from the concept of laws of Nature prevailing in today's science.

In his extensive and scholarly discussion of the differences between today's prevailing science and Goethe's, Carl-Friedrich von Weizsäcker had this to say: "... the taking part of the world of the senses in that of the idea turns in the natural sciences to the validity of the laws, in Goethe it turns into the reality of the symbol".[107] Weizsäcker writes this in the context of his proposition that this difference evolved because Goethe and the dominant natural sciences, while both departing from Plato, have gone in different directions.[108] This view is, incidentally, shared by other physicists like Heisenberg and Heitler.[109] Weizsäcker admits that this suggestion may be a simplification, but he still thinks that noting a common origin could help to eventually overcome the differences between Goethe and the dominant sciences. Leaving aside that it has not become fully clear to me what Weizsäcker understands by the word "symbol" in contrast to that of "scientific law", I retain my doubt that an overcoming of the differences between Goethe's science and the dominant one is possible.[110] In Weizsäcker's case, this hope rests on two misconceptions.

In relation to his first misconception, it is, perhaps, of some significance to point out that Goethe was in as much a declared anti-Platonian as he was a determined non-philosopher.[111] This makes it already somewhat daring to place Goethe in line with Plato. More importantly, however, Goethe's concept of "idea" as being a sensuous reality makes a Platonian interpretation of it dubious. In the present context, it is of even greater weight that a thorough student of Goethe's works, as Weizsäcker certainly is, comes close to seeing Goethe's interest in the "reality of the symbol" as replacing his interest in regularities, if not in laws of Nature. While thinking that this is wrong and that Goethe's interest aims indeed at establishing laws of Nature, we have also to say that even the interest in scientific laws, in a certain way shared between Goethe's and the dominant sciences, does not make their synthesis possible. The reason for this is primarily Goethe's sense of Nature and his creation of mental constructs about her.

Throughout the "Beiträge" and the "Farbenlehre", Goethe points out on almost every page, how under the same or similar conditions equivalent phenomena of colors become visible. He undoubtedly establishes regularities among these conditions and their consequences, arrives at his circle of primary colors[112] and finally comes to express the commonality of all his color experiences under his famous "Ur-Phänomen", i.e. "ground phenomenon" in the often quoted paragraphs 175 – 177 of his "Teachings on Colors".[113] In the first one of these paragraphs, he uses, like on many other occasions,[114] the terms "rules and laws" verbatim. He then adds that "… they [these rules and laws] do not reveal themselves through words and hypotheses to the mind, but simultaneously through phenomenona to the perception". In view of this I wonder whether Weizsäcker misread this important statement or shares in the difficulties that so many of Goethe's students have with his understanding of perception and of the "perceptively guided force of judgement" ("Anschauende Urteilskraft")? This paragraph of the "Teachings on Colors" makes it evident that Goethe's science aims at the formulation of laws in Nature. But there is an aspect involved in Goethe's concept of "rules and laws" that while inseparable from his "perceptively guided force of judgement" is often overlooked. Goethe indicates here that rules and laws as they express themselves in words, must "simultaneously" remain sensuous to deserve acceptance as truth and as being of lawlike reliability. It is this sensuousness as retained in the laws of Nature which definitively separates Goethe's concept of law from that of the prevalent sciences. In the same way, Goethe again correlates the highly abstract with the sensuously concrete in these lines on the "Ur-Phänomen". The "Ur-Phänomen" remains, like his "idea" of the "Urpflanze", i.e., the "original plant", directly accessible to the senses. Beyond any doubt, this way of understanding concepts is irreconcilable with that of modern science.

Goethe's intent to subsume experiences under unifying principles must, furthermore, not be confused with attempts by modern physics to find, for instance, a unifying theory of Nature. Weizsäcker's own work aims at such a theory besides, of course, Einstein's attempt at a "Weltformel", i.e. a "Unified Field Theory". It is not so important for us to see why these attempts were not successful. It is of greater significance to understand the way in which Goethe's search for principles that unify experiences is so distinct from these attempts.

Focusing in this connection on Weizsäcker's own contributions to the creation of a unified theory of Nature, which he published under the title of "Die Einheit der Natur", i.e. "The Unity of Nature", I have first to point out that this unity is explicitly understood by him as the "unity of experience".[115] But, then, I have to add quickly that Weizsäcker speaks here of experience in terms of its conceptualization, i.e. at a level way "above" sense experiences. Furthermore, whatever experimental result he discusses, it has arisen out of a hypothesis guided research conducted at times with enormously complicated equipment. Here is no mentioning or room for a sustained primacy of sensuousness in processes of knowledge formation. Additionally, Weizsäcker's "unity of experience" aims, of course, at the construction of a theory that is conceptually free of contradictions, i.e. is in that sense a unified theory. Such a theory would have little in common with Goethe's sensuously experienced "analogia entis" of all Nature which he, for reasons to be discussed in a moment, did not even plan to get under his mental grip. Therefore, neither unwilling acceptance nor the overcoming of mental contradictions would move modern science anywhere near Goethe's willingness to accept mental "ruptures"[116] in his knowledge of Nature. Goethe's persisting insistence on the "analogia entis" is then all the more perplexing for those who overlook that this analogia refers to a totality of being and not to a unity of thinking, or of "experience" in Weizsäcker's sense. Goethe's laws reflect consistencies in Nature, but he renounces the task of obtaining them when and where Nature's totality is sensed by him as being too great for the human mind in its sensuousness. As Goethe says later in "The Experiment" (paragraph 200,7/201,1), "... no human being has enough abilities to have a conclusive say on any matter". Late in his life, he sees[117] that a final and total knowledge without contradictions is a figment of one-sided thinking. This gave him a strong sense of "renunciation", but it would be a misunderstanding to surmise that this insight kept him from further participation in the dynamics of knowledge creation. The drive to know is for him as synonymous to living as breathing is. Renunciation did not mean for Goethe a giving up of one's own elevation through growth in understanding. Instead, for Goethe, with the growth of understanding in the human subject, the object of our understanding grew as well. However, since known Nature is more than Nature unknown, an identity between object and subject lies, perhaps painfully for most, outside our Nature in the permanently "not-yet". A conceptually unified theory of Nature is, therefore, inconceivable for Goethe. However, a modesty of this kind cannot be found in the sciences that prevailed at least since Goethe's times.

Goethe's emphasis on sensuousness has created yet another problem in the understanding of his way of doing science. It has mislead many to believe that Goethe flatly opposed the use of research equipment, while oftentimes not sticking to that position himself. In view of the paragraph presently under consideration, we would suggest that Goethe speaks here quite clearly about using "the help of a known apparatus" in experiments. And while he considers that "... the machines which have been invented, and ... are being invented every day for this purpose ...", he says that "... we can rightfully admire human ingenuity" in this regard. Reading this in an essay that has been treated as being so representative of Goethe's thought, it can hardly be understood why the view has been widely accepted[118] that Goethe had rejected the help of "machines and apparatuses" in experiments, however inconsistently so, and that he had instead advocated the exclusive use of the human senses. Let us note that in the portion of the text before us, Goethe even admires the progress in the use of such devices. In view of this, one wonders what misled students of Goethe's science to suggest that Goethe's use of equipment was contradictory and ambiguous.[119]

We concede that Goethe detested the use of spectacles, microscopes, binoculars and that he also listened to those who, like Hegel, called the prism a "triangular glass stick" with which "Satan ... has struck the physicists".[120] Furthermore, and equally beyond doubt, Goethe has always insisted, like he does in the letter to Zelter quoted above,[121] that "... man is the best instrument ..." and that "... the separation between man and the experiment is the greatest mishap in modern Physics".[122] But is his own use and even praise of machines and apparatuses and the simultaneous emphasis on the human senses simply an "antinomy", as some say[123] who place Goethe in between backwardness and modernization?

I would suggest that a careful and contextualized reading of Goethe's views allows for a relatively easy explanation of what appears to be Goethe's inconsistency in this regard.

As far as I can tell, nobody has doubted that Goethe saw the human being with his sensuousness as *the* instrument in the study of Nature. Yet, Goethe has always accepted the help of equipment, provided – and this is most important – that the instruments used were merely extensions of the human senses and not their replacement. Goethe was also aware of the problem that this extension of the senses had a limit at which it would come close to their replacement. Goethe indicates the arrival at such a point in a "Warning" which he included as section XXVII of his research report on his work with "Entoptic Colors".[124] In this research, undertaken between 1813 and 1820, i.e., after the publication of the "Teachings on Colors", Goethe moves into increasingly complex manifestations of colors and, therefore, uses an increasingly complicated "apparatus". Since it would take me several pages to describe this "composite" experiment, I have to leave it at saying that it took Goethe about fifty pages (though interspersed with interpretations and remarks on practical applications!) to describe this research.[125] What is, however, of significance here is the circumstance that the steps in the increase of the complexity in the research apparatus are very carefully explicated by Goethe, even though when judged by modern standards the complexity of the equipment used is still rather modest. Goethe describes them as "The Simplest Experiment", "The Second, Elevated Experiment", then the "Additional Elevation" and, finally, "Apparatus, Fourfold Elevated".[126] It is after that point that Goethe sees fit to insert his "Warning". Because of its importance, we wish to present it here without abbreviation. [127]

> How close we get through our fourfoldedly elevated apparatus to the point, at which the instrument, instead of unraveling the secret of Nature, turns her into an unresolvable riddle, may every Nature loving experimenter take to heart. There is nothing to be said against enabling oneself through mechanical contrivances to demonstrate certain phenomena in accordance with will and discretion more easily and more conspicuously; yet, *they do not further essential instruction* (my emphasis), moreover, there are useless and harmful apparatuses through which the perception of Nature is totally darkened, to which also those belong which present the phenomenon partially or out of context These in particular are the ones on which hypotheses are based and by which hypotheses are retained for centuries; since one cannot speak about this without becoming polemical, mention of this should not be done in our peaceful presentation.

Leaving aside the fact that Goethe indicates that he wishes to keep himself from renewing his polemics (probably the one against Newton of about 10 years earlier), he basically writes here that an increasingly "elevated" apparatus is only acceptable as it "furthers essential instruction", i.e. as it helps to ascertain what one's senses have noticed any way. The senses remain the criteria for truth, as he has once said emphatically: "the senses do not cheat, the judgement does".[128] Instruments are only seen as means to confirm through greater detail, "... more clearly and more conspicuously ..." what the senses have noticed already. Goethe, like everybody else, obviously had reason to seek confirmation on occasion for his sense perceptions, but more was not sought by him, when he used instruments; more would have been "useless and harmful". The use of instruments had taught him not to go beyond what he called "essential instruction".

In today's natural sciences, research equipment has grown so complex that it has nothing to do with confirmation of sense perception anymore. In fact, research equipment is supposed to "correct" the senses, or even to invalidate them, as if what is part of our bodily existence were irrelevant for finding the truth, i.e. for finding what Nature is for us as parts of her. Now it is the internal organization of modern "apparatuses and machines" which creates the desired information.[129] The gathering of data from these apparatuses still consists in the truncated yet irreplaceable sensuousness of reading their gauges. These readings, however, inform us about objects, e.g. in the realm of nuclear physics, which are themselves creations of the researcher's hypothesizing mind and not more.[130] Such a research would not be problematic for us, would we only exist as minds. To the extent, however, that our life is grounded in and part of the sensuously accessible Nature, knowledge created in such an abstracted way may easily turn out to be problematic. This is still not to deny that our body and other bodies of Nature could be *conceptualized* as constituted by particles inaccessible to our senses. However, the risks of such conceptualization are obvious by now (see chapter 1).

At this point, we should bear in mind that the development of the sciences in late capitalism is now also under new and further distorting influences. There is now a type of science that structures our whole life in such a way that the urge to stay in an all pervasive competitive race forces scientists to develop research results (including equipment and theories instrumental for it) the raison d'être of which is that it can be "sold". Given this development, the finding of truth is not an issue at all anymore. Traditionally, scientists may have still enjoyed their already abstracted, de-sensualized research, but this has now become structurally irrelevant. Research must primarily sell and thus has, traditionally speaking, only "exchange value"; it carries the Midas touch in it with all of the above mentioned horrifying consequences.

At the same time, concern about the impact of modern scientific research on our daily lives is not all that foreign to people. This concern is shared by those who have studied Goethe and yet fail to go as far as proper understanding of Goethe's views would allow them to go. Instead of taking note of the most modern twists in scientific praxis, some try to give advice to Goethe. They suggest that Goethe should have "... given the sciences a different direction, namely to correct them in terms of the sensuously conceivable ...". Then, so they think, Goethe could have served to shape a science of greater environmental friendliness.[131] But we wonder, can one not read in numerous published volumes that Goethe had tried to humanize the whole project of science? Certainly, Goethe had hardly any public impact. Yet, was this exclusively his fault? Not fully appreciating what Goethe was up against, even less attention is being paid by these critics of Goethe's to what is happening to the natural sciences under the instrumentalistic conditions of late capitalism.

We think it is clear that Goethe knew that there can indeed be something "harmful" about "apparatuses and machines", but not about "apparatuses and machines" per se. I leave aside that an objection against "apparatuses and machines" per se would be untenable and that it could not even be carried to its logical conclusion. One should also consider the question of what would follow from Goethe's views on research equipment for the use of machinery assisting in production, and not just in research activities. We have to bear in mind that so many apparatuses which are helpful in our daily life stem from that kind of science which has gone far beyond our sensuously grounded abilities, be this in physics, chemistry or biology and bio-technology. Being obviously unable to sort out this issue in our present writing, at a minimum we have to suggest this: Having argued so much in favor of concretely grounded thinking makes raising these concerns at the theoretical level a somewhat dubious undertaking. Of course, these questions have to be raised and decided upon, but would an awareness for the primacy of our senses not suggest that these questions need to be dealt with in the concreteness of praxis?

Paragraph 197,6/198,1

Regardless of how valuable any experiment, considered individually, may be, yet it acquires its value only through unification (in German Vereinigung) and connection (in German Verbindung) with others However to unite and to connect two experiments, which have some resemblance with each other, takes more rigor and attention than even astute observers often have demanded of themselves Two phenomena may be akin to one another but by far not as closely as we believe Two experiments may appear to follow one from the other, even when between them a large series [of connections] has to be inserted in order to bring them into an adequately natural connection

The first sentence in this paragraph could have been written by any of the philosophers prominent during Goethe's life, provided the word "experiment" was replaced by the word "statement". The truth value of a statement, for philosophers, requires that the statement be placed into the totality of its context.

Goethe, however, tries to understand Nature, not just statements. The steps necessary to arrive at true statements about her begin at the level of concrete experiments (or experiences), yet like a statement, "... any experiment ... acquires its value only through unification and connection with others", even all others, as is implied by later paragraphs (e.g. 200,5 – 200,7/201,1). This requires the making of a large number of experiments and experiences, since it is the issue to find the real connections among real phenomena in their unforeseeable number.[132] It has been said that Goethe has made more than 3000 experiments on colors alone. At one point, while looking over his own shoulder so to speak, Goethe wonders "... in which direction did I not look?".[133] But it is not just the quantity of experiments and experiences that is important, the quality of the work going into them is of utmost importance as well. Even only to "... unite and to connect two experiments ... takes more rigor and attention than even astute observers often have demanded of themselves". Reading this, one may wonder why "rigor and attention" have to be so explicitly mentioned as requirements. Would someone like Goethe, who was so deeply permeated by the "analogia entis", the common bond of all Nature, need such normative values? Would that kind of a person not follow the connections in Nature "automatically" with "rigor" and "attention"? Dealing with these questions will guide us to a better understanding of those dangers that Goethe sees as easily arising in our minds with which, after all, our Nature is gifted as well.

While Goethe knew that Nature has primacy even in the Otherness of our mind, he also knows, as he says time and again in the text before us (e.g. paragraph 198,2), that spontaneity, the driving force in our mind, is all too often keen to push the mind forward prematurely; this too is part of our "essence" (paragraph 199,2). In the paragraph currently at the center of our attention, we read that phenomena of Nature "... may be akin to one another but by far not as closely as we believe", yet the "rashness" (paragraph 194,3/195,1) of our mind easily misleads us to project close connections into Nature where they do not exist. The point that Goethe tries to make here is obvious. As he says in the "Introduction" to the "Teachings on Colors", our mind is inclined to instantly "theorize" with every glance of our eyes.[134] Our mind does that "... even when between them [the natural phenomena] a large series [of connections] has to be inserted in order to bring them into an adequately natural connection". When ignoring what "has to be inserted", our mind lacks "rigor and attention", but demanding them is still not a repressive prescription for our senses. "Rigor and attention" are properties of one's sensuousness and therefore cannot be repressive, provided, of course, one primarily enjoys the things in Nature (see paragraph 199,2). As Goethe says "the willing belongs to Nature and relates to the world out there ...".[135] Only concepts, when we enjoy them more than Nature, can get into the way of that relation and thus distort the will transcended-and-contained in them. A will distorted that way could perhaps be corrected by normative coercion, but this is not what Goethe advocates. He advocates to pay "rigor and attention" to the task of keeping our mind from interference in one's true enjoyment. Only then can we remain true to our Nature. So, "rigor and attention" remain in as much requirements of a student of Nature as the desire to see his beloved one is a "requirement" for a lover. But, as even a true lover may, on occasion, get confused about his priorities and/or may fall prey to seduction, a student of Nature is also never permanently immune against doing wrong to Nature. Yet, a return to "rigor and attention" correcting occasional "rashness" and "frivolity" (paragraph 198,2) would still have to come from his own true Nature. As C.-F. v. Weizsäcker sees, Goethe's trust in Nature as the source of truth "is not an opinion or a decision, it is a way to be human".[136] This has not always been well understood. For instance, Dennis Sepper does not adequately interpret the meaning of Goethe's concept of rigor in his generally thorough study "Goethe contra Newton", when he writes about a person's "... willingness to submit to the discipline of the phenomena...".[137] This sentence could easily be read as demanding a person's *decision* to *bow* down to the discipline of the phenomena. Understanding Goethe this way would not allow one to appreciate the depth of his understanding of the way in which our will connects us to Nature, and how the "categorical" side of our inner Nature (speaking in Kantian terms) can mislead us in this endeavor. Further critical inspection of Sepper's interpretation of Goethe's understanding of Newton is of help in this connection.

Sepper says in the concluding part of the just quoted sentence[138] "... it is precisely the strongest spirits who are likely to slight the phenomena". Sepper is right, in our view, when he says that Newton was for Goethe "just such a person".[139] The question, however, is what precisely it was in this particular regard that made Goethe speak against Newton. Was it Newton's will or was it Newton's absolutizing of a concept? I think the answer is obvious: it was the latter. Newton's natural spontaneity got distorted in his mental constructs.

Let us recall that the first point of Goethe's objection against Newton was that he approached light in terms of a hypothetical, i.e. (mentally) preconceived assumption, to which Newton gave primacy by bringing it to bear on all of his studies of light and colors.[140] Newton and his followers are unwilling to question this hypothesis, since they think that it is consistently, i.e. without mental contradictions, confirmed by all experiments they make. Giving primacy to the mind by structuring all subsequent experiments in accordance with just one absolutized hypothesis, Newton forces, in Goethe's view, light into conditions which make light conform to that mentally preconceived hypothesis. Of course, Newton would have changed his hypothesis on light and colors, had the result of his experiments contradicted his hypothesis. But this eventuality is not the issue for Goethe, since it would have led only to another hypothesis aiming at the same purpose, namely, that of interpreting Nature in terms of mental constructs. This, of course, does not mean understanding Nature, i.e. coming to know her on her terms.[141]

This brings us to the second point of Goethe's objection against Newton.

While light is for Newton's hypothetical conceptualization a composite of different rays and, thus, indirectly of colors, for Goethe light is one, i.e. not a composite, since it is one for the human eye.[142] The issue for Goethe is that it does not occur to Newton to accept light as what it manifests itself to that human sense that is its Nature given equivalent, namely the eye, but to accept it in its conceptualized form regardless of its sensuous appearance. Goethe says that Newton's whole mistake rests on having placed a complicated assumption about light at the foundation of his understanding of light. Doing this leads Newton to a treatment of light in which its hypothetically postulated Nature is forced to materialize under exceptional and contrived conditions.[143] This is to say that Newton's mistake lies in his studying the Nature of light by putting it through circumstances derived from constructed hypotheses. Not having been sensuously exposed to the Nature of light and colors to the fullest extent, the mind cannot help but engage in the only activity it is capable of, namely create concepts. These concepts, however, only partially and accidentally jibe with Nature, while their persistent application distorts her. Proceeding this way, the mind places a product of itself between man and what he studies; the mind thus distances itself from what it is akin to and without which it could not even be: Nature. In this way, the commonality of mind and Nature is not lost, but relegated to a secondary status. For Goethe, Newton's views are, therefore, a distortion of outer Nature through the imagery of a distortedly practiced inner Nature. Goethe, on his part, approaches Nature, not by letting concepts, but by letting Nature, in the form of the human senses, be what they are: the mediation between object and subject. Therefore, it is somewhat puzzling when Sepper merely notes[144] that "... the use of hypothetical models ... is almost [? !] entirely absent from the 'Beiträge' ...". Their use in the dominantly accepted sense is *completely* absent from the "Beiträge", but not their use per se.

But there is an even greater puzzle involved here which relates directly to Newton and his scientific work.

Newton knows very well that colors are co-produced by the human eye.[145] In that sense, light and colors have their existence only for our kind of eyes. Is it not surprising, given this insight, that Newton still prefers to know what light and colors are primarily for the mind? To be clear, our problem – and we think it is Goethe's problem too – with Newton is: why does Newton not want to know what the Nature of light and colors is for his own Nature? In other words: why does he not desire to elevate the Nature given connection between light and the human eye up to the level of knowledge by retaining the primacy of Nature in the process of coming to know? Is his thinking so far away from his own Nature? For Goethe, this distance is reflected through the way in which Newton sets up his "experimentum crucis". It would seem to be appropriate, at this point, to describe that experiment briefly.

In order to prove the hypothesis that light is composed of different rays, Newton lets sunlight shine through a hole in a wall into an otherwise darkened room. There light is met by a first prism set at a calculated angle. One of the colors emerging at one of the other sides of the prism is then as a ray directed through another small hole in a second wall in the darkened room. A portion of that ray is then allowed to pass through a third hole in a third wall and then through a second prism behind that wall onto a fourth wall. Doing this in a darkened room, Newton succeeds in separating the various rays coming out of the first prism by turning the first prism gradually, so that the various rays coming out of the first prism would hit the hole in the third wall consecutively. This is the crucial experiment, since it delivers, for Newton, the proof of his hypothesis that light is composed of, and thus contains, all those rays which trigger the visible colors in the human eye.

For Goethe, this "experimentum crucis" is, as we said above, by a play on the Latin words, an experiment by crucifixion performed in a dark chamber. Besides being a torture of bright light preplanned by a hypothesizing mind, this experiment is, for Goethe, also "complicated" and "derived".[146] It deprives light of the simplicity of its oneness which light has for our eyes. Under the influence of such treatment, Nature does what she is forced to do: it yields to a human mind alienated from her.[147] Of course, Nature does not always behave as (mentally) expected, but then one has, as a "normal" scientist, to find other ways, e.g. through a change in one's hypothetical concept of her with which she then can comply. No matter how "correct" that science is, i e how mentally consistent the results are that arise out of this "modus procedendi", that science remains untrue to what Nature is for herself and for the Nature that we ourselves are.

An equivalent to Newton's crucial experiment cannot be found in Goethe's "Teaching on Colors", his earlier "Contributions to Optics" or other reports on his color experiences. Goethe instead observes how color emerges under a great variety of conditions in the human eye. He also creates these conditions "artificially" in numerous experiments (and be it the condition of closing one's eyes and then still to see what he called the "Physiological Colors"). Out of these experiences – composed of observations and experiments – he describes these color manifestations in the sequence under which the colors emerge and change in step with the changes of these conditions. This way he comes to know whether "(T)wo experiments ... follow one from the other ..." directly. By "manifolding" (see paragraph 200,7/201,1) his experiences and experiments along these lines, he "...develop[s] the experiences of the higher kind..." (paragraph 202,3), i.e. he detects the conditions of their emergence. By following the sequence of the real connections among phenomena with utmost rigor, Goethe avoids the premature interference of his mind in creating knowledge. He knows that this is the way to proceed, because he has experienced that "(T)wo phenomena may be akin to one another but by far not as closely as we believe. Two experiments may appear to follow one from the other, even when between them a large series [of connections] has to be inserted in order to bring them into an adequately natural connection." It is in this sense that Goethe can say later in "The Experiment" (paragraph 201,2) that the whole of his "Contributions to Optics" with all its experiments and experiences "... constitute *one* (Goethe's emphasis) experiment ... represent just *one* (Goethe's emphasis) experience under the most manifold perspectives". The "Teachings on Colors" are of the same kind. With the rigor of attentively manifolding experiences, Goethe has come to know what colors are, i.e. what their Nature is for us in our elevated experience of them: "deeds of light, deeds and sufferings".[148]

Additional light is shed on Goethe's understanding of rigor in the study of Nature when one briefly goes beyond the limits of the essay "The Experiment".

As we saw, light is one for Goethe, because it is one for our eye. Light in its oneness holds a particularly high position in Goethe's views, since it ultimately emanates from the sun, *the* life giving source. In other words, light is the mediator between the sun and all what the Nature of this earth is. In the last days of his life, Goethe said: "In her [the sun], I worship the light and the procreative (in German: zeugende) power of God, by which alone we live, act and are".[149] It is this light in all its sacredness to which Goethe is obedient. But this is an obedience which comes out of a "passionate attentiveness" (Schmied-Kowarzik) which on its part arises out of the enjoyment of the real phenomena. The rigor of this obedience needs not and cannot be ordered or imposed as an ethical prescription. It is inseparable from the "lust to know". Therefore, it is a way different from the rigor that goes hand in hand with absolutizing concepts in the form of strategically placed hypotheses. Constructs of this kind put a distorting distance between the life giving God in Nature out there and the Nature in us. They ultimately make our relation to Nature a deadly one, since they imply a growth of distortions. Living like that is sinful in Goethe's views, since it goes against the sacredness embodied in Nature. Sin is as little a normative concept here as it is, for instance, in Martin Luther's theology.[150] Our will is either with Nature or it is not with her. It cannot be ordered to either enjoy the conceptualization or the thing (see paragraph 199,2). It can be known that ethics cannot do anything in this regard. Yet, our problems with Nature do more than just reveal our problematic Nature; they hurt. Our suffering may evoke our desire for returning to where we belong: Nature. Goethe knows that, when he says vis-à-vis our aberrations from our Nature that only "life sets us right" (paragraph 194,3/195,1) and "specifies the bearings of the point to which we have to return" (paragraph 203,2).

Paragraph 198,2

Therefore, one cannot be careful enough in neither drawing conclusions too soon from experiments, nor proving something immediately by experiments, nor wanting to confirm some theory by experiments, for it is here at this pass (The published version reads here, in English "like at a pass", and moves this phrase to a later part of this sentence, namely, between "where"   and "   his inner enemies") at this transition from experience to judgment, from the known to the application, where all his inner enemies lie in wait for man (in German dem Menschen) the power of imagination which already at this point lifts him up on its wings while he believes that he still touches the ground, impatience, rashness, self contentedness, rigidity, mode of thinking, preconceived opinion, indolence, frivolity, fickleness, or whatever else this whole horde with its entourage may be called, all of them lie here in ambush and overpower unexpectedly the actively engaged observer, as well as the quiet observer who seemingly is unassailed by all passions

While all parts of Nature are connected with one another and while we are bodily part of that "analogia entis", it does not follow that our mind "automatically" traces these connections properly. We cannot simply trust our Nature, because our Otherness to her affects even our Nature, i.e. our senses. Speaking in biblical terms, we could say that every moment of eating from the tree of knowledge puts us into the danger of leaving the paradise of Nature. Accepting, however, the leadership of Nature in each act of coming to know, we may be able to return to what creation was meant to be. This is to say that each one of us has it in him or herself to find, in the individuated manner that is adequate to our day and age, "the bearings ... to which [we] have to return" (paragraph 203,2). And yet, our Otherness has the sinful urge to "slight the phenomena". This is to say that Goethe ascribes the falsity at work in research to the mentalistic aspect of human subjectivity. The dilemma, however, appears to be that the status of subject is both a requirement and a problem for the process of coming to know.

Goethe knows that we theorize with every glance of our eyes. In the words of today's neuro-physiology, we would say that all that we consciously perceive of is already a construct of our brain.[151] These constructs may easily turn out to be problematic, but we cannot do without constructing concepts. Goethe knowing this, even says that "... the sheer viewing of something does not advance us",[152] our conceptualizations do. And yet, they not Nature may err. While the will connects us with Nature and drives us to "theorize" instantaneously, such "elevation" all too often occurs prematurely. Goethe says that he has "a thousand examples" (paragraph 198,3/199,1) for this. He notes in the present paragraph that it is at the "transition from experiences to judgement ... where all his inner enemies lie in wait for man ...". Our mind conceptualizes connections not only where there may be none, but even treats these concepts as if they were real. In paragraph 716 of the "Farbenlehre", Goethe warns the physicist that "... he should beware of transforming perceptions into concepts ... and to treat these words as if they were objects ...".[153]

Goethe is aware that an "identity" between an object and a concept of it, or between reality and our scientific disciplines, does not exist. Our mathematically formulated sciences try to deal with this problem by speaking of the "adequacy" between object and concept and/or the "equivalency" among the objects quantified and counted. This way our sciences easily lose sight of the circumstances that, firstly, a concept is not the object to which the concept refers, and secondly, that objects do not have the sameness that ideal constructs like numbers have among themselves. The word "rose" is not a rose and roses are too different to be easily added up. Saying this, we are obviously not suggesting that nothing should be conceptualized and/or counted. However, mathematically *guided* research on Nature has to notice all too often that even at mundane levels of experimental sophistication the actually obtained data are "at best" approximations to the mathematically expected ones. Even greater discrepancies show up in the move from the lab-table to industrial application. The meaning of this for our relationship to Nature is not usually explored. Instead, Goethe suggests that one be careful in the transition from objects to their conceptualizations. Conceptualizing objects in a mathematical form poses yet another problem for him, as we shall see.

It may surprise the reader that I, at this point, yield to my wish to briefly inspect the claim of modern physics to do its job without metaphysics. For me, however, and for Goethe - I think - this claim ignores that physics as a mental construct *is* the metaphysics to the physical world. Leaving aside the traditional philosophical discussion of this issue, I would like to refer the reader again to Gerhard Roth's proposal to distinguish between reality (Realität) and the reality of the constructs of our mind (Wirklichkeit).[154] The issue arising here is, how much of the physical world is contained in our "metaphysics". In this regard, it is important to note Goethe's understanding of the experiment as the materially concrete mediation between object and subject. He knows that it takes thousands of observations, experiences and experiments carried out under the guidance of our attentive senses until a concept, an "idea", that does not only "adequately", but truly transcend-and-contain the object of our "lust to know", can arise in one's mind. In the essay "Bedeutende Fördernis...", i.e. "Significant Support...", published like "The Experiment" in 1823, Goethe exclaims "Which series of observation and contemplation did I not pursue until the idea of the Metamorphosis of the Plant emerged in me!".[155] While Goethe knows that the transcendence-and-containment of an object is an elevation of it above the level of concreteness (with which it must not be confused), he also knows that ideas "emerge". As gifts arising from the materially concrete mediation of outer and inner Nature they are true, but as smart fabrications of the mind they are problematic. Certainly, even in the latter case, they are still elevations of Nature (as Adams also knows), but as such they cannot contain Nature in them without distortions. It is in this sense that I ask: how much of Nature is in our culture, or for that matter even, how much of the physical is contained in our concepts, i.e. in our meta-physics?

We will remember that Goethe could *see* "ideas". Their appearance within this world reveals the undistorted relation between mind and Nature. In this sense, ideas of our mind transcend-and-contain the concrete, but they are only existent in the moment of thoughtful perception of the concrete.[156] Goethe has denied, for instance in paragraph 175 of the "Teachings on Colors"[157] that there is anything to be sought behind or "above" the "Ur-Phänomen", his highest abstraction. Therefore, he can leave an exploration of the question of whether these "ideas" are manifestations of a supra-natural world to philosophical minds as, for instance, Schiller and Kant. A meta-physics, or better, a "meta-Nature" is for him still of this world.

Furthermore, it would mean undoing the primacy of Nature, were one "... to prove something immediately by experiments ...", or "... to confirm some theory by experiments ..." or, worse yet, ".... to move from the known to the application ...". In this connection, Goethe advises us, in the paragraphs 202,3 and 202,4/203,1 quite explicitly, to first familiarize ourselves sensuously with all the real connections among the parts in a field of phenomena, before we verbalize, i.e. conceptualize these connections. Certainly, our mind constantly constructs theories, but the rigor arising from an enjoyment of Nature will keep us from making premature conceptualizations. Being mindful of the dangers involved in wanting "to confirm some theory by experiments", man will have less cause to "crucify" reality by trying to "nail it down" conceptually.

The danger of distortions is the greatest when one moves "... from the known to the application ...", i.e. when a theory prematurely built up or taken over from books guides the perception, and, thus, the experience and the arranging of experiments. This is what Goethe opposed so vehemently in Newton's mode of thinking, which moved "... from the idea, from the [conceivably] possible towards reality".[158] While the influence of the brain on perceptions and concepts was obviously clear to Goethe, the same clarity also prevails among modern neuro-physiologists and neuro-philosophers. But the latter treat this problem differently, certainly not by giving primacy to a love for Nature. They acknowledge that the move from mind to reality (this way around!) involves problems in adaptation of man to his environment,[159] but by proposing adaptation as a remedy, they suggest what is undoubtedly an instrumentalistic "fix" to the problem. This is the structurally adequate response of the modern way of thinking to our problems with Nature, as outlined above. But this way of thinking and its dominance are precisely the problem, also for Goethe. As Sepper puts it aptly: " 'Zur Farbenlehre' could not prevail where seeing was pre-empted by theoretical constructs".[160] Today, grounding knowledge in the preemptive strikes of hypotheses and theories supposedly still makes for "good science". Hermann Weyl, the eminent mathematician and philosopher of physics, made it very clear over half a century ago that theoretical constructs are to be "... placed ahead of the really occurring ..."; this is to him fundamental, methodologically and philosophically, for what science is all about.[161] Kant (as is well known) would happily agree with that.[162]

Goethe knows that it is part of "our essence" to move from experience to judgement, but he also knows that at the "pass" which leads "from experience to judgement", a "whole horde" of "inner enemies ... lie[s] in ambush and overpower[s] unexpectedly ... the actively engaged observer, as well as the quiet observer ...", i.e. the strong willed and the patient seeker of truth (perhaps incarnated by Newton and Goethe respectively). This horde looks indeed like a pretty impressive bunch of enemies. While refraining from taking a closer look at each of them, I would still like to note that Goethe seems to warn here in as much against haste as against slowness, even stiffness of the mind. This and also the metaphor of losing one's touch with the ground while studying the Nature of things reminds us of Ernst Bloch's warning of "getting stuck in the [concrete] matters, [or] flying over them, either one is false".[163] At any rate, it is obvious that Goethe indicates that all the enemies of true knowledge are inside the human mind, obviously implying that there is nothing in Nature herself that could keep us from arriving at truth.

Paragraph 198,3/199,1

As a warning against this danger, which is greater and closer at hand than one thinks, I should like to put forward a kind of paradox, in order to stimulate a livelier attention Namely, I dare to assert, that *one* (Goethe's emphasis) experiment, even several experiments viewed as interconnected (in German mehrere Versuche in Verbindung) prove nothing, indeed that nothing is more dangerous than to want to prove some proposition immediately by experiments, and that the greatest errors have arisen precisely because one has not recognized the danger and inadequacy of this method I must explain myself more clearly in order to avoid the suspicion that I wanted to open the floodgates (in German Tor und Tür öffnen) to doubt (The published version would read, in translation " that I wanted to say something peculiar" and ends the paragraph with these words) Each experience which we make, each experiment by which we repeat this experience, is really an isolated element of our knowledge, by frequent repetition we turn this isolated element of knowledge into a certainty Two experiences within the same discipline can become known to us, they may be closely akin to each other, but they may appear even more closely akin, and we usually are inclined to consider them more closely akin to each other than they are This is in keeping with the Nature of the human being, history of the human mind provides us with a thousand examples, and I have noticed in myself that I commit this mistake almost daily

In the first eight to nine lines of this paragraph, Goethe seems to simply repeat, at times literally, what he has said in the previous one. The difference, however, is that he becomes even more urgent here than before, when he says: "... nothing is more dangerous than to want to prove some proposition immediately by experiments ...". This way, "... the greatest errors have arisen, ...because one has not recognized the danger and inadequacy of this method". Goethe admits that this statement requires "... explain[ing] [him]self more clearly in order to avoid the suspicion that [he] wanted to open the floodgates to doubt" or, in the published version "... to say something peculiar". Of course, Goethe is aware that calling what most scientists and philosophers take to be *the* way of proceeding in scientific research "the greatest error" could stir quite a debate. Goethe also knows that Newton's (and others') way of proceeding had been treated by philosophers and scientists as if the final word had been spoken on the proper scientific method. He on his part, however, has never believed that philosophers as "friends of wisdom", and not primarily of Nature, can solve the problem. Scientists cannot do so either, because they have unreflexively fallen prey to the influence of Newton and others of his kind.

In the first sentence of what is a new paragraph in the published version of "The Experiment", a shift is made to introduce a new aspect in the topic of "propositions and their proof by experiments". Goethe unequivocally states that "(E)ach experience ..., each experiment by which we repeat this experience, is really an isolated element of our knowledge". As such, experiences and experiments are points of sensuous connections between the human individual and a particular phenomenon out there. If we conceptualize these points of contact, and if we repeat an experience or an experiment frequently, "... we turn this isolated element of our knowledge into a certainty", meaning that we elevate this sensuous experience to knowledge of how our senses connect with that object out there. Each additional experience has the same status, but, as events relating our subjective senses to objects, they do not tell us much about the connectedness among these objects themselves. This connectedness is yet to be experienced. Goethe writes: "Two experiences within the same discipline can become known to us, they may be closely akin to each other, but they may appear even more closely akin, and we usually are inclined to consider them more closely akin to each other than they are." Our inclination to *consider* them as connected is "... in keeping with the Nature of the human being ..." as "... the history of the human mind ..." tells us in "thousand examples". Goethe says of himself: "... I have noticed in myself that I commit this mistake almost daily." As isolated experiences, however sensuous in themselves, they do not easily reveal the real connections among them to our senses. Therefore, these connections must not be concluded upon before being sensuously traced as such.

Among philosophers, the phenomenologist Edmund Husserl is one of the few who appears, although only at first sight, to come close to Goethe's view when he admits to the isolated status of experiences. For him as well, experiences and experiments are unconnected instances. According to Husserl,[164] the multitude of singular experiences segregates each one of us into the equivalent multitude of experiencing subjects, and it is only our mind that allows us to create order and unity among these phenomena, thus granting us again the unity of our subjectivity. According to Husserl, mental relations are *the* relations among the phenomena. For him, perceptions have a "transcendence immanent to consciousness",[165] i.e. they point beyond themselves in our minds. The role of our materially concrete kinship to objects is, however, hardly brought to bear by Husserl on the activity of coming to know. In other words, we are unaware that Husserl ever adequately appreciated what, e.g., Karl-Otto Apel later called the "body-a-priori" of all knowledge.[166] So, it is here where the similarity between Husserl and Goethe stops. Undoubtedly, as far as the coming to know is concerned, each experience, each experiment remains, for Goethe as well, an isolated part of our knowing, but differing from Husserl, Goethe has experienced that our mind needs the guidance of the senses when it comes to the conceptualization of true material connections among experienced objects. Under such guidance, we can create a knowledge which is not merely a knowledge *about* objects, but it is a knowledge that ties us into the totality and connectedness of the phenomena out there.

I think it is quite telling that the intent of Husserl's thought could so easily be used by Niklas Luhmann in the build up of his theory of sense systems. For him, Husserl's "immanent transcendence" takes place in systems of sense.[167] For Luhmann, real objects "matter" only as senders of information, and hence the recipients of such information are not primarily human subjects, but systems of sense in terms of which human subjects constitute their flexible identity. It is these sense systems which interpret - not the objects - but the information that comes from them. Sense systems, not human subjects, can then point out, in a supposedly detached manner, thinkable alternatives to the information received. Putting Luhmann's position in Adams' terms, one could say that reflexive re-organization of messages received trigger "re-definitions" in minds distorted by their absolutization of power. As we saw above, this leads to a culture to which Nature remains substantially alien. Among a host of questions arising here,[168] there is a particularly serious one, namely, that of how one could account then for a motivation to know.[169] Luhmann's answer to this question is that he introduces the notion of an "interest in functionality". But this notion remains, on its part, unaccounted for.[170] However disastrous the practical consequences of this answer - we saw above that they involve the pseudo-motivation and pseudo-satisfaction of power "games" - , I am wondering whether a sheerly philosophical line of thinking as it goes back via Husserl to Kant had any other choice but to end up in instrumentalism and its praxis.[171] While we certainly have to note, in this connection, that Goethe also sees problems emerging in man's urge to know, I have to underline that these are not the ones that Luhmann, Adams and modern praxis have. Goethe undoubtedly acknowledged the potentially disastrous consequences of our urge to know, but he also knows what these philosophers and modern thinkers do not seem to know: our "lust to know" can elevate us to togetherness in an all embracing sense when and if it arises out of a bodily grounded enjoyment of the objects around us.

It is at this point where we can return to Goethe's significance for modernity, particularly in view of his awareness that experiences and experiments are "isolated elements of our knowledge". As he anticipates here and explicates later in "The Experiment", elevating these isolated experiences to "experiences of the higher kind" (paragraphs 201,3; 202,3) does not mean to force them into systems of mere thought (paragraph 202,4/203,1), but to experience the connectedness among them with our senses as well. Then these higher level experiences imply neither the modern flexibility of sense systems, as they aim for conceptual control, nor do they preclude a pluralism of understanding, as we shall see later.[172] These kinds of experience, as we saw above,[173] do not even deny the material usefulness of knowing Nature. Neither lending support for the capriciousness of modern thought (paragraph 202,3) nor for egofocal gains, Goethe's way of understanding Nature transcends-and-contains modernity by taking egofocal abstractions out of both, the knowing of and the benefiting from Nature.

Since Goethe knew that Nature was more than logic, more than system, theory, etc., he respected her as being greater than our mind. In fact, as Schöne writes,[174] Goethe, in order to obtain the "pure phenomenon", is willing to accept what Schöne calls, with a certain lack of precision, "empirical ruptures". While such ruptures would trouble Goethe, he has, instead, no problems with ruptures in logic.[175] Conceptual ruptures are necessarily perceived as most problematic in sciences that are guided primarily by logic and aim at conceptual systematizations. Heisenberg, among others,[176] has emphatically noted that modern science and specifically physics are systems of conceptual order. According to Heisenberg, our successful technology is proof of the logical coherence and correctness of these edifices of our thought.[177] Our obviously correct technology is, also according to the philosopher Karl Jaspers, a form of knowledge "...we have to embrace, if we wish to live".[178] In the same vain, we heard C. F. von Weizsäcker speak of "The Unity of Nature" which he explicitly understands as the orderliness of physics and not of what physics is about.[179] 50 years later, we find it superfluous to point out the pyrrhic kind of our techno*logical* victory over Nature. We, together with Richard N.

Adams, have ample reason to know that our victory over Nature may very well turn out to be Nature's victory over us.[180] We know that even instrumentalistic attempts to solve this dilemma will not work. As we have reasoned above, new technologies, new legislation or new ethics will not do.

Paragraph 199,2

This mistake is closely akin to another one from which, for the most part, it also arises Man (in German der Mensch) enjoys, as it were, more the conceptualization [of a thing] than the thing itself, or, rather we must say man (in German der Mensch) enjoys something only in so far as he conceives of it, it has to fit into his kind of sense (in German Sinnesart) and howsoever high he might elevate his way of making sense (in German Vorstellungsart) above the ordinary way, howsoever he purifies it, it usually remains still only a way of making sense that is to say, an attempt to bring several objects into a specific intelligible (in German faßliche) relationship with one another which they strictly speaking, do not have, hence the inclination towards hypotheses, theories, terminologies and systems which we cannot disapprove of since these must necessarily spring from the organization of our essence (in German Wesens)

Goethe knows that the "... inclination towards theories, hypotheses, terminologies, and systems ..." is something "... which we cannot disapprove of since these must necessarily spring from the organization of our essence". Given that this is our "essence", Goethe does not moralistically speak against this inclination. Being so used to activate this essence by giving primacy to the mind, the proposition to give primacy to the senses instead may easily come across to most people as a moral prescription. Such reading would imply, however, a fundamental misunderstanding of Goethe's views.

After having spoken in the previous paragraph about the problems in making mental connections that are unfounded in material reality, Goethe calls it flatly a mistake that "(M)an enjoys, as it were, more the conceptualization [of a thing] than the thing itself, or, rather we must say: man enjoys something only in so far as he conceives of it ...". It seems to satisfy man more to proceed that way, although "... it usually remains still only a way of making sense ...", no matter "... howsoever high he will elevate his way of making sense above the ordinary way ...".

I do not think that these lines can be interpreted as expressing a disregard for man's mental abilities; after all an elevation of Nature to knowledge is our and Nature's elevation as well. For Goethe, the sensuous experience, i.e. the sensing of the connections between our inner Nature and outer Nature is such a matter of enjoyment that man cannot truly wish to distort this enjoyment when elevating it to conceptual clarity. We think that understanding this point is of utmost importance, if one wishes to understand Goethe's message on coming to know at all. The point to be emphasized here is that primacy belongs to Nature even in thought and concept formation. It would indeed be absurd to say that primacy in concept formation and thinking belongs to thinking and concept formation. The "punctum saliens" of Goethe's thinking and being, namely that Nature permeates everything there is, i.e. the "analogia entis *omnium*"), is an insight that affects the understanding of this point itself. Therefore, an understanding of Goethe's way of thinking is only true to itself, if it arises out of one's own bodily enjoyment of the concrete things to be understood. The question of whether or not one has this enjoyment can only be answered when having concretely made one's own observations, experiences and experiments. This is the reason why Goethe writes his "Beiträge" and his "Farbenlehre" as invitations to the reader to make all these experiences for her/himself.

I have pointed out, oftentimes by now, that expressions of pleasure accompany Goethe's studies of colors almost on every page of his writings on the matter. For those not desiring to experience this pleasure as well, prescribing it is futile; one either enjoys one's natural drive to sense and then to know or one does not do that. For Goethe, it is clear (as it was for Martin Luther) that there is little one can do about one's drives except accepting them or deviating from them. Not accepting them implies a "second thought" spontaneity, as we called it above. Then "theories, hypotheses, terminologies, systems" etc., have to take the lead. As such, this is not the primary reason for Goethe to reject the mode of thinking underlying them. The primary reason for his rejection is that he senses this mode of thinking as a bodily distortion. To some extent, I agree with C.-F. v. Weizsäcker's statement on Goethe: "... he erred [in his "Teachings on Colors]", because he *wanted* to err".[181] This is to say that I agree with Weizsäcker by making two important provisos: 1.- Goethe erred only in the judgement of a science represented by Weizsäcker and dominated by an abstraction guided mode of thinking; and 2.- Goethe *wanted* his kind of "error", because this wanting did not only connect him directly with Nature through his will, but allowed him to sense himself as a part of her. As we saw, Weizsäcker himself is aware that Goethe's science arose out of his way of being, but we wonder: did Weizsäcker fully sense what way of being Goethe was talking about?

We should remember the insight we gained above,[182] namely that Goethe's way of enjoying Nature places him into a realm in which the Midas touch has no room. Accordingly, he has no problems with seeing Nature as "benefiting" us. At the same time, Goethe spoke about how important it was not to make Nature recalcitrant in our relation to her; then she would not give freely. Here we see that there is nothing instrumental in Goethe's view on this. He does not speak against making Nature recalcitrant, *in order to* benefit from her, instead he proposes to celebrate her and cultivate her through our proper understanding of her. Then she will give freely to us as lovers give to one another naturally. In the light of this, it testifies to the estrangement from Nature of those modern scientists who have held Goethe's intimacy with her against him; they fear that he is mislead by his subjectivism.[183] At the same time, the estranged subjectivism of the romanticists vis-à-vis Nature has found wide-spread positive responses not the least among scientists, provided they are out of their labs. Once again we see that it is a modern and distorted subjectivity that cannot bring together intimacy and sobriety and is also hesitant to accept the pairing of individuality and usefulness.

I admit that the suggestion to keep these pairs together sounds simplistic vis-à-vis modern man's kind of sobriety. But this sobriety has little more speaking for it than the degree to which it has - suicidally - gained dominance in today's society. Benefiting from direct enjoyment of sensuous experiences is so alien to this mode of thinking that observing and experiencing something without these activities being instrumental for something else has become an alien proposition. This finds its expression also in our educational system. The interests of so many, teachers and students alike, are set so much on learning and applying the perspectives and theories that are en vogue (and "sell") that they in their vast majority see it as strange to be asked for their own observations and thoughts. A graduate student said once to one of us that he did not know the difference between a family, a sports team and a gang, because he never had to read about it.

Paragraph 199,3

If, on the one hand, every single experience, every single experiment must be viewed as isolated by their very Nature, and if, on the other hand, the power of the human mind strives with tremendous force to tie together all which is external to it and comes to be known by it, then one easily comes to acknowledge the danger to which one is exposed, if one wishes to connect a single experience with a preconceived idea or if one wishes to prove through singular experiments some connection which is not entirely sensuous, but which the creative power of the mind has already formulated

In the first part of its opening sentence, this paragraph again makes the statement that every experience, every experiment is an isolated event "by their very Nature". And again, Goethe, the skeptic of philosophy, warns against what "the creative power of the mind" may make of these isolated events, namely, tie them together. Goethe has pointed out before that errors cannot arise at the level of the senses. They can do that only when sense perceptions are elevated to judgement. Therefore, caution should all the more be exercised, when experiences are tied together. I think this is what Goethe expresses here by warning against creating any relation "... which is not entirely sensuous ...". This view of Goethe's can only be understood fully when the status of man as a social and cultural being, i.e. when the sociality of man's individuality is fully appreciated. In this connection, the issue is to see the difference (-in-commonality) between what is merely Nature and man's "Other Nature".

Certainly, all animals who, like ourselves, can smell, see, hear and touch objects around them, may still do harm to themselves by, shall we say, falling into traps, falling prey to predators, drowning, etc. Yet by doing so, they do not make a mistake by misinterpreting Nature. In fact, they do not interpret or understand anything at all. They step on traps or thin ice, because the signals their senses get are strong enough to let them act accordingly and do so inescapably. This, of course, relates to the difference between signals and symbols and to the non-100%-feedback in human communication.[184] The total embeddedness of animals (let alone that of plants, rocks, etc.) in Nature precludes individuality in them. As sketched above,[185] this individuality is the most significant condition for being social and having culture, i.e. for having an also symbolically mediated relation to objects and people. In other words, the "analogia entis" as such does not know itself, but we know it and yet remain a part of it. It is precisely because we as human beings transcend and yet contain Nature in us that we can err, sometimes tremendously so.

Goethe, not only as a scientist, but also as a poet and writer, knows that it is through words, i.e. through conceptualizations of phenomena, that understanding among humans becomes possible. Taking off from there, he once pointed out[186] that one cannot give a presentation about anything without using a conceptual-theoretical bond that "ties together" what we wish to communicate. At the level of concepts and communication, mental coherence is obviously a requirement also for Goethe. However, the strife for mental coherence in the process of understanding must not lead, in Goethe's view, to a deification of reason and its imposition on Nature. God is in Nature, but not per se in our minds. As we have heard him say (paragraph 196,5/197,1), Nature is greater than any person's mind. Therefore, Nature must not be forced to appear without "ruptures". And yet, a mental coherence in speech as in all interaction which willingly accepts the greatness of Nature still aims at plausibility among us humans. As such, it still establishes, at the mental level, a common bond among people which is of a "higher kind" than the one in mere Nature. In this sense then, the interaction of people and their relation to the matters at hand are elevations to the socio-cultural level. People, if in communion with Nature, can then form a community grounded in truth. Truth cannot be without this sociality. Only in this togetherness is our life a transcendence of the otherwise hopeless loneliness that comes along with individuation and sheer correctness. Grounding our Nature in the Nature around us implies truthfulness for our social relations as well. Nothing else will. Disaster, however, threatens under two interconnected conditions: First, when we allow "... the power of the human mind ... to tie together ..." single experiences of which each in its concreteness is only an isolated encounter between a single inner Nature and the world, and second, when we gain "admirers and pupils" (paragraph 200,2) for what we fabricate out of such isolated encounters.

One's "transcendence-immanent-to-consciousness" (Husserl, later Luhmann) is, therefore, not only alien to Nature, it remains alien to fellowman as well, since such kind of transcendence is not grounded in what ties all there is together. It lacks that grounding because of it being immanent merely to consciousness. However fictitious such a transcendence may be, it can obviously be practiced. Such praxis is, nonetheless, a matter of evil for Goethe, a matter of trying not to stay within God's creation. As such, it is man's original sin.

And yet, for humans, seeing is theorizing and theorizing is part of our "essence" (paragraph 199,2); to be a "fallen Nature" is part of our Nature. As Goethe puts it here: "... the power of the mind strives with tremendous force to tie together all which is external to it ...". We make experiences then all too easily not on their own terms, but in terms of previously made experiences which are all too often prematurely promoted to frames of reference and then guide us to perceive of yet other objects and theorize further about them. Such false theories spread like wildfire, particularly where sense distortions have become endemic. Then "theories and systems" take over and "... harm the progress of the human mind ...", particularly "... if they survive longer than is right ..." (paragraph 199,4). Then life, the force of Nature, has to "set us right" (paragraph 194,3/195,1) and has to replace the mental contraptions of theories and systems with fresh senses. In other words, a resurrected obedience (in Goethe's sense) to Nature is the primary source of getting our understandings right and to save us from our original sin.

Returning from here to Goethe's distanced relationship to philosophy, we have an opportunity to note that there was more to that distancing than just his objection against the tendency in philosophy to systematize knowledge.[187] Let us note that Goethe had given up on making attempts to get the philosophers and the scientists of his times back to earth and off their wings. He simply practiced the primacy of Nature in his own scientific work. Keeping his theorizing grounded in the "entirely sensuous" has earned Goethe, as will be recalled, one of Schiller's most severe accusation: "he is too sensuous".[188] But through this sensuousness, he had found the few true companions in his life. Yet even more is misunderstood by those opposed to Goethe's sensuousness. They fail to see that sensuousness is part and parcel of Goethe's innerworldly religiosity. This could be brought to light by further exploring Goethe's understanding of the status of concepts.

"Urphänomene", i.e. "ground phenomena", even though concepts of considerable abstraction, remained real for Goethe, since they still corresponded for him sensuously to the world. Goethe could visualize the "Urphänomen" of colors and the "Urpflanze", the archetypal plant, in every manifestation of color and in every plant. In this sense, his concepts, his whole "metaphysics", remained innerworldly. This innerworldliness separates Goethe fundamentally from philosophers and philosophical minds like Kant, Schiller and Carl-Friedrich v. Weizsäcker, to name but a few. They, instead, all assume a higher world behind the one accessible to our senses. For Goethe, things are what they are for us – period! Therefore, talk about what things are "for themselves" or contemplations about the status of noumena "behind" (or above) the phae-noumena, are superfluous concerns for him. He says that there is nothing "behind" the "Urphänomene".[189] Nature as is, is for Goethe God's creation and the Nature we see is a revelation of Him.[190] Understanding Nature in willful obedience to her gives to this elevation of Nature in man its deeply religious dimension. We can understand God in his revelation, i.e. in Nature, not in a final, but in a dynamic though never perfectible sense.

Paragraph 199,4

Through such an effort, most of the time, theories and systems arise which do honor to the sharp-mindedness of the authors, which, however, if they find more acclaim than is appropriate, if they survive longer than is right, immediately (in German sogleich) slow down again and harm the progress of the human mind which they in a certain sense advance

Being aware of Goethe's advocacy for remaining sensuous and down to earth in one's thinking makes it clear that the line saying " ... theories and systems ... do honor to the sharp-mindedness of [their] authors ..." is meant to be quite ironic, if not sarcastic. In view of what Goethe says later about inventive scientists (paragraph 200,2), this sarcasm of Goethe's can only be fully understood if read by persons who are down to earth themselves. To them, it is also clear that Goethe does not turn against sharp-mindedness for theoretical or ethical reasons. Instead, he speaks against it as a false way of being. After all, opposing sharp-mindedness per se would be untenable, simply because an advocacy of the opposite of sharp-mindedness – let us say of dull-mindedness – would obviously be absurd.

Goethe's sarcasm about the problematic use of the mind needs also to be read in the context of what he says later on in "The Experiment" about the question of ". . how the intellect could come to our help in this endeavor ... " (paragraph 200,7/201,1). While not going into detail at that particular moment regarding the role of the intellect as a guardian against daring mental inventiveness, he tells us quite a bit about the requirements of "thoughtfulness" in the "manifolding" of experiments for the validity of scientific research in most of the sections following paragraph 200,7/201,1

The very short paragraph presently under our consideration makes us also want to look again at Goethe's concept of progress. If anything, we have to note that this passage, like others inspected before (e. g. paragraph 194,3/195,1 or 197,5), lends itself much sooner to an advocacy of progress than to an opposition against it. We have to say that such opposition as in the case of sharp-mindedness could not be reasonably argued for either, because an advocacy of its opposite is clearly absurd as well. What Goethe really opposes here is a progress that is based on a sharp-mindedness that breeds "... theories and systems ... which ...", if accepted, "...slow down again and harm the progress of the human mind which they in a certain sense advance". So, instead of repeating that Goethe is an advocate of progress and not an opponent of sharp-mindedness per se, I find it more important to explore how Goethe could speak of a return to what "is right" in knowing Nature, be aware of the deep-rooted difference between his and the dominant kind of science and yet refuse to perceive of that return as a revolutionary event. In this way, the question comes up again: why was Goethe against revolutions? Even though I am not a specialist on Goethe and have certainly not read more than a portion of his writings, I still think that I could propose a few perhaps useful and not too spurious departure points for an attempt to clarify Goethe's position on this issue.

First of all, we should bear in mind that Goethe's opposition against the French Revolution did not mean an approval of the late absolutist society in France (or elsewhere). But Goethe had his strong doubts that the lower classes while being "the closest to God"[191] had suffered from serious deprivation too long to be capable to take on political leadership. It was not just education, i.e. the acquisition of skills, which were lacking, it appears that Goethe did not see that the lower classes were ready to take on what he considered to be a requirement for leadership, namely the ability to "serve". For Goethe, this ability took a way of being which he had been unable to detect in more than a few individuals around him. In this connection, I have to leave it as an open question whether Goethe saw the dreaded bloodshed of the French Revolution as an indication of inadequacies on the part of the revolutionaries. We know, however, with quite a measure of certainty that a revolution in the sciences could only come about in his view with proper cultivation of the people working in them. Their Nature had to return to Nature herself and away from the distorted conceptualizations of her.

It is perhaps from here that we could briefly compare Goethe with Karl Marx, the great advocate of revolution in the Western tradition of thought.

As should be well known, Marx considered himself a "theoretical-critical mind".[192] It was as such that he delivered his critique of capitalism, i.e. by putting his mind first. He saw doing this as a deficiency and accordingly admired the "practical-mental"[193] and even more so the "artistic" approach[194] to society and Nature. These approaches were much more lively and valid in his view, but he did not pursue them; he remained a philosopher. As such, he believed in the power of thought and in the thoughtful power of the working class. But as is clear today, power as such is the problem; not the having or the not having of it.[195] Therefore, taking power away from the powerful by revolution only leads to shifts in power, not to its disappearance. There are indications that Goethe, the politician, unexplored as he is in that role, was aware of this. This is indicated, in my view, especially through his advocacy of "service". If disappearance of power is the issue, then obedience to Nature in us, around us and in fellow human beings is the point of salvation. This is co-terminus with Goethe's praxis of sensuousness. Its cultivation can only occur in a new praxis in which not revolution is the issue but self-preservation of those living this new praxis.

When the philosopher Gernot Böhme suggests that "an interest in a science of this type ...", namely Goethe's "... could be thematized ... where people develop an interest in experiencing themselves in their interaction with Nature...".[196] I would be inclined to agree. But experiencing oneself in interaction with Nature requires something else than it being "thematized"; it needs to be *done*. Goethe did not just ask for an interest in his science; he invited people to do it. A mere adoption of Goethe's science could only occur for the wrong reasons. Following Goethe's words would not only be un-Goethean, it would all too easily provide a means of control for another kind of revolutionary intellectuals.

Paragraph 199,5/200,1

One will be able to notice that a good mind applies all the more artfulness, the fewer the data lying before him, that he, in order to show his sovereignty, as it were, even selects from the available data only a few favoring ones (in German Günstlinge) which flatter him, that he knows to organize the remaining ones in such a way that they do not contradict him directly, and that he, in the end, knows to confuse, to entangle and to push aside the opposing ones so that then the whole does not really resemble anymore a freely functioning republic but a despotic court

In this paragraph, Goethe writes: "One will be able to notice that a good mind applies all the more artfulness, the fewer the data lying before him; that he ... even selects only a few favoring ones (in German: Günstlinge; this word is often used for favorites of a powerful monarch; FWS) which flatter him; that he knows to organize the remaining ones in such a way that they do not contradict him directly". Grounded so narrowly, a theory inevitably turns, particularly if further research can only be incorporated through "artful" maneuvers, into an uninhabitable old castle, resembling more a maze[197] than a home of the free.

As mentioned before, Goethe's knowledge was based on an unbelievable amount of observations and experiences. In 1798, for instance, he remarked to Schiller that he had paper bags made for him to hold the notes on his studies of colors.[198] From the way in which his own mind oscillated in all these studies between ad-hoc-theorizing and sensuously guided revisions of this theorizing, there cannot be any doubt that it was out of a command of such wealth of data that Goethe saw fit to point out here what "a good mind" all too often does in view of the paucity of data at its disposal, namely, to interpret them "artfully", and that is even to say, deceptively (paragraph 200,2).

Goethe's blame of artificiality against Newton has, in a way, its own history which may be of interest here. Goethe had initially granted Newton "youthful overhaste" in absolutizing his fundamental view of light (as composed of all colors).[199] But Goethe changed his mind about him when he noticed that Newton had never considered to let his senses take the lead in the observation of the real connections between light and colors and to structure his theory accordingly. Goethe understands that we theorize all the time and do so instantaneously, but while absolutizing a small and hypothetically grounded data base by forcing it on all subsequent data may be understood in the dominant sciences as an attempt at theoretical consistency, it is for Goethe a matter of a deeply false and careless relation to the Nature of things. This accusation remains the main theme in Goethe's "Polemics" against Newton, pointed out there already in the second paragraph of its "Introduction".[200]

Having based one's "theories and systems" too narrowly and too hypothetically has further consequences. It forces any sharp-minded scientist - "... in order to show his sovereignty, ... to confuse, to entangle and to push aside the opposing ones [of the data] so that then the whole ... does not really resemble anymore a freely functioning republic but a despotic court". At such a court, the "Farbenlehre" could not prevail, as Dennis Sepper once said.[201] Grounded in a maze of sensuously unfounded data, thinking has little to do with life anymore. It oppresses life and sees that as its liberty, a liberty doled out at the despotic courts of correctness in cautiously dosaged chunks.

When Goethe published his "Beiträge zur Optik", he was not fully prepared to find so little response to it, let alone so much animosity as he in fact did.[202] The reason that this publication was met with widespread rejection or deadening silence was obviously related to the circumstance that the scientific and general public was already used to a segregation between Nature and those studying her. Needless to say, the view had been widely accepted that the primary guidance in research had to come from mental constructs. Goethe, furthermore, was not aware of how narrow-minded the "scientific guilds" were, when it came to admitting diverging points of view into the courts of their discussions.[203] In other words, Goethe had to learn the hard way how despotic these courts were. He finally had to acknowledge that there was no chance to realize his hope to demolish these despotic courts, which like the Bastille, had been demolished in the French Revolution (says Goethe, the opponent of the French Revolution!).[204] To the contrary, he had begun to anticipate that matters would get much worse in the future. He visualized that "men with heads on their shoulders" and "not gifted to the highest degree" would come up and take leadership not only in the sciences but in all social and public affairs.[205] Living today under the rule of such "men", one might easily despair over the question of whether "a freely functioning republic" could ever be erected.

At this point, it seems appropriate to make a few remarks on the linkage that Goethe sees between the despotism of correctness and its permanently latent threat to a healthy life.

In a short piece titled "Naturphilosophie", i.e. "Philosophy of Nature", published in 1827,[206] Goethe says that those who study Nature "with preconceptions" (in German: mit Vorsätzen) and expect the world of objects to obey them[207] create an understanding which is not only false, but is infected by death. Goethe does not say that man's misunderstanding of Nature implies the death of all Nature. He does say, however, that the necrosis (in German: das Nekrose), i.e. the death carrying parts in her body, keeps the rest of Nature's living body from healing itself.[208] So the sickness of the distorted Nature in modern man, as a sickness of only a part of the whole body of Nature, will not be able to bring death to all of her body. While this view supports our above stated position that man will not be able to destroy Nature (as some say), we also have to say that this sickness keeps Nature as a whole from being wholesome and healthy. It constantly threatens those who have not fallen prey to modern abstractedness and makes it difficult for them to live in accordance with their Nature. The seriousness of this threat must, of course, be understood from within the awareness of the importance of sociality for truth to prevail.[209]

The danger that Goethe expresses here is not usually acknowledged today, though it is visibly before us. Among the very few who do acknowledge this is the fore-mentioned biologist Bernhard Verbeek. In his "Die Anthropologie der Umweltzerstörung", i.e. "The Anthropology of the Environmental Destruction", he links[210] modern abstractedness, in a way quite reminiscent of Goethe, to a modern kind of nekrophilia and even to a hatred against all that lives. Verbeek sees this nekrophilia emerging together with the modern mode of abstract thinking in quite a variety of places. He saw it not only in the motto of the Spanish fascists, namely, "viva muerte", and in the death cult of Nazi Germany, but he sees it also in the emphasis on rectangularity that expresses itself in concrete slabs and in concrete poured in such a way to be suitable for little more than "efficient" transportation, "modern" housing and "adequate" health care.

Seen from within this context, it is little wonder that the despotism that has evolved in late capitalism has stood on guard against the death it carries with it. Its instrumentalistic self-restraint, an exercise practiced since quite some time in Western society, expresses itself now also in "environmental concerns" and in its various forms of legislating "environmentally favorable policies".[211] This way, the modern despotism tries to keep itself in check technocratically, economically and politically. It may keep itself from committing suicide. But, while perhaps succeeding in this, "Toxic Capitalism" (Pearce & Tombs) keeps on handing out death, if not wholesale then in a constant stream of sickening dosages.

Paragraph 200,2

For a man (in German Mann) who has so much merit there cannot be a lack of admirers and pupils (in German Schüler) who, in the course of time (in German historisch), come to know and admire such a fabric and, as far as it is possible, appropriate their master's imagery (in German Vorstellungsart) Oftentimes, such a teaching gains the upper hand in such a manner that one would be considered defiant and bold, if one would dare to cast doubt on it Only later centuries would dare to approach such a sacred relic, submit the matter under consideration again to common human sense (in German gemeinen Menschensinn), and take the matter a bit more lightly, and repeat about the founder of a sect what a witty mind has once said about a great scientist he would have been a great man, had he not invented so much

I think that this paragraph continues and even exaggerates the themes of irony and sarcasm, and in doing so, anticipates, at the end, the tone of Goethe's later "Polemics" against Newton. But in its course, it also makes a remark that sheds further light on the appropriation and propagation of knowledge.

In the first sentence Goethe acts as if he could understand that "... a man who has so much merit ..." in sharp-minded research, would not "... lack admirers and pupils ..." who, "... as far as it is possible, appropriate their master's imagery". Goethe, who could not learn from books, obviously thinks that one accepts such kind of imagery only, if one does not expose one's own "common human sense" to the natural phenomena in question. Taking the master's word for truth turns people into "pupils", which Goethe hardly ever had, and "admirers", of which Goethe had very many, at times for the wrong reasons. Already in 1793, Goethe saw that there was next to nothing he could do about the wide-spread false appropriation of scientific knowledge. The despotism that goes with it was so willfully accepted that "... one would be considered defiant and bold, if one would dare to cast doubt on it". Noting that it would take centuries before doubt could be cast on it, Goethe switches his tone to a sarcasm which becomes quite nasty through a twist of which one can hardly assume that a verbally so powerful man like Goethe had not intended it.

But before turning our attention to the sarcastic part of this paragraph, I would like to take up the question whether Goethe himself did not try to gain followers for his point of view. Our answer to this question is not a simply negative one, and our answer needs to be understood in the following context: 1.- As I have mentioned before, Goethe largely presented descriptions and only few theoretical conclusions of his own observations, both in the "Beiträge" and in the "Farbenlehre". He did so with the expectation that the reader would make these experiments and observations for him/herself. He knew that this would not make the acceptance of his scientific writings easier. But he could not help this. On 21 Dec 1831, Eckermann asked Goethe why the[212]

> Teachings on Colors" had not found a wider distribution Goethe answered. "It is very difficult to get it [its message] across, because it demands, as you know, not just to be read and studied, but to be done; and this has its difficulties These, however, could not be avoided.

2.- Goethe also expected, as he states in the essay before us (see e.g. its last paragraph) that those in fact doing their own research on the same matter would present descriptions of it so that new "experiences of the

higher kind" could be formulated jointly and would lead to knowledge
shared by a community of researchers. 3.- Goethe furthermore expected
that along these lines not only knowledge true to Nature and ourselves
would materialize, but also one that was not dogmatic and would allow
researchers to form "a freely functioning republic" of pluralist views.
While Goethe's concept of pluralism will have to be discussed later,[213]
it is clear that he longed for such a "republic". But he did not attempt to
spread a new dogma and gain "admirers and pupils". Companions on
the journey to truth, however, would have been more than welcome.

In the last sentence of this paragraph, Goethe, at first, expresses the
hope that "later centuries" could do something about the "sacred relic"
of an undeservedly admired "imagery" of a "great scientist". Then, and
possibly out of a sense of frustration, Goethe treats the sharp-minded
scientist as being worse than a founder of a sect. Let us note what
Goethe does here! He says this: If one can say about a scientist that he
has "invented so much", then the scientist is, in view of his usual claim
to self-abnegating rigor, even more of a dubious and self-centered
figure than the founder of a sect. In other words, a scientist who
structures his knowledge of Nature under the mentalistic guidance of
one arbitrarily chosen theoretical assumption and yet seeks to find
followers for it, presents a worse make-belief than a sectarian quack.
Thus, an unfounded science is worse than the "hocuspocus" of a
sectarian religion.

3b.: Enjoying Nature and Understanding Her Well
(Commentaries on paragraphs 200,3 to 203,2, the end of the essay)

Paragraph 200,3

But it may not be enough to point out the danger and to warn against it It is fair that at least one makes one's opinion public and makes it known how one believes to be able to avoid such an error (in German Abweg), or whether one has found out how someone else before us has avoided it

What we have read in "The Experiment" so far should make it clear that this short paragraph does not conclude, as some readers may think, one part and introduce a second part of a merely mentalistic exercise. This relates to two aspects.

First: The twofold use of the word "how" in this paragraph may easily suggest to a merely intellectual mind that Goethe will finally come to speak about his own scientific methodology. Yet, as should by now be obvious to the reader, the delivery of a methodo-logy as the unfolding of the *logic* of the *way* to truth is not in keeping with the Nature of things for Goethe. As we shall see in greater detail yet,[214] this could not be done by him, since every encounter between object and subject has its own peculiarities even at the level of the merely "common forces and elements" of Nature (paragraph 200,7/201,1). Therefore, his treatment of the "how" of scientific research can only be a description of the material-sensuous course of how Goethe had concretely encountered Nature in his research.

Secondly, when Goethe suggests in this context to "... find out how someone else before us has avoided ..." the errors of mentalistically misguided thinking, then, the man who "could not learn from books" is not now recommending that. Merely reading is not the way of how he had learned what others had written about; Goethe learned from doing. As an example, let us again remember that Goethe came to understand even poetry, in the case of Hafiz, by re-creating it; he wrote his own poems in Hafiz' style. Only then, that poetry became truly his own.

Goethe had certainly read widely on previous and contemporary studies of light and colors, as the two volumes of the "Historical Part" of the "Teachings on Colors" indicate. But he did not just read about them. This then allows us to raise the question for the role that tradition played in Goethe's views.

Sensing himself as standing in a tradition, as Goethe undoubtedly did, does not mean that such a tradition as a merely mental heritage determined how he approached the world of light and colors. Goethe follows the writings of his predecessors by finding himself in an experientially grounded agreement with their experiences. This, of course, strengthens Goethe's confidence (see e.g. the opening of paragraph 203,2) and lets him continue a tradition, but he does so without simply adopting it. This is the way in which living traditions in other human endeavors have been continued as well. Mozart, for instance, did not follow the piano tradition of the "London-Bach" (i.e. Johann Christian's) by subjugating his musical drive to it. He created a continuation of that tradition by composing what is unmistakably his own piano music. True continuity takes human subjects to be truly alive. Imitations are then in as much out of the question as "admirers and pupils".

Paragraph 200,4

Earlier, I have said that I hold as harmful the immediate bringing to bear of an experiment to the proof of any hypothesis, and have thereby given to understand that I hold a mediated bringing to bear of it (in German derselben) as fruitful, and since all depends on this point, it is necessary to explain oneself clearly

First, Goethe briefly notes that he has so far only stated that he "… hold[s] as harmful the immediate bringing to bear of an experiment to the proof of any hypothesis …". This implies for Goethe that he has "… thereby given to understand that [he] hold[s] a mediated bringing to bear of it (in German: derselben) as fruitful …". A proper understanding of these lines requires a bit of a philological exercise.

Different from the English word "it" in this translation, the German word "derselben" makes it perfectly clear to what "it" refers. The word "it" refers here to the "hypothesis"! A translation of "derselben", the genitive case of the female word "dieselben", allows only for a reference to "hypothesis" = "die Hypothese", as the only female noun in the previous part of the sentence; reference to "proof" = "der Beweis" as a male noun or to "experiment" = "das Experiment" as a neutral noun would be wrong. This reference could unfortunately not have been made unambiguous by literally translating "derselben" into its English equivalent "of the same". This is to say that the English translation cannot easily avoid creating confusion about what it is that Goethe means to say here. What comes to light when paraphrasing the

English translation in a way that is compatible to the German original is this: Goethe believes that he has indicated by what he has said so far in "The Experiment" that a *mediated* "bringing to bear" of a hypothesis on an experiment is a fruitful way to conduct research. This means that he considers it as harmful to bring to bear an experiment *immediately*, i.e. without mediation, on the proof of a hypothesis. Doing that would turn the experiment into a servant of a hypothesis. This would take away from the experiment the role of a sensuous mediator between object and subject. To be clear, doing this would not mean changing the experiment into a purely conceptual mediator between subject and object; it only means that its material concreteness which cannot be abolished loses its primacy. A mentally guided experiment is not just an innocent inversion in the relationship between Nature and our Otherness to her, but its distortion. Needless to say that it is this inversion, as it becomes a distortion on its occurrence, that is fundamental for Goethe's distance to all sciences, regardless whether they still sail in the wake of an idealist synthetic philosophy, of an analytical one, or supposedly of none at all.

The danger of what is more than a mere inversion between mind and matter is nevertheless constantly present, since we, as Goethe knows, "theorize with every attentive glance into the world". Goethe also knows that the "... immediate bringing to bear of an experiment to the proof of any hypothesis ..." implies that, under the guidance of hypotheses, our experiments turn into a torture of Nature so that she reveals to us all what we want to see of her on our own mentalistically distorted terms. If not forced however, Nature gives to our "faithful questions" her "honest replies", as Goethe once put it.[215] Moreover, not being made "recalcitrant", she benefits us freely.

One could, of course, come back to the claim that the dominant sciences are also willing to revise their hypotheses and theories if Nature no longer confirms their validity. But even revisions will again be turned into hypotheses that guide the further research. Goethe's kind of research does not preclude the building up of tentative assumptions either, i.e. of hypotheses in the step by step work of inquiries into natural phenomena. They also lead, after a whole realm of natural phenomena has become familiar, to "experiences of the higher kind", even to highly abstract theories. But Goethe's whole theorizing, like in the particular case of his studies on light and colors, is permeated by the awareness that conceptualizations are merely what one aspect of Nature, namely man, can do with aspects of Nature out there.

Secondary as these conceptualizations are in their relation to Nature, they can, therefore, be abandoned much more freely than a hypothesis, let alone a theory à la Newton's. Goethe theorized with "irony"! In the dominant sciences, "revolutions" give birth to new "paradigms" only with pain. This pain is plausible, if indeed man understands himself primarily as mind. Then man, loving the concept of a phenomenon more than the phenomenon itself (paragraph 199,2), is not easily prepared to abandon this strange love of his.

All this indicates that Goethe's science is not simply a mirror opposite alternative to Newton's. There are concepts, hypotheses and for that matter even an equivalent for theories in it as well. But these hold a different position in Goethe's teachings than they do in the dominant sciences. As a consequence, the truth that Goethe's kind of science tries to find is not merely a negation of prevalent concepts of correctness. His truth transcends-and-contains correctness while changing it in the process of a research that respects its own Nature in its own occurrence. Treating the value of respecting Nature like all other values as extraneous to itself gives the dominant science, as Goethe knows, a "far heavier task" (paragraph 194,2) than his science would ever have: it has to curb itself ethically, i.e. for no reason intrinsic to it.

The problems involved in a research that ignores the object-subject mediation become glaringly obvious in the social sciences as they have tried, since quite some time, to emulate what they take to be science. Dealing with objects far beyond "the more common forces" (paragraph 200,7/201,1) of Nature, namely objects that have the status of subjects themselves, should suggest even more intensely than the study of "mere" Nature does, how important it is to understand the commonality-in-difference in the object-subject mediation. As mentioned above, Karl Marx tried to take care of this concern in his "Method of Political Economy".[216] Instead of paying adequate attention to this, today's social research has even adopted the second layer of distortion in understanding, namely the flexibility of late capitalistic instrumentalism. Having turned themselves into connoisseurs of re-definitions, they know what it takes to stay in business: the production of "facts" for a strange market.

Paragraph 200,5

In living Nature, nothing happens which does not stand in connection with the whole, and if the experiences appear to us as being isolated, if we have to view the experiments as

ısolated facts (in German Fakta), ıt ıs not thereby saıd that they are ısolated, the questıon only
ıs how do we find the connectıon among these phenomena, of thıs occurrence

When Goethe says "(I)n living Nature, nothing happens which does not stand in connection with the whole ...", he presents neither a hypothesis nor a fundamental philosophical or theoretical statement, he merely verbalizes and in that sense elevates his bodily made experience of the "analogia entis". Anybody, or better any human body can experience with every breath taken in, with every sight and with every piece of food passing his/her lips that he/she is connected to the world out there, provided of course, he/she has retained (miraculously so these days) his/her "sharp, fresh senses" (paragraph 196,2). For it is only through them that we can trace and conceptualize the connections within Nature out there and thus our connections with her.

We should note that Goethe speaks here of "living Nature". Tracing connections throughout the various levels of being may very well give us a sense of Nature as a living entity, although parts of her, like rocks or distant stars, are not living themselves. Furthermore, there is nothing in Nature that is at a standstill and we as parts of her enter into that process as a part in process ourselves. Awareness of this dynamic complexity reminds the reader all the more that "... no human being has enough abilities to have conclusive say on any matter" (paragraph 205,4) and that only the social connectedness of free individuals can lead to an adequate understanding of the connections in Nature out there.

Emphasizing that experiences and experiments are *made* is more clearly expressed in the German original than in our translation. It also leads in the German original to a subtle play on words which we have not been able to bring out in our translation in the same way as it exists in the original.

In the German text, Goethe speaks of experiences and experiments not just as facts but as "Fakta". While he uses a Germanized spelling of the Latin word "facta", it is beyond doubt that he meant to say that we *make* (in Latin: facere = to do, to make) experiences and experiments and that they only exist to that extent for us. Furthermore, we have to keep apart two levels of making "facts". While made primarily at the materially concrete and this is to say at the individual level, they remain incomplete there even though they are instantaneously elevated. They also require awareness for the commonality of Nature in other human beings. While "every single experience, every single experiment" (paragraph 199,3) are "isolated facts", "... it is not hereby said that they are isolated". If we sensuously follow the connections among objects in Nature and can create concepts of each one of these connections in each one of our minds, we must also be able to speak to fellowman about them; it is only then, as we also saw above, that they turn into truth.

While seeing Goethe looking here at the question of "... how do we find [in German: finden] the connection among phenomena...", we will remember that he speaks at the end of paragraph 200,2 of "a great scientist: [who] would have been a great man had he not invented [in German: erfunden, infinitive form: erfinden] so much". Goethe tries to say here, and that is obvious in the German text, that a scientist has to find, "finden" in German, what there is, not "erfinden" which means to invent what there is not. A scientist who invents does not only fail to find truth, as a verbal inventor and unlike a poet, he turns himself into a liar, sheer correctness of his findings notwithstanding.

Paragraph 200,6

We have seen above that those who sought to connect an isolated fact (in German Faktum) immediately to their power of thought and of judgement were subjected (in German unterworfen) to error from the very beginning Contrary to that, we shall find that those have achieved the most, who do not desist from exploring and working through all aspects and modifications of a single experience, of a single experiment, in accordance with every possibility

Goethe reminds us that we have "seen above" the problematic ways of those who try to "connect" an experience, i.e. "... an isolated fact, immediately to their power of thought and judgement ...". Those who have done that "... were subjected (in German: unterworfen) to error from the beginning". It is in light of Goethe's idea of elevation that the negativity of the word "subjected" (in German: unterworfen, also meaning subjugated) comes to light. Being "subjected to error" refers to researchers that have lost their freedom, in this case the freedom of their sensuously guided judgement. As they rush to judgement, i.e. give in to the urge of hasty conceptualizations, they become, *only in appearance*, elevated in their understanding of Nature. In reality, they gain false sovereignty over her. This pyrrhic victory turns man's status of subject into one of being defeated, of being subjugated.

A way of understanding Nature which transcends-and-contains her implies that we "... do not desist from exploring and working through all aspects and modifications of a single experience, of a single experiment ...". Particularly when reading further into the last part of the sentence which suggests undertaking these explorations "... in accordance with every possibility ...", one comes to see that Goethe does not just speak here of the objectively, i.e. materially existing possibilities of reality, but also of the ones within the human subject. Indeed, Goethe elaborates here on the status of the subject and its properties in scientific research. The crucial words in the German text, "nach aller Möglichkeit", translated by us as "in accordance with every possibility" should be read, if translated more freely, as "according to all one can do". This translation would be in line with Goethe's earlier formulation in this sentence, where he indicates that he speaks of those "who do not desist from exploring ... all aspects ... of a single experience...".

Only doing all one can do elevates one's insight to a knowledge that is true to one's whole self and to the totality of the matter at hand. Of course, proceeding in this way does not arise out of what could be moralized as "diligence". Goethe instead aims at having a knowledge of Nature that contains our drive for belonging. The full unity of experiencing one's own self in and with the experiencing of the objectively given, establishes what Richard Hönigswald once called the attainment of a concretized subjectivity. Therefore, Goethe's emphasis on the manifolding of experiments and experiences is more than a mere methodological principle;[217] it realizes the Nature of the autonomous subject.

Paragraph 200,7/201,1

It merits a future consideration of its own, how the intellect could come to our help in this endeavor Only this much may be said here (The italicized text is not included in the published version of 1823) Since all things in Nature, but especially the more common forces and elements, have an eternal effect and countereffect, one can say of each phenomenon that it stands in connection with countless others, as we say of a free floating glowing point that it sends out rays in all directions (in German auf allen Seiten) Having made such an experiment, having made such an experience, we cannot investigate carefully enough what immediately borders on it, what immediately follows from it, that is what we have to pay more attention to than to what relates to it The manifolding (in German Vermannigfaltigung) of each single experiment is, therefore, the proper duty of a student of Nature (in German Naturforscher) He has the exact opposite duty to that of a writer who wants to entertain The latter will make for boredom, if he does not leave anything to be imagined (in German zu denken), the former must work restlessly, as if he wanted to leave nothing for his followers to do, although the disproportion between our intellect and the Nature of things would soon enough remind him that no human being has enough abilities to have a conclusive say on any matter (in German in irgendeiner Sache abzuschließen)

The first two sentences of this paragraph have not been included in the published version of "The Experiment". We are not aware that Goethe has ever returned to a presumably extended "future consideration" of the question of "... how the intellect could come to our help in this endeavor ...", namely of "... exploring ... all aspects ... of a single experience, of a single experiment ...". This is not to say, though, that he did not make quite a few remarks on this matter. They are scattered throughout his voluminous oeuvre and the essay before us. Drawing some of these statements together will hopefully enable us to better understand Goethe in this regard.

When Goethe says that "... especially the more common forces and elements, have an eternal effect and countereffect ...", he does not mean to suggest that connections at higher levels of existence are not embedded in the "analogia entis". Goethe merely means to indicate that understanding these makes the task of carefully tracing the materially concrete connections among them more difficult. Focusing in "The Experiment" on the "more common forces", Goethe simply has a relatively easier way to convey his point on what is basically required in doing scientific research. Turning to this, Goethe has this to say: "Having made ... an experiment, having made ... an experience, we cannot investigate carefully enough what immediately borders on it, what immediately follows from it; that is what we have to pay more attention to than to what relates to it". It is the connections among objects, i.e. their "bordering on" one another which needs to be traced, not so much "what relates" to this "bordering" in our minds. It is at this dangerous transition where so many enemies "lie in ambush" (paragraph 198,2).

Exercising rigor in demarcating the exact "bordering" of phenomena on one another is for Goethe not a matter of repressing one's sensuousness, but a matter of following it. There is no "abnegation" (paragraph 194,3/195,1) involved here, but the taking of an opportunity to retain and cultivate one's ability to enjoy and to have pleasure. However, this pleasure is, like all pleasures, quite exhausting. In the letter to Jacobi quoted above[218] and written about two years after "The Experiment", Goethe says that "(T)he matter [his studies of colors] ... is ... an exercise of the human mind ..." which "... requires a working-over of my poor self (in German: meines armen Ichs) of which I would not have had any idea that it would be possible".[219] It is easy for anybody to understand that also an exercise of the abnegating kind takes a lot out of oneself. But let us note that Goethe speaks here of another, namely his kind of work. He relates this "working-over of my poor self", i.e. this kind of exhausting work, to his "lust to know", his "pleasure to see" and even to improving his ability to enjoy. As Conrady puts it, his aim is to practice his "exact sensuous fantasy".[220] Anybody who has ever practiced this has no difficulties in sensing his affinity with Goethe's "passionate alertness" in observation.[221]

Goethe makes it oftentimes clear that the primacy of sensuous enjoyment of phenomena has first to lead him to a saturation of his desires for observations and experiences so that he, then overlooking much of a realm of his interest, can begin to take note of the regularities in the connections among these phenomena. In paragraph 37 of the "Beiträge zur Optik", Goethe addresses this point quite specifically when he writes: "I wish that one views these phenomena (in German: Erscheinungen) *until one senses the desire to understand* (in German: einsehen) the law [!] that governs them".[222] This is still not to say that the mind may not try to regulate the senses by drawing conclusions prematurely or by influencing them through prematurely accepted views. But then a lover of Nature has to "pay" for this dearly. Nature then causes us pain and it is in that way that she will "set us right". Then the mind may come to our help by remembering where, when and how we went wrong. The mind itself, however, has no cause to get back to the right course, because it itself cannot suffer (if so, then fictitiously), but the senses of our body can do that and thus mobilize the help of our mind in our longing for being right with Nature. "... [T]hen the mode of proceeding specifies the bearings of the point to which they [the power of imagination and the wit] have to return" (paragraph 203,2). This makes it plausible that the mind guided thinking of late capitalism cannot deal from within itself with what it perceives of as "environmental problems". It may very well be that a mind cannot remember anymore where its dealings with Nature went wrong. This is a thinkable possibility about which I do not dare to speculate.

Since true knowledge of Nature only arises out of intimate familiarity with her, the "manifolding" of experiments and experiences - not their repetition, as we shall see - "... is ... the proper duty of a student of Nature". In view of the requirement of manifolding, I must emphasize two points in connection with both, the "Beiträge" and the "Farbenlehre", on which we have found discussants often mistaken: 1.- One must not assume that the sequence in which Goethe presents his experiences there is the sequence in which these experiences were made. We do not know the sequence of their occurrence, for the discovery of the real connections had in all likelihood to endure quite a few "detours" as a consequence of ad-hoc hypotheses and the mistakes which come along with them (of which Goethe himself has said that he has made them "daily", see paragraph 198,3/199,1). 2.- As presentations of real connections, Goethe even "demands"[223] that anybody reading his work should make himself familiar "... not on a superficial level, but in a thorough way with what he presents". He points out there that he does not just deliver "signs", "letters" or "empty talk", but that he writes about phenomena which "... one has to have before the eyes of body and mind". While I have said this before, I repeat it here for the following reason: Since we have not found any indication that the scientific and philosophical interpreters of Goethe's "Teachings" have actually worked through an appreciable number of these experiences, we wonder whether these writers truly know what Goethe has done and advocated, notwithstanding their usually subtle intellectual discussions of his writings.

In the context of advocating pedantic caution, Goethe returns in this paragraph to the difference-in-commonality between being a writer and being a scientist. Having emphasized the differences in the sociality of their work earlier (paragraph 197,2), he accentuates it here in a new way.

Goethe says again that the scientist in one regard "... has the exact opposite duty to that of a writer who wants to entertain". While the writer "... will make for boredom, if he does not leave anything to be imagined ...", this is still not to say that what the writer leaves out and leaves to the reader's imagination, is something the writer has not to have thought through in detail and has not to have experienced in his own "exact fantasy" before he can start writing. What appears then on paper as a product of an artistic endeavor is certainly also a piece of life, but it does in as little as Nature herself easily reveal how it has grown. While a piece of art is not an analysis of Nature, a piece of science certainly is. This is the difference between science and art, but this is not a difference between mirror opposites. They are both elevations of Nature: Science produces statements which are syntheses between objects out there and man's re-creative mind, while art is a synthetic product of man's creative mind in its celebration of what is around him. Either way, in science and in art, the human mind brings to life what Nature without the human subject would not contain. This is the commonality between them.

Activities in both areas require time, often a lot of it, but they do that in different ways. As I just said, the writer (like all other artists) has first to work through all aspects of what he wants to create. Only then can he eliminate details, put the work together and present it to the public. The scientist, by contrast, has to bring to public attention every step of his experiences hoping from the beginning to find a community of scholars who eventually can help assemble all there is to be known in a given field. Scientists may hope to find truth in co-operation, the artist's work evolves in social seclusion.[224] While the artistic and scientific ways to work run different courses, what they still have in common is that they require time to mature. Either way, today this requirement runs counter to the demands of modern instrumentalism. Results have to be published as soon as possible. The demands of the market have no time to wait, be it for truth or for beauty.

Towards the end of the paragraph, Goethe brings his attention back to the work of the scientist, this time in a way that anticipates his later sense of renunciation. He speaks here of the scientist's work as being "restless"; he has to proceed "... as if he wanted to leave nothing for his followers to do...". Even if scientific work is carried out in co-operation with others, the scientist will soon come to notice the "... disproportion between our intellect and the Nature of things ...". In "Erfahrung und Wissenschaft", i.e. in "Experience and Science", he compares the required intake of experiences with the attempt of drinking all the water of the sea.[225] It is with this sentiment that he ends this paragraph when noting that "... no human being has enough abilities to have a conclusive say on any matter." While appreciating the Nature-man relation as a dynamic one, Goethe saw it already in his forties with melancholy. As a never ending process, elevation has to renounce its arrival at a final stage. Thus, freedom and beauty remain dreams of a now which can "only" long for the not-yet.

Paragraph 201,2

In the first two parts of my Contributions to Optics, I have sought to establish such a sequence of experiments which directly (in German zunächst) border on each other and immediately touch (in German berühren) each other, which, indeed, if one knows and oversees them all exactly, constitute *one* (Goethe's emphasis) experiment, as it were, represent just *one* (Goethe's emphasis) experience under the most manifold perspectives

Goethe's reference to "the first two parts of my Contributions to Optics" and his suggestion that the "sequence of experiments" established there "constitutes *one* experiment" draw the reader's attention again to the differences between Newton and Goethe and, thus, to Goethe's notion of totality.

Colors had been of interest to Goethe since his youth.[226] Not being sufficiently talented to be a painter himself, he still desired to understand the phenomenon of colors. While in Italy, he decided to approach the matter scientifically.[227] Although being aware that his interest had originated in art and not in science,[228] he took it for granted that artists and scientists in general approach Nature in so far alike as both primarily take off from phenomena,[229] i.e. use their senses, in their attempts to celebrate and understand her intricacies. It was from Newton that he was soon to learn that, as far as scientists were concerned, the primacy of the senses was only appreciated in a limited and, thus, distorted way. The circumstance that this was brought home to Goethe in his struggle with Newton may explain why Goethe's rejection of the dominant mode of thinking in the sciences focused so much on Newton, and not on other prominent scientists.

When Goethe, a few years after his return from Italy, wanted to test what he took to be Newton's theory of colors, he came to see that Newton's concept of colors was primarily a product of "sharp-minded" hypothesis construction. With this insight, Goethe came to see where exactly his thinking and that of the dominant sciences began to differ; the point was since then demarcated for him.

His first intense research on colors took place between 1790 and 1792 and was accumulated in the two parts of the "Contributions to Optics". These focus only on a small area of the general field of colors, namely, prismatic studies and comprise only a small portion of his entire "Teachings on Colors". It is not clear to me, why Goethe retained the title of "Contributions to Optics", even though he knew at that time, as indicated by paragraph 18 of the "Contributions, Part I"[230] that Newton's interest was in optics proper and in the avoidance of colors in optical instruments, while his own was not. To the best of my knowledge, it was only in his "Confession" of 1810 that he, for the first time, admits to the title as being a misnomer.[231] It strikes one as strange that Goethe never changed the title. Could it be that he did not do that, because he wanted to keep it obvious that his views were opposed to those of Newton's, the renowned physicist?

When Goethe says in the paragraph before us that the "... Contributions ... establish a sequence of experiments ...", then we should bear in mind that this sequence is as a description of real connections among real phenomena a theoretical presentation.[232] The actual observations and experiments preceding this conceptually created order could not, however, have been made in that sequence. All Goethe could do was to make these experiences "... under the most manifold perspectives". This is to say that it was not a "theoretical" perspective which guided Goethe's research but manifolded sensuous perspectives in the concrete sense of the word. This is further to say that the sequenced and conceptualized result of these experiences guarantees the transcendence-and-containment of the sensuous experiences in a way undistorted by mentalistic preconceptions.

Moreover, these experiments put together that way "... constitute *one* (Goethe's emphasis) experiment, as it were, represent just *one* (Goethe's emphasis) experience ...". In their oneness, they form a totality of natural phenomena in a sense entirely different from the totality envisioned, for instance, in the conceptual "Unity of Nature" by C.-F. v. Weizsäcker or the "Weltformel", i.e., a formula conceptually unifying the world, intended by Albert Einstein.

The "Contributions" demonstrate that one has to rise from ever more experiences and experiments to an ever more comprehensive concept of natural phenomena. "... (U)nder the most manifold perspectives ...", as he continues in the next paragraph, "... an experience ... of a higher kind" will be made, "represent[ing] the formula through which innumerable single cases are being expressed" (paragraph 201,3). When he published his "Teachings on Colors" in 1810, he could at last spell out the "Ur-Phänomen", the "ground phenomenon", under which *all* appearances of colors known to Goethe could be subsumed.[233] He could see the "idea" of light and colors, i.e. their totality, in each one of their manifestations. While "unifying" experiences as well, it appears to be doubtful that Goethe ever expected to arrive as a scientist at an "idea" unifying all of Nature, let alone at a concept cognitively uniting all there is. It was only in poetic terms that he would wonder "what holds the world together, there at its inmost core".[234]

Paragraph 201,3

Such an experience which consists of several others is evidently of a higher kind It represents the formula through which innumerable single cases (in German Rechnungsexempel) are being expressed To work towards such experiences of the higher kind, I hold to be the duty of the scientist (in German Naturforscher) and the example of the most eminent men (in German Männer) who have worked in this discipline points us in this direction (At this point, a paragraph has been made by Goethe in the published version of 1823), moreover the thoughtfulness (in German Bedächtlichkeit) in joining the next only to the next or rather, in deducing the next from its immediate antecedent (in German aus dem Nächsten) we have to learn from the mathematicians, and even there where we do not dare to calculate, we always have to go to work as if we were accountable to the most demanding geometrician (in German Geometer)

The "one experience" presented by the "Contributions", and the "Urphänomen" presented in the "Teachings", are "... evidently [experiences] of the higher kind" in so far as they represent "... innumerable single cases ...". And yet, even as abstractions, they must not be understood as sheerly mental principles. However, given the dominant way of thinking, the "Urphänomen", i.e. the "ground phenomenon", has been understood that way. We saw above[235] how Werner Heisenberg tried to place such concepts as "double helix" and "elementary particles" into the same class as the "ground phenomenon". He fails to see that, as "secondary concepts" of the modern sciences, these have no reality outside the mind,[236] while even the meaning of Goethe's most elevated concepts remains manifest to the naked eye in their "innumerable single cases", for instance, in each manifestation of colors and also of plants.

When Goethe suggests that "(T)o work towards such experiences of the higher kind I hold to be the duty of the scientist ...", then this duty is in as little a normative prescription as it is a suggestion of "authorities" to be followed, when he says that "... the example of the most eminent men who have worked in this discipline points us in this direction,...". Reading the "Historical Parts" of Goethe's "Teachings on Colors",[237] one is inundated by cases of studies on color in which Goethe soberly checks out with whom, for reasons of shared sensuous experience, he can agree or with whom he has to disagree. Goethe accepts good examples, but he does not ideologize a tradition or submit to false "authorities".

As I have pointed out time and again Nature - according to Goethe - will not truly reveal herself under torture. The question of how to avoid distortions in our understanding of her leads Goethe to suggest "... thoughtfulness in joining the next only to the next..." phenomenon while exploring every single connection among these appearances. While it may have already been surprising for some that it is his love for Nature which implies rigor for Goethe, it may even be strange that he now relates a rigor associated with love to the "thoughtfulness" that we "... have to learn from the mathematician". This brings us to the widely discussed and widely misunderstood relation that Goethe had to mathematics.[238]

In this connection, we should, first of all, note that Goethe refers here to mathematics in connection with areas "... where we do not dare to calculate ...", but where "... deducing the next from its immediate antecedent ..." is required. In other words, the mathematical *method* is recommended here, not the application of numbers in areas "where we do not dare to calculate". This method is later contrasted (paragraph 202,2) to the capriciousness of those who want to "dazzle" the mind "through the wit and power of imagination", i.e. through quick "sharp-mindedness". Goethe, instead, recommends (see paragraph 206,3) "... the mathematical method, because of its thoughtfulness and purity ...", which "... reveals at once each leap in assertion". It is the mathematical way of proceeding step by step which is to be followed in discovering what precisely is connected directly in Nature. This way one comes to know what makes light shift the color experiences in our eyes, however minutely so.

In the "Teachings on Colors", specifically in the paragraphs 722 – 729, titled "Relation [of the "Teachings on Colors"] to Mathematics",[239] Goethe indicates that he accepts the use of mathematics in the sense of "measuring and calculations" only for the field of "Optics", but he explicitly rejects it also there for "Chromatics". Again his hesitation to use mathematics relates to the application of numbers to phenomena, but not to mathematical "thoughtfulness".[240] Chromatics, however, has only suffered from having been treated numerically and from having been confused with "Optics".[241] Leaving aside that Goethe was also among those who had originally confused these two areas, he ascribes the continued application of numbers to studies of colors to the circumstance that "a great mathematician" (obviously Newton) had "sanctioned the mistakes he has made as a student of Nature" by his outstanding skills "as an artist in measurements".[242] In his "Confession of the Author" (of the "Teachings of Colors"), he adds,[243] while speaking of physicists in general, that "a mathematician, as soon as he enters the field of experience, is as much subjected to error as anybody else is". In other words, the mathematician better follows the connections as they exist in Nature in the same spirit as he follows his deductions in mathematics proper. Thoughtfulness in each field is required, not however the mixing of these two distinct fields.

While preparing his "Contributions to Optics", Goethe remembers how surprised he was to see "... that people appeared to have no idea anymore about a Physics without Mathematics".[244] For Goethe, mathematics belongs fundamentally to the world of sheer thinking. As such, it shares its property of uninterrupted sequentiality with an other great field of human ingenuity, namely that of music.[245] Since this sequentiality also prevails in Nature's "analogia entis" and since it is these sequential connections which Goethe wishes to uncover, the "thoughtfulness" of mathematics is of help. However, the "calculating" application of mathematics to an understanding of natural phenomena remains as problematic for Goethe[246] as the application of music would be to fields external to it, e.g. to propaganda and advertisements.

Keeping mathematics and physics separate *in the process of research* has been demanded by Goethe oftentimes, e.g. in his "Maxims and Reflexions", paragraphs 632-661,[247] in Book I, chapter 10 of "Wilhem Meisters Lehrjahre"[248] and in paragraph 724 of the "Teachings on Colors".[249] Nowhere do these references suggest that Goethe has no respect for mathematics, as has been claimed. To the contrary, he has "… deplored his reputation as an apparent opponent of a subject (i.e. mathematics, FWS) that no one can hold in higher esteem …" than he does.[250] In his "Maxims and Reflexions", he says for instance "… one may speak of Mathematics as the highest and most certain Science,[251] "but", so he continues, "it cannot make anything true than what is true".[252] Mathematics as the art of "calculating" may be brought in to help the student of Nature once the truth has been found, but not before that.

As Goethe says at the end of the paragraph presently under our inspection, accounts of our understanding of Nature must satisfy "… the most demanding geometrician". If so, our trust in Nature can derive its strength not from the mere correctness of our scientific understanding, but from its sense of being itself a part of Nature. "Experiences of the higher kind", if arrived at through our "perceptively guided judgement", will be equally, if not more certain than Nature herself. This is what Goethe once wrote to Henrik Steffens, a student of Schelling's.[253] And this is what allowed Goethe to say in paragraph 197,3 of "The Experiment" that his method "… proceeds most advantageously and most securely".

How to go about the creation of such secure knowledge is what Goethe unfolds in the rest of "The Experiment" and this is introduced, in a highly condensed fashion, in the next paragraph.

Paragraph 202,1

For, properly speaking, it is the mathematical method which, because of its thoughtfulness and purity, reveals at once each leap in an assertion, and its proofs are really only detailed (in German umständliche) explications, that what is presented in connection was already there in its simple (in German einfachen) parts and in its whole sequence, that it has been surveyed in its entirety and found to be correct and irrefutable under all conditions And thus its demonstrations are always rather presentations, recapitulations than arguments Since I make this distinction here, I may be permitted to take a look back

The certainty, even infallibility of Nature of which I have spoken before[254] can only be transcended-and-contained in our knowledge of Nature by having our own Nature follow the ways in which her components are connected at all levels including the level of culture and society. Treating the mental, however, "as if" (Adams) it were outside Nature, and still as somehow applicable to her, contributes, within the context of our serious problems with Nature out there, also to the problems we have with the Nature of our fellow human beings. Tracing connections also at the elevated level of culture and society as faithfully as mathematicians follow the connections among the entities making up their fields, we may hope to establish the dynamic and yet reliable commonality not only between objects "out there" and our concepts of them, but also the dynamic and yet trustworthy commonality among human beings. This way, the "analogia entis" among Nature, man as Other Nature and fellow human being as Alter Other Nature could become a known and lived reality.

When Goethe writes here again about the "thoughtfulness" of the mathematical method, he introduces new aspects of scientific work by suggesting that the "thoughtfulness" of the mathematical method and its "purity ... reveal(s) at once each leap in assertion". Then he turns to an inspection of "proof" in science and does so by connecting it to the requirement of totality and sociality in processes of knowledge creation.

Scientific studies that aim to be thoughtful and pure deliver, strictly speaking, proofs in as little as mathematics does. Mathematics delivers "... really only detailed explications ..." of what "... was already there in its simple parts and its whole sequence ...". The words "was already there" used in connection with mathematics does not only indicate that Goethe assigns reality, and not an "as if" status, to mathematical entities, he also emphasizes that mathematical explications are, like explications on any matter, only "... found to be correct and irrefutable under all conditions ..." when "... what is presented ... has been surveyed in its entirety ...". This is to say that single observations or just a few of them hardly yield irrefutable scientific certainty. Undoubtedly with an eye on Newton and his "experimentum crucis", Goethe emphasizes that the true understanding even of a single field of Nature requires understanding of that field in its totality; partial understanding, even if sensuous, does not count.

Surveying a field of Nature in its entirety requires, inter alia, co-operation among many people, since "… no human being has enough abilities to have a conclusive say on any matter" (paragraph 200,7/201,1). This adds to the reason that studies of Nature, as they try to do justice to her "… are always rather presentations, recapitulations than arguments". As arguments or proofs, they do not do justice to the Nature in fellow human beings; they overwhelm. There is nothing to be argued, however, when scientists jointly survey a matter in its entirety and share, as expected by Goethe, their observations before articulating general statements (paragraph 202,3). Shared enjoyment of the matter under consideration does away with the antagonistic "truth"-claims of singularized and individuated arguments. To "dazzle" others with a partial "proof" (paragraph 202,2) then becomes a relic from a distorted world.

While Goethe sketches in the paragraph before us how unity with Nature and sociality among people can be established uno actu, he also announces that he wishes to unfold all that in the remainder of "The Experiment" by taking "a look back" on what he has dealt with earlier. This way, he can better yet contrast his method with the one of those who deliver merely clever arguments. While trying to further clarify his method, we must, however, not expect that the topic of "Goethe and Mathematics" will receive further (and required) attention. I nevertheless hope that enough has been said to make it clear that Goethe could never have accepted Kant's view that "… teachings on Nature (in German: Naturlehre) do only contain as much proper Science as Mathematics is applied in it".[255] This was stated in Kant's "Primary Metaphysical [!] Foundation of Science", first published in 1786, the year when Goethe fled to Italy, not the least to purify his senses.

Paragraph 202,2

One sees the great difference between a mathematical demonstration which takes the first elements through so many connections and the proof which a clever speaker could bring forth through arguments Arguments can contain quite isolated interrelations and yet they can be brought together into *one* (Goethe's emphasis) point through wit and power of imagination, and, surprisingly enough, the appearance of a right (in German *eines* Rechts) or a wrong (in German Unrechts), of a true or a false is fabricated (in German hervorgebracht) The same way one can, in support of a hypothesis or theory, compile singular experiments like arguments and deliver a proof which is more or less dazzling

The most fundamental difference between a demonstration and a proof lies, for Goethe, in the difference between the two subjectivities and the interests of the two human subjects "behind" them. Both human subjects are concerned with the same world of objects out there, but these objects differ in their way of being for and between these two subjects. This implies that proofs originate in a subjectivity which turns to Nature on the basis of, first a mentally preconceived hypothesis and of, second, the intent of proving it more out of love for this hypothesis than out love for the objects at hand. While this way of proceeding is structured to be in keeping with one's own mental product, i.e. one's hypothesis, and thus easily paves the way to egofocal self love, it undoubtedly still involves the mental as an elevation above Nature, regardless of whether this is acknowledged or not. But in this form, elevation is an estrangement from the Nature that the human subject wishes to understand. This is not to say that Goethe's approach to Nature - Goethe representing the other kind of human subject - is void of theorizing and of hypothesizing, but arising out of manifolded sensuous encounters with Nature, his theorizing and hypothesizing elevate the commonality of object and subject to a knowledge that remains within Nature.

Arguments and proofs require "artfulness" (paragraph 199,5/200,1). Accordingly, there is little regard for the question whether the aspects selected are as closely akin as one believes they are (paragraph 197,6/198,1). The issue is whether aspects "... can be brought together into *one* (Goethe's emphasis) point through wit and power of imagination,..." and, whether "... the appearance ... of a true or false is fabricated." Of course, "... one can, in support of a hypothesis or theory, compile", as Newton did, "singular experiments like arguments and deliver a proof which is more or less dazzling". Through "dazzling", one can then impose one's views onto others, but then "judgment is ... deviously obtained, if ... not entirely mired in doubt" (paragraph 202,4/203,1).

In this connection, one should again note the circumstance that keep the "Teachings on Colors" from becoming "dazzling" themselves: they are meant to be *done* by the reader with his/her own hands and not to be grasped just mentally. They should become material evidence to be produced right there in people's own court of judgement. This then leads to a sharing of knowledge which puts all social interaction on a footing that is entirely different from the one "based" on proofs. It allows the actively experimenting reader to follow the sequences of his/her own experiences by tracing "the next from its immediate antecedent" paragraph 201,3). The damage done by not having students learn to follow their own experiences and spontaneity can be observed daily in our educational institutions. The result is that people can be "dazzled" so easily. Being easy prey for re-definitions, one wonders whether they will ever become free citizens in a free republic.

Goethe's "Teachings", instead, deliver a map, so to speak, on which the connections among color phenomena can be traced. On that map, anybody can start anywhere and, like in "... a mathematical demonstration which takes the first elements ..." - where one starts - "... through ... many connections ...". Then one can take one's path through the universe of colors as one pleases. Doing so, one is not at a "despotic court" at which one has to follow the hallways of an "old castle". All of one's own single observations and experiments can come together like tones do which, otherwise single, can then form a melody, another "experience of the higher kind".[256] Such experiences can be enjoyed in a virtually infinite number of ways, not only in music, but also in the art of painting.

Paragraph 202,3

The one, however, to whom it matters to proceed in his work in honesty (in German redlich) to himself and to others, will try to develop the experiences of the higher kind through the most careful arrangement of singular experiments These allow themselves to be articulated through brief and comprehensible statements, to be put side by side to one another, and the more of them are generated, the more they can be put into an order and into such a relation that they can stand unshakably alone or together as well as mathematical statements do The elements of these experiences of the higher kind, which are many single experiments, can then be investigated and tested by anyone, and it is not difficult to determine whether the many singular pieces can be expressed through a general statement, for here there is no room for capriciousness

Speaking about "(T)he one ... to whom it matters to proceed ... in honesty" ..., this paragraph sets out to deal with a kind of human being that, for structural reasons, is not only out of place in modern society, but is also hardly imaginable for the modern mind. I read the eight to nine lines of this paragraph as addressing the issues of honesty and sobriety in counterdistinction to what Goethe calls "capriciousness", a feature which we take to be most typical for late capitalism.[257] To fully grasp what Goethe is saying here, one has to keep it present in one's mind (even before one's eyes) that Goethe does not live at all out of such a capriciousness but out of a sense for the all pervasiveness of Nature. Coming from there, honesty is the elevation of Nature's infallibility to the symbolic and thus the social realm, and sobriety is what arises from "passionate alertness" or, as Goethe called it in the previous paragraph, from willful acceptance of the mathematical method in research. Do we have to say again that honesty and sobriety are further examples of Goethe's "re-evaluation of values", and not moralistic admonitions?

When, for instance, C.-F. von Weizsäcker says: "No peace with Nature without peace among humans",[258] then he reveals himself as being one of those concerned citizens who get matters upside down. Should we become honest with one another in order to avoid the unavoidable "arms races" among and within power structures? A small step separates Weizsäcker's suggestion from an instrumentalistically grounded moralism expressing itself in peace movements and so-called "Green Parties" which try to constrain and channel an understanding of Nature merely viewed then as a "natural resource". Such an understanding of Nature still implies intense social control. The real issue, however, is whether people come to sense the beauty of the creation and their own being as a part of it. If so, then moralism will be replaced by an aesthetics (Maxim Gorki) which will also terminate the lament over the di-lapse of correctness and truth.

Turning once more to the social dimension of truth, Goethe has this to say in the paragraph before us.

The truths of single experiments, set up in Goethe's way, cannot only "stand unshakably alone and together", they also "... allow themselves to be articulated through brief and comprehensible statements ...". This is what Goethe has done in the hundreds of paragraphs of the "Beiträge" and the "Farbenlehre". Elevated this way to "experiences of the higher kind", they also connect us truthfully to our fellow human beings when communicated to them. But this communicability has its own significant condition. Although having mentioned it before, it deserves being repeated.

Goethe obviously expects that his experiments and their results would be "investigated and tested by anyone", as he puts it here. He assumes in all people the joy of seeing for themselves what Nature looks like. Studies carried out this way do not exclude mutual correction (see paragraphs 197,2 and 200,5 for instance), but expecting enjoyment to carry the process of coming to know, Goethe also assumes that people do not wish to be "dazzled" or to "dazzle" others by mere words. This indicates that Goethe speaks here of a sobriety that arises out of a solidly grounded and yet lustfully motivated drive for knowledge and togetherness. It is not a sobriety that arises out of the mutual doubts and distrusts that permeate our life today.

It is out of our own experience that we share Goethe's view on the linkage between mere intellectual skepticism and non-sensuous ways of knowing. In this connection, I would like to mention an observation which, in our view, is more than just anecdotal. Over the years, we have come across quite a few people who had read Goethe's "Teachings on Colors" and the "Contributions to Optics". Almost all of those to whom we spoke about Goethe's science found it "really interesting" and saw in it "an entirely different position". Yet nobody among them had even thought of following Goethe's numerous invitations to do these experiments for themselves. With a smile typical for intellectuals, they admitted to that, apparently seeing Goethe's invitations as yet another one of his idiosyncracies and left it at that.

Goethe thinks that the clearly established connections among single phenomena in Nature "... allow themselves ... to be put ... into such a relation that they can stand unshakably alone and together as well as mathematical statements do". In other words, it is only an extension of Nature's clarity into the social realm to speak about matters in such a way that they "... not be removed from the horizon of so many human beings" (paragraph 203,2), but remain accessible to their senses. This is obviously not possible in modern science, not only because of its problematic abstraction, but also, in recent times, because of its intended capriciousness. This makes us raise the question as to how many people could be found today who would desire to listen to "brief and comprehensible statements", let alone, to check out their concrete meaning with their own hands? Our own experience of the "culture of power and immunity" tells us that doing so as a form of resistance against the abstracted capriciousness of late capitalism will take a while yet to materialize in a societally relevant number of people. Without a sober sense for the Nature of things, our sense for the Nature of fellowman will remain distorted. There is no peace among humans, unless it is contained in our peace with Nature.

Paragraph 202,4/203,1

With the other method, however, by which we wish to prove something that we assert through isolated experiments in the same way as through arguments, the judgement is often deviously obtained, if it is not entirely mired in doubt If one, however, has compiled a series of experiences of the higher kind, then one may exercise one's intellect, one's power of imagination and one's wit on them, as one wishes This will not be harmful, indeed, it will be beneficial That first endeavor cannot be undertaken carefully, diligently, vigorously, indeed pedantically enough, for it is undertaken for the world and the posterity But these materials must be ordered and presented in sequence, not be put together in a hypothetical manner, not be used for forming systems (in German nicht zu einer systematischen Form verwendet) Then it sets everybody free to connect them according to his way and to form a whole from it which in general will be more or less comfortable and pleasant to the human way of making representations (in German der menschlichen Vorstellungsart) This way, what is to be distinguished is distinguished, and one can enrich the collection of experiences much more speedily and purely than if one has to put the later experiments aside unused like stones which have been gathered after a building has been completed

The first sentence of this paragraph will be misunderstood if read by adherents of today's dominant mode of thinking. If it is read, however, in terms of Goethe's way of thinking and by someone "… to whom it matters to proceed … in honesty …" (paragraph 202,3), then Goethe's words take on an entirely different quality. Two aspects then come out with clarity: 1.- Not following Nature with our senses produces truncated insights, and 2.- accepting guidance in our studies of Nature from our imagination and wit "… one must arrive at hypotheses, theories, systems and … other representations" (paragraph 194,3/195,1) which are misleading to oneself and to others. Inevitably then, "… judgement … is deviously obtained, …" and thus "… mired in doubt". Goethe, instead, suggests that the first endeavor in the making of observations and experiments has to be that one does them "… carefully, diligently, vigorously, indeed pedantically …", so that one comes to see what phenomenon "immediately borders" for our senses on the next one. All experiments must be done that way, "… for it is undertaken for the world and the posterity".

Having become thoroughly familiar with a whole field of phenomena this way, these "… materials must be ordered and presented in sequence …", needless to say, in the sequence that they have for our senses. In other words, they better not "… be put together in a hypothetical manner, … be used for forming systems". If approached with the latter intent, the order of Nature would again be in the danger of being distorted. In a short note, titled "Probleme" (i.e. "Problems"), published 1823, Goethe says in the very first sentence: "Natural system, a contradictory expression" and continues by emphasizing: "Nature has no system, she has, she is life…".[259] Proceeding this way in one's scientific work, the productive force of thinking, our otherwise problematic "sharp-mindedness", practices its awareness of itself as being only "a moment in the productivity of Nature".[260]

I think it should be noted that Goethe sees yet another advantage in his "method". Proceeding in "(T)his way …", he writes, "… what is to be distinguished is distinguished, and one can enrich the collection of experiences much more speedily and purely than if one has to put the later experiments aside unused like stones which have been gathered after a building has been completed". In other words, proceeding with careful attention while thoroughly and thoughtfully familiarizing oneself with the connections that exist in an area of one's interest would also allow for efficiency in scientific research. Following Nature's inner connections with openness from the beginning contributes greatly to avoiding detours which the rashness of our speculative mind so easily suggests.

Elaborating on this, we would first like to underline that Goethe did not just advocate sensuousness, but an *attentive* sensuous awareness. He did not only take in the world around him and lose it then, as so many of us do, he brought so enormously much of it to his conscious awareness by writing it down, i.e. by verbalizing these experiences in his diaries, in letters or in short notes. Enjoyment of verbal articulation came close to finding its match in his enjoyment of phenomena in Nature around him. These experiences, elevated to conscious familiarity, contributed to a large extent to Goethe's productivity, both in the sciences and beyond.[261] Remembering experiences and their sensuously noted connections helped him to avoid experiments that had become superfluous this way.

Today, we claim to be efficient as well. We do so with respect to practically all aspects of our life and yet, even on a moment's inspection, we have to acknowledge the conspicuous absence of efficiency from our life. As we have elaborated upon in the first chapter, it is an outstanding feature of our activities that we make huge energy investments in most of our activities with usually "miniscule results" (Richard N. Adams). We usually ignore how inefficient so many of our implements are, ranging from jet engines to electrical can openers and to cars. The latter often employ hundreds of "horse powers" to carry the 150 (or so) pounds of our own weight around. Research equipment can often easily compete with these implements regarding its "efficiency". Claiming efficiency and yet overlooking its truly existing wastefulness are both consequences of our strangely abstracted ways of knowing and being. Goethe instead produced so much with so very little.

Turning now to the issue of pluralism in Goethe's views on science, I would first like to note that it has usually been misunderstood, if not been denied outright.[262] This probably stems from Goethe's indeed implacable rejection of Newton. And that is to say, his advocacy of pluralism got lost in his passionate attack against that mode of thinking which is now dominant and, with its emphasis on correctness and efficiency, is not pluralist at all (though infinitely flexible in its most recent variation). The only author whom we have seen dealing seriously with Goethe's pluralism is the American philosopher Dennis Sepper.[263] While we agree with Sepper that there is a pluralism in Goethe's science, we must still admit that we share his thoughtful analysis of Goethe's pluralism only in part.

First of all, I take it to be a sign of a pluralist stance that Goethe, in the presently inspected paragraph, invites "... one's intellect, one's power of imagination and wit ..." to be exercised in research "... as one wishes". At the same time, I would like to note that Goethe has warned quite strongly against these powers of the mind before. In view of the possibility that this could be seen as a contradiction, I think it is important to underline the difference in the stages of research at which Goethe cautions us against the power of the mind and the one at which he advocates it. Goethe, we will remember, cautions us against a mode of proceeding in which "... isolated interrelations ...[are]... brought into *one* (Goethe's emphasis) point through the wit and power of imagination ..." (paragraph 202,2) and thus lead to premature construction of theory and hypothesis. In the present connection, however, where Goethe speaks about a later stage in research at which "... one has compiled a series of experiences of the higher kind, ... it sets everybody free to connect them according to his way and to form a whole from which it in general will be more or less comfortable and pleasant to the human way of making representations". In other words, if and after materially real connections have been elevated to properly sequenced statements, i.e. when reality has entered the conceptual level truthfully, one can play with these higher level insights freely. It is in this sense that Goethe, in his later years, speaks of his own "Farbenlehre" as a teaching that could have been different. He says this often also in the "Historical Parts" of this work. Substantiating, in a moment, these indications of pluralism with a few examples, we should also get a better insight into his reasons for not extending his pluralism to Newton.

First, I would like to give an example of how Goethe has played with higher level insights.

In the "Second Part" of the "Teachings on Colors",[264] Goethe deals with the physical colors (as distinct from the physiological and chemical colors, dealt with in Part I and Part III respectively). Among them, he distinguishes "katoptrical", "paroptical", "dioptrical" and "epoptical" types, meaning colors that emerge respectively when light is reflected from surfaces, when light hits edges of solid bodies, when light goes through an object that one can see through and when light appears on a colorless surface under a variety of conditions.[265] Goethe presents what are obviously "sequenced" descriptions of singular experiments on each of these physical types of colors. This ordering represents an application of "imagination and wit" and goes beyond descriptions of singular sensuous experiences. It ties each of these singular experiences together into "experiences of the higher kind".

The order in which the different types of colors are described as well as the various appearances of colors within each type is not a matter simply given by Nature out there; the human subject Goethe definitely had his hands (or better: his body and mind) in it. We may already note at this point that not everybody else would have given his experiences that order. While it is certainly important to note that Goethe delivers his reason for his kind of ordering and sequencing, e.g. on every occasion when he moves from one type of color to the next,[266] it is perhaps even more important to point out that Goethe is not only aware of the subjectivity of his ordering, he also sees and admits that his subjectivity in presenting this particular order is historically shaped; it tries to speak to a historically specific circumstance. This is expressed with particular clarity in the "Transition" from his treatment of "dioptrical" to that of "katoptrical" colors.[267] He admits there that he has dealt with "dioptrical" colors too "extensively" (his treatment of the other three took him a fraction of the space as even a brief look into the table of contents of the "Farbenlehre" reveals). He reasons about it by saying that this was a "need of the time". The need of the time was to refute "the presentation of phenomena in false connections, ... so that one could apply a completely prepared work to ... polemic ... treatments ...", needless to say, of Newton's explanation of colors. In other words, his "Teachings on Colors" would have been different without that historically specific interest.

Obviously, Goethe does not leave any doubts about what determines his subjectivity at the time of his research and writing, namely his anger, if not his wrath, towards Newton. It too was a force that he accepted as shaping his subjectivity. In his "Experience and Science", Goethe admits that scientific work is even influenced by highly personal circumstances like "moods (or dispositions) of the mind" (in German: Geistesstimmung), "the disposition of the organ [or sense] at a given moment ... and a thousand other circumstances ..." without treating these subjective dispositions as blurring the reality (or should we say "Wirklichkeit"?) of Nature.[268] For him, these dispositions are constitutive for the Nature as she is and as she includes our subjectivity at that moment. Goethe, appreciating Nature as inescapably containing us, simply concludes that one has, therefore, to make as many experiences as humanly possible and to note them completely and carefully in order to understand a phenomenon fully and under all circumstances (including the one the researcher finds himself in). If so, and not bothered by self-doubt, Goethe was "... set(s) ... free to connect ... [his experiences] ... according to his way and to form a whole ... more or less comfortable ... to the human way of making representations". He leaves the making of different presentations happily to others, be it "... to a serenely active present (in German: Mitwelt) or posterity".[269] In this sense, Goethe's "Teachings on Colors" is a product of freedom, not a product of an arbitrary liberty. By the same token, his "Teachings on Colors" can grant to anybody the freedom of proceeding in research in his/her way along the multiple lines of Nature. These ways are not matters of prescription for Goethe. This is his pluralism.

But this is still not to say that Goethe included Newton and his approach into that circle of pluralism. We think it is quite important to see why precisely he did not do so. This will come to light, we hope, if one follows Dennis Sepper in his quite far reaching, yet ultimately insufficient attempt to clarify why Goethe did not tolerate Newton.

Sepper thinks that Newton stirs Goethe's furious objection, since Newton "... ruled over the minds and experiences of scientists, and laymen alike".[270] Elaborating on this,[271] Sepper rightfully emphasizes that what Goethe called "the human way of making representations" are properties of all human subjects. Sepper, hence concludes that "(T)he world as experienced is plural" and that, by the same token, dominance must not be given to just one "Vorstellungsart", i.e. to one way of making representations and be it one claimed by a mind like Newton's.

In my view, this interpretation of Goethe's advocacy of pluralism and of his objection to Newton does not go to the heart of the matter. In the first place, it turns Goethe into a moralist who more than anything else opposes what one ought not to do, namely dominate others. Since a moralist is so clearly what Goethe was not, we do not wish to deal with this matter. Secondly, and of greater importance, Sepper comes into the danger of having Goethe implicitly perpetuate an object-subject-segregation, i.e. the old Cartesian split, when he ascribes pluralism to human experience and oneness to the world of Nature. This split, however, cannot be reconciled with Goethe's praxis and concept of elevation. For Goethe, human experience at whatever level of elevation remains part of what it is about, namely Nature. Above, we have expressed this by saying that man is not only the material condition for knowledge to be, even knowledge has being only in those moments at which it is actively thought, i.e. when it is "done" by a human brain.[272] Even when man forces Nature under his conceptual grip, under his hypotheses, he still does not enact a real segregation between the mind, let alone its carrier man, and Nature; he only acts upon the distorted notion that such a segregation exists. When Sepper writes[273] that Goethe's pluralism, particularly in his later years, was a consequence of resignation over the apparent impossibility to find the one and only truth, so that Goethe sought consolation in the insight that "the plurality of experience" is still "unified by the object", then Sepper gives away that he not only misunderstands Goethe's renunciation,[274] but also and more importantly so, Goethe's praxis and concept of science. Sepper fails to see and appreciate what is quintessential for Goethe's thinking and being: the commonality-in-distinction between object and subject. Missing this also underlies what leads to man's arrogant and dumb claim that he and his knowledge are beyond Nature. This is what infuriates Goethe and this is what sustains his implacable wrath against Newton.

Given the importance of this point, I would like to approach it in yet another way.

Goethe knew, as Newton did (!), that colors have no objective existence of their own; they emerge when rays of light stir the human eye to generate colors in the eye's perception. I do not think that Newton ever appreciated this circumstance in its significance for the praxis of scientific research. In other words, his own insight that colors as materially-concrete, pre-conceptually occurring phenomena are co-produced by the human eye was not honored and carried over by Newton into his scientific work. With Goethe, we can say that colors are just one example for the circumstance that our own Nature already in its sheer bodily aspects co-creates the Nature around us. But our Nature goes even further than that. As our senses as parts of Nature creatively connect with other parts of Nature, also our mind better be honest enough to follow its Nature given urge to trace these connections. Our mind better does so by retaining awareness that the symbolic creations of our mind are little more than re-creations of Nature at a new level. In this sense, we co-produce what Nature is in every moment of our being, namely those of our sense perceptions *and* of our thoughts. But we never leave Nature behind in these acts. In other words, we create a worked-over Nature (a "Wirklichkeit") already at an earlier stage than the one of the technological application of our knowledge. We create Nature as our Nature already in every moment of sense perception. Since we tend to "theorize" these perceptions instantaneously, we have to conceptualize Nature with the kind of caution that Goethe recommends. Then we have a possibility to arrive at truth. There cannot be another truth beside this one. But this truth appears in 1001 different ways. These ways depend on the particular personal and/or historical circumstance in which Nature is encountered. Therefore, Goethe grants individual uniqueness in understanding Nature to each of us. This kind of pluralism opens up a way to transcend-and-contain what otherwise would end up in monological individuation and/or tyrannic unification by dogma. It is from here that we can appreciate Goethe's message today, in an age that has replaced true pluralism and true freedom by an attempt to globalize the liberty of making up one's own re-definitions. Late capitalism could only break out of this distorted mode of thinking, would it appreciate its own insight into the diversity of us humans as exemplified by our awareness that speech can never be a 100%-feedback interaction. Above we have discussed,[275] how today's awareness for the uniqueness of each individual is distorted by a deranged sensuousness. Being stuck in such derangement, the pluralism that Goethe practiced cannot even be recognized, let alone be realized. True pluralism strikes most moderns strangely enough as "utopian" and not as a "concrete utopia" in Ernst Bloch's sense. At the same time, we today have both the historically greatest need and greatest potential to realize the utopia of freedom and pluralism. This is so, simply because their perversions - liberty and re-definitions - cause us pain and confusion.

Goethe knew that Nature in us and out there does not only grant, but lives off diversity-in-commonality. Thus, human individuality within Nature is for him the source of a "rich cultural life", to use Rudolf Bahro's words.[276] The pluralism arising from this awareness could, of course, not be extended to Newton, not just because his domination of others is bad - after all, they accepted it - but because it is false; it distorts and empoverishes the truthful elevation of Nature in us in its individual (not individuated!) multitude. Goethe's sustained furor over Newton and his followers was also accompanied by his deep seated fears for what was still in the future for him.[277] And yet, he who had learned to despair, as he admitted,[278] also knew that words could not prevent the upcoming disaster.[279] It is "life" which has to "set us right"; advocacy cannot do it.[280]

One's understanding of Goethe's pluralism can be enriched by reading the "Historical Parts" of Goethe's "Teachings on Colors". There one can learn so much about the reasons for his positive and negative reactions towards "eminent men", not only of those who had concerned themselves with light and colors. To name but a few examples, one could point out his positive reaction to Pythagoras,[281] his only qualified acceptance of Pythagoras' followers,[282] his appreciation of Galilei (particularly because this mathematically inclined mind had stayed away from the study of colors),[283] his strong resentment of Tycho Brahe's orthodoxy, e.g. in matters of astronomy[284] and, finally, his feelings about the sorry state of the "German Learned World" and the mechanistic ways of thinking prevailing in it (which, to a large part, was not even able to adequately understand Newton).[285] Not being able to take a closer look here at all these reviews made by Goethe and collected in two volumes, we can only point out that the common themes among all these evaluations of scientific works are the criteria of sensuousness and of willful acceptance of Nature. To those to whom these criteria do not apply, Goethe does not extend his pluralism.

Coming to the end of our inspection of this paragraph, I would like to point out the position that the making of experiments occupies in Goethe's scientific studies. Spelling out their place in research further helps one to understand Goethe's pluralism.

It is crucial for an understanding of Goethe's science that the experiment *follows* observation. It is sensuous experiences made in daily careful observations and not hypotheses which guide Goethe to experiments. In them, he merely re-creates and cautiously varies the conditions under which the color phenomena emerge that his senses have come across before in observations. In this way, Goethe tries to carry an aspect of observation over into the experiment, namely, the avoidance of a primarily mind guided interference in Nature. He does, of course, not aim at avoiding interference in Nature while experimenting; this would go against the Nature that we are. Observation, thus, does not hold a minor or merely preliminary status in Goethe's ways of coming to know, it guides the doing of experiments.

However, much of Nature is only accessible by observation. In fact, there are areas where experimental analysis would distort observation, e.g. in plants, animals, let alone in human biology and culture. But this circumstance does in no way preclude or even lessen the potential for gaining true knowledge about these areas. As an example for the validity of close observation far "below" the level of human beings, one could point out how meaningless the analysis of the ph-value of a farm field is. Leaving aside the already serious problem of getting soil samples that are truly "representative" for a whole field, the observation of the kinds of plants and "weeds" that grow on them will tell the well trained eye of the farmer much more about a field than any lab test could. Attentive observations guide the farmer to know what is wrong or right with his fields, what must be done with them and what can be left alone. How much more ludicrous sample studies on socio-cultural matters therefore must be, is a matter too obvious to deserve elaboration here. Yet: the often factually existing applicability of such studies today cannot be denied either. This makes us raise a somewhat fearful question: Could it not be that the "really existing" applicability of so much sample research in the social sciences gives us a measurement for the distortion of those human beings from whom they are obtained?

Paragraph 203,2

> The view of the most eminent men and their example let me hope that I am on the right path, and I wish that my friends may be satisfied with this explanation, who ask me sometimes what actually my intent is in my optical endeavors? My intent is to collect all experiences in this discipline, to perform all experiments myself and to conduct them in their most manifold variety (in German Mannigfaltigkeit) so that they can easily be repeated and not be removed from the horizon (in German Gesichtskreis) of so many human beings (in German Menschen) And then to put forward (in German aufzustellen) statements through which the experiences of the higher kind can be expressed, and to wait and see in what way these too can be subsumed under a still higher principle If, however, the power of imagination and the wit sometimes run ahead impatiently, then the mode of proceeding itself specifies the bearings of the point to which they have to return

This final paragraph summarizes Goethe's considerations on scientific research in such a way that the specific Nature and consequences of his motivation for engaging in research are placed into focus.

As Goethe has said, time and again, it is not a preconceived, mentally prefabricated, general hypothesis or theory that brings his study of Nature onto its way, but a "lust to know". He desires to understand what he feels akin and drawn to: Nature. In other words, it is not a yet unattained mentally projected goal lying ahead of him that drives his research, but a force that lies inside of him and aims at uniting him in a distinct commonality with the objects of his attention. This is to say that he acts out of a motivation from which the attainment of his goal of understanding remains distinct yet not segregated. Here, goal attainment and motivation are not confused as is the case so often when the goal to be attained has to substitute for motivation. This is to say that Goethe's scientific investigations must, also in this regard, be distinguished from instrumental*istic* undertakings in which the intended purpose lying ahead of oneself has to take the place of the absent internal drive to know.[286]

Different from instrumentalism, its pseudo-motivation and its unavoidable Midas syndrome, Goethe finds true satisfaction *in* his scientific investigations, not just in their results. As a sustained drive, it prepares itself for ever new and "higher" tasks. From here, one can see again that diligence, care, rigor, attentive alertness, etc., are not self imposed values, instrumentalized to repressive norms for labor and study; they are willfully derived from Goethe's inner self. Out of this sense for the forces in him, his research remained an ongoing affair throughout his life, in fact until the morning hours of his final day on March 22, 1832. This drive to know, this longing is, to use Friedrich Gundolf's perhaps somewhat outdated word, Goethe's "daemon".

This "daemon" makes him work restlessly and makes him talk and write in such a rich way that others may feel invited to see the wonders of Nature for themselves. Yet, this reaching out to others is a purpose that must not be understood in segregation from its motivation either. His desire to connect through his work and its sensuousness to other people was part of his Nature; it was not the product of a calculated purpose at having social "connections". He could have joined the "scientific guilds", but this, as he came to see, would have come only at the cost of losing his sense for being at one with Nature and himself. This made him lonely, perhaps even unusual, but it did not make him "abnormal".

Goethe's invitation to others to join him in his endeavors was inseparable from his hope that his scientific work would not "… be removed from the horizon of so many human beings". How illusory such a hope would be vis-à-vis the sciences of today needs not to be underlined. Indeed, Goethe had soon come to see, with resignation and yet correctly, that the number of those longing for first hand sensuous knowledge of Nature would even dwindle in the future and create a knowledge unbecoming to so much of her. And yet, this anticipation did not keep him from trying to make it clear to his friends, "what actually my intent is in my optical endeavors". It is, not the least, his intent to be in good company with others when pursuing them.

Pursuing matters in his way, Goethe admits that "(T)he view of the most eminent men and their example let me hope that I am on the right path…". As discussed above,[287] this hope does not make Goethe simply follow a tradition (or to join "guilds"). But he is obviously delighted and consoled to see that he is not alone in his ways of studying. This certainly gives him also a sense of tradition, but this sense arises out of a doing that on its occurrence happens to continue a tradition. He does not ground himself in a tradition but in Nature. This is, as we saw from a different angle before, why Goethe is so important for us today. We have no tradition left in which we could ground ourselves. It is only the occurrence of individual sensuous encounters with Nature and their elevation to communicable insights that can help us in the constant renewal of our life as social beings. Our evolution to modernity has freed us to this insight. If this initiates a new tradition, we have to say: all the better. But this will not be a tradition that perpetuates the primacy of the mind, as it has dominated the West since the times of the pre-Socratics. Instead, it points to horizons of Goethe's innerworldly spirituality.

The question is whether we, indeed, pick up "... the bearings of the point to which [we] have to return". In this regard, Goethe had learned to despair. In a world controlled by "men with heads on their shoulders", his way of being and thinking had, and still has, not much of a chance. Gernot Böhme has pointed out that Goethe's "Teachings on Colors" could only gain "actuality", if it would enter "into the network (in German: Zusammenhang) of practically defined interests".[288] Some may suggest that interests akin to Goethe's are altogether absent these days. I do not think they are. However small in number, there is a resistance against the distortions of the late capitalist regime. It must not be overlooked that, for instance, Rudolf Steiner, the former editor of Goethe's scientific writings, and the Anthroposophical Movement founded by him, try to live in ways that are like Goethe's work in keeping with Nature. Their praxis has yielded remarkable results in areas like medicine, agriculture, pedagogy and pharmacology. While integrating Goethe's innerworldliness with ideas going perhaps daringly beyond its concreteness, the question is not whether a going beyond Goethe must not occur, but whether one retains one's groundedness in Nature wherever one goes.

Notes

[1] See pp. 148n65

[2] To the best of my knowledge, a reading of this title adequate to Goethe's thinking, has hardly ever been proposed, a few exceptions like Wolfdietrich Schmied-Kowarzik, 1986, and perhaps Alfred Schmidt, 1984, notwithstanding

[3] See, in this regard, also Trunz, 1948ff, XIII, p 618

[4] Heitler, 1970, p. 20.

[5] See also p. 174-175.

[6] Quoted according to Unseld, 1998, p. 30; my translation.

[7] Böhme, 1993, p 137 and Weizsäcker, in Trunz, 1948ff, XIII, p 551 note this, in their way, as well.

[8] See Schöne, 1987, pp 122ff.

[9] See Sixel, 1995, pp. 4f

[10] Goethe, 1988, III, p 232

[11] See p. 112.

[12] Trunz, 1948ff, XIII, pp. 617f.

[13] See pp. 304-310 Regarding neuro-physiology and neuro-philosophy, see Roth, 1994, pp. 303ff; see also Damasio, 1994 and Spitzer, 1996.

[14] However, he speaks of it very often throughout the "Contributions to Optics" and the "Teachings on Colors"

[15] This reminds one directly of Karl Marx, who said once that for man "Nature is his body", Marx, 1975, p. 276

[16] See, as examples, Heisenberg, 1975 [1967], Heitler, 1970, Schieren 1998, Sepper, 1988, Weizsäcker, in Trunz, 1948ff, XIII

[17] Schöne, 1987, p. 133

[18] ibid., pp. 134f.

[19] Schieren, 1998, p 86

[20] Goethe, 1988, I, pp 264f.

[21] See Goethe, 1988, I, p. 55; see also Goethe, 1988, II, pp 15, 16, 47; 1988, III, pp 243, 260.

[22] Goethe, in Trunz, 1948ff, XIII, p 37; my translation Incidentally, for anybody only slightly familiar with Kant's philosophy, it is quite likely that Goethe's use of the word "Vorschriften", i.e. of "prescriptions" to Nature, could be read as a somewhat sarcastic reference to that philosopher who indeed thought that man's categories "prescribe" to Nature how she has to appear "for us".

[23] See pp. 220-221

[24] See p. 289.

[25] In German. "anhaltende Beschäftigung"; my translation, see, for instance, Goethe, 1988, I, p. 55f

[26] Goethe, in Trunz, 1948ff, XIII, p 617; my translation

[27] Quoted according to Sepper's translation, see Sepper, 1988, p 89.

[28] See p 150.

[29] See pp. 258, 272.

[30] Goethe's study of Kant's Critiques was taken up in the winter of 1790/91, i.e. well before he wrote this essay; see e g Schieren, 1998 p. 43

[31] See e.g. pp. 195, 222.

[32] See e.g. p 261.

[33] Most of those mentioned on p 189.

[34] For instance, those of Ernst Bloch, Wolfdietrich Schmied-Kowarzik and Alfred Schmidt

[35] Schieren, 1998, 29ff

[36] ibid., p 77

[37] ibid., p. 80.

[38] See pp. 158-159, 162

[39] See paragraph 197,6/198,1.

[40] Quoted, in our translation, according to Schöne, 1987, p 134, Heisenberg, 1975 [1967], p 124 also points out that Goethe saw today's problems with Nature as being related to man's distance from Nature

[41] See e.g. Weizsäcker, in Trunz, 1948ff, XIII, p. 538. Habermas, 1973, pp. 18ff places Hegel's concept of the role of the human subject in the process of coming to know into close vicinity to an "organon theory" Habermas notes this not without lamenting that this Hegelian concept has eventually led to dissolving the constitutive role of the human subject in the creation of knowledge.

[42] Roth, 1994, p. 314.

[43] Quoted according to Schöne, 1987, p. 134, my translation

[44] See pp. 245, 248-252.

[45] See e.g. E. U. v. Weizsäcker, 1992, passim; Verbeek, 1994, passim; and, in a more theoretical vein, Heitler, 1970, e g p. 22.

[46] See Goethe, 1988, III, p 234.

[47] Weizsäcker, 1994, p. 236

[48] ibid , p. 244

[49] Weizsäcker, 1994, pp. 243ff

[50] Verbeek, 1994, p 243 where he quotes Vogel, 1988, p 217; my translation

[51] Pearce & Tombs, 1998, passim present highly significant examples for this

[52] Trunz, 1948ff , XIII, p 563, my translation

[53] Not too long ago, the "bracketing" of subjectivity in social research used to be recommended by sociologists and anthropologists claiming to be informed by phenomenology. See, for instance, Geertz, 1969, p. 37, Geertz, 1973, passim; Psathas, 1972, pp. 132ff; Strasser, 1967, passim. To "bracket" one's subjectivity is, of course, a proposition that is as infected by ambiguity as "abnegation" is. Instead of trying to answer the question of how much or how little subjectivity is permissible, Marx, in his "Method of Political Economy", rather discusses the question of how subjectivity is mediated with the objects around the researcher; see Marx, 1973, pp. 100ff; see also Sixel, 1995, pp. 69ff.

[54] See e.g. Heisenberg, 1975 [1967], p 124; Sepper, 1988, p 97

[55] Goethe, 1988, I, pp 47f; my translation.

[56] See p. 256.

[57] Goethe, 1902ff, IV, p 164; my translation.

[58] He speaks of Newton's teachings on light and colors at one point as an old castle in which one gets lost, or as a "Bastille" that has to give room for freedom, see Goethe, 1988, I, pp 48f.

[59] See pp 13-26.

[60] Goethe, 1988, III, p 232

[61] See pp. 204-207, 209-210, 214-215

[62] See pp. 248-252.

[63] Goethe, 1988, III, p. 232

[64] This has also been argued by Carl-Friedrich von Weizsäcker when he, in the context of his philosophical interpretation of Goethe's "The Experiment",

returns to the first conversation between Goethe and Schiller, see Weizsäcker, in Trunz, 1948ff, XIII, pp. 537ff, p 542 in particular.

[65] See pp 259ff, 263ff, 273ff, 278ff

[66] See p. 150.

[67] See pp. 221-222, 226.

[68] Weizsäcker, in Trunz, 1948ff, p. 550; my translation.

[69] Heisenberg, 1975 (1967), pp 131f, 139.

[70] ibid., pp. 138ff.

[71] ibid., p. 128.

[72] ibid., see also Goethe, 1902ff, IV, p 168

[73] See paragraphs 194,2-194,3/195,2; and pp 213ff, 218ff

[74] See pp 87-88.

[75] See my treatment of this in Sixel, 1988, pp. 85ff, see also the literature mentioned there.

[76] See paragraph 203,2 and pp. 311ff, also pp. 281f.

[77] See pp. 175, 175n197

[78] Thomas Mann brings this to life in a long monologue delivered by Dr. Riemer in his novel "Lotte in Weimar", 1940, p. 80

[79] Unseld, 1998, pp 82ff

[80] Regarding the latter, see Unseld, 1998, pp 87ff.

[81] We think, incidentally, that the metaphor of "rising water" can be read as another indication that progress in science was definitely not understood by Goethe as a revolutionary one He saw progress as a steady growth, though not without dangerous deviations potentially occurring in it Getting off such deviations may be sensed as revolutionary by those embarking on them, but this did not apply to Goethe Therefore, we do not know what to make of Schöne's suggestion – see Schöne, 1987, pp. 114f – to understand Goethe's "Teachings on Colors" in the sense of Thomas Kuhn's "scientific revolutions" Furthermore, how Schöne can reconcile this interpretation of Goethe's science with his understanding of Goethe's "Theory of Colors" as a "Theology" is beyond us.

[82] Newton's and Leibniz' "discovery" of calculus is an outstanding example of this. Another example would be the co-discovery of the "principle of natural selection" by Charles Darwin and Alfred Wallace

[83] See e.g. pp. 178-179, see also p. 325.

[84] Goethe, 1988, III, pp. 252f.

[85] See p. 132.

[86] Litt, 1959, p. 137.

[87] Schmied-Kowarzik 1986, pp. 72f, who has drawn our attention to Litt's views, places it into the context of Goethe's and Marx's thought and, thus, comes to doubt whether a theoretical synthesis is sufficient

[88] Sepper, 1988, p. 190 comes to a similar conclusion, but when he places his hope in politics as the arena for finding solutions, he becomes too optimistic for us.

[89] This often overlooked status of science will be dealt with more closely later, e.g. in the commentary on paragraph 198,2.

[90] Goethe, in Trunz, 1948ff, pp. 32ff, 567f.

[91] See Schmied-Kowarzik, 1986, p 68 and 1996, pp 37ff, 66ff.

[92] Goethe, 1988, III, pp. 238ff.

[93] Quoted in Trunz, 1948ff, XIII, p. 563; my translation.

[94] Schmied-Kowarzik, 1986, p. 69.

[95] See pp. 189-190

[96] See pp. 304-310.

[97] See also Goethe, 1988, II, p 133

[98] Goethe, 1988, I, p. 81

[99] See our commentary on the title of "The Experiment", pp. 204ff

[100] Newton, 1979, pp 124f.

[101] Goethe, 1988, I, p 45.

[102] Goethe, 1988, I, p. 57; my translation.

[103] Goethe, 1988, I, p 57, my translation.

[104] Goethe, 1988, I, p 56

[105] Roth, 1994, pp 227ff, Verbeek, 1994, pp 15ff

[106] Roth, 1994, pp 303ff

[107] Weizsäcker, in Trunz, 1948ff, XIII, p 538, my translation

[108] Ibid.

[109] Heisenberg, 1975 [1967], p 137.; Heitler, 1970, p 18

[110] See p 235.

[111] See Sixel, 1999, passim; see also Schieren, 1998, pp. 152ff and the literature mentioned there.

[112] Regarding Goethe's color circle and its significance for art, see his "Encore" (in German: Zugabe) in the "Teachings on Colors" and Philipp Otto Runge's letter on this matter; see Goethe, 1988, I, p. 311.

[113] ibid , pp 115f

[114] See e g Goethe, 1988, II, pp 33, 39, to name but a few

[115] Weizsäcker, o.J., p 13

[116] This is Schöne's term. See also below p. 266.

[117] See pp. 176-177.

[118] In fact, we cannot name one publication that does not share this view.

[119] Schöne, 1987, pp. 127ff and additional examples mentioned there.

[120] Quoted according to Schöne, 1987, p. 129; my translation

[121] See p. 216.

[122] My translation; see also Conrady, 1993, II, p 304

[123] Schöne, 1987, p. 129 and others mentioned there

[124] Goethe, 1988, II, pp 192-194; this warning is also quoted in Schöne, 1987, p. 163 as endnote 375, it is surprising that Schöne relegates such an important statement of Goethe's into the fine print of an endnote, although it speaks directly to Schöne's considerations.

[125] See Goethe, 1988, II, pp. 165-216.

[126] See ibid., pp. 169, 170, 178, 189
[127] Goethe, 1988, II, pp. 192ff; my translation.
[128] Goethe, as quoted by Trunz, 1948ff, XIII, p. 617; my translation. See also his objection to the notion of "optical illusions" referred to above p. ...
[129] So also seen by Böhme, 1993, p 147.
[130] Regarding their status as "secondary concepts", see p 294
[131] Quotation from Schöne, 1987, p 131; my translation, see also Böhme, 1993, p 150.
[132] Since we have commented on this in connection with the previous paragraph, we leave aside here that aiming at the totality of the context of a phenomenon is, for reasons related to the dialectics between object and subject, a never ending process
[133] Goethe, in Trunz, 1948ff, XIII, p. 37.
[134] Goethe, 1988, I, p 47.
[135] Goethe, 1988, III, p 232.
[136] Weizsäcker, in Trunz, 1948ff, XIII, p. 550; my translation
[137] Sepper, 1986, p. 96
[138] ibid.
[139] ibid.
[140] Goethe, 1988, III, p. 13
[141] Our friend, the physicist and mathematician Hans Kummer has reminded us that speaking about the differences between Newton or for that matter, the dominant natural sciences, and Goethe in terms of mental constructs preferred by the first and sensuousness by the latter, is not easily plausible for practitioners of today's natural sciences. It is much more common in today's sciences to speak about the difference between objects in reality and objects as conceptualized and to do so in terms of distinguishing between "substance" and "form". The sciences have given their articulation of natural phenomena a specific mental, very often mathematical "form" which is, of course, a transformation of the "substance" of real phenomena. I have obviously not agreed to formulate the difference between Goethe's science and that of mainstream science in those terms I have not done so for two reasons· Firstly, Goethe has not used that terminology and, secondly, Goethe's distinction between enjoyment of a "conceptualization of a thing" and the enjoyment of a thing itself (paragraph 199,2) contains the distinction made in today's science between "form" and "substance". See also Zajonc, 1976, p 330
[142] Although Schöne points out this distinction between Newton and Goethe with admirable clarity - see Schöne, 1987, pp. 63ff, 74, 85ff, 89ff - he still fails to relate this distinction to Goethe's life long understanding of Nature as unity and to his resentment of revolutions
[143] Goethe, 1988, III, p. 251
[144] Sepper, 1988, p. 62.
[145] See p. 241
[146] Goethe, 1988, I, p. 55

[147] So also Heitler, 1970, p 20

[148] Goethe, 1988, I, p 45

[149] Eckermann, 1984, p. 665, under the date of 11 March 1832, my translation

[150] See Luther, 1954, passim.

[151] Roth, 1994, p. 306

[152] Goethe, 1988, I, p. 47

[153] Goethe, 1988, I, p. 259, my translation.

[154] Roth, 1994, pp. 278ff.

[155] Goethe, in Trunz, 1948ff, XIII, p. 39, my translation, see also notes on p. 569

[156] See in this connection also pp 108-110

[157] Goethe, 1988, I, pp 115f.

[158] Goethe, 1902ff, IV, p 164, my translation

[159] See Roth, 1994, pp 308ff; Spitzer, 1996, pp. 211ff

[160] Sepper, 1988, p. 99.

[161] Weyl, 1934, 1f, 42f

[162] See also pp 272, 298.

[163] Bloch, 1959, I, p. 256, my translation.

[164] Husserl, 1986, pp. 56f; see also Schieren, 1998, pp 91f with the same reference to Husserl.

[165] See Sixel, 1988, p 81 and the literature mentioned there

[166] Apel, 1963, passim.

[167] See Sixel, 1988, pp. 80ff, also for additional literature on this matter.

[168] There are, for instance, the questions related to Luhmann's differentiation of ethics and aesthetics from knowledge and from each other, see Luhmann, 1983, passim and, as a reaction to this proposal, Sixel, 1983, passim

[169] Sixel, 1981, passim.

[170] Sixel, ibid

[171] This praxis is described as the life-world of the "last man" in Nietzsche's "Zarathustra", see, in this connection, also Dannhauser, 1987, pp. 841f with whom I, however, disagree regarding his politico-philosophical conclusions.

[172] See pp. 304-310

[173] See pp. 208-210.

[174] Schöne, 1987, p. 110

[175] An attempt to subsume Goethe's "world view" under the label of "postmodernism", by arguing that he does not follow the "enlightened" emphasis on reason and systematic ("rupture-free") knowledge is, in our view, not worth an iota of thought The simple reason for this is that the postmodernists, while doubting the reasonability of Reason, have no appreciation for the primacy of Nature and its consequences on our reasoning Goethe knows why knowledge cannot be free from logical ruptures. Does postmodernism know that? Their co-optation of Goethe would be as futile an attempt as the one that treats Ernst Bloch, a kindred spirit to Goethe, that way

This has been pointed out, with all necessary clarity, by Schmied-Kowarzik; see Schmied-Kowarzik, 1995, p. 217.

[176] Trunz, 1948ff, XIII, p. 615; see also Helmholtz, who in his "Popular Scientific Lectures", 1962 [1853], p. 21, speaks of "the machine of matter".

[177] Heisenberg, 1975 [1967], pp 129ff.

[178] Jaspers, 1949, p. 9.

[179] Weizsäcker, o.J , p. 13

[180] Adams, 1975, p 282.

[181] Weizsäcker, in Trunz, 1948ff, XIII, p. 537, my translation and emphasis.

[182] See pp. 208-210.

[183] This is noted, for instance, by Zajonc, 1976, p. 327; see also Heisenberg, 1975 [1967], pp 134ff.

[184] See pp. 19-20, 105.

[185] See p. 118 in conjunction with pp. 19-20.

[186] Goethe, 1988, I, p. 45.

[187] Sixel, 1999, passim.

[188] See p 153.

[189] Goethe, 1988, I, p. 116, paragraph 177, see also Zajonc, 1976, p 330.

[190] Goethe has made many remarks indicating this view In his old age, he connected them with the fear that God may not find enjoyment anymore in mankind and His creation; see Eckermann, 1984, p 600

[191] See p. 146.

[192] Marx, 1973, pp. 101f; see also Sixel, 1995, p. 77

[193] Marx, ibid.

[194] Marx 1973, pp 101f; see also Sixel, 1995, pp. 97ff.

[195] See pp. 111-124

[196] Böhme, 1995, p 150.

[197] Goethe, 1988, I, pp. 48f.

[198] See Trunz, 1948ff, XIII, p 606

[199] Goethe, 1988, I, p. 48.

[200] Goethe, 1988, III, p 13

[201] Sepper, 1988, p. 99.

[202] Goethe, 1988, III, p 252

[203] Ibid

[204] Goethe, 1988, I, p 49

[205] Goethe in a letter to Zelter, quoted according to Heisenberg, 1975 [1967], p 130

[206] Goethe, in Trunz, 1948ff, XIII, pp 44f, notes on p. 571

[207] This could be seen as a side cut aiming at Kant

[208] Ibid., p. 45

[209] See pp. 297-298.

[210] Verbeek, 1994, pp. 201ff.

[211] Pearce & Tombs, 1998, passim, pp. 280ff in particular

[212] Eckermann, 1984, p 436; my translation. In this connection, one should point out that John Neubauer captures the uniqueness of Goethe's writings on science very well in his essay titled by a quote from Goethe, namely, "Ich lehre nicht, ich erzähle", i.e., "I do not teach, I narrate" [experiences and experiments]"; see Neubauer 1997.

[213] See pp. 304-310.

[214] See e.g. pp. 306-307.

[215] Quoted according to Heitler, 1970, p 20; my translation

[216] Marx, 1973, 100ff, see also Sixel, 1995, 69ff.

[217] As some think it is, e.g. Schieren, 1998, pp 81ff, Sepper, 1988, p 70.

[218] See p. 238.

[219] Quoted in Trunz, 1948ff, XIII, p 563; my translation.

[220] Conrady, 1993, II, p. 370.

[221] Schmied-Kowarzik, 1986, p. 69.

[222] Goethe, 1988, II, p. 28; my translation and my emphasis.

[223] See e.g. paragraph 242 of the "Teachings on Colors", in Goethe, 1988, I, p. 134.

[224] See our remarks about Goethe's work on "Hermann und Dorothea" on p 168.

[225] Goethe, 1988, II, p.132.

[226] See Goethe, 1988, II, p. 22.

[227] Goethe, 1988, III, p. 244.

[228] Goethe, 1988, II, pp 21f.

[229] Goethe, 1988, III, p 253

[230] Goethe, 1988, II, p. 22.

[231] See Goethe, 1988, III, p. 252; he says this also in the short note "Well to be considered" (in German "Wohl zu erwägen"), publ. in vol 1, no 4 of his "On Natural Science", 1817-23; see also Goethe, 1988, II, p 14

[232] For the meaning of this Goethean concept, see pp 270-271

[233] See the paragraphs 174-177, in· Goethe, 1988, I , pp 115f.

[234] Goethe, 1976, p 22

[235] See p. 229

[236] See also Zajonc, 1976, p. 330.

[237] Goethe, 1988, IV and V; for a few examples taken from there, see pp. 309-310.

[238] To name but a few who have dealt with this matter, see Blasius 1979, Bloch, R 1957, Cassirer 1961, Gundolf 1918, Heitler 1970, Sepper 1987 and 1988, Steiner 1926

[239] Goethe, 1988 I, pp 262ff.

[240] See ibid., paragraph 727, see also Goethe's remarks on mathematics and its misuse in Eckermann, 1984, pp. 164ff.

[241] Goethe, 1988, I, paragraph 725

[242] ibid., paragraph 726, my translation.

[243] Goethe, 1988, III, p 252.

[244] Goethe, 1988, III, p. 252; my translation.

[245] Regarding mathematics, see also Schieren, 1998, p. 119; regarding music, see also Brady, 1977, p. 157. Goethe does not discuss, here, the peculiar being of mathematics, let alone that of music. While I am inclined to point out that they share an existence of zero-dimension with other "merely" mental constructs, e.g. concepts, I have to leave aside an inspection of the ways in which all these are elevations of Nature.

[246] See Goethe, in Trunz, 1948ff, XII, pp 452ff; see also Heitler, 1970, p. 15, see also p. 260.

[247] See Goethe, in Trunz, 1948ff, XII, pp. 451ff.

[248] Goethe, in Trunz, 1948ff, VIII, pp 126ff.

[249] Goethe, 1988, I, p. 262.

[250] Quoted according to Stephenson, 1995, p. 6, see also Goethe in Eckermann, 1984, p. 165f.

[251] It should be borne in mind in this connection that the English "science" is not identical in meaning to the German "Wissenschaft" used by Goethe. The "humanities" are in German the "Geistes*wissenschaften*" and this is where mathematics belongs.

[252] Goethe, 1948ff, XII, paragraph 636, p 452; my translation.

[253] According to Schöne, 1987, p 107

[254] See p 270

[255] Kant, 1997, IV, p 470; my translation

[256] It is Jost Schieren who speaks of this so nicely. See Schieren, 1998, p. 212

[257] See chapters 4 &5 passim.

[258] Weizsäcker, in Scheffner & Vogt, 1998, p. 7.

[259] Goethe, in Trunz, 1948ff, XIII, pp 35ff; see also the notes there on pp 568f

[260] Schmied-Kowarzik, 1986, p. 70; my translation.

[261] He even asked people around him to make notes for him regarding all kinds of their experiences.

[262] Quite explicitly so, e.g. by Schöne, 1987, passim

[263] Sepper, 1988, particularly pp. 91ff.

[264] Goethe, 1988, I, pp 104ff.

[265] See for these distinctions, Goethe, 1988, I, paragraph 140, p 106

[266] ibid., paragraph 178, p. 117; paragraph 299, p. 151.

[267] ibid., paragraph 358, p. 169.

[268] Goethe, 1988, II, p. 132; my translation.

[269] Goethe, 1988, I, paragraph 358, p 169; my translation

[270] Sepper, 1988, p 19

[271] ibid , 93ff

[272] See pp. 19-20, 105

[273] Sepper, 1988, pp 96f

[274] See pp. 176-177

[275] See chapters 4 & 5 passim.

[276] See Bahro, 1977, pp. 484f.

[277] See e.g. p. 177.

[278] See Müller, 1982, p. 193.

[279] See also Goethe, 1988, I, pp 57f.

[280] It may also be helpful for one's understanding of pluralism and freedom, if one were to draw upon the example of mathematics, its method and its presentations. There cannot be any doubt that the elements in all fields of mathematics stand side by side to one another in an unshakable order. However, the unshakable order of mathematics does in no way limit the uncountable multitude of games one can play with its elements. This expresses itself, for instance, in the overabundance of introductions to mathematics While the precision and truth of its equations do not grant any liberty, the enjoyment of creating the multitude of mathematical connections in one's own mind gives one a sense for what freedom is all about

[281] Goethe, 1988, IV/V, p. 24.

[282] ibid., pp 97ff

[283] ibid., pp. 190ff.

[284] ibid., p 192

[285] ibid., pp. 423ff.

[286] See the discussion of reason and purpose in Sixel, 1988, pp 23ff

[287] See pp. 309-310

[288] Böhme, 1993, p 150; my translation

AFTERWORD

There are a few things we wanted to say in this book and a few others that we did not.

What we wanted to say was that Nature is for us what she is for us as being Nature ourselves. As such we are connected to her primarily through our senses. Not sensing and practically acknowledging this primacy implies relating to all there is falsely.

Having said that, we would like to underline that it has not been our intent to deliver a blueprint for life. In fact, we think that from behind our desks no advice can be given in such matter. Solutions have to evolve in a new praxis carried by those no longer willing to endure the distortions of their Nature.

Could it then be said that we have tried to deliver an argument for the primacy of Nature and that people better accept it?

It looks like we did. As an argument, however, it would merely aim at turning the primacy of Nature into a guiding principle again. Our concept of Nature, however, does not primarily matter, only what we are does.

Therefore, we can only state our hope that those who sense themselves as parts of Nature will join forces in a new praxis. Then the Eighth Day of creation may not be the last one after all.

Bibliography

Adams, Richard N.: Energy and Structure - A Theory of Social Power - London, Austin (Texas), 1975.

Adams, Richard N.: The Eighth Day - Social Evolution as the Self-Organization of Energy - , Austin (Texas), 1988.

Apel, Karl Otto: Das Leibapriori der Erkenntnis, in: Archiv für Philosophie, vol. 12, no. 1-2, 1963.

Ayres, Robert U. & Indira Nair: Thermodynamics and Economics, in: Physics Today, vol. 37, no. 11, 1984.

Bahro, Rudolf: Die Alternative - Zur Kritik des real existierenden Sozialismus - , Frankfurt, 1977.

Bahro, Rudolf (Hg.): Rückkehr - Die In-Weltkrise als Ursprung der Weltzerstörung - , Berlin, Frankfurt, 1991.

Bateson, Gregory: Steps to an Ecology of Mind, New York, 1972.

Binswanger, Hans Christoph: Geld und Magie - Eine Deutung von Goethes Faust - , in: Bahro, Rudolf (Hg.): Rückkehr, Berlin, Frankfurt, 1991.

Blasius, Jürgen: Zur Wissenschaftstheorie Goethes, in: Zeitschrift für philosophische Forschung, vol. 33, 1977.

Bloch, Ernst: Das Prinzip Hoffnung, 2 Bde., Frankfurt, 1959.

Bloch, Ernst: Geist der Utopie (1918), Frankfurt, 1973.

Bloch, Robert: Goethe - Idealistic Morphology and Science - , in: American Scientist, vol. 40, 1952.

Böhme, Gernot: Ist Goethes Farbenlehre Wissenschaft?, in: Böhme, Gernot (Hg.): Alternativen der Wissenschaft, Frankfurt, 1993.

Brady, Philip: On not being Intimidated: Socialist Overhauling of a Classic, in: Wilkinson, M. (ed.): Goethe Revisited, London, 1984.

Brady, Ronald: Goethe's Natural Science – Some Non-Cartesian Meditations - , in: Schaefer, Karl E., Herbert Heusel and Ronald Brady, (eds.): Toward a Man - Centered Medical Science, New York, 1977.

Carson, Rachel: Silent Spring, Boston, 1962.

Cassirer, Ernst: Freiheit und Form – Studien zur deutschen Geistesgeschichte – , Darmstadt, 1961.

Center for Transportation Analysis Publications: Transportation Energy Data Book, Edition 18, Oak Ridge National Laboratory, 1998.

Conrady, Karl Otto: Goethe - Leben und Werk, Band I, Frankfurt, 1992.

Conrady, Karl Otto: Goethe - Leben und Werk, Band II, Frankfurt, 1993.

Damasio, Antonio: Descartes' Error – Emotion, Reason and the Human Brain - , New York, 1994.

Damm, Sigrid: Goethe und Christiane, Frankfurt, 1996.

Dannhauser, Werner: Friedrich Nietzsche, in: Strauss, Leo & Joseph Cropsey, (eds.): History of Political Philosophy, Chicago, London, 1987.

Delouche, John C.: Seed Change VIII, in: Seedman's Digest, August 1983

"Deutschland Nachrichten", New York, Issue of 27 Oct 1995.

"Deutschland Nachrichten", New York, Issue of 28 Dec 1995.

Eckermann, Johann Peter: Gespräche mit Goethe, hg. von Regine Otto, München, 1984.

Fairley, Barker: A Study of Goethe, Westport (Conn.), 1947.

Frisken, William B.: The Atmospheric Environment, Baltimore, 1973.

Furnham, A. & C. Smith,: Choosing alternative Medicine: A Comparison of the Beliefs of Patients Visiting a General Practitioner and a Homeopath, in: Social Science and Medicine, vol. 26, no. 7, 1987.

Gadamer, Hans Georg: Truth and Method, New York (in German: Wahrheit und Methode, 1961), 1976.

Geertz, Clifford: Religion as a Cultural System, in: Banton, M. (ed.): Anthropological Approaches to Religion, London, New York, 1969.

Geertz, Clifford: The Interpretation of Cultures: Selected Essays, New York, 1973.

Goethe, Johann Wolfgang v.: Sämtliche Werke, Jubiläumsausgabe, Band IV, Stuttgart, Berlin, 1902ff.

Goethe, Johann Wolfgang v.: Reineke Fuchs, in: Goethes Werke, hg. von Trunz, Emil, Band II, Hamburg, 1948ff.

Goethe, Johann Wolfgang v.: Faust II, in: Goethes Werke, hg. von Trunz, Emil, Band III, Hamburg, 1948ff.

Goethe, Johann Wolfgang v.: Wilhelm Meisters Lehrjahre, in: Goethes Werke, hg. von Trunz, Emil, Band VII, Hamburg, 1948ff.

Goethe, Johann Wolfgang v.: Wilhelm Meisters Wanderjahre, in: Goethes Werke, hg. von Trunz, Emil, Band VIII, Hamburg, 1948ff.

Goethe, Johann Wolfgang v.: Dichtung und Wahrheit, in: Goethes Werke, hg. von Trunz, Emil, Band IX, Hamburg, 1948ff.

Goethe, Johann Wolfgang v.: Maximen und Reflexionen, in: Goethes Werke, hg. von Trunz, Emil, Band XII, Hamburg, 1948ff.

Goethe, Johann Wolfgang v.: Der Versuch als Vermittler von Objekt und Subjekt, in: Goethes Werke, hg. von Trunz, Emil, Band XIII, pp. 10-20, Hamburg, 1948ff.

Goethe, Johann Wolfgang v.: Bildungstrieb, in: Goethes Werke, hg. von Trunz, Emil, Band XIII, pp. 32-34, Hamburg, 1948ff.

Goethe, Johann Wolfgang v.: Freundlicher Zuruf, in: Goethes Werke, hg. von Trunz, Emil, 1948ff Band XIII, pp. 34f, Hamburg, 1948ff.

Goethe, Johann Wolfgang v.: Probleme, in: Goethes Werke, hg. von Trunz, Emil, Band XIII, pp. 35-37, Hamburg, 1948ff.

Goethe, Johann Wolfgang v.: Bedeutende Fördernis durch ein einziges geistreiches Wort, in: Goethes Werke, hg. von Trunz, Emil, Band XIII, pp. 37-41, Hamburg, 1948ff.

Goethe, Johann Wolfgang v.: Naturphilosophie, in: Goethes Werke, hg. von Trunz, Emil, Band XIII, pp. 44f, Hamburg, 1948ff.

Goethe, Johann Wolfgang v.: Erläuterungen zu dem aphoristischen Aufsatz "Die Natur" in: Goethes Werke, hg. von Trunz, Emil, Band XIII, pp. 48f, Hamburg, 1948ff.

Goethe, Johann Wolfgang v.: Entwurf einer Farbenlehre, in: Goethes Werke, hg. von Trunz, Emil, Band XIII, pp. 315–523, Hamburg, 1948ff.

Goethe, Johann Wolfgang v.: Faust I, translated by Randall Jarrell as "Goethe's Faust, Part I", New York, 1976.

Goethe, Johann Wolfgang v.: Theory of Colours, translated by Charles Lock Eastlake, Cambridge (Mass.), 1982.

Goethe, Johann Wolfgang v.: Maximen und Reflexionen, in: Goethe, Berliner Ausgabe, Band XVIII, Berlin, 1984.

Goethe, Johann Wolfgang v.: Historischer Teil 1, in: Goethe: Farbenlehre, hg, von Ott, Gerhard & Heinrich O. Proskauer, Band IV, Stuttgart, 1986.

Goethe, Johann Wolfgang v.: Historischer Teil 2, in: Goethe: Farbenlehre, hg. von Ott, Gerhard & Heinrich O. Proskauer, Band V, Stuttgart, 1986.

Goethe, Johann Wolfgang v.: Zur Farbenlehre, in: Goethe: Farbenlehre, hg. von Ott, Gerhard & Heinrich O. Proskauer, Band I, pp. 43-318, Stuttgart, 1988.

Goethe, Johann Wolfgang v.: Wohl zu erwägen, in: Goethe: Farbenlehre, hg. von Ott, Gerhard & Heinrich O. Proskauer, Band II, p. 14, Stuttgart, 1988.

Goethe, Johann Wolfgang v.: Beiträge zur Chromatik (Optik), in: Goethe: Farbenlehre, hg. Von Ott, Gerhard & Heinrich O. Proskauer, Band II, pp. 15-93, Stuttgart, 1988.

Goethe, Johann Wolfgang v.: Der Versuch als Vermittler von Objekt und Subjekt, in: Goethe: Farbenlehre, hg. von Ott, Gerhard & Heinrich O. Proskauer, Band II, pp. 119–131, Stuttgart, 1988.

Goethe, Johann Wolfgang v.: Erfahrung und Wissenschaft, in: Goethe: Farbenlehre, hg. von Ott, Gerhard & Heinrich O. Proskauer, Band II, pp. 132-134, Stuttgart, 1988.

Goethe, Johann Wolfgang v.: Newtons Persönlichkeit, in: Goethe: Frabenlehre, hg. von Ott, Gerhard & Heinrich O. Proskauer, Band III, pp. 229-237, Stuttgart, 1988.

Goethe, Johann Wolfgang v.: Konfesssion des Verfassers, in: Goethe: Farbenlehre, hg. von Ott, Gerhard & Heinrich O. Proskauer, Band III, pp. 238-256, Stuttgart, 1988.

Goethe, Johann Wolfgang v.: Bedeutende Förderniss durch ein einziges geistreiches Wort, in: Goethe: Farbenlehre, hg. von Ott, Gerhard & Heinrich O. Proskauer, Band III, pp. 257-261, Stuttgart, 1988.

Goethe, Johann Wolfgang v.: The Experiment as Mediator between Object and Subject, in: Goethe, Johann Wolfgang v.: Scientific Studies, edited and translated by Miller, Douglas, New York, 1988.

Goethe, Johann Wolfgang v.: Die Metamorphose der Pflanzen, in: Goethes Morphologische Schriften, hg. von Troll, Wilhelm, pp. 127-186, Jena, o.J.

Goethe, Johann Wolfgang v.: Glückliches Ereignis, in: Goethes Morphologische Schriften, hg. von Troll, Wilhelm, pp. 265-269, Jena, o.J.

Goethe, Johann Wolfgang v.: Einwirkungen der neueren Philosophie, in: Goethes Morphologische Schriften, hg. von Troll, Wilhelm, pp. pp. 285-288, Jena, o.J.

Goethe, Johann Wolfgang v.: Anschauende Urteilskraft, in: Goethes Morphologische Schriften, hg. von Troll, Wilhelm, pp. 289-290, Jena, o.J.

Guardian Weekly, Overseas Edition, 20 Aug, 1995

Gundolf, Friedrich: Goethe, Berlin, 1918.

Guyol, Nathaniel B.: Energy in the Perspective of Geography, Englewood Cliffs, 1971.

Habermas, Jürgen & Niklas Luhmann: Theorie der Gesellschaft oder Sozialtechnologie, Frankfurt, 1971.

Habermas, Jürgen: Erkenntnis und Interesse, Frankfurt, 1973.

Heisenberg, Werner: Goethe's View of Nature and the World of Science and Technology, (Lecture to the Goethe Society in Weimar, 21 May 1967, translated by Peter Heath), in: Heisenberg, Werner (ed.): Across the Frontiers, New York, 1975.

Heitler, Walter: Die Naturwissenschaft Goethes. Eine Gegenüberstellung Goethescher und modern-exakter Naturwissenschaft, in: Berliner Germanistentag. Vorträge und Berichte, hg. von Borck, Karl-Heinz & Rudolf Henn,, Heidelberg, 1970.

Helmholtz, Hermann: On Goethe's Scientific Researches – A Lecture delivered before the German Society of Königsberg in the Spring of 1853 – in: Popular Lecture on Scientific Subjects, selected and introduced by Morris Kline, New York, 1962.

Hoerres, W.: Der Wille als reine Vollkommenheit bei Duns Scotus, München, 1962.

Holz, Hans Heinz: Technik und gesellschaftliche Wertordnung, in: Verein deutscher Ingenieure (Hg.): Werte und Wertordnungen in Technik und Gesellschaft, Düsseldorf, 1975.

Holz, Hans Heinz: Historischer Materialismus und ökologische Krise, in: Gärtner, E. & A. Leisewitz (Hg.): Ökologie – Naturaneignung und Naturtheorie - , Köln, 1982.

Husserl, Edmund: Analyse der Wahrnehmung, in: Held, Klaus (Hg.): Phänomenologie der Lebenswelt, Ausgewählte Texte, Stuttgart, 1986.

Jaspers, Karl: Unsere Zukunft und Goethe, Bremen, 1949.

Jha, A. K.: Conserving Bio-Diversity: Need for Statutory Support, in: The Economic and Political Weekly, 11 March 1994.

Kant, Immanuel: Metaphysische Anfangsgründe der Naturwissenschaft, in: Gesammelte Schriften, hg. von der Königlich Preußischen Akademie der Wissenschaften, vol. IV, Berlin, 1902.

The Kingston Whig-Standard, Kingston, 24 Nov 1995.

Klemperer, Victor: I Will Bear Witness – A Diary of the Nazi Years 1933 – 41, New York (publ. in German 1995), 1998.

Kloppenburg, J. R.: First the Seed, Cambridge, New York, 1990.

Koch, K.-H.: Architektur und Umwelt,, in: Calließ, J. & E. Lob (Hg.): Praxis der Umwelt-und Friedenserziehung, vol. I, Düsseldorf, 1987/8.

Krippendorff, Ekkehart: Goethe - Politik gegen den Zeitgeist - , Frankfurt, Leipzig, 1999.

Litt, Theodor: Goethes Naturanschauung und die exakte Naturwissenschaft, in: Litt, Theodor (Hg.): Naturwissenschaft und Menschenbildung, Heidelberg, 1959.

Lotka, Alfred: Contribution to the Energetics of Evolution, in: Proceedings of the National Academy of Sciences, vol. VIII, 1922.

Luhmann, Niklas: Soziologie der Moral, in: Luhmann, N. & St. Pfürtner (Hg.): Theorietechnik und Moral, Frankfurt, 1978.

Luhmann, Niklas: Die Ausdifferenzierung von Erkenntnisgewinn, in: Stehr, Nico & Volker Meja (Hg.): Wissenssoziologie, (Sonderheft der Kölner Gesellschaft für Soziologie und Sozialpsychologie, 22), Opladen, 1981.

Luhmann, Niklas: The Differentiation of Society, New York, 1982.

Luhmann, Niklas: Liebe als Passion: Zur Codierung von Intimität, Frankfurt, 1989.

Luhmann, Niklas: Die Realität der Massenmedien, Opladen, 1996.

Luther, Martin: Dass der freie Wille nichts sei, in: Martin Luther: Ausgewählte Werke, hg. von Borcherdt, H. H. & G. Merz, München, 1954.

Maclean's, Canada's Weekly Magazine, Toronto, 7 Feb 2000.

Mann, Thomas: Lotte in Weimar, Stockholm, 1940.

Martin, Gottfried: Kant's Metaphysics and Theory of Science, Westport, 1974.

Marx, Karl: Grundrisse, Frankfurt, Wien, o.J.

Marx, Karl: Grundrisse, translated by Nicolaus, Martin, New York, 1973.

Marx, Karl: The Economic and Philosophical Manuscripts of 1844, in: Marx, Karl & Friedrich Engels, Collected Works, vol. III. New York, 1975.

McGregor, K. & Peay, E. R.: The Choice of Alternative Therapy for Health Care: Testing Some Propositions, in: Social Science and Medicine, vol. 43, no. 9, 1994.

Mommsen, Katharina (Hg.): Goethe - Märchen - , Frankfurt, 1984.

Müller, Kanzler Friedrich v.: Unterhaltungen mit Goethe, hg. von Grumach, Renate, München, 1982.

Neubauer, John: "Ich lehre nicht, ich erzähle", Geschichte und Geschichten, in: Goethes natur-wissenschaftliche Schriften, Goethe Jahrbuch, vol. 114, Weimar, 1994.

Newton, Isaac: Opticks, Or A Treatise of the Reflections, Refractions, Inflections & Colours of Light (based on the Fourth Edition London 1730), New York, 1979.

Nietzsche, Friedrich: Werke, 3 Bde., hg. von Schlechta, Karl, München, 1954 – 56.

Odum, Howard: Environment, Power and Society, New York, 1971.

Parikh, Jayoti: North-South Issues for Climatic Changes, in: The Economic and Political Weekly, 5 – 12 Nov, 1994.

Pausch, Alfons & Renate Pausch: Goethes Juristenlaufbahn, Köln, 1996

Pearce, Frank & Steve Tombs: Toxic Capitalism - Corporate Crime and the Chemical Industry - , Aldershot, 1994.

Psathas, George: Ethnomethodology and Phenomenology, in: Manis, J. G. & B. N. Meltzer (eds.): Symbolic Interaction, Boston, 1972.

Roberts, Eugene: Disinhibition as an Organizing Principle in the Nervous System, in: Roberts, E, T. N. Chase and D. B. Towers (eds.): GABA in Nervous System Function, New York, 1975.

Roth, Gerhard: Das Gehirn und seine Wirklichkeit – Kognitive Neurobiologie und ihre philoso-phischen Konsequenzen- , Frankfurt, 1994.

Rousseau, Henry: The Social Contract and Discourses, (first publ. 1762), New York, 1950.

Rousseau, Henry: Emile, or On Education, (first publ. 1762), London, 1986.

Scheffran, Jürgen & Wolfgang Vogt (Hg.): Kampf um die Natur - Umweltzerstörung und die Lösung ökologischer Konflikte - , Darmstadt, 1994.

Schieren, Jost: Anschauende Urteilskraft – Methodische und philosophische Grundlagen von Goethes naturwissenschaftlichem Erkennen - , Düsseldorf, Bonn, 1998.

Schmidt, Alfred: Goethes herrlich leuchtende Natur – Philosophische Studien zur deutschen Spätaufklärung - , München, 1982.

Schmied-Kowarzik, Wolfdietrich: Ist Goethes Naturanschauung noch eine Herausforderung gegenüber der heute herrschenden Naturwissenschaft, in: Leviathan, Zeitschrift für Sozialwissenschaft, Jahrgang 14, Heft 1, 1982.

Schmied-Kowarzik, Wolfdietrich: Ernst Bloch. Suche nach uns selbst ins Utopische, in: Fleischer, Margot (Hg.): Philosophen des 20. Jahrhunderts, Darmstadt, 1995.

Schmied-Kowarzik, Wolfdietrich: "Von der wirklichen, von der seyenden Natur", - Schellings Ringen um eine Naturphilosophie in Auseinandersetzung mit Kant, Fichte und Hegel - , (Schellingiana Band 8), Stuttgart-Bad Cannstadt, 1994.

Schmied-Kowarzik, Wolfdietrich: Annäherungen an Hönigswalds transzendalanalytischer Systematik der Philosophie, Ms.

Schöne, Albrecht: Goethes Farbentheologie, München, 1987.

Sepper, Dennis: Goethe against Newton: Towards Saving the Phenomenon, in: Amerine, Frederick, Francis J. Zucker & Harvey Wheeler (eds.): Goethe and the Sciences: - A Reappraisal - , Dordrecht, Boston, Tokyo, 1986.

Sepper, Dennis: Goethe contra Newton - Polemics and the project of a new science of color – , Cambridge, New York, Sydney, 1988.

Shiva, Vandana: Biotechnology, Development and Conservation of Biodiversity, in: The Economic and Political Weekly, 30 Nov, 1991.

Simmons, I.G.: Changing the Face of the Earth: Culture, Environment, History, Oxford, New York, 1991.

Sixel, Friedrich W.: Motivation und Wissen, in: Stehr, Nico & Volker Meja, (Hg.): Wissenssoziologie (Sonderheft der Kölner Zeitschrift für Soziologie und Sozialpsychologie, 22), Opladen, 1981.

Sixel, Friedrich W.: Beyond Good and Evil? - A Study of Luhmann's Sociology of Morals - , in: Theory, Culture and Society, vol. 2, no. 1, 1983.

Sixel, Friedrich W.: Crisis and Critique: On the 'Logic' of Late Capitalism, Leiden, New York, 1988.

Sixel, Friedrich W.: On Adams' Monistic Concept of Social Evolution, in: Cultural Dynamic, vol. IV, no. 2, 1991.

Sixel, Friedrich W.: Understanding Marx, Lanham, London, 1995.

Sixel, Friedrich W.: Goethe: Nicht-Philosoph aus Koketterie?, in: Eidam, Heinz & Frank Hermenau (Hg.): Zur Problematik menschlicher Emanzipation heute, Lüneburg, 1994.

Society of Biodynamic Farming and Gardening in Ontario, Newsletter, Dec, 1995.

Society of Biodynamic Farming and Gardening in Ontario, Newsletter, Summer, 1999.

"Der Spiegel", Hamburg, Issue of 23 Oct, 1995.

Spitzer, Manfred: Geist im Netz – Modelle für Lernen, Denken und Handeln - , Heidelberg, Berlin, Oxford, 1996.

Steiner, Rudolf.: Goethes naturwissenschaftliche Schriften, Dornach, 1926.

Stephenson, Roger H.: Goethe's Wisdom Literature – A Study in Aesthetic Transmutation - , Bern, Frankfurt, New York, 1983.

Stephenson, Roger H.: Goethe's Conception of Knowledge and Science, Edinburgh, 1995.

Strasser, S.: Phenomenology and the Human Sciences, in: Kockelmans, J. J. (ed.): Phenomenology, the Philosophy of Edmund Husserl and Its Interpretation, Garden City, 1967.

Summers, Claude M.: The Conversion of Energy, in: Energy and Power. A Scientific American, Book, San Francisco, 1971.

Sylvester, E. J. & L. C. Klotz: The Gene Age: Genetic Engineering and the Next Industrial Revolution, New York, 1983.

Taylor, Mark: Alteraty, Chicago, 1987.

Toronto Star, 30 Sept, 1995.

Transportation Energy Data Book, Edition 18, publ. by Center for Transportation Analysis Publications, Oak Ridge National Laboratory, 1998.

Troll, Wilhelm: Deus sive Natura, in: Troll, Wilhelm (Hg.): Goethes Morphologische Schriften, Jena, o.J.

Unseld, Siegfried: Goethe und der Gingko, Frankfurt, 1998.

Verbeek, Bernhard: Die Anthropologie der Umweltzerstörung – Die Evolution und die Schatten der Zukunft - , Darmstadt, 1994.

Viëtor, Karl: Goethe, the Thinker, Cambridge, 1950.

Vipond, Shayne: The Process of Involvement: Discovering Complementary Health Care, Unpubl. M.A.-thesis, Queen's University, Kingston, 1998.

Vogel, Ch.: Gibt es eine natürliche Moral? Oder: Wie unnatürlich ist unsere Ethik?, in: Meier, R. (Hg.): Die Herausforderung der Evolutionsbiologie, München, Zürich, 1986.

Vorländer, Karl: Kant, Schiller, Goethe, Leipzig, 1907.

Wehler, Hans-Ulrich: Deutsche Gesellschaftsgeschichte, vol. I, München, 1989.

Weizsäcker, Carl-Friedrich v.: Die Einheit der Natur, Berlin, Darmstadt, Wien, o.J.

Weizsäcker, Carl-Friedrich v.: Nachwort [zur Farbenlehre], in: Trunz, Emil (Hg.): Goethes Werke, Band XIII, pp. 537 – 554, Hamburg, 1948ff.

Weizsäcker, Ernst U. v.: Erdpolitik – Ökologische Realpolitik an der Schwelle zum Jahrhundert der Umwelt - , Darmstadt, 1994.

Werner, David: Turning Health into an Investment: Assaults on the Third World Health Care, in: The Economic and Political Weekly, 21 June, 1994.

Weyl, Hermann: Mind and Nature, Philadelphia, 1934.

Wiese, Benno v.: Schiller, Stuttgart, 1959.

Wilson, A.: New World Order and the West's War on Population, in: The Economic and Political Weekly, 20 Aug, 1994.

World Resource Institute, Washington, D.C., 1989.

Zajonc, Arthur G.: Goethe's theory of color and scientific intuition, in: American Journal of Physics, vol. 44, no. 4, 1975.

"Die Zeit", Overseas Edition, Hamburg, Issue of 1 Dec, 1995.

Selected Readings
Related to Part II

The publications listed below have been studied by us in connection with a variety of projects. Some of these projects date back to our doctoral research decades ago. Others relate to research carried out by the "Political Economy Group" that existed at Queen's University (Kingston) around 1980. Yet others are connected to our more recent publications on late capitalism and Marxist thought. Only some of the suggested readings have been studied in direct connection with Part II of this book.

We do not claim that our list is representative for the current state of historical and developmental (evolutionary) research. But we do believe that this list is helpful for those who wish to explore, more thoroughly, particular issues and the general trend of our argument presented in Part II.

This reading list is subdivided into two sections. In the first section, we list literature of a more general historical or developmental interest. In the second section, we list publications which are more specific to particular states and societies. Of course, a clear cut segregation of the various pieces of literature along this dividing line could not always be made. In such cases, we have placed a given publication in accordance with what we see as being its emphasis.

Finally, we would like to point out that publications *quoted* in Part II are *not* included in this reading list. The reader will find their bibliographical data in the "Bibliography".

1.- Publications of general historical or developmental interest:

Anderson, Perry: Passages from Antiquity to Feudalism, London, 1974
_____ : Lineages of the Absolutist State, London, 1974

Barudio, G.: Das Zeitalter des Absolutismus und der Aufklärung, 1648 - 1779, Frankfurt, 1981

Beckerath, H. v.: Großindustrie und Gesellschaftsordnung, Tübingen, Zürich, 1954

Beloff, Max: The Age of Absolutism 1660 - 1815, New York, 1954

Bendix, R.: König oder Volk – Machtausübung und Herrschaftsmandat - , Frankfurt, 1980

Benz, W. & H. Graml (Hg.): Weltprobleme zwischen den Machtblöcken, Frankfurt, 1981

_____ : Europa nach dem Zweiten Weltkrieg, Frankfurt, 1983

Bergeron, Louis, F. Furet und R. Koselleck: Das Zeitalter der europäischen Revolution 1780 – 1848, Frankfurt, 1969

Billaçois, F.: La crise de la noblesse europeén 1550 - 1650, in: Rev. d'hist. mod. et contemp., XXIII, 1976

Bloch, Marc: Feudal Society, Chicago, 1968 (in French 1939)

Braudel, Fernand: Europäische Expansion und Kapitalismus 1450 - 1650, in: Schulin, E. (Hg.): Universalgeschichte, Köln, 1974

The Cambridge Economic History of Europe from the Decline of the Roman Empire, 3 vols., Cambridge, 1941 - 1963

Chandler, A. D. & H. Dahms (eds.): Managerial Hierarchies - Comparative Perspectives on the Rise of the Modern Industrial Enterprise - , Cambridge, 1980

Dülmen, Richard van: Entstehung des frühneuzeitlichen Europa 1550 - 1646, Frankfurt, 1982

Friederici, G.: Der Charakter der Entdeckung und Eroberung Amerikas durch die Europäer, 2 Bände, Stuttgart, 1925 - 36

Fürstenberg, F.: Gestaltwandel der Unternehmen, in: Nürnberger Abhandlungen zu den Wirtschafts- und Sozialwissenschaften, Heft 4, Berlin, 1954

Ganshoff, F. L.: Was ist das Lehnswesen?, Darmstadt, 1961

Habermas, Jürgen: Geschichte und Evolution, in: Habermas, J.(Hg.): Zur Rekonstruktion des Historischen Materialismus, Frankfurt, 1976

Hanke, Lewis: Aristotle and the American Indians, London, 1969

Harnack, Adolph v.: Mission and Expansion, New York, 1961

Hilton, Rodney H.: Transition from Feudalism to Capitalism, in: Science and Society, XVIII, no. 4, 1953

Hogan, Michael: The Marshall-Plan - America, Britain and the Reconstruction of Western Europe 1947 – 1951 - , New York, 1987

Le Goff, Jacques: Das Hochmittelalter, Frankfurt, 1965

Kennedy, Paul: The Rise and Fall of the Great Powers - Economic Change and Military Conflict from 1500 to 2000 - , New York, 1989

Lis, C. & H. Soly: Poverty and Capitalism in Pre-Industrial Europe 1350 - 1850, Hassocks, 1979

Luhmann, Niklas: The Differentiation of Society, New York, 1982

Marx, Karl: Das Kapital, vol. 1, (various editions)

Mauro, F.: Towards an 'International Mode', European Overseas Expansion between 1500 and 1800, in: Econ. Hist. Rev., XIV, 1961

Mauro, F.: Histoire de l'économie mondiale, Paris, 1971

Michalka, Wolfgang (Hg.): Der Erste Weltkrieg - Wirkung, Wahrnehmung, Analyse - , München, Zürich, 1994

Mommsen, Wolfgang J.: Das Zeitalter des Imperialismus, Frankfurt, 1969

Parsons, Talcott: The System of Modern Societies, Englewood Cliffs, 1971

Pirenne, Henry: Economic and Social History of Medieval Europe, London, 1963

Polanyi, Michael: The Great Transformation, Boston, 1944

Rabb, Th. K.: The Struggle for Stability in Early Modern Europe, London, New York, 1975

Sixel, Friedrich W.: Die Entdeckungen und die Erweiterung des geographischen Weltbildes Europas (bis Ende des 18. Jahrhunderts), in: Saeculum Weltgeschichte, Bd. VI, Freiburg, Basel, Wien, 1971

Sixel, Friedrich W.: "Christoph Columbus war kein Freund von mir", in: Kohl, Karl-Heinz (Hg.): Mythen der Neuen Welt, Berlin, 1982

Slicher van Bath, B.: The Agrarian History of Western Europe, London, 1963

Sweezy, Paul M.: The Theory of Capitalist Development (particularly "Part Four"), New York, London, 1970

Tilly, Charles (ed.): The Formation of National States in Western Europe, Princeton, 1975

Wallerstein, Immanuel: The Modern World System, vol. I, New York, 1974; vol. II, New York, 1980

Weber, Max: The Protestant Ethic and the Spirit of Capitalism, New York, 1958

_____ : Economy and Society, New York, 1968

2.- Publications focusing on the development of specific countries:

England:

Ashton, T. S.: The Industrial Revolution 1760 - 1830, London, 1948
Bolton, G.: Britain's Legacy Overseas, London, 1973
Bullard, R. W.: Britain and the Middle East, London, 1951
The New Cambridge Modern History, vol. X, 1960, vol. XI, 1962, vol. XII, 1960, all publ. in Cambridge
Chambers, J. D.: Enclosures and Labour Supply in the Industrial Revolution, in: The Economic History Review, vol. IX, 1958
Chambers, J. D.: Population, Economy and Society in Pre-Industrial England, London, New York, 1972
Cowan, H.: British Emigration to British North America - The First Hundred Years - , Toronto, 1961
Craig, G.: Lord Durham's Report, Toronto, 1963
Douglas, D. C.: William the Conqueror - The Norman Impact upon England - , Berkeley, London, 1964
Daniel-Rops, H.: The Church in the Age of Revolution, London, 1967
Easterbrook, W. T. & H. G. J. Aitken: Canadian Economic History, Toronto, 1970
Gallagher, J. & R. Robinson: The Imperialism of Free Trade, in: The Economic History Review, vol. VI, no. 1, 1953
Harlow, V. T.: The Founding of the Second British Empire, vol. I, London 1952, vol. II, London, 1964
Hill, Christopher: Protestantism and the Rise of Capitalism, in: Fisher, F. J. (ed.): Essays in the Economic and Social History of Tudor and Stuart England, London, 1960
Hobsbawm, E.: Industry and Empire, Middlesex, 1968
Knorr, K. N.: The British Colonial Theory 1570 - 1850, Toronto, 1944
MacFarlane, Alan: The Origins of English Individualism: The Family, Property and Social Transition, Oxford, 1978
Nef, John: Industry and Government in France and England, 1540 - 1640, Ithaca, 1957
Thompson, E. P.: The Making of the English Working Class, London 1963
_____ : The Peculiarities of the English, in: Miliband, R. & J. Saville, (eds.): The Socialist Register, No. 2, 1965

Wheare, K. C.: The Constitutional Structure of the Commonwealth, Oxford, 1962

Wilson, D. M.: The Anglo-Saxons, London, 1960

Stone, L.: The Causes of the English Revolution 1529 - 1642, London, 1972

France:

Bergengruen, A.: Adel und Grundherrschaft im Merowingerreich, Wiesbaden, 1958

Bloch, Marc: French Rural History, Berkeley, 1966

Clapham, J. H.: Economic Development of France and Germany 1815 - 1914, Cambridge, 1961

Deschamps, H.: Les Méthodes et les Doctrines coloniales de la France, Paris, 1953

Duby, Georges & Robert Mandrou: Histoire de la civilisation française, 2 vols., Paris, 1958

Goubert, Pierre: Louis XIV and Twenty Million Frenchmen, New York, 1970

Lot, F.: L'Invasion barbares et peuplement de l'Europe, 2 vols., Paris, 1937

Miquelon, D. (ed.): Society and Conquest - The Debate on the Bourgeoisie and Social Change in French Canada 1750 – 1850 - , Toronto, 1977

Nef, John: Industry and Government in France and England 1540 - 1640, Ithaca, 1957

Rioux, M. & Y. Martin (eds.): French Canadian Society, vol. 1, Toronto, 1964

Sieburg, Heinz-Otto: Grundzüge der französischen Geschichte, Darmstadt, 1997

Taylor, G. V.: Non-capitalist Wealth and the Origins of the French Revolution, in: The American Historical Review, January 1967

Germany:

Boehme, H.: Deutschlands Weg zur Großmacht, Köln, Berlin, 1966

Conze, W. & D. Groh: Die Arbeiterbewegung in der nationalen Bewegung - Die deutsche Sozialdemokratie vor, während und nach der Reichsgründung - , Stuttgart, 1966

Hamerow, Th. S.: Restoration, Revolution, Reaction - Economics and Politics in Germany 1815 – 1871 - , Princeton, 1958

Jäckel, Eberhard: Das deutsche Jahrhundert - Eine historische Bilanz - , Darmstadt, 1996

Knapp, M., W. Link, H.W. Schröder, K. Schwalbe, K. (Hg.): Die USA. und Deutschland 1918 - 1975, München, 1978

Kruedener, J. v.: Economic Crisis and Political Collapse - The Weimar Republic 1924 - 1933 - , New York, 1990

Kuczynski, J.: Die Bewegung der deutschen Wirtschaft von 1800 bis 1946, Berlin, 1947

Larres, K. & T. Oppelland (Hg.): Deutschland and die USA im 20. Jahrhundert, Darmstadt, 1997

Niethammer, L.: Entnazifizierung in Bayern - Säuberung und Rehabilitierung unter amerikanischer Besatzung - , Frankfurt, 1972

Nolan, Mary: Visions of Modernity - American Business and the Modernization of Germany - , New York, 1994

Schoenbaum, D.: Hitler's Social Revolution, Garden City, 1966

Thamer, H.-U.: Verführung und Gewalt - Deutschland 1933 – 1945 - , Berlin, 1986

Wehler, H.-U.: Deutsche Gesellschaftsgeschichte 1700 – 1914, Bände I - III, München, 1989ff.

India:

Banerjee, A. C. & D. K. Ghose (eds.): A Comprehensive History of India, vol. IX (1712 - 1772), New Delhi, 1978

The Cambridge Economic History of India, vol. II (in particular Parts I - VI), Cambridge, 1982

Spear, Percival: A History of India, vol. II, London, New York, 1990

Panikhar, K. M.: The Foundation of the New India, London, 1963

Sutherland, L. S.: The East India Company in Eighteenth Century Politics, Oxford, 1952

The Netherlands:

Barbour, Violet: Capitalism in Amsterdam in the 17th Century, Ann Arbor, 1963
Geyl, Pieter: The Netherlands in the 17th Century, vol. I, London, 1961; vol. II, London, 1964
Glamann, K.: Dutch Asiatic Trade 1620 - 1740, Copenhagen, 1958

Japan:

Allen, G.: A Short Economic History of Japan, London, 1962
Beasley, W.: The Modern History of Japan, London, 1963
Maruyama, M.: Thought and Behavior in Modern Japanese Politics, New York, 1963

Russia (USSR):

Fainsod, M.: How Russia is Ruled, Cambridge, 1963
Geyer, D.: Die russische Revolution, Stuttgart, 1968
Goehrke, K., M. Hellmann, R. Lorenz, P. Scheibert: Rußland, Stuttgart, 1972
Jasny, N.: Soviet Industrialization 1928 - 1952, Chicago, 1961
Robel, G.: Vom Tod Stalins zur Ära Breshnew - Die RWG - Staaten seit 1953 - , in: Benz, W. & H. Graml (Hg.): Europa nach dem Zweiten Weltkrieg, Frankfurt, 1983

Spain:

Elliott, J. H.: Imperial Spain 1469 - 1716, London, 1969
Gomez Hoyos, Rafael: La Iglesia de América en las Leyes de Indias, Madrid, 1961
Hanke, Lewis: The Dawn of Conscience in America: Spanish Experiments and Experiences with Indians in the New World, in: Proceedings of the American Philosophical Society, vol. CVII, no 2, 1963

Höffner, J.: Christentum und Menschenwürde - Das Anliegen der spanischen Kolonialethik im goldenen Zeitalter - , Trier, 1947

Konetzke, R.: Das spanische Weltreich, München, 1943

Konetzke, R.: La Legislación sobre Immigración de Extranjeros en América durante el Reinado de Carlos V, in: Colloques Internationaux de Centre National de la Recherche Scientifique, Paris, 1959

Madariaga, S. de: The Rise of the Spanish American Empire, London, 1947

_____ : The Fall of the Spanish American Empire, London, 1947

Pike, Frederick: Public Work and Social Welfare in Colonial Spanish American Towns, in: The Americas, XIII, 1956/7

Smith, Robert: The Spanish Guild Merchant: A History of the Consulado 1200 - 1700, New York, 1972

Vicens Vives, Jaime: An Economic History of Spain, Princeton, 1969

_____ : Approaches to the History of Spain, Berkeley, 1970

USA:

Baran, P. & P. Sweezy: Monopoly Capital - An essay on the American Economic and Social Order - , London, 1965

Bell, Daniel: Marxian Socialism in the United States, Princeton, 1967

Blum, John et al.: The National Experience: A History of the United States, New York, 1973

Burman, St.: America in the Modern World - The Transcendence of United States Hegemony - , New York, 1991

Conkin, Paul K.: The New Deal, New York, 1975

Dahms, H. G.: Grundzüge der Geschichte der Vereinigten Staaten, Darmstadt, 1997

Dembinski, M., P. Rudolf und J. Wilzewski (Hg.): Amerikanische Weltpolitik nach dem Ost-West-Konflikt, Baden-Baden, 1994

Diefendorf, Jeffry M. & A. Frohn, H.-J. Rupieper (eds.).: American Policy and the Re-Construction of West Germany 1945 - 1955, Cambridge, 1993

Ermarth, M.: America and the Shaping of German Society 1945 - 1955, Princeton, 1993

Franklin, John Hope: From Slavery to Freedom, New York, 1974

Gaddis, John L.: The United States and the Origin of the Cold War 1941 - 1947, New York, 1972

Gimbel, John: The Origins of the Marshall Plan, Stanford, 1976

Higgs, Robert: The Transformation of the American Economy 1865 - 1914, New York, 1971

Jacobs, Wilbur: Dispossessing the American Indian, New York, 1972

Kirkland, E.: American Economic History since 1860, Northbrook, 1971

Morgan, Howard W.: America's Road to Empire: The War with Spain and Overseas Expansion, New York, 1965

Nadworthy, Milton J.: Scientific Management and the Unions 1900 - 1932, Cambridge, 1955

Pessen, Edward (ed.): Three Centuries of Social Mobility in America, Lexington, 1974

Taylor, George (ed.): American Economic History before 1860, Northbrook, 1969

Temin, Peter: Iron and Steel in Nineteenth Century America, Cambridge, 1964

De Tocqueville, Alexis: Democracy in America, London, 1994

Woodruff, W.: America's Impact on the World - A Study of the Role of the United States in the World Economy 1750 – 1970 - , New York, 1975

Young, Alfred F. (ed.): The American Revolution, Dekalb, 1976

Index

Note: Some entries that appear throughout major parts of the book, such as "Goethe", "Nature", "culture", "knowledge", "human being" are not listed in the Index.